Terrorism

Terrorism

Terrorism
The Bottom Line

Nathan I. Yungher, Ph.D.

PEARSON
Prentice
Hall

Upper Saddle River, New Jersey, 07458

Library of Congress Cataloging-in-Publication Data

Yungher, Nathan I.
    Terrorism : the bottom line/Nathan I. Yungher. — 1st ed.
        p.   cm.
    Includes bibliographical references.
    ISBN 0-13-156800-0 (alk. paper)
    1. Terrorism.   I. Title.
    HV6431.Y85 2008
    363.325—dc22

                                                    2007021662

Editor-in-Chief: Vernon R. Anthony
Senior Acquisitions Editor: Tim Peyton
Editorial Assistant: Alicia Kelly
Marketing Manager: Adam Kloza
Production Liaison: Joanne Riker
Cover Design Director: Jayne Conte
Cover Design: Brucekenselaar
Cover Illustration/Photo: Getty Images, Inc.-Image Bank
Full-Service Project Management/Composition: Integra Software Services, Ltd.
Printer/Binder: RR Donnelly & Sons

Pearson Education LTD.
Pearson Education Australia PTY, Limited
Pearson Education Singapore, Pte. Ltd
Pearson Education North Asia Ltd

Pearson Education, Canada, Ltd
Pearson Educación de Mexico, S.A. de C.V.
Pearson Education-Japan
Pearson Education Malaysia, Pte. Ltd

10 9 8 7 6 5 4 3 2

ISBN-13: 978-0-13-156800-6
ISBN-10:   0-13-156800-0

To Fran

Contents

Illustrations

Preface

I am petrified of flying. When I was young, I parachuted out of airplanes dozens of times, but years of work for airport and airline security instilled in me an acute fear of flying. Just as some restaurant workers who know the facts of the back kitchen are reluctant to ever eat out, my knowledge of the dangers lurking causes me anxiety at airports as boarding time approaches.

It did not help much that when I taught about terrorism at an Ivy League university in the mid-1980s, there was little public awareness of the subject. Suitable textbooks were rare. I used to collect the few published articles that dealt with terrorism and bring them to class to share with my students. And I felt as if I had a monopoly over the dread of airports and flying. What a contrast a few years make! Terrorism is on the minds of many, and so many articles on terrorism appear daily that I have stopped reading or collecting them all. Terrorism is no longer the obscure subject it once was and textbooks on the subject abound.

Years of teaching experience has opened my eyes to the reality of college education; unfazed by quizzes, midterms, and final exams and successfully fighting off the temptation posed by in-class movies and guest lecturers, too many undergraduate students tend to view the assigned readings as an amusing suggestion. This may not always be the students' fault. A myriad of wonderful textbooks published in recent years resemble sophisticated encyclopedias on terrorism, complete with charts, graphs, "additional recommended readings," key concepts, appendices, maps, recommended websites, long summaries, and so on. This massive amount of information possibly overwhelms and turns off some students. This is unfortunate. Properly told, the subject of terrorism should be riveting.

The book you are now holding is specifically designed for undergraduate students. I wrote this book using common terms—at times as if it was a class lecture—and added anecdotes, questions aimed at enticing readers to think for themselves, case studies, and—when I thought they would help clarify the explanations in the text—a few simple diagrams. The book is written in what I consider a reader-friendly fashion, with the expectation that an easy-to-read, hopefully entertaining, yet educational guide for learning about terrorism will motivate students to want to learn more about the subject of terrorism.

METHODOLOGICAL NOTES

1. To maximize the suitability of this textbook to the rigors of the academic calendar, it is structured in a way that offers enough material to cover all of the meetings planned for the semester. Thus, if a class meets twice a week, each meeting during the semester is covered by a chapter, or parts thereof. (Some chapters, such as those on Islam and weapons of mass destruction, require more than one meeting.) This design makes sure to leave open some meetings for guest speakers, a movie, midterms, and so on. In cases where the course features approximately 15 weekly meetings, the textbook offers professors the flexibility to skip a couple of chapters according to their preference.

2. When quoting luminaries such as Shakespeare, Churchill, Gandhi, and so on, I refrained from providing exact references for such general knowledge citations in order to keep the flow of the reading uninterrupted.

RECOGNIZED WITH APPRECIATION

The well-meaning and frightfully talented individuals who have graciously donated their time and skills to this project are too many to be mentioned in a way that will do justice to their labors and goodwill. Suffice it to say that if not for the combined efforts of academics and practitioners, this textbook would not have been possible. The discerning reader will do well to keep in mind that any error this textbook may contain is in spite of these individuals' best efforts, learned advice and, on occasion, strong pleas.

Ellen Coleman discharged her duties as editor of this project with uncompromising zeal to ensure accuracy in detail and substance. A formidable independent thinker, she stood her ground on issues that went beyond grammar and syntax, repeatedly challenging the banal and speculative in favor of balance and fact. Her immense contribution to this book, a mixture of expertise and intellectual conviction served with constructive diplomacy, is deeply appreciated.

Lastly, to the reader of this textbook: Terrorism is a scourge with which we are doomed to cohabitate for decades to come and, consequently, with which it is wise to become better acquainted. My hope is that this book will help clarify many of the causes and ramifications associated with terrorism, thus providing one with not just a smoother ride on life's journey, but a safer one as well.

PART I

TAKING STOCK

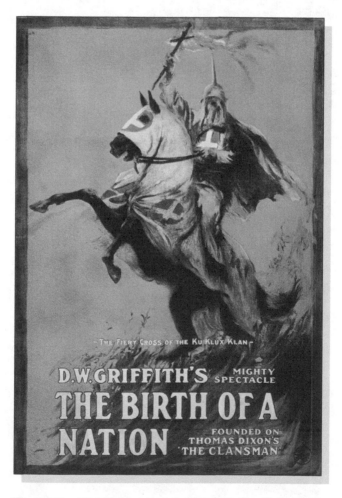

The 1915 film, *The birth of a nation,* glorified the Ku Klux Klan and white supremacy
Source: The Granger Collection.

1

Deliberate Confusion

Defining Terrorism

To get anywhere, you have to walk over the corpses.

Illyich Ramirez Sanchez, the terrorist known as "The Jackal."

❖❖❖

On November 13, 1974, the Palestinian leader Yasser Arafat addressed the General Assembly of the United Nations and declared in an artful speech, "whoever stands by a just cause and fights for the freedom of his land . . . cannot possibly be called terrorist . . ."[1]

❖❖❖

Before discussing definitions, we need to understand, at least in a general sense, why terrorism exists at all. In the coming chapters, you will learn important theories about the sources of terrorism, but first a sneak preview of the basic reasons why terrorism exists in the first place is necessary; the discussion of the finer points of terrorism can wait for later chapters.

Writing on the subject of terrorism, Clifford Simonsen and Jeremy Spindlove attribute the phenomenon to its four basic goals:[2]

1. To bring awareness to an alleged grievance by performing shocking acts that create attention.
2. To use the media to maximize people's knowledge of the cause.

3. To influence the public's reaction to acts of violence by spreading fear.
4. To produce policy changes through acts of violence that weaken governments' resolve.

Whatever we think of the strategy of terrorism, we should keep in mind that terrorism is not a new phenomenon. It has been used for thousands of years for the simple reason that many times it works. Terrorism, especially in the modern era, can make governments appear unfit and sometimes outright stupid. Since terrorists get to choose any target they wish and use the most brutal methods, the result makes them look more capable than the government, which has to "play by the rules."

The fear factor is important in all acts of terrorism and has been the focus of many analysts. H. H. A. Cooper, for example, notes that as television and other media have exposed the public to a gruesome diet of death and destruction, "the audience has become increasingly difficult to shock."[3] This numbness represents a challenge to terrorists, who must keep their audience's morbid attention. The fact is that, excluding *state* terrorism on the scale seen in Nazi Germany, the USSR under Stalin, or, recently, Rwanda, the non-governmental terrorist organizations' butcher bill is not characterized by very high numbers. This understanding necessarily raises the question of what terrorists will be willing to do to recapture people's interest. With the need for even higher death tolls to gain the media's and the world's attention, the chances that terrorists will use weapons of mass destruction increase with time.

Still, horrific scenes of terrorist handiwork tend to succeed in getting our attention; the media make sure that they do. Simonsen and Spindlove suggest an order for the degree of shock audiences show, a scale based on the identity of the victims.[4] The public can stomach to a certain extent acts of terrorism carried out against soldiers, less when the violence is directed at government officials—possibly members of the establishment—and least of all when the victims are civilians, who are not connected to the conflict, and so a clear pecking order emerges. Thus, to register the maximum impact with the public, civilians become terrorists' preferred targets.

Agonizing Dilemmas

The following situation has taken place many times in a number of countries: Imagine that you are a member of a government faced with the gut-wrenching choice of deciding the proper response to the bald-faced demands of terrorists holding civilians hostage. The stakes are very high—the terrorists demand the release of jailed comrades and threaten to murder hostages unless their demands are met.

In 1977, the Dutch government faced just such a problem. Terrorists belonging to the Free South Moluccan Organization tried to bring attention to the Indonesian takeover of South Moluccas by hijacking a passenger train and seizing a nearby school, taking their occupants hostage. In this case, the Dutch decided on a military solution and successfully sent in commando teams to end the takeover and rescue the hostages.

TOWARD A DEFINITION OF TERRORISM

You need to know two things about terrorism. One is that terrorism is *always* a strategy, *never* a goal. In the words of Simonsen and Spindlove, terrorism is "a means to an end—nothing more and nothing less . . ."[5] The second thing you need to know is that *terrorism* is a word that is very hard to pin down and define.

Perhaps the perfect definition is so elusive because of the diverse causes such a definition needs to cover: political, religious, revolutionary, nationalistic, separatist, state violence, and many others. Make no mistake. There are hundreds of definitions of the word *terrorism*, but finding one that covers precisely every possible situation is nearly impossible. In fact, so difficult it is to define terrorism that even the Federal Bureau of Investigation (FBI), the U.S. Department of Defense, and the U.S. State Department, three governmental organizations in the same country and culture, use different definitions.[6]

In spite of the temptation, I will not impose on you the usual long list of definitions. Instead, I offer just two to give you an idea of scholars' basic thinking on this issue. In addition, we will discuss the four parts that any good definition of terrorism usually includes, which will help you use your own judgment to determine what action is, or is not, terrorism.

Terrorism: On Strategies and Causes

The idea that terrorism is only a strategy is very important. In fact, it is so important that if you remember only one idea presented in this entire book, it is that *terrorism is never about the cause, but always about the strategy used to win it.* After all, each side of a conflict is certain that it is in the right, which makes the meaning of "cause" nothing but a biased feeling. The only way to protect innocents from self-righteous parties is to place clear rules on the use of violence, excluding all "moral beliefs and sociological-political mumbo-jumbo."[7] This point cannot be overstated: *terrorism is never about the cause; it is always about the methods used.*

When scholars try to define terrorism, a number of words always seem to appear. The following is a top-ten list of the most important words such definitions include: *violence, political, fear, threat, psychological impact, methods of combat, violation of accepted rules, coercion, publicity,* and *randomness.* In different combinations, most definitions of terrorism use these words.[8]

For this reason, the two definitions I am about to offer may be imperfect, but they are still helpful. Just remember that these are only two out of hundreds of unique and creative attempts to define the term. Writing about terrorism and the rule of law, Richard Pious defined terrorism as "The use (or threat of the use) of force against noncombatant (i.e., innocent) civilians with means that violate criminal laws or the laws and customs of war, often on a random basis, with the goal of terrorizing and immobilizing the population in its economic, social, and cultural activities."[9] H. H. A. Cooper, also eminent in the field, defined terrorism as "the intentional generation of massive fear by human beings for the purpose of securing or maintaining control over other human beings."[10] As mentioned, as good as these definitions are, they are lacking. This is an unsatisfying situation for those wishing for a tool, or a model, that will help them decide which violent political act is or is not terrorism.

THE COMPONENTS OF TERRORISM: AN OPERATIONAL MODEL

Short of a perfect definition that works well to describe every single situation, we are best served by knowing what the components of an act called "terrorism" are. Once we know what they are and can put them together, we create a tool, or a model, that is more helpful than wordy definitions. Such a model helps us judge which acts qualify as terrorism. Professor Cindy Combs, from the University of North Carolina at Charlotte, gives us such a model. She offers a loose definition that has four parts essential for identifying terrorism. According to Combs,[11] a terrorist act

- is an act of *violence*
- has a *political* goal
- is carried out against *innocent* people
- is intended to frighten the *larger audience*

In my view, an act of terrorism can also be carried out against soldiers. This happens when the act of violence is in violation of the codes of war and its purpose is to affect the larger audience in order to change policy. To understand how soldiers can also become victims of terrorism, we need to set apart cases involving *war crimes* from acts of terrorism. For example, a commando unit *secretly* killing its prisoners during a raid engages in a war crime, not in terrorism, whereas those who violate the rules of war by *publicly* beheading prisoners of war (POWs) in order to influence a larger audience and therefore governmental policy engage in terrorism.

Jurists may engage in endless debates about individual cases, but this operational model provides a good rule of thumb to establish the meaning of a violent act quite easily, as is shown in the next section.

Applying the Model

The following two cases will help you understand the usefulness of this model for deciding whether a violent political act is terrorism or not.

The Real Irish Republican Army (Real IRA)   On August 15, 1998, a car bomb in Omagh, Northern Ireland, killed 29 civilians and wounded roughly 220 others, many of them women and children. The Real IRA, an offshoot of the

Scene of Omagh, Northern Ireland, after the Real IRA terrorist attack in 1998
Source: Courtesy of Empics.

Provisional Irish Republican Army (IRA) had opposed the peace process that ended in the April 10, 1998, Good Friday Agreement and planted the bomb to derail the accord. How can we tell if this act of violence qualifies as terrorism or as a bloody military operation by, say, freedom fighters?

Using Professor Combs's four-part model, we find that this attack definitely qualifies as a terrorist act. First, it was an act of violence. Second, it had a political motive. Third, the victims were innocent. Fourth, the real target was not the actual victims but the public at large, which was to be terrorized by the Real IRA's continued campaign of violence. Case closed.

The American bombing of Mage el-Deeb in Northwestern Iraq   Some would later describe this May 19, 2004, air attack, which resulted in scores of dead and injured, as an attack on a "wedding party." With contradictory accounts given by survivors and by the American military about the identity of the victims, those harboring ill will toward the United States were quick to accuse it of terrorism because innocent people were killed. Even if the victims were innocent non-combatants, was the American bombing an act of terrorism?

Combs's model easily establishes that the incident was not one of terrorism. It meets two, possibly three, of her criteria: it was an act of violence, in a political context, which may have harmed innocents, but the United States did not purposely attack civilians in order to influence the larger public opinion. In fact, following the incident, the United States wished nobody had ever heard about it. As in any war, the Iraq war has had incidents in which civilians became the unintentional victims of the hostilities. This is not terrorism.

What Do YOU Think?

The period between the end of World War II in 1945 and the establishment of the state of Israel in 1948 was a bloody one in Palestine, strewn with violence involving Arabs, Jews, and the British, who were in control of the land. As part of their struggle for independence, the Jewish group Etzel, the Hebrew acronym for "National Military Organization," decided to blow up the King David Hotel in Jerusalem, in which the British Military Command was stationed. The act was carried out on July 22, 1946, when—after warning the authorities that a bomb was to go off imminently—a huge explosion ripped through the hotel and killed 91 people, mostly Arab and Jewish civilians who happened to be staying at or working in the hotel, as well as 28 British personnel.

   Does this attack, executed by men wearing civilian clothes against a military command center located among non-combatants, qualify as "terrorism"? Explain your position.

Terrorism: Dirty Word or Badge of Honor?

As you will see in the next chapter, "terrorism" was not always a bad word. In fact, only a hundred years ago, some considered the word *terrorism* a badge of honor. Today, individuals, organizations, and states are reluctant to admit that their actions add up to terrorism. Why? To spare you long-winded explanations, I will sketch the four main reasons:

   1. *Image:* Terrorist organizations wish to present their struggle, even if for cynical purposes, as a legitimate one. The cause such organizations fight for will be damaged by the negative associations with the word *terrorism*. Of course, public relations aside, in reality terrorists' actions never fail to prove Gandhi's point that "morality is contraband in war."

   2. *International law:* Even as it continues to be practiced around the world, being associated with the label "terrorism" is far less in vogue today than it was a few decades ago. The main reasons are international law and judicial institutions such as the International Criminal Court in The Hague, in charge of prosecuting those accused of genocide, crimes against humanity, and war crimes. This concern applies not only to terrorist organizations, but also to governments using what amounts to "state-terrorism" or "state-backed" terrorism. No governmental official wishes to be taken to task for involvement in terrorism even if the chances of such an eventuality are quite remote. The example of the years-long international hunt for former Serbian officials suspected of war crimes as Yugoslavia disintegrated is likely to serve as a cautionary reminder to others around the world that, regardless of how implausible it is, they will have to face justice. Still, it is important that you keep in mind that such concerns, while perhaps present in the back of one's mind, are in fact very limited.

3. *Idealism:* Terrorists see their struggle through the idealistic lens of good versus evil and genuinely reject any negative depiction of them or what they do. In their view, the struggle is between total right and absolute wrong with no gray area left to negotiate over. Benito Mussolini had the same idea: "violence is profoundly moral—more moral than compromises."

4. *Prejudice:* Some argue that the origins of the critical label "terrorism" come from suspect sources that have a built-in bias against the weak party to a conflict. Since the codes of war are the product of international law that has been strongly influenced by the colonial powers, these rules carry an unfair bias against "freedom fighters" worldwide. For example, guerillas fighting an occupying power while carrying insignia that identifies them as fighters—as international law requires—face a short life expectancy. Yet, if the guerillas do not follow the rule and blend into society rather than set themselves apart from the non-combatants, they are unfairly labeled "terrorists."

Reflecting Edward Bond's contention that "law and order is one of the steps taken to maintain injustice," members of such organizations reject as unfair attempts to classify them as terrorists. Moreover, these critics point to recent history as proof of the Western powers' hypocrisy. During World War II, they charge, Britain and the United States—two of the leading world democracies—bombed German and Japanese population centers and killed millions of civilians in the process. The bombing raids over Germany targeted cities full of non-combatants although German soldiers were at the front, not in Dresden, for example. Similarly, Japanese soldiers were not in Hiroshima when its civilian population met its nuclear fate. Their war over, critics note, these same powers turned their attention to movements struggling for independence, pointing an accusatory finger at the freedom fighters and labeling them terrorists when they strike non-combatants.

In reality, while it may be unfashionable to admit to committing terrorism, do not confuse the perpetrators' dislike of the label with the actual practice. The accusations, the defiant countercharges, and the cynical manipulation of the word *terrorism* have dulled the impact of the term. In his 1969 well-known *Handbook of Urban Guerilla War*, the Brazilian Marxist leader Carlos Marighela blatantly advised his followers that "the word . . . 'terrorist,' no longer mean[s] what [it] did. . . . To be called . . . a terrorist . . . is now an honor to any citizen . . ."[12] Years later, and similarly scornful of Western-inspired international codes of war that do not agree with his methods, Osama bin Laden shrugged off the meaning of the label "terrorism" with crudely deceitful logic: "If killing the ones that kill our sons is terrorism," he declared after September 11, 2001, "then let history witness that we are terrorists."[13]

The Blame Game

Often terrorists blame authorities for the bloody resolution of an armed standoff that they themselves initiated. It is also a regular practice for terrorists and their supporters to confuse the issue by equating their own behavior with that of their hated opponent as a justification for an atrocity.

September 1, 2004, was the first day of the new school year in Beslan, the third largest town in the republic of North Ossetia-Alania of Russia. Thirty-two Chechen terrorists stunned the world by taking some 1,200 people at the school hostage; most of them were school children. Fifty-two hours later, an unfortunate chain of events involving a botched rescue operation ended with 330 hostages dead, about half of them school children. In an interview with the American television network ABC in July 2005, the top commander of the Chechen terrorists, Shamil Basayev, refused to be singled out as a terrorist if no blame was to be placed on Russia: "I admit, I'm a bad guy, a bandit, a terrorist . . . but what would you call them [the Russians]? . . . If they are antiterrorists, then I spit on all these agreements and nice words."[14]

A Label in Need of Clarity

Terrorism exists and in order to deal with it, we need to be able to identify it. This can only be done if, to use baseball lingo, we "call 'em like we see 'em," ignoring our political sympathies. Given human nature, doing so is easier said than done. Terrorists and their supporters routinely—and on too many occasions, successfully—use smoke screens and verbal acrobatics to confuse the public's common sense.

Combs's model should make it relatively easy to sort out legitimate conflict from political excuses and apologies that are little more than red herrings. In fact, doing so ought to be common sense rather than a complex intellectual challenge. H. H. A. Cooper unmasked the self-righteous veil of terrorism best, stating, ". . . as with obscenity, we know terrorism well enough when we see it."[15] Clichés to the effect that "one man's terrorist is another's freedom fighter" and that "terrorism is the weapon of the weak," and the "root causes" justification are fig leaves for excusing strategies that deliberately target the innocent and violate the rules of war.

One must judge violent acts by the way a group with perceived grievances carries out its struggle rather than by its "cause." At the end of the day, whether just or not, "causes" are infinite; one can find individuals and groups dissatisfied with certain aspects of their lives in almost every corner of the globe. The fact that people can organize for violent political action cannot excuse acts that violate the laws of war. The reason is simple: "cause" is a one-sided word that is never truly objective and may or may not be valid. If we accept that a self-declared cause justifies the use of all means possible—meaning, the use of terrorism—then we can be certain that terrible suffering will come to innocents in the name of that cause. Historian Victor Davis Hanson takes issue with the excuses terrorists use to justify their causes. Describing the elusive nature of those expressed by Islamist terrorists, for example, he writes, "The killers always allege particular gripes—Australian troops in Iraq, Christian proselytizing, Hindu intolerance, occupation of the West Bank, theft of Arab petroleum, the Jews, attacks on the Taliban, the fifteenth-century re-conquest of Spain, and, of course, the Crusades. But in most cases . . . the common bond is not poverty, a lack of education or legitimate grievance. . . ."[16]

As an example of the confusion that one's outlook on an issue can cause, consider the war in Iraq. In this conflict, political sympathies for one side or the other shape the labels used to describe the opposing parties. For example, in recent years Syrian officials and the country's state-run news organizations have criticized the United States' military operations in Iraq as "terroristic." At the same time, U.S. officials have named those fighting the coalition forces in Iraq "terrorists" and "jihadists." Some Western news organizations, reflecting popular opinion, have described those fighting coalition forces in Iraq as "insurgents" or as the "resistance." If the circumstance were not so bloody, this name-calling might be amusing. What is worse, this situation confuses the audience. Failing to describe those in Iraq who intentionally bomb mosques, target marketplaces, and have slaughtered tens of thousands of innocent civilians in violation of the rules of war as terrorists obscures the true nature of that party to the conflict.

The need to stay clear of political sympathies is very real; people die because of it. For example, in July 2005 the United Nations failed to reach an agreement on defining terrorism. The breakdown was the final blow to the effort that had been languishing in a United Nations committee since 1996. This failure is a classic example of rejecting a definition based solely on the nature of the violent act because of sympathy for a particular political cause. In this instance, Arab countries' insistence that Palestinian suicide bombings of Israeli civilian population centers not be considered terrorism because the cause—fighting "foreign occupation"[17]—is just, has been derailing the United Nations' attempts to define terrorism. In any political situation, the question of "who decides" clouds the issue. In this case, the question of who is to decide exactly which territories are "occupied"—Arab countries? Israel? the PLO? Hamas?—illustrates the danger of an approach based on political backing or sympathies.

Refusing to define terrorism in order to excuse the behavior of a favored group is a conscious attempt to confuse the issue and to allow exceptions to the rules. This dangerous trend of getting around clear legal restrictions for the benefit of a political cause can result in absurd situations. For example, if exceptions to the codes of war are made for Palestinians, allowing them to target Israeli civilians, the same allowance should be made for others who, perhaps justifiably, claim a pressing cause of foreign occupation. Following this logic, Tibetans should be permitted to plant bombs in Chinese universities, Chechens to hijack Russian planes, and Kurds to take Turkish schoolchildren hostage.

No Apologies

To terrorists, there are no innocents. Confronted with the fact that hundreds of Muslims perished in the course of the September 11 attacks, captured al-Qaeda members were unmoved. From their point of view, if the dead Muslims were "good Muslims," then the attackers had just quickened the arrival of the dead to paradise. However, if the dead were not "good Muslims," then they deserved to die. Either way, the terrorists did not think that they were guilty of any wrongdoing.

A Brief Reminder of International Law

Following the rules of war is clearly a major issue in discussions of terrorism. Many organizations use subjective titles, such as "guerillas," "freedom fighters," or "national liberation movement" to represent their struggle. How are we to distinguish between the "good" freedom fighters, who fight by the rules—perhaps Fidel Castro's 26th of July Movement during the Cuban Revolution—and the "bad" ones, who use terrorism? A clear difference exists between guerillas and terrorists: their policy regarding the international rules of war. To be considered guerillas, fighters must set themselves apart from the non-combatants by wearing uniforms, armbands, or other symbols that identify them as combatants. They must also carry their arms in the open, not hidden. Most important, guerillas have to honor the rules of war, which, among other conditions, means not deliberately hurting civilians and treating enemy POWs according to the series of Conventions on Warfare signed in Geneva and The Hague between 1860 and 1949.

Since a strategy of terror violates international law, anybody using it is a terrorist. It should not be too difficult to identify these people: if they target civilians on purpose, take hostages, mistreat their prisoners, etc., they do not follow the codes of war and are therefore terrorists. Yasser Arafat's statement that "whoever stands by a just cause and fights for the freedom of his land . . . cannot possibly be called terrorist," with which this chapter begins, was in fact wrong regardless of the nature of his cause. He might have been the father of the Palestinian nation, a diplomat, president of the fledgling Palestinian Authority, a

---

What Do YOU Think?

A fierce battle took place in Fallujah, Iraq, in November 2004, between U.S. forces supported by Iraqi troops on the one hand and local fighters opposed to the coalition presence in Iraq on the other. In one incident, a U.S. Marine was photographed shooting an apparently unarmed enemy combatant, out of uniform, lying badly wounded in a mosque from which he and some of his comrades had been firing at the advancing troops. In your opinion, was the Marine innocent or guilty of terrorism?

husband, and a father, but because he used political violence against civilians in ways that violate the rules of war, he was also a terrorist.

The Contrast

The contrast between Arafat's statement and that of Ali Ahmeti, a leader in the Macedonian National Liberation Army, is instructive: "I am a freedom fighter," Ahmeti said. "That person cannot be a terrorist who wears an army badge . . . who respects the Geneva Convention and the Hague Tribunal, who acts in public with name and surname and answers for everything he does. . . ."[18]

SUMMARY

In this chapter, you have learned the following:

1. Defining terrorism is very difficult.
2. The reasons for this difficulty range from a mixture of legal disagreements, contradictory precedents, and cynical manipulations in support of a favorable party.
3. One workable solution to this confusing state is the use of a model consisting of four parts. When all four parts of the model are present in a violent act, then the act fits the definition of terrorism.
4. While at present the term *terrorism* has an unpleasant connotation, in reality those using the practice view it more as an undesirable nuisance than as an actual inhibitor.

As our journey continues, it is time to turn our attention to the history of terrorism. Knowing how we got here will help us understand the present better and perhaps shed light on what is awaiting humanity down the road.

💣💣💣

The unique nature of a terroristic strategy is vividly demonstrated by the following episode. On the night of October 12, 1984, two bombs went off at the Grand Hotel in Brighton, England, where the Conservative Party headed by Prime Minister Margaret Thatcher was holding a conference. Although five people were killed in the attack, including one conservative Member of Parliament, the Prime Minister herself and all members of her cabinet survived the assassination attempt. The following day, the IRA issued a statement that with time would turn into a classic: "Today we were unlucky, but remember we only have to be lucky once. You have to be lucky always."

💣💣💣

14   CHAPTER 1   Deliberate Confusion

Notes

1. For Arafat's speech, see "Arafat's Speech to the United Nations (13 November 1974)" http://electronicintifada.net/bytopic/historicalspeeches/305.shtml (accessed July 18, 2006).
2. The four motives can be found in Clifford E. Simonsen and Jeremy R. Spindlove, *Terrorism Today: The Past, The Players, The Future*, 2nd ed. (Upper Saddle River, NJ: Prentice Hall, 2004), pp. 8–9.
3. For H. H. A. Cooper's contention, see "Terrorism: The Problem of Definition Revisited," in Gus Martin, ed., *The New Era of Terrorism: Selected Readings* (Dominguez Hills, CA: Sage Publications, 2004), p. 59.
4. For the escalating order of the shock factor, see Simonsen and Spindlove, *Terrorism Today*, p. 8.
5. Simonsen and Spindlove's contention that terrorism is a means to an end is found in Ibid., p. 7.
6. For the differences between the definitions of the FBI, the Department of Defense, and the State Department, see Bruce Hoffman, *Inside Terrorism* (New York: Columbia University press, 1998), p. 38.
7. For the expression regarding "sociological-political mumbo-jumbo," see Simonsen and Spindlove, *Terrorism Today*, p. 7.
8. For a more complete list of terms defining aspects of terrorism, see Alex P. Schmidt and Albert J. Jongman, *Political Terrorism: A New Guide to Actors, Authors, Concepts, Data Bases, Theories, and Literature* (New Brunswick: Transaction Books, 1988), pp. 5–6.
9. For Pious' definition of terrorism, see Richard M. Pious, *The War on Terrorism and the Rule of Law* (Los Angeles, CA: Roxbury Publishing Co., 2006), p. 2.
10. Cooper's definition is found in p. 56.
11. For Cindy Combs' "loose definition," see Cindy C. Combs, *Terrorism in the Twenty-First Century*, 3rd ed. (Upper Saddle River, NJ: Prentice Hall, 2003), p. 10.
12. Carlos Marighela's advice is quoted in Bruce Hoffman, "Defining Terrorism," in Russell D. Howard and Reid L. Sawyer, eds., *Terrorism and Counterterrorism: Understanding The New Security Environment* (Guilford, CT: McGraw-Hill/Dushkin, 2003), pp. 13–14.
13. Bin Laden made this claim in an October 21, 2001, interview, as quoted by James S. Robins, "Bin Laden's War," in Russell D. Howard and Reid L. Sawyer, eds., p. 355.
14. Shamil Basayev's outburst can be found in "Chechen Guerrilla Leader Calls Russians 'Terrorists'," ABC News, July 29, 2005, http://abcnews.go.com/Nightline/International/story?id=990187&page=1 (accessed July 18, 2006).
15. Cooper's comparison of terrorism to obscenity can be found in H. H. A. Cooper, *Terrorism*, p. 62.
16. Victor Davis Hanson's quote can be found in "Enough Is Enough," *Washington Times*, July 22, 2005.
17. For an example of the perspective that views Palestinian acts of terrorism as fighting "foreign occupation," see Mustafa al Sayyid, "Mixed Message: The Arab and Muslim Response to 'Terrorism'," in Gus Martin, ed., pp. 64–71.
18. Ali Ahmeti is quoted in Timothy Garton Ash, "Is There a Good Terrorist?" in Charles W. Kegley, Jr., ed., *The New Global Terrorism: Characteristics, Causes, Controls* (Upper Saddle River, NJ: Prentice Hall, 2003), p. 61.

2

What's Old Is What's New

A Brief History of Terrorism

History is a vast early warning system.

Norman Cousins

💣*💣*💣*

The *Thugees* (Thugs) were worshipers of the Hindu goddess Kali. She, like all goddesses, exacted a steep cost, but hers was very steep—the ritual sacrifice of human beings. As word spread of the danger posed by the Thugees, people stopped traveling with strangers for fear of being kidnapped, and the Thugees were forced to come up with ever-more creative ways to outwit their suspicious prey. One successful ruse was to organize caravans in which, secretly, every single traveler was a *Thugee*. Would-be victims who had to travel but were too scared to do so alone for fear of the Thugees would approach the leaders of the caravan and plead to be allowed to join the caravan on the dangerous trip . . .

The Thugees kidnapped and murdered about one million people during their 1,200-year existence, from the eighth century to the nineteenth century. The British managed to wipe them out by the end of the nineteenth century and saved the terrorized population.

💣*💣*💣*

ONCE UPON A TIME: A TOUR DE FORCE

As creatures of our time with limited patience for the past, how far into the past should we look to understand the problem of terrorism?

In the previous chapter, we discussed the many definitions of terrorism, and learned that different experts employ different definitions. Thus, some historical events are called "terrorism" by certain writers while others do not see the events that way. For example, some scholars trace terrorism back by at least 2,000 years, to the deadly antics of the Jewish *Sicariis*, who were attempting to expel the Romans and their allies from ancient Judaea. Similarly, the assassinations of Julius Caesar and Tsar Alexander II of Russia are also classified as acts of terrorism. These may not fit neatly with our own operational model (an act of violence, for political reasons, against innocents, to influence the larger audience), but readers need to be aware of the large variety of definitions and historical examples of terrorism, even if they are not always compatible with our model.

Only in recent decades did the assassination of political leaders come to be defined as terrorism. The acceptance of this definition has presented an exciting windfall of opportunities for scholars. With no time constraints and with ample stories of killings, they were quick to peek far into the past and to designate a variety of assassinations as acts of terrorism. The biblical figure of Jael, who used her feminine charms to slay the unsuspecting General Sisara, for example, would have been surprised to know that some 3,000 years later her act would be considered "terrorism." Continuing along that timeline, discussions of the origins of terrorism never fail to mention Greek philosophers, such as Aristotle, who encouraged people to earn their freedom by assassinating the tyrants who ruled them. Scholars point to similar attitudes expressed by Roman writers. Seneca, for one, advised that "no sacrifice was as pleasing to the gods as the blood of a tyrant." Cicero was of the same opinion, arguing that tyrants always attract a violent act. Even the unfortunate Brutus was "an honorable man" for killing Julius Caesar, until history and Shakespeare conspired to change this image following his act of terrorism.[1]

Scholars usually identify the Jewish Sicarii terrorist group, which existed some 2,000 years ago, as that point in history where individual acts of terrorism graduated to terrorism orchestrated by organized groups. David C. Rapaport contributed a much-cited work about the evolution of terrorism from the Sicarii of ancient Judaea through the Assassins in northern Persia around the end of the first millennium to the Thugees in India mentioned earlier.[2] We will discuss these three groups in detail in Chapter 6, when we explore the link between terrorism and religion.

Enter the French Revolution

Just as tales of ancient conspiracies and intriguing Byzantine accounts of deadly deceptions are sure to rekindle a dying conversation at a cocktail party, the saga of the House of Medici has also been known for its value as a social icebreaker.

None of these accounts, however, will help us to understand modern terrorism. For that, we need to fast forward to the French Revolution. Credit for the term *terrorism* is attributed to the French revolutionary Maximilien Robespierre. Having established the Committee of General Security and the dreaded Revolutionary Tribunal to protect the fruits of the French Revolution against counterrevolutionaries, Robespierre enacted what became known as the *regime de la terreur*. It may be difficult to understand from today's perspective, but Robespierre was actually proud of the state-terrorism that was supposed to ensure justice and democracy. "Terror is nothing but justice, prompt, severe and inflexible; it is therefore an emanation of virtue," he argued.[3] French state-terrorism would ultimately cost the lives of hundreds of thousands of people, ending only when Robespierre himself had his date with the guillotine in 1794. Thereafter, the word *terror* was associated with horror, injustice, and criminality.

Constitutional Democracy, Radical Democracy, Anarchism, and Terrorism

The influence of the French Revolution was more important than could be understood at the time. The underlying message of the Revolution about people's rights gradually spread to the rest of Europe and was transformed into a struggle for a moderate, constitutional democracy. As one writer put it, "the French revolution did not bring democracy; it brought Napoleon. Under the surface, however, democratic ideas continued to grow."[4] This European preoccupation with greater freedom kept mounting but, as time went by, the exact nature of the freedoms sought kept changing.

Still, there was no one unified movement of freedom-seeking democrats with a clear agenda. In the mid-nineteenth century, much of Europe and the United States bubbled with the energy of the Industrial Revolution. Accompanying the rapid industrialization were many ills, naked injustice, and brutality. Amidst the great social changes that affected all aspects of life, opinions among those looking for change varied. If some middle-class activists advocated greater constitutional freedoms, other democrats turned their attention to the economic sphere, demanding not just political liberty, but also a more just division of wealth. These radical democrats became known as *socialists*. They were radical in outlook, but did not advocate the use of violence to achieve their goals.

Karl Marx and Terrorism

A famous socialist during that period was Karl Marx (1818–1883). Intellectually, he foresaw an inevitable future in which the working masses would rise up against their exploiters. Yet, he did not advocate, or believe in, using terror to bring about that future.

The year 1848 is known as the *Spring of the Peoples*. What began in that year as a mini-revolution in Paris quickly spread to other European capitals and even reached as far away as Brazil. The democratic forces driving these revolutions, however, were disorganized and lacked workable strategies for achieving clearly defined objectives. Consequently, they were crushed in short order by the threatened monarchies and upper classes. As the ruling elites managed to stave off the revolutionaries by force, many radical democrats lost hope that a revolution would ever be brought about by peacefully distributing pamphlets and giving speeches. Instead, these radical democrats (socialists) turned violent (militant socialists).

Keep in mind that not all radical democrats were violent, but those who were, embarked in the second half of the nineteenth century on a campaign of political violence throughout Europe. Assassinations, bombings, and incidents of arson became commonplace to the point that some took to using the word *terrorism* to describe the wave of deliberate political violence unleashed by the militant socialists.

Some socialists who did not support violence, yet despaired of ever trusting any government to do right by the people, advocated the peaceful and gradual elimination of centralized government and leaving the people alone to fend for themselves as families and communities. They came to be known as *anarchists* (derived from Greek, meaning "without ruler"). There were some anarchists, though, who believed that people had to hasten the arrival of that utopian democracy by using violence, rather than waiting passively for it to happen sometime in the future. Together with the militant socialists, they became known as *anarchist-terrorists*.[5]

Early, Selective Terrorism

Toward the end of the nineteenth century, some European intellectuals were encouraging their contemporaries to use terrorism with ideological justification and with impatient calls for action. A noted example was the Italian Anarchist Carlo Piscanae, who is credited with turning the slogan "propaganda by deed" into an ideological action plan for future terrorists. His call for prioritizing the use of the bomb and the gun over continued passivity gained much appeal among European revolutionaries.

Did You Know?

The Russian Social Revolutionary Party, organized in 1900, quickly added an "armed wing" to conduct terrorist operations. After a successful six-year run in which they committed dramatic acts of terrorism, the Russian authorities managed to penetrate the organization very thoroughly. In a textbook case of counterterrorism, the authorities managed to not only plant informants within the group, but also to have an undercover police officer, Yevno Azef, become the leader of the organization! Betrayed and on the run, members of the organization could not withstand the wave of arrests, executions, and exile that followed and the group faded away. Terrorism in Russia found itself on a slow burner until the 1917 Revolution.

By the end of the nineteenth century, Russia became the most fertile ground for revolutionary terrorism. Some early Russian anarchist-terrorists formed a terrorist group called *People's Will*. The organization had no defined program, but it carried out political killings culminating with the assassination of Tsar Alexander II in March of 1881. This successful act of terrorism also spelled the demise of the group as the Russian authorities hunted down its members and had all of them executed within a short period. In a 1909 article ominously titled "Why Marxists Oppose Individual Terrorism," the Bolshevik leader Leon Trotsky argued against the type of terrorism used by the People's Will because it was "outdated by history."[6] The state-terrorism the Marxists would practice once in power would make the People's Will look innocent and amateurish indeed. Nevertheless, the People's Will succeeded in being an early role model for the second wave of Russian revolutionaries. The process would end in the 1917 Bolshevik Revolution, which ushered in the communist era.

Pre–World War I terrorism was not limited to Russia, of course. The practice had spread internationally—even as far as Japan and India—turning into a headline-grabbing, frequent occurrence. The assassinations of French President Sadi Carnot in 1894, Spanish Prime Minister Antonio Canovas in 1897, the Austrian Empress Elisabeth in 1898, King Umberto of Italy in 1900, and President William McKinley in 1901 are a few famous examples of the wave of global anarchist-terrorism during that era.

Later, attention turned to the boiling pot that was the Balkans. There, two groups that used terrorism gained special notoriety before World War I: (1) the anti-Ottoman Inner Macedonian Revolutionary Organization (IMRO) in the last decade of the nineteenth century, and (2) the pan-Serb, People's Defense organization that was established in 1908 to resist the Hapsburg Empire's rule. In 1911, a more radical splinter group emerged from the People's Defense

The assassination of U.S. President William McKinley in 1901
Source: Courtesy of Picture Desk, Inc./Kobal Collection.

called the *Black Hand,* which, with some covert support from the Serbian government, devoted itself to a campaign of terrorism against Austro-Hungarian rule in Bosnia.

This early terrorism was selective and refined in comparison to the indiscriminate terrorism practiced today. The terrorists were idealistic young men and women who, along with their fervent ideological zeal, carried with them the middle-class values with which they had been raised. They considered political assassination an instrument for eliminating selected members of the hated establishment and for stirring the masses to further action, but they functioned along self-imposed moral limits they tried not to cross. Young Russian terrorists, with idealism that from today's vantage point can only make one nostalgic for the terrorism of that era, were known to abort missions if they discovered that their intended target was accompanied by his wife or child.

State-Terrorism

Using political violence to gain and maintain power reached its peak in the first half of the twentieth century. Only this time there was a twist in the unfolding story of terrorism. The old idealistic bands of anarchist-terrorists, who had so inflamed the hopes of some and the fears of others for over half a century, gave way to centralized, state-run terrorism. The latter, in turn, created new standards of mass repression and murder, terrorizing the mostly innocent at a level unheard of in the modern era. Writers usually identify Fascist Italy under Benito Mussolini, Hitler's Nazi Germany, and the Soviet Union under the leadership of Joseph Stalin as the classic examples of this episode in history. Mussolini best expressed the utter disregard with which such states held their real or imagined opponents. Denying his regime used terrorism against its people, he protested that the state actions were merely "social hygiene, taking those individuals out of circulation like a doctor would take out a bacillus."[7] The irony of this development meant that terrorism had come full circle to the days of the French Revolution, with its infamous *regime de la terreur*, and states were once again using their power to terrorize their own people.

The internal terror practiced by the Soviet Union, Italy, and Germany is well known and documented. Yet, with far less fanfare and public awareness—but with similarly horrific results—state-terrorism was also taking place elsewhere in the world. Turkey used terrorism against its Armenian population and the fascist military regime in Japan did not shy away from using violence against internal dissidents opposed to the chauvinistic direction of its policies.

Post–World War II Anti-Colonial Terrorism

The process of decolonization accelerated after World War II in many parts of the world. Often, indigenous people managed to rid themselves of their colonial occupiers by means of terror. State-terrorism in the years between the two world wars came to be viewed as an interruption of what would have been a natural progression—a direct line connecting the ideological anarchist-terrorist to the new nationalist-terrorist movements resisting foreign occupation. In other words, in their attempt to fight the stronger powers ruling over them, nationalist movements were quick to adopt the violent methods used in the past by ideological terrorists. After all, they argued, if terrorism could be used for a certain type of struggle, surely oppressed people fighting for independence from foreign occupation had no less right to do the same. This line of reasoning merged the moral justification for terrorism of both anarchists and nationalists into one.

Nationalist Terrorism and Ethno-Separatist Terrorism

Two types of movements have used terrorism as part of their struggle for independence in the postcolonial era:

1. Nationalist movements trying to gain independence from colonial occupation.
2. Ethnic movements trying to separate themselves from majorities of a different ethnicity.

Examples of nationalist movements range from the Vietnamese' struggle against the French, Cypriots' fight against British rule, to the Algerian war for independence from France. Four reasons explain the rush to decolonization after World War II:

1. The growing reluctance of the colonial powers' own citizens to rule over other people.
2. The near bankruptcy of the colonial powers as they emerged from the war, which forced them to question the cost-effectiveness of continued colonialism.
3. The promises made by the allies during World War II in a document known as *The Atlantic Charter* of 1941, in which the United States and Britain hinted that after the war colonies would gain independence. When the war ended, people everywhere sought to redeem that promissory note.
4. The fall, in February 1942, of Singapore, Britain's most formidable garrison in Southeast Asia, had a huge impact on colonized people everywhere. This shocking Japanese victory demonstrated that, propaganda to the contrary notwithstanding, white people were not superior and enjoyed no special right to continue ruling colonized populations.[8]

┌───┐
│ **What Do YOU Think?**
│
│ Do you agree with the notion that with the possible exception of the American
│ experience, not *one* violent revolution in world history was a true success, justify-
│ ing the suffering involved and living up to the optimistic expectations of the peo-
│ ple? Explain your position using examples.
└───┘

Examples of ethno-separatist terrorism abound; among them, the two-decade campaign of the Kurdistan Workers' Party (PKK) against Turkey (mostly from 1978 to 1995); the Armenian Army for the Secret Liberation of Armenia (ASALA), which was active between 1975 and 1985; and the Basque Euzkadi Ta Askatasuna (ETA), with its ongoing struggle against Spain.

The main reason for the glut of movements seeking separation from a larger ethnic majority is self-evident. In an era in which fighting for independence or self-government is sanctified by many as legitimate and even heroic, it is inevitable that various ethnic groups demand similar rights.

Ideological, Religious, and Criminal Terrorism

As nationalist-terrorism was triumphing in all corners of the world, terrorism morphed again. This time terrorism changed direction and again became ideological, later religious in nature, and, still later, intermingled with criminal terrorism. It is significant that these three new variations are *transnational* in essence, a notable departure from the previous state and parochial nature of terrorism. In the late 1960s, the general dislike of the Vietnam War and the imperialism it seemed to represent alienated the peaceful mainstream in the United States and elsewhere in the West. Radical fringe elements, however, opted to express their frustrations by joining left-wing terrorist organizations, such as the Red Army Faction (RAF) in West Germany and the Red Brigades in Italy. Following the collapse of the Soviet Union and the exposure of the bankruptcy of communism, left-wing terrorism declined, largely replaced by its right-wing counterpart, especially in Europe.

This ideological terrorism, as we will see in subsequent chapters, was fragmented and of relatively limited influence. By the early 1990s, it was overshadowed by a much more menacing and organized international form—religious terrorism. Completing the transition is the newest plague on the stage of modern terrorism—criminally inspired. In this category, one usually finds narco-terrorists and various organized international networks of criminals that ally themselves with other terrorists and cooperate with them for profit. We will explore the origins, nature, and unique threat these three new types terrorism pose to the West in Chapters 5, 6, and 7.

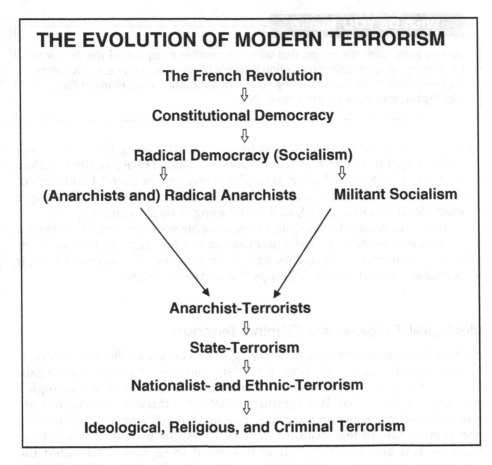

THE EVOLUTION OF MODERN TERRORISM

The French Revolution
⇩
Constitutional Democracy
⇩
Radical Democracy (Socialism)
⇩   ⇩
(Anarchists and) Radical Anarchists   Militant Socialism

Anarchist-Terrorists
⇩
State-Terrorism
⇩
Nationalist- and Ethnic-Terrorism
⇩
Ideological, Religious, and Criminal Terrorism

SUMMARY

In this chapter, you have learned the following:

1. Our model for defining an act of terrorism differs from that of many other definitions.

2. Scholars trace a great many instances of terrorism through the millennia.

3. The origins of modern terrorism can be traced back to the aftermath of the French Revolution.

4. Terrorism evolved and changed over time until it completed a full circle when it again became associated with state-terrorism circa World War II.

5. The decolonization process following World War II witnessed the adoption of terrorism by nationalist and separatist movements.

6. Ideological terrorism has been widespread in recent decades.

7. Terrorism has morphed lately into religious and criminal forms.

💣💣💣

Perhaps no group better exemplifies the transition of terrorism from that practiced by the anarchists a century ago to the present brutal mixture of ideology, religion, and criminality than the Lord's Resistance Army (LRA). Based in Uganda, where it has been trying to overthrow the government for the last two decades, the true nature of the LRA is hard to define: While practicing a twisted version of Christianity, its members pray like Muslims. The organization maintains its power base by kidnapping thousands of children each year to turn the boys into fighters and the girls into sex-slaves. The LRA's murderous brutality is legendary. Its fighters are known to hack to death the inhabitants of villages and to rape and torture on a large scale. The young abducted fighters often are ordered to kill their own relatives and friends—and sometimes to cook and eat their bodies. Terrorism has come a long way, yet according to some, we have seen nothing yet of what the future holds.

💣💣💣

NOTES

1. More on the ancients' attitude toward killing of tyrants can be found in Walter Laqueur, ed., *The Terrorism Reader: A Historical Anthology* (Philadelphia, PA: Temple University Press, 1978), pp. 10–19; and in Walter Laqueur, *The New Terrorism: Fanaticism and the Arms of Mass Destruction* (New York: Oxford University Press, 1999), p. 10.

2. See David C. Rapaport, "Fear and Trembling: Terrorism in Three Religious Traditions," *American Political Science Review*, Vol. 78, No. 3 (September, 1984), pp. 658–677.

3. Robespierre is quoted in R. R. Palmer, *The Age of the Democratic Revolution: The Struggle*, Vol. 2 (Princeton, NJ: Princeton University Press, 1964), p. 126.

4. The quote about the aftermath of the French Revolution can be found in Jonathan R. White, *Terrorism: An Introduction*, 4th ed. (Belmont, CA: Wadsworth/Thomson Learning, 2002), p. 67.

5. For an excellent discussion of the evolution of this process, see Ibid., pp. 67–71.

6. Trotsky's article can be found in Leon Trotsky, "Why Marxists Oppose Individual Terrorism," at http://www.socialistparty.org.uk/Trotsky/againstterrorframe.htm (accessed July 19, 2006).

7. Mussolini is quoted in Walter Laqueur, *Terrorism* (Boston, MA: Little, Brown and Company, 1977), p. 71.

8. The points about the impact of the Atlantic Charter and the fall of Singapore were made by Bruce Hoffman, *Inside Terrorism* (New York: Columbia University Press, 1998), pp. 45–47.

PART II

REBELS WITH LOTS OF CAUSES

FOUNDATIONS OF MODERN TERRORISM

Blowing up houses of worship to please God

PART II

REBELS WITH LOTS OF CAUSES

FOUNDATIONS OF MODERN TERRORISM

Motives that Don't Meet the Eye

Psychological Reasons for Terrorism

We are the people our parents warned us about.

Anonymous

A botched bank robbery in 1973 in Stockholm, Sweden, in which four people were taken hostage, marked an important milestone in the study of the link between psychology and terrorism. After a six-day standoff, police stormed the bank to end the crisis. The hostages reacted to the rescue attempt in a way that surprised the police—they physically resisted the rescue operation. Later, the former hostages refused to testify against their captors and even raised money to help pay their legal costs.

Although this chapter deals with the psychology of terrorists, not of victims, and with incidents of terrorism, not robberies, this event has been significant in the study of terrorism in general. The behavior exhibited by the hostages, while strange, is not inexplicable and has been observed over the years in different cases involving terrorism. Helpless and facing possible death, the hostages come to be completely dependent on their captors, and, as a result, undergo a process of identification with those in control of their lives to the point of losing their own identity. The victims come to understand, sympathize with, and even justify the actions of the criminals or terrorists who can decide their fate.

You may recognize this type of behavior by the name it acquired after that failed bank robbery in Sweden, the *Stockholm Syndrome*.

THE GREAT DEBATE: IS IT ALL IN THEIR HEADS?

Students of terrorism who enjoy a lively disagreement between scholars should look no further. A serious debate has been raging between those who think that we can learn a great deal about terrorism by studying the psychology of individuals and those who pretty much pooh-pooh the idea. At the heart of this debate is the question of whether or not psychology can help us understand terrorists and their motives. In this chapter, we will examine the two differing schools of thought: Those who think that terrorists are motivated largely by psychological reasons call terrorist acts *expressive*, as in lashing out spontaneously in ways that express a basic reaction without much thinking. Scholars who disagree with this approach refer to terrorism as *instrumental*, which means that acts of terrorism are deliberate, rational, and guided by a calculated plan.

The Expressive View: Terrorism as Spontaneous Combustion

Those who hold this point of view believe that terrorism is an expression of some individuals' psychological makeup and needs, rather than a thought-out approach based on cost–benefit calculations. Professor of psychiatry and political psychology Jerrold Post belongs to this camp. In his opinion, "political terrorists are driven to commit acts of violence as a consequence of psychological forces."[1] Importantly, he argues that terrorists rationalize acts of terrorism that, in reality, they were psychologically compelled to commit anyway.

Supporting this outlook, according to Post, is the strange similarity of the rhetoric used by terrorists everywhere. Wherever and whoever they are, terrorists' expressions of their cause and motives are similarly "polarizing and absolutist . . . a rhetoric of 'us versus them.' " These terrorists look at their political world only in shades of black and white and perceive themselves as righteous freedom fighters. At the same time, they see the other side, the "them," as an evil that must be destroyed because there can be no compromise with so wicked an enemy that is responsible for the wrongs the terrorists fight against. Equipped with this knowledge, asks Post, how can we possibly argue the opposite, that terrorism is the logical product of well-balanced individuals who rationally choose terrorism as a strategic means?

Post warns against jumping to the conclusion that terrorists are necessarily abnormal people with serious psycho-pathological issues. As an example, he points to studies of the terrorist organizations National Liberation Front (FLN) in Algeria and the Irish Republican Army (IRA) which found no evidence to suggest that their members suffer from any psychological abnormalities. In fact, findings show that individual terrorists who actually enjoy killing and inflicting violence are relatively unimportant figures within their terrorist organizations and tend to be followers rather than leaders. Other individuals join terrorist organization not out of psychopathic reasons or from ideological conviction, but because they enjoy the "high" associated with the danger of terrorism. Moreover, comparative studies of different terrorist groups do not show "a particular psychological type, a particular personality constellation, a uniform terrorist mind."

If this is the case, how can Post advance the idea that psychology is, after all, closely linked to terrorism? The answer, suggests Post, is that some individuals have a psychological makeup that makes them join a terrorist group because doing so provides them with the opportunity to carry out violent acts that they really want or need to do. Those who agree with this school of thought believe psychology can provide important clues about types of terrorists, what makes them "tick," and how authorities should deal with them.

One fascinating explanation for the relationship between psychology and terrorism, according to Post, is the phenomenon of *splitting* or *externalization*. These terms refer to individuals with a borderline personality disorder in which "an individual with this personality constellation idealizes his grandiose self and splits out and projects onto others all the hatred and devalued weakness from within. . . . They need an outside enemy to blame." This means that unlike most humans, some individuals cannot have both the good and bad, strengths and weaknesses, co-exist within them. Such individuals resolve the issue psychologically by splitting the two parts: They assign to themselves everything that is good and project onto someone else (externalize) all that is wrong. Similarly, terrorists who suffer from this borderline disorder take credit for the

"Splitting": An Example

Some analysts speculate that Adolph Hitler may have suffered from this borderline personality disorder. He considered himself the God-sent knight in shiny armor to the German people. As such, he claimed all of the credit for the early successes of his policies. When the fortunes of war turned against him, he disavowed all responsibility for the setbacks and, instead, blamed all that went wrong on others: the Jews, his subordinates, and even the German people, who, he complained, were unworthy of him.

positive things in their lives, while blaming others (the establishment, the enemy, "them") for everything that has gone wrong with their lives. This theory provides an interesting explanation for the absolutist, black-and-white, angry state of mind of some terrorists. Post maintains that the phenomenon of splitting is represented in disproportionately high percentages among terrorists.

Citing research on mostly left-wing terrorists conducted in West Germany, Post describes findings that show the following: A high ratio of the terrorists came from broken families; 24% of the subjects studied had lost a father prior to the age of 14; almost 80% of the terrorists questioned told of severe conflict with their parents while growing up; and a third had been convicted in juvenile court. The pattern that emerged is of life-long failure in everything.

Other Psychological Explanations

Another interesting psychological aspect worth pondering is the "incidence of birth." It has been noted that some of the most famous conquerors in history had not been born into the nation that they would turn into empires. For example, Alexander the Great was not a genuine Greek, but a Macedonian. Similarly, Napoleon was born in Corsica, Adolph Hitler in Austria, and Joseph Stalin in the Caucasus, in Georgia. The psychological impact of being an outsider, or member of a minority, seems to be at play with certain terrorists as well. For example, citing research conducted about the Basque terrorist group Euzkadi Ta Askatasuna (ETA), Post shows that while only 8% of the Basque population were born to mixed Basque–Spanish parents, no less that 40% of the ETA members originate from such mixed couples. Can the psychological factors behind this phenomenon be ignored?

Jessica Stern, a terrorism expert at Harvard's John F. Kennedy School of Government, also believes that terrorism can be an expressive outburst against an enemy without the benefit of a well–thought-out program. Stern classifies al-Qaeda's September 11, 2001, attack as an example of expressive terrorism because the attack had no realistic chance of achieving its political goals; the organization's stated grievances have been changing constantly (such as the loose talk of lost Andalusia in Spain or the questionable calls for a worldwide jihad), and the attacks were carried out by the cynical exploitation of like-minded but uninformed young Muslims.[2]

Another scholar, Richard Rubinstein, does not agree that a psychological approach offers a sufficient explanation for terrorism, but he believes that understanding certain psychological aspects can be useful. "Most efforts," he writes, "to explain terrorist thinking and behavior on the basis of psychological theories still seem overly general and of uncertain applicability."[3] But not all. Rubinstein cites the concept of "chosen trauma," developed by Vamik Volkan, a professor of psychiatry at the University of Virginia. "Chosen trauma" is a partial explanation of terrorism that views violent political behavior as the result of a painful historical experience.[4] A chosen trauma registers a deep impact on an individual or on a certain collective that triggers a disproportionately violent reaction to a similar event. For example, the Crusades left a bitter residue among Arabs and Muslims that has lasted to this day. The rage exhibited against the West in the Middle East nowadays cannot be fully understood without realizing the influence of that chosen trauma—the Crusades—on the psyche of Middle Easterners. Similarly,

---

What Do YOU Think?

How do you feel about individuals from either religious or secular terrorist groups who purposefully kill themselves for their "cause"?

"Palestine" has evolved into a powerful chosen trauma for many in the Middle East.

Rubinstein contributes an interesting psychological explanation of terrorism by focusing on the outcome of the interplay between *temptation* and *intimidation* in certain societies—especially among young people. Temptation is represented by Western culture: television shows, movies, the Internet, clothes, music, alcohol consumption, and so on. Intimidation is represented by the conservative forces of the society in which they live. Occasionally, temptation contradicts central religious tenets of that society, such as dating or drinking alcohol, which are viewed as outright blasphemy. Sooner or later, some "sinners" feel the need to get back into the good graces of their society. Accomplishing such a reversal may require an outstanding act of "self-purification" that cleanses all of one's sins and feelings of guilt. This remarkable act can be achieved in a heroic struggle, or martyrdom, against the temptation, against those who brought it about (Westerners), and even against locals who participated in it. This psychological explanation can help us understand a good many cases of suicide bombings around the world.

No discussion of the psychology of terrorists can be complete without a quick peek into a widely cited typology of terrorism developed by the psychiatrist Frederick Hacker. In an attempt to profile terrorists and understand what make them tick, Hacker classified terrorists into three categories: crusaders, criminals, and crazies, and within each, he identifies the terrorists' motives, their expectations, and what these mean for the authorities that deal with them.[5]

Crusaders commit terrorism in the service of what they believe is a higher cause that will please their God or benefit the collective on whose behalf they toil. Their struggle, these individuals believe, is not for selfish purposes. It is next to impossible for law enforcement officials to negotiate with crusader-terrorists because the latter will not compromise on their God's will or negotiate away their sacred mission. For example, if while on a suicide mission, members of the terrorist group Liberation Tigers of Tamil Elam (LTTE) in Sri Lanka are surrounded, they cannot be expected to strike a deal with the authorities to save themselves because doing so would betray their people's cause.

Criminals commit terrorism for personal gain. Since they are interested only in their own well-being and profit, it is easiest for law enforcement to negotiate with this type of terrorists. Officials can deal with them rationally and offer a deal that makes sense to criminals interested only in survival and profit. For example, think of a member of a Russian criminal organization who tries to smuggle Russian military components to Europe for sale to an international terrorist group. Something goes wrong and the besieged criminal finds himself holed-up in a house and holding hostages. An offer for safe passage or money, or both, is likely to end the crisis peacefully. Raphael Trujillo, who was the dictator of the Dominican Republic from 1930 until his assassination in 1961, terrorized his people for decades for criminal purposes. As Frederick Hacker puts it, Trujillo was not a sadist or mentally ill; he terrorized his nation for normal criminal gain. "He was a thief, pimp, informer, and convicted forger before he became the benefactor of the people, genius of peace, savior of the country, protector of workers, and father of all Dominicans, as his people had to call him."[6]

Crazies commit terrorism for reasons known only to them. Since their reasoning ability is, well, unusual, it is very difficult for authorities to manage a crisis involving them. Hacker quotes the former dictator of Uganda, Idi Amin, a man who murdered perhaps 250,000 people and who was universally considered less than balanced, as writing to Tanzania's distinguished president Julius Nyerere, "I love you very much and if you had been a woman, I would have considered marrying you although your head is full of gray hairs. But as you are a man, that possibility does not arise."[7]

One should not confuse, however, "crazy" with "dimwitted." As we all know, crazies' logic may be different than ours, but some of them may be brilliant otherwise. This makes it more difficult to establish an understanding of the motives or wishes of a volatile bomb-carrier in a shopping mall, for example. Negotiating with this type of a terrorist requires a negotiator who can form some sort of common bond with the terrorist, encouraging the terrorist to believe that he or she is understood and taken seriously. The process and outcome of such negotiations are dangerous as they are strewn with potential surprises.

Irony

During a lecture on this typology, a student once quipped, "Isn't it crazy, or criminal, that Islamist terrorists belong in the *crusader* category?" Ironic indeed.

The Instrumental View: Terrorism—Cool, Calm, and Calculated

On the other side of the debate is the school of thought that maintains that psychology is not a very useful tool for understanding terrorism. Walter Laqueur—and to a lesser extent Walter Reich—argues that attempts to understand terrorism by focusing on its psychological origins are for the most part useless because terrorism is too varied and widespread geographically and historically.[8] Adding the large influence of different cultures and religions dooms to failure attempts to come up with psychological profiles of terrorists' behavior. The opposite of the psychological approach, the instrumental view, holds terrorism as a logical strategy based on a cost–benefit analysis.

Strategic Calculation

During the Algerians' war against French rule (1954–1962), rebels would manipulate the French soldiers into counterproductive behavior. The rebels would choose to ambush a French military convoy next to preselected villages or towns, knowing that following the ambush the enraged comrades of the attacked soldiers would conduct brutal sweeps and searches of these places. Predictably, after humiliating encounters with the ill-mannered soldiers, more local young men would head to the hills to join the rebels.

Professor Martha Crenshaw of Wesleyan University offers one of the best representations of the instrumental view. Crenshaw maintains that the available data on terrorists suggest that they are usually normal people. In her view, terrorism is a deliberate, rational strategy, even if not always calculated purely on a cost–benefit basis. However, she agrees, certain psychological aspects are important when analyzing the terrorist group's influence on individuals' behavior. Crenshaw finds the preoccupation with psychological motives that cause individuals to join terrorist organizations unhelpful: there are simply too many reasons why they join. Dwelling on this question may be unproductive, but asking ourselves why terrorists *stay* in such organizations can prove useful.[9]

To understand terrorism, we need to explore the factors that gave rise to the need to use the strategy of terrorism in the first place. For Crenshaw, two things make up this background: the *environment* in which terrorists exist and function, and the role *politics* and *economics* play on that society. Crenshaw suggests that we can best understand them by studying the three parts that form the environmental and political/economic settings: The *situation* in places where terrorism exists, the *reasons* for terrorism, and the role of the *individual* terrorist.[10]

Situation

The situation has two aspects: *preconditions* (for example, poverty or a society prone to violence) and *precipitants* (for example, a triggering event such as the killing of a family member by the authorities, or humiliating treatment by soldiers searching the neighborhood). Elaborating on preconditions, Crenshaw provides three explanations: The first is the "permissive causes of terrorism," which enable the creation and spread of terrorism. Think of improvised explosive devices and the Internet and you get a good idea of technology as a permissive cause of terrorism. "Urbanization" is the second precondition. A terrorist's delight, urbanization enables terrorists to target crowded skyscrapers, markets, and universities, which contain large numbers of people in small spaces. Last, Crenshaw cites "social habits and historical traditions." Consider the "Wild North," an area in northern Pakistan bordering on Afghanistan, where armed local tribesmen have always roamed free, defying authorities when wishing to do so to the extent that even Pakistani soldiers do not dare set foot in certain areas. Little wonder, bin Laden, who is said to be hiding somewhere along that frontier and enjoying local tribal protection, has never been caught.

Discussing the second aspect of the situation, *precipitants*, Crenshaw goes beyond the environment that made terrorism possible in the first place to explain what in that environment provides motivation and direction for terrorists. Differently put, this explanation deals with the reasons for terrorism rather than with the opportunities for terrorism.

The importance of precipitants can be seen in the result of a government action, when it puts down a riot or suppresses some display of political dissatisfaction too harshly. "Black Friday," as the event came to be known in Iran, is a powerful demonstration of a precipitant. On Friday, September 8, 1978, huge crowds flooded the streets of Teheran to demonstrate against the rule of the Shah. In a tremendously counterproductive decision, authorities responded with live fire, allegedly using machine guns, tanks, and helicopter gunship fire to break up the demonstration, killing hundreds in the process. The disproportionately harsh response to this demonstration galvanized much of the population and made the Iranian Revolution inevitable.

"Political Oppression" as a Relative Concept

Terrorism is not always a reaction to actual political repression. For example, the left-wing terrorist organizations that plagued Western nations in the 1960s and 1970s, such as the Italian Red Brigades, the West German Red Army Faction, the French Direct Action, or the Japanese Red Army, did not function within repressive political environments, at least not as we understand the term.

The Reasons for Terrorism

Since a great number of groups with widely different ideologies have resorted to terrorism, Crenshaw suggests that a common denominator can be found by examining their short-term goals. Regardless of the ideology or the exact audience the terrorists try to reach, Crenshaw finds that groups which use terrorism share the following seven motives:

> ## What Do YOU Think?
>
> Professor Martha Crenshaw speculates that "perhaps terrorism occurs precisely where mass passivity and elite dissatisfaction coincide."[11] Explain the significance of this observation and try to come up with a few cases in modern history that support your opinion.

1. *To publicize the cause*—some terrorist operations are planned to match the media scheduling routine.

2. *To disrupt establishments' normal functioning*, and, by doing so, to show how inept the government is.

3. *To create public sympathy* for the cause or to spread fear among potential enemies.

4. *To provoke a harsh response from the government*, which will alienate the public.

5. *To add cohesion, boost morale, and galvanize* the group for continued struggle.

6. *To counter the greater military power* of the government.

7. *To capitalize on a unique historical opportunity* that requires immediate action.

With this understanding, it is time to explore the importance of the third part of Crenshaw's thesis—the role of the individual.

The Role of the Individual

The school of thought that does not attach much importance to psychological factors in the study of terrorism is quite naturally not overly concerned with the unique differences among individuals. On the other hand, it is illogical to completely overlook the role of individual terrorists as if there are absolutely no lessons that can be learned from studying this significant aspect. The compromise that scholars, including Crenshaw, came up with is to look at common characteristics of terrorists in order to better understand their shared traits.

Crenshaw identifies several attributes that seem to be common to many terrorists: First, the sense of personal danger that typifies all terrorists who risk life, limb, and liberty in the course of their struggle. Either because of a high level of commitment or for love of the thrill, members of terrorist groups show high tolerance to risk. Second, due to the high stress accompanying a life on the run, terrorists come to rely a very great deal on the group. Interactions with the group, writes Crenshaw, may be more important than particular psychological characteristics. Third, the quest for vengeance for jailed or slain comrades becomes the engine that feeds further acts of terrorism. As Crenshaw put it, "A government that creates martyrs encourages terrorism."[12] Fourth, terrorists usually seem to posses a sense of guilt, which makes them constantly justify their actions and seek understanding for their behavior. Guilt can lead to deliberately risky behavior and acts of self-sacrifice. Trying to imagine one such individual brings to mind Winston Churchill's immortal one-liner: "He has all of the virtues I dislike and none of the vices I admire." Edgar O'Ballance lists shared characteristics of terrorists who do well in their chosen field:[13]

1. *Dedication to a political belief or cause:* Part-time efforts do not lead to success. One needs to immerse oneself totally in the terrorist lifestyle and its uncompromising demands.

2. *Willingness to self-sacrifice:* Being a terrorist presents dangers that are not for the light of heart. A commitment to being a terrorist means that any given time one might be killed, jailed, or tortured.

3. *The ability to suppress normal emotions:* By definition, terrorists hurt innocents. It takes a deviant personality to be able to suppress all emotions and murder in cold blood unarmed, helpless victims.

4. *Reasonably high intelligence:* Fools cannot get far in this high-stake game. To plan and carry out missions while constantly keeping one step ahead of the authorities requires a higher level of intelligence than is usually realized.

5. *Education:* In the era of international terrorism, to be successful one needs to have the know-how and refinement to travel inconspicuously to foreign destinations without rising suspicion.

6. *Access to resources:* Successful terrorists have access to money, publicity, sanctuaries, and other logistical support.

SUMMARY

In this chapter you have learned that

1. A debate exists among scholars whether terrorism results from spontaneous acts of aggression or from rational calculations.

2. Concepts such as "incident of birth," "chosen trauma," and "temptation and intimidation," and the classification of terrorists into the categories of crusaders, crazies, and criminals can explain much about terrorism.

3. Terrorism can be analyzed according to the "situation," the "reasons," and the "role of the individual."

4. Certain personal traits characterize "successful" terrorists.

This chapter began with an explanation of the Stockholm Syndrome. It is time to conclude this chapter with one of the most celebrated examples in American history of this psychological phenomenon. Once again, although the focus of this anecdote is on the victim's psychological state, rather than on the terrorists', students of terrorism need to be aware of it.

A sensational case of political terrorism took place in California in February of 1974. Patricia Campbell Hearst, granddaughter of the famous newspaper publisher William Randolph Hearst, was kidnapped from her apartment by a bizarre, left-wing terrorist group called the Symbionese Liberation Army (SLA). Amidst the greatest manhunt in history until then, the captors kept Patricia Hearst blindfolded in a closet for two months, abusing her physically, sexually, and psychologically. Tortured, isolated from the world, and brainwashed, an armed Patricia Hearst was seen on April 15, 1974, actively participating in a bank robbery in San Francisco along with members of the SLA. During the year before she was caught and on the run, she participated in other armed robberies, disseminated SLA propaganda, and appeared to have wholeheartedly embraced her captors' political agenda. Even during her trial, she refused to incriminate fellow members of the SLA who were also in police custody.

In her defense, Hearst's legal team tried to use the Stockholm Syndrome concept to explain her actions, but following an extremely high-profile trial, Hearst was sentenced to seven years' imprisonment. She would serve 21 months.

Patricia Hearst depicted in three photos
Source: Courtesy of Corbis/Bettmann.

NOTES

1. Post's argument, as well as the other aspects and concepts discussed by him and mentioned in this chapter, can be found in Jerrold Post, "Terrorist Psycho-Logic: Terrorist Behavior as a Product of Psychological Forces," in Walter Reich, ed., *Origins of Terrorism: Psychologies, Ideologies, Theologies, States and Mind* (Washington, DC: Woodrow Wilson Center Press, 1990), pp. 25–40. The quote is on page 27.

2. Jessica Stern, "Understanding Terrorism," in *Harvard Magazine* (January–February, 2002), accessible at http://www.harvardmagazine.com/on-line/010262.html (accessed October 5, 2006).

3. Richard Rubinstein's article is to be found in "The Psycho-Political Sources of Terrorism," in Kegley, Jr., ed., *The New Global Terrorism: Characteristics, Causes, Controls* (Upper Saddle River, NJ: Prentice Hall, 2003), pp. 139–150.

4. Dr. Vamik Volkan's "chosen trauma" concept is cited in Ibid., pp. 139–140.

5. Frederick J. Hacker, *Crusaders, Criminals, Crazies: Terror and Terrorism in Our Time* (New York: W.W. Norton & Company, Inc., 1976).

6. The description of Trujillio is found in Ibid., p. 23.

7. Idi Amin is quoted in Ibid., p. 11.

8. See Laqueur's discussion of the terrorist personality in his book *Terrorism* (Boston, MA: Little, Brown and Company, 1977), p. 120, and that of Walter Reich, ed., "Understanding Terrorist Behavior: The Limits and Opportunities of Psychological Inquiry," pp. 261–279.

9. For more on Crenshaw's position that terrorism is not expressive, see Martha Crenshaw, "The Logic of Terrorism: Terrorist Behavior as a Product of Strategic Choice," in Walter Reich, ed., pp. 7–24.

10. Crenshaw's explanation of the situation, the reasons for terrorism and the role of the individual terrorist are found in "The Causes of Terrorism," in Kegley, Jr., ed., pp. 92–105. The examples in the current discussion are provided by me.

11. Crenshaw's speculation of when terrorism occurs is found in Ibid., p. 95.

12. Crenshaw's quote that martyrs create more terrorism, is found in Ibid., p. 102.

13. For the list of characteristics of successful terrorists, see Edgar O'Ballance, *Language of Violence: The Blood Politics of Terrorism* (San Rafael, CA: Presidio Press, 1979), pp. 299–302.

4

Dogmatic Reasoning

Sociological Aspects of Terrorism

Every story has three sides to it—yours, mine and the facts.

Foster Meharny Russell

Aum Shinrikiyo was a Japanese terrorist group that developed biological and chemical weapons and launched several deadly attacks in Tokyo and throughout Japan in the 1990s. It originated in the 1980s as a religious group that adhered to a complex mixture of Buddhist doctrines combined with Hindu teachings and other self-developed principles. Eventually, the group evolved into a doomsday cult. The group's leader, Shoko Asahara, sold clippings from his beard for $375 and his dirty bathwater for $800 a quart. Surprisingly, many of the group's members were physicians, scientists, and engineers from the best universities in Japan. After the authorities moved in and dismantled the terrorist operation, they interrogated group members, trying to understand how these bright analytical minds could succumb to such fantastic, irrational demagoguery. Mostly embarrassed, they had trouble explaining how they had relinquished their most basic sense of judgment and morality once they became part of the group. To this day, hardcore followers of the founding leader Asahara refuse to renounce him.

Two factors are important for understanding the influence sociological forces have on terrorism. One factor is the terrorist *organization*. It consists of two categories: *groups*, such as the French Direct Action and the Japanese Red Army, and *national movements*, such as the Liberation Tigers of Tamil Elam (LTTE) in Sri Lanka and the Palestine Liberation Organization (PLO). Groups are usually driven by ideology, and attempts to understand them center on the relationship between each group's values and its ideology. In contrast, movements that are driven by patriotic motives enjoy greater popular support than ideological terrorist groups do. The second factor is the *society* in which terrorist groups exist and function.

In this chapter, we first look at characteristics of typical terrorist organizations to understand better their impact on the authorities' ability to fight terrorism. We then examine the role of society in the development and support of terrorism to understand how the norms of a society can spell success or failure in the fight against terrorism.

SOCIOLOGY AND TERRORISM: THE INSIDE STORY

Fascinating things happen when an individual joins a terrorist organization. A new set of relationships develops between the person and the organization, one that results in a drastic change in the thinking and behavior of that individual. This is one important reason that sociological aspects make it so difficult for law enforcement to deal with terrorism.

When they join a terrorist organization, individuals change to adapt to the group's demands and expectations. Merging into the organization provides some of them with the feeling of belonging to a "family" for the first time in their lives. The shift in self-esteem can be dramatic. A new sense emerges within these individuals that they are significant and that their opinion and actions count. At the same time, the opposite is taking place: having joined an organization, the dynamics of the group begin to exert strong influence over the individual's judgment. This is a well-known phenomenon and characterizes groups of all sorts, including the military, business, or education. Therefore, contends Jerrold Post, it is only natural to expect that similar processes take place inside terrorist organizations as well.[1] Where does this progression lead? According to Professor Cindy Combs, "modern terrorists are, for the most part, fanatics whose sense of reality is distorted."[2] Who then are these modern terrorists, really?

Characteristics of Terrorist Organizations

Ideological and nationalist terrorists end up crossing a psychological threshold as they move underground and detach themselves from family and friends, creating a family for themselves within the new group. Living isolated lives underground means that the organization becomes their only source of reliable information, a confirmation of everything they believe, and the foundation of their security. This is especially true of the more isolated ideological terrorists.

> **Did You Know?**
>
> Terrorists tend to be young, and increasingly so in recent years. However, terrorists who are members of ideological organizations are normally better educated than their counterparts in nationalist movements.

Post states that this creates a pressure cooker atmosphere within the terrorist organization. Powerful sociological forces come into play, moving everybody in the direction of ever-increasing radicalism.

How does this pressure cooker work? As the terrorists incorporate their individual identities into the group, a "group mind" emerges. The external pressures, the daily dangers, and the constant sacrifices tend to increase group solidarity. This situation is similar to a divided nation that rallies around the flag in the face of an external threat. Inevitably, a feeling of common destiny sets in. This condition affects the belief system the organization adopts, the nature of the targets chosen, and the members' commitment to self-sacrifice. The result of this dynamic is that no doubts are tolerated and that anybody questioning the group's decisions or methods risks being expelled or killed.

Inside terrorist organizations, all questions concerning the morality of terrorist acts receive blanket justification. Having surrendered their individuality, the organization's morality now becomes the individuals' morality. As in many cults, individual morality is strictly forbidden; consequently, the more isolated individuals were before joining the group, the more dependent upon it they become. In addition, they become less likely to question the organization's positions and tactics. For such individuals, truth is no longer found outside the group; it exists only in the perceptions of the organization, even if the perceptions are illusions. The French-American historian Jacques Barzun said it best, "In any assembly the simplest way to stop the transacting of business and split the ranks is to appeal to a principle." Such group morality enables terrorist organizations to indoctrinate their members to fight for what their adherents believe are—and what may be—noble principles but not to live up to them.

Group Discipline

Post cites the experience of a new recruit in the German Red Army Faction (RAF) who was horrified when he learned of the group's plan to firebomb a department store. When he protested that innocents would get hurt, a hostile silence descended upon the room and the new recruit quickly realized that one could not question the group's consensus. As a result, group pressure compelled an idealistic individual to target innocent civilians. Doubts were dismissed with the cliché that the department store was "where the bourgeoisie shops," which the group turned into a fact beyond question.

What Do YOU Think?

In light of the findings that moderate leaders of terrorist organizations do not last long, consider the following: Is it realistic to expect that if new leaders emerge for right-wing American terrorist groups, such as the Aryan Nation, they might pursue more moderate policies than their predecessors? Can you think of anything that might change the usual group dynamic and cause new leaders to tone down their ideological rhetoric?

In this atmosphere of conformity, any leader or moderate contender for a leadership position loses to the person who advocates more shocking acts of violence. History points clearly in this direction and examples abound of leaders of terrorist organizations who increase the harshness of their actions in order to maintain their leadership positions. Instinct and experience have taught them that exhibiting flexibility and restraint is hazardous to their life.

Groupthink

Understanding the basic aspects of "groupthink" will provide an outside observer a better grasp of the "mind" of the terrorist organization and the frustration that comes from expecting its members to demonstrate opinions different from those held by the group. Members trapped in a groupthink state exhibit four main symptoms: feeling of invulnerability, certainty in the organization's morality, simplistic perception of the enemy as evil, and intolerance toward any internal dissent. Combined, they make the fight against terrorism far more difficult than an outsider looking in would think.

Feeling of invulnerability: Research into decision-making shows that terrorist organizations adopt far riskier courses of action than their members, asked individually, would have considered wise. This group distortion of common sense is particularly disturbing, and is why experts express growing alarm over terrorists' access to weapons of mass destruction. Their anxiety is accompanied by a declining hope that moral restraint will deter terrorists from using these weapons.

Certainty in the organization's morality: "Cognitive dissonance" is a term that describes the human tendency to reject information that contradicts what one believes. The result is a feeling of absolute confidence in one's cause. Therefore, fighting for the cause justifies all means. This explains the lack of genuine remorse by members of terrorist organizations after conducting particularly gruesome operations. In one of his video messages taped post-September 11 and broadcast on al Jazeera, bin Laden stood by his cause, proclaiming that if others wished to label members of his organization "terrorists," so be it. For him and his supporters, there was no cognitive dissonance because they rejected anything that challenged al-Qaeda's cause, and it therefore enjoyed a complete monopoly over the moral high ground. This absolute certainty leaves no room for doubt or mercy for the thousands of innocent victims.

Simplistic perception of the enemy as evil: The organization's rigid outlook results in a black-and-white perception of its enemies. Since the organization's cause and morality are unquestionably superior, it only stands to reason that the other side is wicked and thus deserving of its fate.[3] Even pro-Palestinian observers are at a loss to explain the terrorist group Hamas's (Islamic Resistance Movement) practice of referring to Israelis as "the sons of pigs and monkeys"; however, the answer is disturbingly obvious. Just as alluding to Jews as "units" made it easier for the Nazis to dispatch their victims to death camps, dehumanizing Israelis makes it easier for Hamas's suicide bombers to kill them all, including women and children.

Intolerance toward any internal dissent: As we have seen, the organization creates social and ideological unity that limits its members to a single way of interpreting events and processes. Dissenting opinions are not encouraged or allowed. Post described the explanation a jailed member of the RAF gave for the lack of independent thinking within his organization: "The way to get rid of the doubts was to get rid of the doubters."

The Threat of Victory

What happens to a terrorist organization once its struggle has met with success and it has achieved its goals? Can we expect it to disband and to lay down its arms? Will its members join mainstream society? This is a critical issue for anybody who studies terrorism and tries to draw conclusions about its future. Studies of both groups and national movements reveal a pattern that points toward a more sober perspective. Pessimism may be out of vogue, but a healthy dose of realism can prevent much grief down the road.

From biology, we learn that a priority of any organism is survival; sociology tells us that this is true of organizations as well, and terrorist organizations are no exceptions to this rule. When a terrorist organization achieves its goals, its very reason for being is threatened, and a fear of victory sets in because of the consequence of success to the future of the organization. As a result, the terrorist organization prefers to be successful enough to record some heroics, to perpetuate its name recognition, to attract new members, and to keep the organization going, but never to win the war. If it acknowledges triumph, what is the organization to do the next day? For individuals involved in the exciting world of conspiracy, danger, and the pursuit of a noble cause, terrorism expresses the essence of their self-worth. As a result, terrorists neither disarm nor voluntarily stop their campaign. Instead, they respond by escalating their demands to ensure the continuation of the organization.

After Victory

The Lebanese Shi'i group Hezbollah, considered by the United States a terrorist organization, claimed as its *raison d'être* the ejection of Israel from South Lebanon. When Israel withdrew from Lebanon in 2000, Hezbollah refused to disarm and disband. Instead, it set ambitious new goals for itself, such as political prominence in Lebanon. Thus, in spite of clear UN recognition that since 2000 Israel has not been present on a single inch of Lebanese territory and in defiance of subsequent UN resolutions to disband all militias in Lebanon, Hezbollah remains a powerful political and military presence in Lebanon. The organization's successful campaign against Israel in the summer of 2006 motivated it to seek an even greater share of political power in Lebanon.

It is difficult to exaggerate this fear of victory. Consider the following example: the 1993 Oslo Accords laid the foundation for peace between Israel and the Palestinians. However, Palestinian policy under the late president of the then budding Palestinian Authority (PA), Yasser Arafat, seemed more focused on preparations for a renewed campaign of violence than on building the infrastructure of a self-sufficient and peace-oriented Palestinian nation.

Some Middle East experts attributed Arafat's implicit acceptance of the worsening situation on the ground to his "fear of victory." Prior to signing the Oslo Accords with Israel, Arafat had been admired as a revolutionary, a freedom fighter, father of the Palestinian nation, and a welcome statesman in international capitals; with the signing of the Oslo Accords, life for Arafat became dismal. Instead of registering heroic exploits on the battlefield and in the political arena, leadership for Arafat became associated with the mundane tasks of balancing budgets, managing garbage collection, and meeting other civil responsibilities. As success lost its luster, the alternative of keeping up the struggle gained appeal.

Demonizing the Enemy

In trying to explain the ability of terrorists to plan and execute the most brutal acts of violence against innocents, Professor Michael Barkun discussed the terrorists' practice of "demonizing" their rivals.[4] His idea has three parts:

- scapegoating
- conspiratorial explanations
- identification of a co-conspirator

What Do YOU Think?

Based on this understanding of terrorists' dread of victory, consider the following: If the West were to capitulate to al-Qaeda's demands to leave the Middle East and abandon Israel, would the organization cease to exist or would it just raise its demands?

Let's look at each of the components: *Scapegoating* involves projecting everything that is negative onto somebody else and rejecting the possibility that the party doing the finger pointing might be in any way responsible for the problem. This observation helps explain terrorists' reactions to bloody stand-offs with law enforcement, especially when an episode results in casualties. Almost invariably, the surviving terrorists blame the authorities for the car-nage, protesting that no harm would have come to the victims if the authorities had given in to their demands.

Successful demonizing is not an easy undertaking, so *conspiratorial expla-nations* are added to the brew to make the demonizing more convincing and acceptable. As a result, events are routinely interpreted in ways that suggest that there is more to them than meets the eye, that a plot is unfolding. Take the 2003 Iraq war, for example. Militant Islamic groups have viewed the U.S.-led war in Iraq as fertile ground for conspiracy theories. Chief among them is the assertion that the war had very little to do with liberating the Iraqi people or even with the search for weapons of mass destruction. Rather, they argue, the war was merely an American conspiracy to take over Iraq's huge oil deposits. Relentlessly promoted by al-Qaeda, affiliated extremist groups, certain Islamic clergy, and anti-American elites, this assertion has gradually taken root and become enormously popular all over the world, especially in the Middle East.

I am often surprised at the persistence and genuine conviction with which even some U.S. university students believe this claim. A basic calculation of how much revenue the United States would have to obtain from the sale of Iraqi oil to make the war effort profitable points to the fallacy of this conspiracy theory. The sales would have to be in the trillions of dollars just to break even with the hundreds of billions of dollars the war has cost! During a lecture, I tried to discredit this accusation by questioning its logic. I asked my class of undergraduates, "If the Americans are so interested in Middle Eastern oil, why did they invade powerful and problematic Iraq instead of just taking over defenseless oil-rich Kuwait?" Unfazed, one of the students responded, "Because the U.S. already owns Kuwait." Conspiracy theories die hard, if at all.

For claims of a conspiracy to appear reasonable, one needs to add meat to the skeleton of the unfolding plot. The accusation needs supporting details, new information that supposedly has become available, and exciting rumors to make the conspiracy believable—enter the *co-conspirator*. As con men know, the larceny in people's hearts is what makes the success of a scheme possible. Therefore, they provide information their victims want to believe. Similarly, to demonize the enemy effectively, terrorists need to do two things: They have to attribute wicked plans to the policy in question and then make the charge more believable by adding an already distrusted party as co-conspirator to the fictional allegation. It lends greater credence to the conspiracy.

To demonize the United States for its alleged conspiracy against Iraq, rumors about co-conspirators plotting with the United States to achieve its dreaded goals abound. In the Middle East, these range from the Israelis to the "crusaders" of the West. The conclusion is clear: Since the United States allied itself with the worst co-conspirators imaginable, it becomes an enemy richly deserving of brutal punishment.

Intentional deception is not always the purpose of accusing others of conspiracies. Often, terrorists sincerely believe the conspiracy theory they advocate and, in turn, try to convince others to share those beliefs. On other occasions, terrorists do not shy away from cynically manipulating public opinion with deceptions and deliberate fabrications.

The Making of a Conspiracy

The phenomenally successful fabrication that the September 11, 2001, attacks were carried out by none other than the CIA and the Israeli intelligence agency, the Mossad, is an excellent illustration of demonization. Days after the attacks, word of an American–Israeli conspiracy aimed at discrediting Arabs and Muslims spread throughout the Islamic world. Hundreds of millions of Muslims were said to believe this falsehood for months after the events took place, and one can only wonder how many millions still do in spite of the fact that following the attacks the Qatar-based al Jazeera news organization broadcast a video of bin Laden in which he all but took responsibility for orchestrating the attacks.

The supposed conspiracy had all of the required elements to appear credible to receptive ears and minds: the United States as the scapegoat, the plot to tarnish the reputation of Arabs and Muslims everywhere, and, finally, the Israeli co-conspiratorial angle. It took over a year to trace the source of this trumped-up story as the brainchild of Hezbollah's satellite television station al Manar, which purposely originated the story as part of its propaganda campaign against Israel and the United States.[5] In some parts of the world, honest reporting and accountability either do not exist or are a farce.

Separating the Military from the Political

A historic development has taken root among nationalist terrorist movements in recent years. The trend is toward separating the political and military wings of the movement. Doing so allows the political leadership to distance itself from the atrocities committed by the military wing, and since national movements represent large sections of the population, the international community finds itself in a bind. On the one hand, these movements use terrorism as a strategy. On the other, they present themselves as legitimate political organs with massive popular support. In some cases, the movement engages in humanitarian activities, gaining both political and monetary support from abroad using the pretext that the funds are to be used for charitable purposes. This was true of the PLO of old, as well as of the Lebanese Hezbollah today.

Splitting the two wings works quite well for national movements when dealing with democracies. The arrangement confuses democracies and provides them with a convenient pretext for dealing with the movement. The deception also helps countries avoid hard choices, such as having to brand nationalist movements as terrorist organizations. If a separation between the military and the political wings did not exist, governments would be compelled to enact harsh measures against such movements, a course of action governments are not always eager to impose. Saudi Arabia financed the terrorist group Hamas for years saying that its funding was earmarked only for Hamas's welfare programs, not its military arm. The Saudis were never seriously taken to task over this cynical policy, a clear demonstration of the difficulties democracies confront in combating terrorism.

Some movements excel in using this illusionary division. The Irish Sinn Fein ("We Ourselves," in Gaelic), under Jerry Adams, is a good example. Having presumably separated the political party from the militant Irish Republican Army (IRA), Adams has managed to gain entry into the political mainstream and the halls of governments, including the White House, in spite of protests from Britain. Professing complete detachment from the violent operations of the armed wing works because it serves both the terrorist organization and the interests of other governments.

Dual "Wings"

Hamas has taken this tack of splitting its political and military arms for years. This protected the movement's political leadership from the fury of Israeli retaliation, while its armed wing, the Izz al-Din al Kissam, continued to carry out terrorist operations mostly against Israeli civilians. Hamas killed hundreds of innocents and wounded thousands more while its leaders claimed innocence, arguing that they only determined policy, raised money for operations, recruited fighters, and ordered attacks. Since they did not know the exact sites of the operations or the precise identity of the would-be suicide-bombers, they could not possibly be held responsible for the attacks launched by the armed wing.

This sham worked for a while. As the attacks increased in frequency and ferocity, the Israelis tired of the charade and began hunting down, arresting, or killing the political leaders of Hamas. The climax of the Israeli countermeasures came in 2004 when successive Israeli air strikes killed the political leaders of Hamas, Shaykh Ahmad Yasin and later his replacement, Abd al Aziz al Rantisi. The relentless Israeli targeting of specific Hamas political and military leaders proved successful for a while. Its leadership decapitated, Hamas was rudderless for the next several months and the frequency and quality of its terrorist operations were drastically affected for a while.

SOCIETY AS THE BACKBONE OF TERRORISM

The second factor in the discussion of sociological forces is the society itself. Both factors—the terrorist organization and the social environment—pose serious challenges to law enforcement, but it is the society and its attitude toward the terrorists' cause that is the most problematic. With few exceptions, the main reason the war on terrorism appears to be an increasingly uphill, losing battle is the level of support a society provides for the terrorists.

A quick glance at recent history shows that nationalist movements usually win if they use terrorist tactics and enjoy wide and genuine popular support. The success of such movements in cases ranging from Cyprus to Algeria to apartheid-era Rhodesia is apparent. One can point to exceptions, such as the British success in putting down the communist rebellion in Malaya in the late 1940s and early 1950s, but this happened because the British were not fighting an indigenous nationalist movement but rather a Chinese minority group. It is too early to tell whether the more contemporary experiences of the Chechens, the Palestinians, and the Tamils of Sri Lanka will succeed or become exceptions to the rule. These struggles are still unfolding processes whose result we are yet to witness.

The crucial factor in the success of an antiterrorist campaign is the *nature* of the society within which the terrorists operate. For example, religious terrorists strongly believe that their acts are justified based on divine law that supersedes any set of rules created by human beings. If the society shares a similar belief system, this will enhance the terrorists' motivation and resolve. In other words, if society gives heinous acts the cloak of legitimacy and reinforcement, neither police action nor military intervention will succeed, as the Tamils' struggle in Sri Lanka demonstrates. Conversely, if society rejects the terrorists' actions and the values that guide them, such as in the case of the French Direct Action, the terrorist group is almost certain to fail in the end. This shows us that we need to look beyond "cost effectiveness" calculations or explanations that focus on the individual terrorist in order to understand terrorism better. If we are to gain meaningful insights into the phenomenon of terrorism, we should focus on the societal aspects.

Popular Support

The difficulties the international community has encountered in wiping out al-Qaeda prove the uselessness of fighting terrorist groups that enjoy wide popular support. Grassroots backing by the sympathetic Muslim population residing along the border regions of Pakistan and Afghanistan has made attempts to capture or kill bin Laden and his top aides fruitless. In contrast, the Greek Marxist–Leninist terrorist group known as 17 November was put out of business by Greek authorities in 2002. The organization's failure to mobilize the Greek masses to its cause resulted in an abrupt liquidation of the group when the authorities managed to arrest one of its members.

A street vendor in Pakistan selling pictures of Osama bin Laden in 2001
Source: Courtesy of Peter Arnold, Inc.

The Collapsing State System

A realistic understanding of terrorism must take into account the ever-worsening global economic situation, which has resulted in hundreds of millions of desperate people hardly able to subsist. The French satirist Sebastian Chamfort's quip that "Society is composed of two great classes: those who have more dinners than appetite, and those who have more appetite than dinners" is becoming more relevant by the day.

To make things worse, in some regions of the world such as western Africa, states that cannot provide for their citizens are collapsing. Countries like Sierra Leone, the Ivory Coast, and Ghana serve as eye-opening examples of this trend. The process is already underway, and as societies disintegrate along tribal, regional, or religious lines, the need for survival takes the form of the kind of violence we label "terrorism." Labels notwithstanding, this violence is increasingly becoming the norm in those regions. Although this low-level brutal conflict is beginning to spill over into some neighboring countries, a solution to the problem is nowhere to be found, and this alarming process is expected to deteriorate further.

The noted military historian Martin van Creveld believes that we are headed toward a future in which warfare will be largely conducted by terrorists, guerillas, bandits, and robbers. He predicts that war and crime will become undistinguishable, and legal and moral values as we know them today will no longer exist in many parts of the world. Indiscriminate destruction and abuse of the enemy will become the new standard.[6]

Take politicians' words about "the war on terrorism" and the imminent victory for the shiny knights of law and order over the abominable forces of terrorism with a grain or a boulder of salt. Demographic, economic, religious, and political forces—beyond the ability of the international community to control—all but guarantee that victory over terrorism is not likely in our lifetime.

Governments' Dilemmas

For centuries, a tempting strategy in the fight against terrorism has been the physical elimination of a large segment of the society. Some regimes have succeeded in campaigns against terrorists by applying ruthless methods against entire portions of a population. In 1982, the Syrian regime of Hafez Assad successfully suppressed a rebellion by Muslim fundamentalists in the city of Hama, brutally killing at least 20,000 residents of the city in the process. Similarly, Slobodan Milosevic's Serbia tried to annihilate the mutinous Albanian Muslim population in Kosovo, elements of which did terrorize the Serb countryside. Only the U.S.-led military intervention saved the entire Muslim population of Kosovo from elimination by death or expulsion. However, such strategies are unattractive choices nowadays even for the most tyrannical regimes because instant media exposure and the certain public outcry to follow make these brutal options problematic.

However, what was good for the goose was rarely possible for the gander. Authoritarian and dictatorial regimes may have successfully defeated any attempts at terrorism within their countries, but applying similar measures to quell the masses is a nonstarter for democratic societies. The revulsion of the democratic societies of Britain, France, and the United States may have been more responsible for the success of rebel movements in pre-Israel Palestine, Algeria, and Vietnam than was the terrorism practiced by the indigenous forces. As a result, while there are no terrorist organizations operating successfully in North Korea, The People's Republic of China, or Syria, one can easily conceive of cases of terrorism plaguing democratic societies from Germany to Japan and from India to Italy. The fact that democratic societies cannot use the same murderous methods that dictatorial regimes employ helps explain why terrorism persists. Democratic societies that are targets of terrorism appear indecisive and to be on the defensive.

What Do YOU Think?

The Israeli–Palestinian context provides fertile ground for lessons about the fight against terrorism. One of these lessons is the overwhelming obstacle that a supportive population poses to authorities. Survey after survey shows that 50% to 75% of the Palestinian people—depending on when the polls are conducted—endorse the goals and methods of the terrorists. With the populace providing the terrorists with logistical, political, and moral support, will the Israelis ever succeed in eliminating Palestinian terrorism by standard law enforcement methods?

SUMMARY

In this chapter, you have learned the following:

1. Terrorist organizations consist of groups and national movements.
2. The group plays a unique role in the life of terrorists, providing them with a sense of family, security, and purpose.
3. Neither disagreements nor expressions of moderation are welcome in terrorist organizations.
4. Terrorist organizations tend to demonize their enemies and fear the possibility of actually achieving their declared goals.
5. Some terrorist organizations find it convenient to separate their military and political wings in order to give leaders the ability to deny connivance in terrorist acts.
6. Authorities have had difficulties winning wars against terrorist organizations that enjoy their societies' support.

💣 💣 💣

In 2001, a *Wall Street Journal* reporter writing an article about the phenomenon of madrasahs, or religious Islamic schools, interviewed an 11-year-old Pakistani student. Asked whether a man had ever walked on the moon, the boy replied, "This isn't possible." "What is two times two?" Silence. Eager to impress, though, he announced that dinosaurs exist: "The Jewish and American infidels have created these beasts to devour Muslims."[7] Pakistani madrasahs teach about 700,000 students, indoctrinating many into the world of anti-Western Jihad.

Over the years, the 8,000 madrasahs have graduated many students who now hold key positions in Pakistan. The country has nuclear weapons.

💣 💣 💣

NOTES

1. Post's speculation that sociological forces at play in various types of organizations also affect terrorist groups, his discussion of the pressure cooker atmosphere inside terrorist organizations, the characteristics of "group think," and terrorists' fear of victory, which are discussed later, are found in Jerrold Post, "Terrorist Psycho-Logic: Terrorist Behavior as a Product of Psychological Forces," in Walter Reich, ed., *Origins of Terrorism: Psychologies, Ideologies, Theologies, States and Mind* (Washington, DC: Woodrow Wilson Center Press, 1990), pp. 25–40.
2. For the assertion that terrorists are essentially fanatics with a distorted sense of reality, see Cindy C. Combs, *Terrorism in the Twenty-First Century*, 3rd ed. (Upper Saddle River, NJ: Prentice Hall, 2003), p. 61.
3. An excellent insight into the dehumanization of victims is found in Albert Bandura, "Mechanisms of Moral Disengagement," in Walter Reich, ed., pp. 180–182.

4. Michael Barkun, *A Culture of Conspiracy: Apocalyptic Visions in Contemporary America* (Berkeley, CA: University of California Press, 2003).

5. More on the role Hezbollah's TV station, al Manar, played in promoting the 9/11 conspiracy can be found in Terence Tao, "The Case of the Missing 4000 Israelis," self-published article, last updated August 8, 2003. Available online at http://www.nocturne.org/~terry/wtc_4000_Israeli.html. See also, Michael Dobbs, "Myths Over Attacks on U.S. Swirl Through Islamic World—Many Rumors Lay Blame on an Israeli Conspiracy," *Washington Post*, October 13, 2001. According to the *Pew Global Attitude Project* conducted in 2006, the majority of Muslims in countries surveyed still believed that Arabs did not carry out the September 11, 2001, attacks. See Meg Bortin, "Poll Finds Discord Between Muslims and Western Worlds," *New York Times*, June 2006, p. A3.

6. Martin van Creveld, "The Transformation of War," in Richard W. Mansbach and Edward Rhodes, eds., *Global Politics in a Changing World: A Reader*, 2nd ed. (New York: Houghton Mifflin Company, 2003), pp. 35–45.

7. Peter Fritsch, "With Pakistan's Schools in Tatters, Madrasahs Spawn Young Warriors," *Wall Street Journal*, October 2, 2001.

5

On Behalf of the Sheep and for the Like-Minded

Left-Wing and Right-Wing Terrorism

In a war of ideas, it is people who are killed.

Stanislaw Lec

💣💣💣

Political ideology is divided between the *left* and the *right*, but what is the origin of these everyday terms and what do they *really* mean?

It all began in the days of the French Revolution (1789–1799). Those who believed in forming a republic (referred to as republicans, but having no relationship to present-day American Republicans) in the National Assembly (the French legislature) were opposed to the old order, who supported France's absolute monarchy, represented by the conservatives and the aristocracy. Since the republicans were seated on the left side of the Assembly Hall, the name *left* stuck.

Over the next 200 years, the meaning of political left has undergone many changes, but it usually denotes those who sympathize with the less privileged classes. In recent decades, the political left has come to be associated with liberalism, social democracy, or socialism.

In contrast, "right" was a label attached to those French legislators favoring the interests of the "old order," the conservatives and aristocrats, because they sat on the right side of the Hall. Today, *right* is a term associated with those who favor free markets, capitalism, and a number of conservative positions on social issues.

💣💣💣

IDEOLOGICAL TERRORISM: SIMILARITIES BETWEEN THE LEFT AND THE RIGHT

While there are more than two types of terrorism that are motivated by "ideas," this chapter limits *ideological terrorism* to terrorists of the left and of the right. We will explore other types of terrorism, such as religious and criminal, in later chapters.

Left-wing terrorists see themselves as champions of the downtrodden everywhere, particularly of the poor in the third world. Right-wing terrorists are more concerned with issues of nationalism or their race. That said, they share many commonalities: Equally unhappy with the social structures of modern industrial societies, they see themselves as "revolutionaries" and dislike parliamentary democracy. "All cruelty springs from weakness," wrote Seneca prophetically some 2,000 years ago. Indeed, terrorists see their enemies as more powerful than they really are, while viewing themselves as weak and without options, most often to a point that, in their eyes, justifies spectacular atrocities against innocent members of the "enemy." In other words, both types of terrorists look at the world through biased lenses that make them feel above normally accepted morality. Therefore, they act as if regular standards of behavior do not apply to them. Whether on the left or on the right, terrorist groups find ways to identify the victims of their operations as members of the enemy and, consequently, deserving of the violence inflicted upon them.

Left- and right-wing terrorists have inspired nationalist and separatist terrorists to adopt the ideologues as their model in their own struggles for independence. Naturally, some important differences—mainly in their goals—do exist between ideological and nationalist types of terrorism.[1]

Terrorists of both the left and right disagree with the existing social and economic structures of their societies, especially in their industrial-capitalist manifestations, and hope to replace them with a new order. Nationalists, however, appreciate modern industrialization and hope to maintain this system after winning independence. For example, the Palestine Liberation Organization (PLO) has no problem with capitalism or industrialization; its top concern is winning Palestinian independence.

Interestingly, despite their rhetoric, terrorists of the left and right are not shy about collaborating with international terrorists who do not share their point of view. Both have taken advantage of the wealth of terrorist-training opportunities available in the Middle East even when the ideologues' interests and basic values were in conflict with the religious or nationalist values of their hosts. In fact, on many occasions the same Middle Eastern terrorist group that trained and supported terrorists from the left provided equal hospitality to their bitter opponents from the right. Ideological terrorist groups, in turn, have provided logistical and operational support to various Middle Eastern terrorist groups, mainly in Europe.

Intellect versus "Guts"

A major difference between left- and right-wing terrorism is in the intellectual level of their philosophies. Leftist ideologies often seem to require much reading of theoretical works, analysis, and debate. Early Marxists, for example, were usually intellectuals who published articles, debated them, countered publications of colleagues with articles and books of their own, and were passionate students of history. Generations of followers of Marxism were exposed to a constant barrage of theory alleging the superiority of that ideology. Communist-era masses, factory workers, peasants, and students had to attend periodic meetings for indoctrination in these teachings. Left-wing ideology has been challenging the intellect of its followers to this day. Leftist terrorists still attempt to base their ideology on Marxist and other theoretical bodies of work, such as "dependency," "neo-Marxism," "world capitalist system," and so on.

In contrast, right-wing ideologies aim at the heart rather than the intellect. Mass rallies and bonding with similar people substitute the intellectual approach of the left with a mob mentality driven by sentiment or "gut" feelings. In this type of politics, overcharged senses replace thinking with a desire to have like-minded people unite against supposed outside enemies of the collective, which is probably best illustrated by the Nazi rallies of the 1930s. One would be hard-pressed to find serious theoretical works by leading Nazis. With a few exceptions, the same is true of modern right-wing terrorism.

LEFT-WING TERRORISM

The Rise

The origins of post–World War II leftist terrorism in Europe can be traced to the anti–Vietnam War climate of the 1960s. The growing opposition to the war found its first radical voice in West Germany and quickly spread to other countries, including France, Italy, Spain, and Belgium. In these countries, as well as in others around the world, the ideological resistance to the war morphed into a militant anti-American rage that targeted the wider issues of imperialism and capitalism itself.

History has a disturbingly long tradition of small elites who view themselves as the self-appointed benefactors of those they treat like sheep. Similarly, leftist terrorists everywhere assume that they, the small combative elite, represent the masses' interests and know what is good for them, whether or not the people understand or agree with them.

In Western Europe, the newly formed terrorist cells modeled themselves on the urban terrorism strategy of the pioneering Tupamaros in Uruguay, who had introduced a campaign of bank robberies, kidnappings, and assassinations in the early 1960s. Later in their evolution, these terrorist groups would develop close ties with Palestinian groups in the Middle East, mainly in

What Do YOU Think?

Imagine that you are a young Russian about 100 years ago. When you look around, you see horrific social injustice: The vast majority of the people live in abject poverty, families are unable to provide for their children, and famine and disease are common. Children work from dawn to dusk in mines to help their families eke out a subsistence living. While free universal education or access to health care for the masses is a fantasy, a tiny percentage of the population—rich beyond all proportion—controls almost all the assets and resources of the country. Those complaining about the situation are certain to be exiled to Siberia by a tyrannical regime that tolerates no political dissent.

One day, friends invite you to attend a meeting. There, you are introduced for the first time to the writings of Karl Marx and Frederick Engels and told that their theory has an "iron logic" that is beyond dispute. You meet other young people who speak of a just future in which the working people, not the few rich, will own the means of production and men and women will work according to their individual abilities and will be paid according to their needs. All children will receive free education, and everyone will be entitled to jobs, free medical care, and participation in the political process.

At this point in our imaginary script, you do not know about future gulags, the true face of a "dictatorship of the working people," and large-scale murderous political purges. Most important, communism itself is not then a bankrupt ideology. As a young and idealistic person who wishes to create a more just society, would you risk life and freedom and join the communist party to actively help bring about that utopian future?

Lebanon. The Palestinians would provide the training and the Europeans would reciprocate with logistical and operational assistance for Palestinian operations in Europe.

So fervent was the leftist ideology among the young of the 1960s and beyond that much of it was incorporated into the propaganda of nationalist movements. Terrorist organizations with a clearly nationalist agenda such as the IRA, the Basque ETA, and some Palestinian groups adopted the slogans of antiimperialism and of working-class solidarity in their literature, communications, interviews, and even in the political indoctrination of new recruits. The reality, however, was very different. The nationalist movements did not understand or care for the leftist agenda they seemed to endorse, but it was fashionable and useful to appear to be a part of the universal anticapitalist and antiimperialist struggle.

Expectedly, the Soviet Union was not too upset about this development; in fact, it enthusiastically supported some of these anti-Western leftist movements. Sometimes indirectly through its communist allies and sometimes directly, the Soviet Union provided left-wing European terrorists logistical and political support.[2]

Hannah Arendt observed that "ideas, as distinguished from events, are never unprecedented." Indeed, Europe was not the only domain of left-wing terrorist groups; they had been preceded and later followed by terrorists of the same persuasion the world over. Although leftist ideology and leftist terrorism have been around for over a century, some left-wing terrorist groups have been more infamous than others. Among the most noted examples of left-wing terrorist groups in the post–World War II era is an impressive list of groups that earned a celebrity status in their heydays. The following smorgasbord provides us with a quick glimpse of leftist terrorist organizations in Europe, Latin America, Asia, and the United States: After the pioneering Tupamaros of Uruguay came the West German Baader–Meinhoff, later to be renamed Red Army Faction (RAF). Additional European terrorist organizations came into the scene, making a name for themselves: the Red Brigades of Italy, the French Direct Action, the 17 November group in Greece, and the Turkish Dev Sol. Latin America has continued to contribute important movements to this list: From the Revolutionary Armed Forces of Colombia (FARC) and the smaller National Liberation Army (ELN) in Colombia to the Marxist Shining Path and Túpac Amaru Revolutionary Movement (MRTA) in Peru, to name but a few. The Japanese Red Army (JRA) made a name for itself internationally, while left-wing terrroism in the United States was best represented by the Symbionese Liberation Army (SLA) and the Weather Underground.

Celebrity Terrorists

One of the most famous European left-wing terrorist organizations was the West German Baader–Meinhof group, later known as the RAF. Andreas Baader, a drug addict, and Ulrike Meinhof, who had suffered from early brain damage, led the group during its heyday between 1968 and 1977. During that period, the RAF grabbed international headlines with its terrorist exploits and gained celebrity status in West Germany. The young terrorists, usually from comfortable middle-class backgrounds, presented themselves as working-class people and claimed it was on their behalf they were terrorizing the country. To sound "blue-collar," members used a great deal of profanity, and to demonstrate their defiance of bourgeois standards of morality, they engaged in sexual orgies. Declared sympathies with the working class notwithstanding, Baader–Meinhof members used only BMWs as their getaway cars.

The West German authorities managed to arrest most of the important leaders of the group by 1972, and by 1977, all three leaders had committed suicide. Surprisingly, the RAF continued to function in spite of its repeated failures and the persistent arrests of its new leaders until 1998, when the group formally announced its own dissolution.

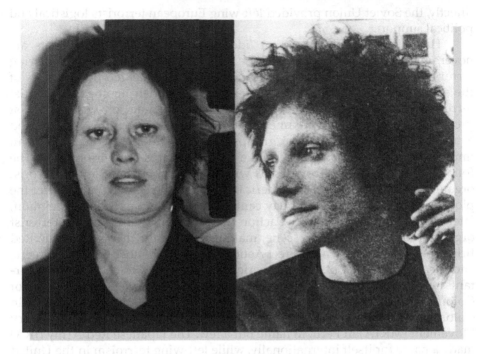

Ulrike Meinhof and Gudrun Ensslin of the Baader–Meinhof terrorist group
Source: Courtesy of Getty Images Inc.-Hulton Archive Photos.

Latin America has also seen the successful proliferation of leftist terrorist groups. The obvious example is the Columbian Marxist FARC, which has been fighting the government quite successfully since 1964, when the local communist party established it. Currently, the FARC is in control of a substantial portion of the Colombian countryside, with a well-trained, armed, and motivated force. Similarly, the radical Maoist Shining Path terrorist group in Peru is still alive and active despite serious setbacks in recent years. This group prepared for its campaign of terrorism for ten years, and, once launched, gained notoriety for its particularly brutal practices that left over 30,000 Peruvians dead. Although its founder and leader, Abimael Guzman, has been in jail since 1982, the group has not withered away.

The Peruvian Hostage Rescue Operation

They secretly dug tunnels under the house, followed every move the terrorists holding the hostages made by bugging the house with electronic devices, frequently deceived the terrorists, and spent months preparing a military raid to free the hostages. They even found out that all four terrorist leaders, along with other members, played soccer every afternoon on the first floor of the building.

The crisis began on December 17, 1996. The Japanese Ambassador to Peru was hosting some 400 Peruvian and foreign dignitaries for a diplomatic reception when 14 members of the Peruvian leftist terrorist group MRTA seized the house and took everybody hostage. The young terrorists, some of them teenagers, demanded the release of comrades from Peruvian jails. The 126-day crisis that ensued ended on April 22, 1997, when President Albert Fujimori ordered a well-planned rescue operation to commence. Using the tunnels that had been dug under the house, the Peruvian commandos burst in during the terrorists' soccer game. When it was over, all the terrorists, one hostage and two soldiers were killed.

The brilliant rescue operation was later tainted by accusations that some of the terrorists were killed in cold blood after their surrender.

And Fall

It is thought that European left-wing terrorist groups began their rise in 1968, peaked during the next two decades, and, for the most part, passed from the scene by 1995. Jonathan White argues that three key events changed the course of European politics and explain the decline in leftist terrorism:[3] (1) the fall of the Berlin Wall in November 1989 and the subsequent unification of Germany, which diffused much of the appeal of left-wing terrorism; (2) the emergence of the newly liberated peoples of the former Yugoslavia, which diverted left-wing energies from abstract Marxist goals to the region's actual ethnic conflicts; (3) the collapse of the Soviet Union in 1991, which took the wind out of the sails of leftist ideology in Europe both by eliminating logistical support and by revealing the bankruptcy of the Marxist ideology. This decline took place against the backdrop of a thriving capitalistic system in Europe that opened unprecedented channels for political participation and dissent. These developments removed whatever incentive or need some might have felt previously for resorting to terrorism. Victor Hugo wrote that "No army can withstand the strength of an idea whose time has come." The time of the idea that Marxism is a failed ideology came and leftist European terrorism became passé.

Old habits don't die easily. Hardened left-wing terrorists did not simply give up and go away, turning their backs on decades of conviction and struggle. As the decline of left-wing terrorism in Europe accelerated, its leaders tried desperately to avoid total collapse and elimination. In 1985, news surfaced about attempts by major West European left-wing terrorist organizations to unite, pool their resources, and create a mega leftist terrorist network. Authorities and analysts were first alarmed at the prospect, but this fear turned out to be misplaced. This last hurrah of the terrorists was more a symbol of weakness, a last-gasp effort to stay alive than a sign of an ambitious campaign to come. European left-wing terrorist organizations would fold one by one in the years to come, but their demise did not herald a new era of terrorism-free European peace and stability. Instead, there was a switch to right-wing terrorism, brutal ethnic terrorism in the Balkans, and the emergence of criminal terrorist organizations.

Walter Laqueur notes the ironic twist that accompanied the decline of left-wing terrorism. Initially, when European terrorism came from the left, Western intellectuals like Jean-Paul Sartre and Noam Chomsky "understood" the use of terrorism. Using creative verbal acrobatics, some intellectuals formulated an assortment of rationalizations to explain and sometimes justify terrorism; for example, that the capitalist system was the real villain—that it used terrorism against the people, or that terrorism was some sort of a liberating act aimed at helping the masses in the long run. What a difference a few years make. As the political left in Europe declined and terrorism became increasingly associated with the right, Western intellectuals found themselves embarrassed by having to explain why terrorism was not, after all, such a progressive political act, and was, in fact, wrong. Suddenly, "the old wisdom about one person's terrorist being another person's freedom fighter was no longer heard."[4]

Left-wing terrorism in Europe failed because the mainstream never understood the terrorists' naïve political agenda, did not identify with it, did not sympathize with the terrorists themselves, and was never even close to joining the struggle. Walter Laqueur summed it up, "left-wing terrorist discourse proceeded on a level of higher lunacy, divorced from all reality . . ."[5] Under these circumstances, the European leftist terrorists found themselves isolated and on the run, and, as a result, the end came as no surprise.

It is important, however, to understand why left-wing terrorist organizations continue to thrive in many parts of Latin America and Southeast Asia. The rhetoric of such terrorist groups has a lasting appeal despite their shortcomings, brutality, and failures. The reason is deeply rooted in the dismal economic conditions in these regions, in contrast to conditions in Europe. As long as people live amidst great poverty and injustice, the lure of communist ideas of equality to all and a more just distribution of land and wealth will continue to fall on the eager ears of those unable to feed their children. The hope for a better future has proven more powerful than the fear of the authorities, and left-wing terrorism around the world will not disappear anytime soon.

RIGHT-WING TERRORISM

Some see European right-wing terrorism as a backlash against its predecessor on the left. Globally, in this category are religious extremists, neo-fascists, neo-Nazis, various racist groups, and certain types of violent hooligans, such as "skinheads." These groups are not concerned with universal values; they care only for those who look like them, worship like them, and think like them. However, not all right-wing terrorism is alike. The United States, with its many white supremacist groups, is a violent society in which people have easy access to firearms and explosives, and Latin America has had its own share of deadly right-wing paramilitary groups. However, there has been relatively little organized right-wing terrorism in Europe since World War II.

There have been few rightist European organizations engaged in serious and systematic campaigns of terrorism. Yet, there have been many lethal cases of arson, racial, and xenophobic attacks throughout the European continent by those associated with the political right. At the same time, certain cases identified as European right-wing terrorism resemble the violent behavior of European soccer hooligans more than they do terrorism.

Still, right-wing European terrorism does exist. Right-wingers, like all other terrorists, tend to depersonalize their enemy, viewing everyone on their opponent's side identically, without distinction of gender, age, and politics. According to Combs, this approach frees terrorists from thinking of their victims as individuals and makes it easier for them to target anybody who belongs in the big block of people known as the *enemy.*

In the case of right-wing terrorism, negative images of the enemy collectively enable the terrorists to inflict violence on entire groups of "undesirables": journalists, lawyers, students, or intellectuals that the terrorists consider "liberal," "progressive," or "socialist." Homing in on the enemy and destroying it is more problematic if terrorists thought of their victims as individuals—someone's child, parent, wife, or an innocent passer-by.[6] Consequently, over the last two decades, rightist political violence in Europe has resulted in the deaths of dozens of innocents in a political context aimed at sending a message to wider audiences—the unmistaken characteristics of terrorism.

Mass Murder in Bologna

Saturday, August 2, 1980, was a hot and humid day in Bologna, Italy, a city known for its culture as well as for its left-leaning politics. Bologna's train station is one of the busiest transportation centers in the country and on that fateful morning, huge crowds packed the air-conditioned train station, seeking refuge from the intense August heat. The terrorists struck at 10:25 A.M. A huge explosion ripped through the train station, inflicting carnage on travelers and employees. Eighty-five people were killed and over 200 were wounded in the most lethal post–World War II terrorist outrage in Europe to that date.

The identity of the terrorists was engulfed in mystery at the time. It appears, however, that the perpetrators were right-wing neo-fascists, who had decided to punish all of the people living in, passing by, or doing business with Bologna. In a classic demonstration of terrorists who view the "enemy" as a depersonalized, monolithic group, the terrorists selected Bologna for a target because of the city's pro-communist political leanings.

The devastating terrorist attack that shattered the peace of that tranquil Saturday morning became the most infamous example of European right-wing terrorism. But this incident proved rare as there have been no other instances of rightist terrorism of this magnitude in Europe.

Germany: A Case Study of Right-Wing Terrorism

In Europe, right-wing terrorism is thought to have originated in 1987. From that humble beginning, the trend gradually changed as individuals and groups classified as "rightist" became better organized. In some cases, they began moving into the open, seeking political legitimacy and greater mainstream recognition. The German reunification process in the 1990s and the accompanying rise of various right-wing groups was of huge importance. Their number peaked in 1992, but declined sharply by the middle of that decade.

The organization, philosophy, and activities of these German groups look a lot like that of the brown-shirts in Nazi Germany. This combination of skinheads, neo-Nazis, old Nazis, and neo-Fascists follows a well-trodden historical path: "purification" of Germany from foreigners, fervent nationalism, racial purity, anti-Semitism, and general hatred of non-Germans. After the fall of the Berlin Wall in 1989 and the subsequent German unification, youths from the poor regions of the former East Germany became eager recruits for these right-wing groups. Consequently, the groups grew stronger, coordination among them increased, and some of them developed tentacles internationally to collaborate with like-minded groups elsewhere, especially in the United States. Like their predecessors some 60 years before, these young right-wingers tried to dominate the street by violence in order to frighten away their ideological opponents.

In contrast to the left-wing terrorists, who were mostly the product of German universities, these right-wing hoodlums emerged from bars and street corners. In addition, while left-wing terrorists in general attempt to study theoretical works relevant to their ideologies, German right-wing terrorists have not been disposed to ideological discourse, intellectual debates, or to reading theoretical works. They follow a simplistic belief system that claims racial superiority and advocates the expulsion of all foreigners from Germany. For them, elaborate theories and sophisticated intellectual guidelines are useless. Falling back on the Nazi doctrine is sufficient. As Laqueur notes, the fact that both Russian and American right-wing extremists have been borrowing their ideas from Germany regardless of the geographic and cultural differences between them proves how unimportant ideological theory is for right-wing radicals.[7]

The Luge Olympian Incident

In a headline-making incident on October 29, 1993, local skinheads viciously attacked two American luge Olympians training for the winter Olympics in the east German town of Oberhof. Robert Pipkins, an African-American, and his white teammate, Duncan Kennedy, were punched, kicked, and pummeled by 15 neo-Nazi skinheads, who assaulted them as they were leaving a local disco. The incident, thought to be indicative of right-wing violence in Germany, has received much attention.

Since the 1990s, Nazi groups in Germany have engaged in street riots and demonstrations and physically attacked foreigners and minorities. The mob-like mentality of these rightists demonstrates the seventeenth-century British physician Thomas Fuller's observation that "The mob has many heads but no brain." Undoubtedly, for these German thugs fury is a product of xenophobia—the fear of strangers—and the fact that millions of Muslim immigrants, asylum seekers, and foreign workers living in Germany present, disturbingly, an especially attractive target.

Another noteworthy curiosity is that German right-wingers, like their European counterparts but unlike right-wing terrorists in the United States, disavow any connection with religion, theology, or clerics. On the other hand, massive beer drinking is a well-known characteristic of young, right-wing Germans. Often undereducated, some possess a lower than average intelligence and come from broken homes. Some exhibit symptoms that suggest that they may be psychopaths. It is, therefore, not surprising that many of them are unemployed or hold menial jobs.[8] This description brings to mind the words of the American social philosopher Eric Hoffer, "Passionate hatred can give meaning and purpose to an empty life."

German right-wing hoodlums engage in low-level violence, but on a part-time basis. In comparison, left-wing terrorists engage in the practice on a full-time basis, which helps explain why the right's violence in Germany is more sporadic, fragmented, spontaneous, and "primitive" compared to the more effectively structured and managed leftist terrorism. However, the fact remains that these right-wingers are hooligans who engage in random acts of terrorism. Hurting foreigners, setting an immigrant's house ablaze—sometimes to the delight of the local community—and marching provocatively are not simple criminal acts but political statements designed to terrorize the larger community of foreigners living in Germany. This type of fanatic and racist hatred and terrorism has resulted in no less than 80 deaths between 1990 and 1994 alone. One needs to bear in mind Nietzsche's eternal warning that "Insanity in individuals is rare—but in groups, parties, nations . . . it is the rule." Currently, these hooligans represent only a potential danger of wide-scale, organized terrorism; however, things could change and they could be galvanized into structured terrorist groups operating systematically with a centrally determined national agenda.

It is somewhat reassuring that for the time being, German right-wing groups have experienced a decline. If these movements improve their recruitment techniques and the quality of their operations at all, it will happen because the social causes responsible for the emergence of these groups—migration, unemployment, and so on—still exist. If the economy suffers a painful recession, the situation could worsen quickly and drastically. In addition, it is not impossible that German right-wing extremists could capitalize on a public backlash to Islamist violence and that their activities could escalate from their present low-level into full-fledged terrorism.

SUMMARY

In this chapter, you have learned the following:

1. The designation of political *left* and *right* goes back to the era of the French Revolution.
2. Left-wing terrorism began in the 1960s in reaction to the Vietnam War and the Western imperialism it was perceived to represent.
3. By the mid-1990s, left-wing terrorism was essentially over in Europe, but it has continued and strengthened in other parts of the world, notably in Latin America.
4. Right-wing terrorism emerged as a backlash to leftist terrorism in Europe.
5. Although deadly, currently right-wing terrorism in Europe is more a potential danger than a present, substantial menace.

💣💣💣

Left-wing terrorist organizations are known to network with each other for training, and logistical and operational support. A noted case took place on June 27, 1976, when a combined team of the German RAF and a Marxist Palestinian group, the Popular Front for the Liberation of Palestine (PFLP), conducted a joint terrorist operation that resulted in one of the most celebrated airline hijackings in history.

Shortly after Air France Flight 139 took off from Athens en route to Paris, it was commandeered by the combined terrorist team and diverted to the airport at Entebbe, Uganda, which was then governed by the dictator Idi Amin. The hijackers freed all but 103 Jewish and Israeli passengers and demanded the release of comrades jailed in Israeli and European prisons, threatening to murder all hostages unless their demands were met. It soon became apparent that Ugandan soldiers at the airport were working with the terrorists, aiming their rifles at the hostages rather than at the terrorists.

The Israeli government ordered its military to launch a rescue operation. In a unique raid, Israeli commandos secretly flew thousands of miles and landed in the Entebbe airport on the night of July 4, 1976, storming the airport before the hostage-takers or the Ugandan soldiers realized what was happening. The raid was a success; the commandos killed all of the terrorists, immobilized the Ugandan soldiers, and took off with the rescued hostages to Tel Aviv. Along with three dead hostages, the Israelis suffered only one fatality, Lieutenant-Colonel Jonathan Netanyahu, ground commander of the operation and the older brother of Benjamin Netanyahu, who would later become the prime minister of Israel. This daring rescue, which has also been immortalized in several Hollywood movies, has become an operational inspiration for counterterrorist forces around the world.

💣💣💣

NOTES

1. An interesting discussion of the differences between nationalist and ideological terrorism is provided by Raymond R. Corrado , "Ethnic and Student Terrorism in Western Europe," in Michael Stohl, ed., *The Politics of Terrorism* (New York: Marcel Dekker, Inc., 1979), pp. 191–257.

2. For a sample insight into the Soviet role in fostering left-wing terrorism, see Claire Sterling, *The Terror Network: The Secret War of International Terrorism* (New York: Holt, Reinhart and Winston, 1981), pp. 286–297.

3. Jonathan White's explanation of the decline of leftist terrorism in Europe is found in Jonathan R. White, *Terrorism: An Introduction*, 4th ed. (Belmont, CA: Wadsworth/Thomson Learning, 2002), pp. 172–175.

4. Laqueur's description of the embarrassing development for these Western intellectuals is in Walter Laqueur, *The New Terrorism: Fanaticism and the Arms of Mass Destruction* (New York: Oxford University Press, 1999), pp. 106–107.

5. For the quote about the irrationality of the European leftist-terrorists, see Ibid., p. 122.

6. The discussion of "images" held by right-wing terrorists of the enemy as monolithic is found in Cindy C. Combs, *Terrorism in the Twenty-First Century*, 3rd ed. (Upper Saddle River, NJ: Prentice Hall, 2003), pp. 42–44.

7. For Laqueur's observation of the ideological similarity characterizing right-wing terrorists in various countries, see Laqueur (1999), pp. 122–123.

8. Much of the information concerning right-wing terrorists in Germany is found in Ibid., pp. 119–126.

Fanatics in the Service of God

Religiously Inspired Terrorism

I consider myself a Hindu, Christian, Moslem, Jew, Buddhist, and Confucian.

Gandhi

Operation Bluestar was launched in June 1984. The Indian government of Prime Minister Indira Gandhi had accused a religious Sikh movement in the state of Punjab, led by Jarnail Singh Bindranwale, of fostering ethnic separatism and involvement in terrorism against Indian officials and moderate fellow Sikhs, allegations the Sikhs have denied to this day. Indira Gandhi ordered Operation Bluestar to arrest the armed Sikh group that had barricaded itself in the Sikhs' holiest shrine, the "Golden Temple." Scores of Sikhs were killed in the attack, including the revered Jarnail Singh Bindranwale. The holy Golden Temple itself also suffered damage. Sikhs claim that thousands were murdered by Indian security forces in sweeps conducted throughout villages and towns in Punjab in the aftermath of the fighting at the Temple, charges the Indian government has denied.

Religious fanatics have a long memory and an unforgiving nature. As part of a series of acts aimed at avenging the desecration of their holiest site and of the killing of their religious leader, Sikh members of Indira Gandhi's own bodyguard contingent assassinated her in her residence in November of that year. In addition, on June 23, 1985, Air India Flight 182 on route from Canada to India exploded over the Atlantic Ocean, killing all 239 passengers on board, including 82 children. This act of terrorism is believed to be the work of revenge-seeking Sikh expatriates living in Canada, but no convictions have ever been secured.

🖤🖤🖤

Members of Aum Shinrikyo marching along a street in Japan, wearing identical masks
Source: Courtesy of The Yomiuri Shimbun.

AN OMINOUS DEVELOPMENT: RELIGION'S DARK SIDE

Each religion seems to have within it two undercurrents: One sanctifies life, promotes moderation, forbids killing, and acknowledges the humanity within all humankind, in the form of concern for the "least among us" or by reminding us, "thou shalt not kill." The other streak lurking within each religion is one that is dark and forbidding. This one sanctions killing and urges a rigid, purist approach, rejects all alternative interpretations of sacred scripture, and has few inhibitions against using violence against "sinners" or non-believers. History is burdened by too many examples of adherents of this severe and unyielding approach, who misuse religion by interpreting it in a way that serves political causes.

Early Religious Terrorism: The Sicarii

The bragging rights for the first organized religious terrorist group belong to the ancient Jewish Sicarii. Judaea, in the first century A.D., was a harshly governed Roman province whose population was awash with messianic visions of imminent heavenly salvation. The Sicarii terrorists operated in Judaea, especially in Jerusalem, in the second half of the first century. Eager for independence, they believed that humans could force God's hand to expedite the salvation by initiating a revolt against the Romans, thus compelling God to intervene on behalf of his people. Named Sicarri, or "men-of-the-dagger" in Hebrew, they used this weapon to murder Jewish moderates who disagreed with their militancy, as well as Roman officials. Through terrorism against fellow Jews and murderous provocations against the Romans, who tried to avoid war, the Sicariis successfully forced a military showdown with Rome on a reluctant Jewish majority.

The rebellion ended in disaster. The mass destruction, the devastation of Jerusalem, the rivers of blood spilled, and the burning of the Temple became the precursor for the future. Within 60 years, a subsequent rebellion inspired by the Sicarii precedence would result in the final exile of the Jews from their land.

Religious Terrorism Today

The recent increase in religiously inspired terrorism has come as a surprise to many. Until circa 1980, few would have believed that people might once again revert to terrorism in the name of religion. This new back-to-religion trend is surprising in the face of centuries of steady movement away from clerical domination of society. One can only contemplate with wonder the genius of the American founding fathers, who understood the importance of trapping the genie of religion in the bottle called "separation of church and state." Unprecedented and somewhat counterintuitive for many at that time, this separation is the key to the American experience, this great marriage of liberty and power. Instead of adopting the American model, however, a worldwide religious renaissance has been taking place in recent decades. Religion has been making a comeback, and with vengeance! Unfortunately, in many cases religion has been accompanied by that most unwelcome of guests—terrorism.

Fundamentalism exists within each religion and is not part of the problem of terrorism. The pious desire to go back to the basics and live according to one's religious dictates is irrelevant to our discussion of religion and terrorism. Therefore, one must not confuse or associate Islamic fundamentalism, for example, with terrorism. Each religion has its own brand of fundamentalists. Mormons, Quakers, and Hassidic Jews, for instance, also are "fundamentalists," but no one will confuse them with terrorists.

The Original Assassins

The Assassins were an Islamic shi'i cult that existed from 1090 to 1275. They viewed themselves as enforcers of proper Islamic conduct, which included killing public officials and other prominent individuals who were deemed to have strayed from the right path of Islam. Residing in fortified cities in what is today northern Iran, they spread their terror throughout the Middle East. They used deception and elaborate trickery to gain the confidence of would-be victims in order to be able to kill them later. The Assassins were conditioned by their dispatchers never to be caught alive; for that purpose, they used weapons that ensured that they would not be able to escape after the killing, such as daggers rather than arrows. Legends of the exploits of the Assassins and their ability to always reach their target assumed epic proportions during that era, usually for good reason. For example, one method for preparing an Assassin was to indoctrinate children in the ways of the Assassins and to send them to grow up in certain locations where they were to establish themselves over the years as reliable local residents. Years later, when they received the order, the Assassins would kill their prey. Because horrified Muslims of the period could not understand the fanaticism of these killers and assumed that they must have carried out their suicidal missions while drugged, they referred to them as "hashashins," as in "hashish eaters." In time, Europeans would corrupt the word into "Assassins."

The Assassins murdered relatively few people, compared to the Thugees in India, for example, but their impact throughout Muslim society was great and lasted for two centuries. The Mongols invaded the region late in the thirteenth century and destroyed the Assassins.

How the Genie of Religious Terrorism Got Out of the Bottle

To understand why religious terrorism has suddenly made its unexpected reappearance onto the stage of history, seemingly from nowhere, we need to go back a few decades to the Iranian Revolution. In 1979, a new theocracy took power in Iran, a powerful, oil-wealthy, and strategically located Middle Eastern country. Its new leaders, extremist Shi'i clerics inspired by the Grand Ayatollah Khomeini, made no bones about the new regime's priorities. Chief among them was to actively help Muslims engaged in a struggle anywhere in the world. Prohibitions on the strategies used in the course of that support, such as the ones posed by international law, would not be a high priority.

The new religious fervor swept down from Iran and infected the rest of the Middle East as well as areas beyond that region with a revival of religious enthusiasm that, combined with the spiritual, political, and financial support from Iran, inspired tens of millions of other Muslims. Decades passed before the full meaning of the process dawned on the West. However, while Western societies may have been slow to understand the finer points and the implications of this new development, elements within these societies and in other religious groups were quick to adopt the new Iranian model in their own struggles. The subsequent progression of modern religious terrorism is noteworthy; nearly all of these phenomena have taken place after 1979.

Poisoned Salad Bars

One of the most bizarre cases of religio-biological terrorism took place on American soil in 1984. A cult following the teachings of a guru from India, named Bhagwan Shree Rajneesh, bought an old ranch in Oregon and established a religious center there in 1981. Soon thereafter, thousands of orange-robed disciples descended on the place. Tensions flared and friction developed as local Oregonians in nearby counties became increasingly unhappy with the influx of strangers sporting a private security force and engaging in strange practices.

In 1984, Rajneesh's followers allegedly attempted to take over the Wasco County Commission by poisoning as many local people as possible on the day of the elections so that the cult's own candidates would win. To accomplish this feat, cult members poisoned the salad bars in ten restaurants with salmonella and other dangerous organisms in The Dalles, the town designated by history as the end of the Oregon Trail. Seven hundred and fifty one people took ill, rendering the event the largest germ attack in modern American history.

Despite the strong suspicion of a deliberate plot, it took federal authorities a full year before they could establish with certainty that the incident was indeed a terrorist attack of mass poisoning. By 1985, the guru had been deported and, faced with a multitude of felony investigations, the American subsidiary of the cult all but collapsed.

The rise of religious terrorism in recent decades has been accompanied by a corresponding decline in terrorist activity by separatist movements.[1] There are several reasons for this phenomenon: whereas religious terrorism has been experiencing a global boom, many separatist and ethnic movements had already achieved their respective goals, especially after the fall of the Soviet Union, and no longer needed to use terrorism to achieve their goals. Topping the priority list of such former terrorists has been the need for legitimacy and using terrorism is counterproductive to this aspiration. In addition, newly liberated peoples have been busy fighting with conventional means other newly liberated neighboring peoples and no longer have a need to resort to terrorism.

COMMON DENOMINATORS OF RELIGIOUS TERRORISM

Not all religious terrorist groups are identical, yet surprising parallels common to all do exist. The noted terrorism expert Bruce Hoffman suggests that religious terrorists see the world as a battlefield between the forces of good and evil. Therefore, winning is described not in political terms but in absolute terms that necessitate that the enemy be wiped out completely. Killing, for such "holy warriors," is a sacred religious act. As an example, Hoffman cites Islamist terrorists whose goals are to kill the "enemies of God" or to convert them to their own brand of Islam. To these terrorists, such lofty goals mean that they are on a special mission from God.[2]

Equally important to all religious terrorists is the historical precedent. All religions view the early years of their faith as some sort of a "golden age" that is to be aspired to and emulated. As the historical precedent becomes the obligatory model for subsequent generations, particular modes of behavior are mandated on the faithful by the usually self-appointed gatekeepers of the religion. Such fanaticism can only arouse sympathy for the anonymous writer who exclaimed, "I am an atheist. I don't believe in Zeus." For staunch believers, however, patterns of behavior from thousands of years ago are sacred and are models for present conduct. For example, the biblical concept of Total War employed by the ancient Hebrews when they conquered the Holy Land guided the Sicarii in their terrorist war against Roman occupation and moderate Jews a thousand years later. Similarly, during his early years in Medina, before he developed a formidable conventional army, Mohammad encouraged assassinations to eliminate his political rivals. Centuries later, the Assassins, who were Shi'i residing in what is today northern Persia, elevated the technique to new heights, claiming that they were following the precedent set by Mohammad during the struggling early days of the Muslim religion.

The Algerian Civil War

The gruesome civil war in Algeria between the government and the Islamist terrorists highlights the use of the "historical precedent" argument by religiously inspired terrorists. Asked how his forces could deliberately massacre Muslim children, a senior leader of Algeria's Armed Islamic Group (GIA), Antar Soubari, expressed no remorse. Going back to the founding days of Islam, he wrapped himself in scripture to prove that Mohammad's prohibition against killing children did not apply because it did not include children who acted in a way that "encouraged the enemy." Repeating a saying attributed to Mohammad, he said, "I am innocent of those killed, because they are associated with those who had to be fought."[3]

Religious terrorists of all stripes consider their struggle divinely inspired, an apocalyptic struggle of cosmic proportions that will change the course of history. Because they participate in this end-of-days war between good and evil, believers feel exempt from the bonds of man-made laws and other norms of behavior that limit their all-out struggle against the enemy and its supporters. This abandonment of any sense of proportion by religious zealots on the one hand and the advent of unprecedented destructive technology on the other does not bode well for the future of humankind.

Where Civilizations Collide

What happens when the visions of competing religious groups that share so many common denominators come into conflict? Professor Samuel Huntington's famous phrase the "clash of civilizations" is important to our understanding of much of the religious terrorism around the globe.[4] Huntington pointed out eight different areas of the world, each with its own unique civilization—Western, Confucian, Japanese, Islamic, Hindu, Slavic-Orthodox, Latin American, and African. Huntington argues that peace is threatened in "torn countries," those regions where more than one civilization exists within a single area and frictions develop between the different civilizations. The potential for clashes between competing civilizations in those regions stems from respective zealots trying to impose their points of view on everybody else by using national myths and symbols that sanctify the cause.

SECULAR VERSUS RELIGIOUS TERRORISM: THE DIFFERENCES[5]

We know that religious terrorists of various faiths share surprisingly similar characteristics. However, the telltale differences between *secular* and *religious* terrorists are truly thought provoking. Secular terrorists, such as ideologues from the left and the right, operate within the sphere of their own political and cultural framework. This means that while they wish to replace the political system with a better one, they nevertheless campaign for this goal according to the norms of the society within which they live and function. For example, West European terrorists from both the left and the right are not likely to use a

---

Did You Know?

According to Walter Laqueur, a noted scholar of political violence, guerrilla warfare, and terrorism, if we exclude tribal warfare in Africa, Muslim states or Muslim minorities are involved in 90% of all sub-state terrorist conflicts worldwide.[6]

nuclear warhead or other weapons of mass destruction against their own societies, or those of other countries, in order to improve the quality of peoples' lives. Such inhibitions do not limit the ambitions of some religious terrorists as demonstrated by the Aum Shinrikyo's March 20, 1995, biological attack on the subway system in Tokyo that resulted in 12 dead and 5,500 injured. Religious terrorists look at the world as an arena in which good is engaged in a constant battle against evil.

Other major differences exist between religious and secular terrorists. Whereas secular terrorists use terrorism in an attempt to create theater for the consumption of the larger audience—society at large—religious terrorists do not cater to a wider audience, with the exception of co-religionists, whose approval of the cause and material support the terrorists crave. They act on behalf of God, not for an audience of people. Therefore, for religious terrorists there is hardly a reason to restrain the ferociousness of their attacks. As a Hezbollah leader Hussein Mussavi once quipped about his organization's fight against the Israeli presence in South Lebanon, "We are not fighting so that the enemy . . . offers us something. We are fighting to wipe out the enemy."[7]

Abusing Corpses in the Name of God

Lebanon is composed of a bewildering array of competing ethnic groups, which are usually organized along religious lines. For about a decade, beginning in the mid-1970s, a particularly cruel civil war raged among the various religious denominations. Tracking the unfolding events was difficult because of the mind-boggling and frequent shifts in alliances among the warring sides. One day pitched against their former allies, the next on the same side as their former nemesis were Christian militia, Sunni militia, Shi'i militia, Druze militia, the PLO, and conventional military forces from the neighboring countries of Israel and Syria.

Given the religious dimension of the fighting, there was little moderation, mercy, and differentiation between civilians and combatants. Sometimes, members of a militia victorious in a battle—any militia, regardless of its identity—would tie the bodies of fallen enemy fighters behind their vehicles and drag them through the dirt for a few days. The explanation for this barbaric behavior was sincere and unapologetic: Doing so to God's enemies, they said, was certain to please God.

Secular would-be terrorists tend to move from issue to issue until they find the one that best fits their thinking and emotional needs. For example, a woman may consider joining a group fighting for environmental causes or one that advocates independence for her ethnic group before opting for a left-wing terrorist organization because the latter champions women's rights. Obviously, this is not the case with religious terrorists. For them the purpose of the campaign, the methods used, and the targets selected are vividly clear, since they are based on historical precedent, scripture, or clerical guidance. Moreover, secular terrorists engage in violence as an unpleasant task that involves inflicting harm on the few but will benefit the many. In contrast, religious terrorists regard killing as a sacramental act and do not care about inflicting mass casualties on the enemies of God; as long as doing so advances the cause of the faith, killing in the service of God is a righteous deed. Secular terrorists are on a self-appointed mission on behalf of the collective. Religious terrorists are on a mission from God.

Secular terrorists demonize their enemies. We are all familiar with the epithet "pig" for police officers. It was popular with yesteryear's liberal anti-establishment crowd and was widely used by American leftist-terrorists during the 1970s and 1980s. However, secular terminology is mellow and kind compared with the terms religious terrorists use to describe their enemies—"children of Satan," "mud people," "infidels," and many more. Since in the eyes of religious fanatics their enemy also happens to be the enemy of God, name-calling is much harsher because it prepares the terrorists for what lies in store for such despicable creatures. Simply defeating their enemy is not sufficient; the enemy has to be completely eradicated. Frequent and methodic reference to the enemy as dogs, monkeys, pigs, and so on dehumanizes and delegitimizes the victims, which makes killing them easier and more justifiable.

Therefore, it is very difficult to reason with religious terrorists, who filter all information through the lens of their fanaticism and analyze it in ways that are valid only to them and those who think like them. They fight according to their own rules, are uncompromising, and have no timeframe for ending that war. Some of these struggles are meant to last for generations, or until some Messiah comes on some sort of a judgment day.[8] Religious terrorists are uncomfortable negotiating and compromising because doing so, in their eyes, means living with half-truths of man-made laws that contradict God's wishes.

For this reason, the argument about the "root causes" of religious terrorism, often voiced as an excuse or apology for this type of terrorism, is fallacious. Closer examination of these "root causes" reveals that they are immaterial pretexts. In reality, the terrorists have particular references, justifications, and motivations that drive their actions, which casual observers cannot easily understand. Thus, although no compromise or mutual understanding is a valid option for religious terrorists, their propaganda is nonetheless too often treated as a fact by outsiders.

MODERN GLOBALISM AND RELIGIOUS TERRORISM

In an important article, Professor Mark Jurgenmeyer of the University of California at Santa Barbara examines the links between religious terrorism and globalism, a worldwide phenomenon dominated mainly by a secular Western culture.[9] Jurgenmeyer contends that all religious terrorist groups share a common denominator: their hatred for secular globalism and the fight against it, which gives meaning to their lives.

Not surprisingly, these groups reject liberal values and secular institutions and do not respect the limits societies set for religion (considering one's faith a private concern, for example). Significantly, these religious terrorist groups also reject the more moderate version of their own faith as practiced by the mainstream adherents and try to replace it with a more radical and vibrant version. From this perspective, according to Jurgenmeyer, Osama bin Laden is no more representative of mainstream Islam than Timothy McVeigh, the white supremacist who blew up the Alfred Murrah Federal Building in Oklahoma City in 1995, is of Christianity or the founder of the Japanese Aum Shinrikyo, Shoko Asahara, is of Buddhism.

Secularism may have proclaimed the death of religion, but these religious forces wish to proclaim the death of secularism. For them, fighting secularism globally translates into an epic transnational war for the soul of the universe. For Islamists, for example, the events of September 11, 2001, were part of a cosmic struggle between everything that is good and sacred and that which is evil, secular, and alien. The reason religious terrorists fear and hate globalism so much has to do with the current international structure and the advent of technology.

Although the countries in which they live or from which they come may have their independence, borders, and other trappings of sovereignty, in their view, the morals and values of Western secular democracy have penetrated them, infecting their societies with consumerism, videos, and fashion. The political commentator Henry Louis Mencken observed, "Puritanism is the haunting fear that someone somewhere may be happy." As if to give truth to his sarcasm, stern religious forces within these societies have been fighting with increasing success this invasion of secularism, which they see as a threat to their traditional values and religious dogma.

What develops is a problem of legitimacy for the respective governments. The Western cultural invasion threatens the old traditions and marginalizes local religions. As the situation reaches a point where very little seems to work or make sense, the legitimacy of the government of the country in which this new social order is emerging comes into question. Because the economic conditions in such countries are often harsh, it is not difficult to understand the

---

Did You Know?

A *sect* is an offshoot of an established religion, the way Hassidic Jews relate to Judaism or Quakers to Christianity. Sects either grow into larger denominations or wither away. They are moderate and avoid aggressive patterns of behavior. In contrast, a *cult* is led by a charismatic leader for whom becoming a major denomination is not important, and who directs the group's energies in aggressive new directions. Jim Jones's doomsday cult was one such vibrant and dangerous group.

potential for internal strife. When the government routinely fails to provide sufficiently for the needs of its population, the prospect of political change becomes very attractive.

Since the solution to the problems is achievable only by drastic changes in the entire socio-political system, the appeal of those advocating a divinely mandated cure can be irresistible to those whose children go hungry. The process of change leads through a cosmic, all or nothing war between the present evil and the forces seeking change, and, as a result, the war is viewed as different from other, more typical, conflicts. As society's rules regulating the use of violence become irrelevant, the struggle often becomes cruel. For believers, the duty to carry out God's will is more important than man-made laws and, therefore, the war becomes sacred and absolutist with total moral self-justification.

Divine Law versus International Rules

Explaining why the use of violence to spread Islam all over the world was divinely sanctioned, the Shi'i theologian Ayatollah Baqer al-Sadr wrote, "the world as it is today is how others shaped it. . . . We have two choices: either to accept it with submission . . . or to destroy it, so that we can construct the world as Islam requires . . . We are not fighting within the rules of the world as it exists today. We reject all those rules." [10]

This is not a hypothetical discussion. In many parts of the world, even in the United States and Japan, many have grown disillusioned with their governments' ability to guide and to provide for them adequately and, as a result, view their governments as the enemy. It is not difficult to imagine the impact this "loss of faith" [11] in the secular Western culture has had on various governments in the vast parts of the world where conditions are quite appalling. The appeal of new forces that advocate the silver bullet of religious identity to guide their nations is similarly easy to understand. In recent decades, these religious appeals have gained increasing popularity.

Some religious terrorists go even further. Al-Qaeda, for example, does not pursue a religious form of government; rather, its goal is a world ruled by religious law. Thus, concludes Professor Jurgenmeyer, transnational terrorists like bin Laden can be thought of as guerilla antiglobalists. [12]

CHRISTIAN TERRORISM: *THE TURNER DIARIES*

Religious terrorism is not limited to Islam. For example, in a northeastern state of India, Nagaland, Christian separatists have been fighting for independence from the Hindu-majority secular state since the early 1950s. But to understand

Christian terrorism we do not need to look at remote corners of the world; Christian-inspired terrorists abound in our own backyard in the United States. American right-wing fanatics, who compose the ranks of the various "patriot," "militia," neo-Nazi and other terrorist groups are usually very religious. Much of their racist ethos is related to their identity as Christians and their hatred for those who are non-Christian or not white.

The Turner Diaries powerfully illustrates the beliefs of these religious terrorists. The author is the white supremacist William Pierce, who published it in 1978 under the pseudonym Arthur Macdonald. It soon became a mega-hit with ultra-right racist Americans, who treated this fictitious work as a sacred scripture. The tale reflects standard Nazi stereotypes and premises, but with a heavy religious emphasis, a phenomenon that has always distinguished American right-wingers from their European counterparts. It tells the story of a white man who is drawn into a white "order" to fight an epic war on behalf of white people against the government and its Jewish and non-white allies. The language the author uses to describe these enemies of God and his real chosen people, the whites, is dreadful. The "happy ending" comes with the swift victory of the "good guys," the racists, who use nuclear weapons to wipe out their enemies, restore order on earth, and make God happy again.

One could call the premise silly if it were not for the Nazi precedent, which began with similar hallucinatory-sounding ramblings, and the large number of armed, right-wing American terrorists eagerly fantasizing about such an end of days. The book is a classic among its intended audience and very influential. Timothy McVeigh was a connoisseur of the book, which is said to have had a great impact on him.

The core beliefs of the American Christian terrorist groups center on several interesting premises: (1) Jesus was not a Semite but an Aryan; (2) the lost tribes of Israel were not Jewish, but blue-eyed Aryans; (3) the Anglo-Saxons, not the Jews, are the real "Chosen People"; and (4) the United States is the real

Did You Know?

When interviewed afterwards, the most common recollection of survivors of suicide-bombings carried out by Muslim terrorists is of the killers' smile just before they detonated themselves. "Bassamat al-farah," it is called in Arabic, "the smile of joy." Islamist suicide-bombers are indoctrinated to meet death with a happy smile because for their martyrdom they now will be rewarded by Allah with a blessed eternal life in Paradise. The logic instilled in them by their dispatchers is that they should not just die while killing the enemy, but face their imminent death with a cheerful attitude that expresses genuine delight in the opportunity to die in the service of God.

"Promised Land."[13] Logically flowing from this perspective is a great hatred toward the American government and its officials, loathing of Jews—who are believed to control the government, banks, and the media—and a fixation on racial superiority.

STATE-SPONSORED RELIGIOUS TERRORISM

We can conceive of the existence of non-state organizations of religious fanatics using violence against perceived and real enemies and terrorizing them for various reasons, but that states, part of the modern international community of countries, engage in this practice is more difficult to fathom. Yet the phenomenon exists in several countries possibly because it is relatively easy for states to use the country's resources and capabilities to terrorize minorities within their territory and then hide or deny the facts. In addition, sometimes countries escape censor from the international community by receiving the automatic support of other states that share the same ideology or religion with the offending country. The religiously inspired state-terrorism by Sudan provides us with a timely example of this practice.

Sudan contains two distinct ethno-religious groups: the Muslim Arabs in the north, who make up about 70% of the population, and the Christian/Animist Africans in the southern part of the country, who make up about 30%. The northern Muslims have tried to convert the southerners to Islam for centuries and these efforts intensified after Sudan gained its independence from Britain in 1956. That year marks the beginning of a prolonged, on-and-off civil war that might be the longest in modern history. After the Iranian Revolution, Sudan became heavily influenced by the theocratic government in Teheran. In 1982, the Sudanese government tried to impose the Islamic law, Shari'a, on the south, further escalating the conflict. Confronting the Arab government of Sudan are mainly two major non-Muslim guerilla groups that are ethno-African: the Sudanese People's Liberation Army (SPLA) and the armed wing of the Sudanese People's Liberation Movement (SPLM). The fight is not an equal one. The Arabs in the north enjoy clear numerical and geographic superiority, as well as the resources of the country, including trained military and relatively overwhelming economic capabilities.

Between war and famine and with the instruments of conventional military force and murderous Arab-Muslim militias, the Islamic government of Sudan has inflicted millions of casualties on the south. In an attempt to terrorize the Africans to convert, the Islamic government has enabled the abduction and enslavement of tens of thousands of non-Muslim Africans. This fierce devotion to fight the infidel brings to mind the saying by the late American satirist Ambrose Bierce that an infidel in New York is someone who does not believe in the Christian religion, or—in Constantinople—one who does.

SUMMARY

In this chapter, you have learned the following:

1. Each religion contains an aggressive and a moderate streak.
2. Fundamentalism is found in all religions and has nothing to do with terrorism.
3. The Iranian Revolution of 1979 opened the floodgates of religious terrorism everywhere.
4. Religious terrorism is vastly different from other types of terrorism.
5. Recent religious terrorism can be thought of as a war against globalism and its social and economic consequences.
6. Right-wing American terrorists tend to be religious.
7. Certain states practice religiously inspired terrorism.

It was circa 1980 and Israeli Jewish zealots unhappy with the policies of the Israeli government formed a terrorist underground. The premise of the group's 20 members was shockingly ambitious: to bring about an epic change in the situation by blowing up Islam's third holiest shrine in the world, the Dome of the Rock on the Temple Mount in Jerusalem, an event of cosmic proportions that would usher in the long-awaited "redemption" of the Jews and culminate in replacing the secular Israeli government with a theocracy. The plot was foiled in 1984 by Israeli authorities who arrested the conspirators and brought them to justice. The perpetrators rationalized their plot with startling conviction: The planned terrorist act would have sparked an apocalyptic chain of events certain to expedite the arrival of the Messiah.[14]

NOTES

1. The observation regarding the rise in religious terrorism and the decline of separatist terrorism is made by Bruce Hoffman, *Inside Terrorism* (New York: Columbia University press, 1998), p. 91.
2. The discussion of the common denominators of religious terrorism is based in part on Hoffman, pp. 94–95; and Jonathan R. White, *Terrorism: An Introduction*, 4th ed. (Belmont, CA: Wadsworth/Thomson Learning, 2002), pp. 51–56.
3. The quote by the Algerian rebel leader is found in Hoffman, p. 98.
4. For the "clash of civilizations," see Samuel P. Huntington, *The Clash of Civilizations and the Remaking of World Order* (New York: Simon & Schuster, 2003).

5. Part of the discussion of the differences between secular and religious terrorism is based on Hoffman, pp. 94–95.

6. Laqueur's contention that 90% of all sub-state conflicts involve Muslims can be found in Walter Laqueur, "Left, Right, and Beyond: The Changing Face of Terror," in James F. Hoge, Jr. and Gideon Rose, eds., *How Did This Happen: Terrorism and the New World* (New York: Public Affairs Reports, 2001), p. 75.

7. The *Hezbollah* leader is quoted in Amir Taheri, *Holy Terror: Inside the World of Islamic Terrorism* (Bethesda, MD: Adler and Adler Publishers, 1987), p. 16.

8. See more on the eschatology of terrorism in White, pp. 53–54.

9. For the discussion of religious terrorism as a violent response to globalism, see Mark Jurgenmeyer, "The Religious Roots of Contemporary Terrorism," in Kegley, ed., *The New Global Terrorism: Characteristics, Causes, Controls* (Upper Saddle River, NJ: Prentice Hall, 2003), pp. 185–193.

10. Ayatollah Baqer's explanation for not fighting the war according to current international law is found in Taheri, p. 15.

11. The "loss of faith" concept was coined by Jurgenmeyer, p. 190.

12. Jurgenmeyer's equation of al-Qaeda with antiglobalism forces is found in Ibid., p. 191.

13. The core beliefs of the American Christian terrorists are discussed in Hoffman, pp. 105–120.

14. For more on the Temple Mount plot, see Ian S. Lustick, *For The Land And The Lord: Jewish Fundamentalism in Israel* (New York: Council on Foreign Relations, 1988), pp. 69–70, 96–97, 168–176; Ehud Sprinzak, *The Ascendance Of Israel's Radical Right* (New York: Oxford University Press, 1991), pp. 94–99, 252–261.

Unholy Alliances

The Irresistible Lure of Money

The creatures outside looked from pig to man, and from man to pig, and from pig to man again; but it was impossible to say which was which.

George Orwell, *Animal Farm*

What the world does not need is terrorists, politicians, insurgents, and drug lords working as a team, but this phenomenon has become increasingly frequent in recent decades. A fascinating precursor to such groups was the international "dream team" put together by Carlos Lehder Rivas, co-founder of the infamous network known as the Medellin Cartel. Lehder, an American citizen, amassed billions of dollars from narcotics trafficking, even while declaring his Marxist orientation for a while. Between 1978 and 1984, approximately, Lehder took care of the distribution and marketing of the drugs, the Colombian drug lord Pablo Escobar handled the production and supply, the Ochoa family greased the wheels of the political process, and senior members of Fidel Castro's government helped protect the smuggling routes. They were all implicated in the November 6, 1985, Marxist Colombian M-19 Movement attack on the Palace of Justice in Bogotá. This terrorist raid was instigated and financed by the Medellin Cartel to force the authorities to repeal recently instituted laws permitting the extradition of drug lords to the United States. The raid and the siege that followed ended in a spectacular blood bath with over 100 dead, among them the President of the Supreme Court and 10 justices.

To analyze issues concerning terrorism, we neatly categorize explanations and concepts in order to provide greater clarity to the discussion. Psychological sources of terrorism, for example, are discussed separately from sociological ones and ideological causes are artificially differentiated from those that stem from religion. The reality, however, is different. Sometimes causes and processes are intertwined and mixed in ways that boggle the mind. In the real world, seemingly impossible alliances form and result in terrorist strategies that to the casual observer seem counterintuitive. As Antonio Costa, Executive Director of the United Nations Office on Drugs and Crime, said in late 2005, "The world is seeing the birth of a new hybrid of organized crime-terrorist organizations."[1]

Instead of the clear-cut terrorist typology the world was accustomed to and, therefore, could understand and try to combat, the growing new menace integrates criminal activity with terrorism. This unwelcome development has given rise to an octopus of threats whose tentacles embrace the world and whose objectives are becoming increasingly murky and more difficult to counter. The enormous flood of criminally gained capital that supports terrorism may already be too much to control, and it is conceivable that the West has already lost much of the battle over the financing of terrorism.

THE NEW WORLD DISORDER: THE ECONOMICS OF TERRORISM[2]

The strategy of containing terrorism by severing terrorists from their financial resources appears doomed. The world has changed. The worldwide underground economy which provides much of terrorism's fuel is booming, making hopes of winning the war by targeting finances unrealistic.

In her groundbreaking work, *Terror Incorporated*, economist Loretta Napoleoni analyzes terrorism from an economic point of view. Her conclusions are startling. Between what she terms the "terror economic network" and non–terrorism-related international criminal enterprises a total of $1.5 trillion per year, or 5% of the entire world's gross domestic product, is transacted![3] While this underground economy is in apparent conflict with Western capitalism, much of the money is laundered, becomes legal, is incorporated into Western financial institutions and, eventually, returns to the underground economy. Because of their participation in the process, legitimate Western financial institutions become dependent upon these colossal—albeit illegal—sums. According to Napoleoni, it is not clear that Western capitalism can afford to lose an annual injection of $1.5 trillion, regardless of its origins.[4] As Voltaire cynically observed almost three centuries ago, "When it is a question of money, everybody is of the same religion."

Terrorism Financing: Fighting Back

Any discussion of the struggle by U.S. and international law enforcement entities to combat terrorism is incomplete without mentioning two leading organizations that spearhead these efforts. Domestically, the Financial Crimes Enforcement Agency (FinCEN) of the U.S. Department of the Treasury, founded in 1990, is an organization whose purpose is to "safeguard the financial system from the abuses of . . . terrorist financing." FinCEN is a network that helps law enforcement agencies in the regulatory and financial communities share relevant information. In the international arena, the EGMONT Group merits special mention. Established in 1995, the group consists of Financial Intelligence Units (FIUs), one per country, whose mission is to coordinate international efforts to combat financial criminal activities. From 2004, the mandate of EGMONT was specifically extended to include terrorism financing.

Revenue for terrorist organizations and activities comes from several sources:[5]

1. *Criminal activities*: Capital from activities such as smuggling, kidnapping, robbery, narcotics, extortion, counterfeiting, and protection fees, among others.

2. *Legitimate business*: Income derived from investing this illegally earned capital in legal financial institutions and businesses.

3. *Illegally obtained funds*: Monies gained from practices such as tapping into foreign aid, creating front organizations to obtain funds received from NGOs, or circumventing legislation by other means in order to obtain government allocations.

4. *Contributions from related ethnic and religious groups*: Individuals and organizations that sympathize with the terrorists' agenda donate funds.

5. *State support*: States provide financial assistance to terrorist groups in order to advance their own interests.

Financing Terror

The most crucial link between terrorism and criminal activity is financing. It costs a great deal to support a terrorist organization. Expenses include safe houses, cars, and equipment and communication hardware necessary for its networking and surveillance operations, as well as the purchase of arms and explosives. In addition, life's mundane necessities, such as providing members with housing, food, clothing, and so on is costly.

This need for capital explains the strange connection between terrorists who believe they are fighting for a noble cause on the one hand and their cynical involvement in criminal activities on the other. Excuses, explanations, and rationalizations for this behavior abound, but the fact remains that some of those fighting to spread God's will or to better society often use old-style Mafia-like methods to finance their causes. Sometimes, the line separating the terrorists from common criminals becomes so blurred that it is no longer possible to tell whether an organization is using terrorism to get rich, or whether it resorts to crime in order to continue its violent political campaign.

Entrepreneurship and Its Rewards

To finance its terrorist operations, the Irish Republican Army (IRA) needed a constant and substantial flow of money. Over the years, the organization perfected illegal schemes that yielded so much money that the IRA's problem became laundering the vast amounts coming in.

Money came from a variety of illegal operations, including forcing companies and businesses to pay "protection"; robbing banks, post-offices, and armored-trucks transferring cash; counterfeiting alcohol, DVDs, designer-clothing, and jewelry; providing consulting services to other terrorist groups, like the Palestine Liberation Organization (PLO), the Revolutionary Armed Forces of Colombia (FARC), and the Basque Euzkadi Ta Askatasuna (ETA); smuggling fuel, cigarettes, electrical appliances, and even livestock; and committing mortgage fraud on behalf of unqualified applicants, for a fee.

These ventures were so successful that the IRA had to launder these substantial revenues by muscling its way into and taking over many cash businesses such as taxi companies, pubs, restaurants, nightclubs, and gas stations, as well as by investing considerable amounts in overseas real-estate holdings.[6]

It was not always so. A century ago, terrorists were usually so cash starved that they were hard-pressed to finance the purchase of a single pistol or a train ticket for the getaway. Most stuck by their principles and were quite successful in resisting the seduction of ill-gotten money. This trend would change by the mid-twentieth century as nationalist terrorists, such as the Popular Movement for the Liberation of Angola (MPLA) and the National Liberation Front (FLN) of Algeria, with their greater resources entered the picture, only to be followed by state-supported terrorism, as in the case of Iran.

Later in the century, globalization brought with it international networking and the opportunity to possess more money than earlier terrorists would not even have fantasized about. This influx of substantial amounts of capital changed the scope of the terrorists' ambitions, and created an alarming cycle in which terrorists felt the need for evermore funding and, once raised, for a corresponding increase in the ferocity of their attacks in order to demonstrate the need for raising more money. From here, the road to unapologetic criminal activity became short.

Criminal activity can take many shapes and the focus can be on different moneymaking venues. Some terrorist organizations engage in smuggling arms and humans, others favor counterfeiting and money laundering, while still others prefer armed robberies, kidnapping, extortion, and similar activities. But of the entire gamut of criminal activity, by far the most lucrative has been the drug trade. Its tremendous potential has made it the lynchpin of terrorism and crime, which earned it the term *narco-terrorism*. So tempting is this new plague that, to paraphrase Walter Laqueur, every entity that has had the opportunity to engage in the drug trade has done so despite Marx, Prophet Muhammad, or patriotic fervor. Indeed, one would be hard-pressed to find a terrorist organization that lives up to its pure, noble, and self-righteous rhetoric. From the Golden Triangle, where Laos, Thailand, and Myanmar (formerly Burma) meet, to the Lord's Resistance Army in Uganda, to Chechen nationalists, the standards are always the same. As the Portuguese proverb suggests, "laws go where dollars please."

CRIME AND TERROR: THE PLAYERS

Two types of forces drive this criminal-terrorist activity: (1) *criminal groups*, for example the Chechen gangs and the *Medellin Cartel*, which combine criminal activity with terrorism and (2) *terrorist organizations* such as the Shining Path in Peru and the Palestinian Popular Front for the Liberation of Palestine (PFLP). Both are occasionally helped by politicians and government officials, such as those of Syria, Cuba, and the former Panamanian regime of Immanuel Noriega, who had turned his country into the center of drug trafficking in the region.

Through complex international networks and personal contacts developed over the years, these criminal-terrorists smuggle arms, launder money, exchange intelligence information, provide each other counterfeit travel documentation, share safe houses, and assist each other in any way possible. The convergence of interests among previously antagonistic entities has created alliances with unprecedented potential for carrying out complex global terrorist activities. This chapter explores the two central elements in this new development: criminals engaged in terrorism and terrorists using crime to finance their terrorist activities.

Terrorism in Buenos Aires

On July 18, 1994, a car bomb carrying 880 pounds of high-grade explosives was detonated in front of the Argentine Jewish Community Center in Buenos Aires, Argentina. Of the employees who were providing social services to the needy, 85 were killed and 240 others wounded. Following a thorough investigation by the Argentinean intelligence services, the Investigating Judge issued a special report of the findings in March 2003.

The report established that Iran, using some of its diplomats stationed in Argentina, along with the Lebanese terrorist group Hezbollah carried out the atrocity. They were helped, according to the report, by criminal elements among the Shi'i immigrant community who lived in the crime-infested region of the Triple Border triangle that connects Argentina, Brazil, and Paraguay; some of them, according to the report, have also been members of Hezbollah's infrastructure in South America. Overall criminal activity in this region alone generates approximately $12 billion annually.[8]

Those accused denied the charges but the evidence documented in the report implicating higher-ups in the Iranian government was irrefutable. The names, the methods, and the motives of all those involved were well established. Among those accused of personal involvement in the atrocity were the Iranian spiritual leader, Ali Khamenei; Iran's president, Rafsanjani; the then Iranian ambassador to Argentina, Hadi Soleimanpour; and the Iranian intelligence minister, Falahian. Argentina issued international warrants against some of the Iranians implicated in the crime, but this judicial exercise has thus far proven futile.[9]

The Role of Organized Crime in Terrorism

Sometimes for profit, other times as a joint venture with a terrorist group, occasionally out of patriotic motives, and often for reasons of religious affinity, criminals have been crossing the line into terrorism with growing frequency. Recent years have witnessed several demonstrations of this unholy alliance. Following are two cases that exemplify the wider phenomenon of criminals engaged in terrorism.

D Company   Dawood Ibrahim was once the most senior crime figure in India. With a large criminal organization that he himself had built, his business extended into more than a dozen countries and included the regular "product lines"—smuggling, extortion, arms trafficking, contract killing, and money laundering using banking and construction companies as fronts.

Then he stopped being a nice guy and turned serious. A Muslim, he organized a one-day series of bloody attacks in Bombay on cafés, restaurants, the bazaar, the airport, and other crowded areas of the city, apparently to avenge an earlier anti-Muslim wave of riots in the city. The March 12, 1993, onslaught was initiated by the Pakistani Inter-Services Intelligence agency (ISI), which supplied the explosives to Ibrahim's network. When the dust settled, 257 innocent civilians were dead and over 700 injured. Currently, Dawood Ibrahim lives in Dubai, in the United Arab Emirates, from which he continues to run his crime syndicate. Ominously, Ibrahim has decided to tie his fate with al-Qaeda and put his organization's expertise and resources at the terror organization's disposal, merging a life of crime with one of terrorism.[10]

A Strange Marriage of Convenience

A report in *U.S. News and World Report* suggests that Islamists who smuggle North African immigrants into southern Europe as a means of financing their terrorist operations cooperate with European criminal organizations. For example, the Report cites the Napoli-based branch of the Italian Mafia, the Neapolitan Camorran, which is said to arrange safe houses and facilitate arms deals for the Islamists.[11]

The Russian Mafia   An unanticipated outcome of the disintegration of the Soviet Union is the impact it has had on the rise in criminal activity throughout that country's former areas. The term *Russian Mafia* has come to include the entire criminal enterprise operating in the region of the former Soviet Union, not any one particular group.

Russian organized crime organizations are said to consist of over 100 transnational criminal groups operating in about 40 countries. Tens of thousands of their members are believed to control about 50% of the Russian economy, with many enjoying alliances with terrorist groups worldwide as well as with other criminal entities, especially those involved in the profitable narcotics business. According to Napoleoni, Russian organized crime has been instrumental in transferring $500 billion out of Russia for safekeeping in Western financial institutions throughout the 1990s.[12]

There is also evidence suggesting that the Russian Mafia has not been shy about trading in arms with terrorist groups possessing the cash for the transactions. That elements of the Russian Mafia exhibit no hesitation about selling arms to anybody who has the cash is very worrisome since it is conceivable that if these groups obtain weapons of mass destruction they will sell them to terrorists, provided the price is right. This scenario is particularly disturbing because the poverty and corruption of present-day Russian society is an invitation for trouble. Can underpaid Russian law enforcement personnel be entrusted with safeguarding the country's vast arsenal of weapons of mass destruction? It may be naive to think so given the reality of ruthless and well-financed criminals specializing in extortion and bribery. Laqueur's cautionary words that "the extent of Russian army and police corruption is virtually unprecedented in history"[13] eloquently point to the magnitude of the danger.

Chechnya: A Case Study of the Russian Mafia

Few examples better illustrate the link between criminals and terrorists than the Chechen criminals who also happen to be Muslim Chechen patriots. While numerous criminal organizations operate nowadays all over central Asia and the Caucasus, the major Chechen criminal organizations are based in Russia, especially in Moscow. Of the estimated 100 main criminal organizations operating in Moscow in recent years, six are particularly large and lethal.

These organizations are structured and organized along guidelines that resemble multinational corporations on the one hand and law enforcement agencies on the other. Exceptionally cruel and sophisticated, each of these large criminal enterprises boasts thousands of members, with organizational structures consisting of departments for operations, intelligence, and legal affairs. Since they operate transnationally and are well connected and networked all over the world, the location of choice for their international headquarters is London. Of the six sizeable Russian criminal organizations, no less than three are Chechen.[14]

Briefly revisiting the events in Chechnya since the collapse of the Soviet Union helps make sense of the unfolding of the conflict in that small, unfortunate nation. Essentially, the Chechen people won their war of independence against Russia in the first Chechen war of 1994–1996. The remnants of the once invincible Red Army were untrained, underequipped, demoralized, and poorly led and, therefore, defeated soundly by the fiercely committed Chechen fighters. Instead of thanking their lucky stars for the historical coincidence that saw the mighty Soviet Union replaced with a struggling Russia too preoccupied with its own problems to seriously care about Chechnya, the Chechens largely squandered the fruits of their victory.

A state of anarchy descended on the land as lawlessness and banditry replaced the previous order. When waves of robberies, kidnappings, and wide-scale thievery began to spill into neighboring Russian republics, the latter were forced to take notice. More worrisome for the Russians was the Islamization of the Chechen campaign. Independence was no longer the Chechen goal. Influential elements among the Chechens shifted their objective from mere Chechen independence to the creation of an independent Islamic country that would also include, even if without consent, the neighboring Russian state of Dagestan. To pursue this cause, the Chechens resorted to terrorist attacks. This escalation forced the Russian government to engage in a renewed war in order to end this intolerable situation.

The second Chechen war, from 1999 to 2002, was a bloody undertaking whose true end is still far from known. Chechen criminal organizations in

A Brazen Act of Terrorism

The long saga of brutal terrorist attacks that over time may have dulled the public's sense of outrage registered one memorable milestone in June 1995. On June 14, during the first Chechen war, the Chechen warlord Shamil Basayev led a group of 150 terrorists into the Russian city of Budenovsk, seized the local hospital, and took over 1,000 hostages—hospital patients! They demanded that the Russians leave Chechnya completely, or else . . .

Refusing to yield to blackmail, the Russians launched a costly rescue attempt, which failed when the terrorists used the patient-hostages as human shields. Nearly 120 hostages were killed and a negotiated compromise followed. The terrorists released most of their victims, but, with the Russians providing safe conduct, kept over one hundred as hostages during their return to Chechnya. Upon reaching Chechnya, the terrorists were greeted with a triumphant heroes' welcome, and then released their remaining hostages.

Chechen terrorists concluded that the Russians were vulnerable to this type of blackmail and would capitulate again in future standoffs involving large numbers of hostages. The Russian authorities, for their part, learned the opposite lesson: to never again give in to hostage-taking terrorists. Two subsequent mass hostage-taking incidents ended with gruesome results: the October 2002 Moscow Theater carnage and the September 2004 Beslan school massacre. In both cases the Chechen terrorists expected the Russians to cave in to their demands, while the Russians were determined to avoid just such an outcome.

Russia have provided the oxygen that helped finance, organize, manage, and even perpetuate the Chechen terrorist campaign. At bottom, the Chechen criminals are also Chechen patriots and fellow Muslims. Many of them returned to Chechnya to fight the Russians during the second war and used the capital obtained from their criminal endeavors to buy arms and to provide for Muslim volunteers who flocked to Chechnya to help their coreligionists.[15]

***

Reasons for terrorist activities by criminals are plentiful, but from Latin America to the Balkans and from the Caucasus to the Middle East, criminals typically use terrorism in order to influence the political process. Awash in cash, especially from the narcotics trade, some criminal organizations have been vying for control of the judicial system and law enforcement agencies in their respective countries. Given the fortunes involved, using terrorism to manipulate politics in some societies has become both possible and inevitable.

TERROR AND CRIMINAL ACTIVITIES

Money is the lifeblood of terrorism. Most international terrorism would come to a halt if terrorist organizations were deprived of capital for their operations and existence. Accordingly, since the September 11 attacks, the United States has led the global effort to combat terrorism by attempting to cut-off these financial supply lines. The success of these efforts has been limited, however.

In fact, terrorists have adapted successfully to the interruptions in their financial support by resorting to criminal ventures in order to become financially independent. One cannot overemphasize the point that the lines separating terrorism and crime have become so blurred that sometimes it is difficult to determine what the *raison d'être* for the continued existence of some of these organizations really is. As the British playwright Henry Fielding dryly noted, "Money is the fruit of evil as often as the root of it."

The Revolutionary United Front

The Revolutionary United Front (RUF) of Sierra Leone is a political party with a gruesome history. For about a decade, between 1991 and 2002, it terrorized the countryside with extreme cruelty, killing an estimated 50,000–200,000 people in the process. The group began as a social protest movement by urbanites discontented with the government but evolved into a new and puzzling form.

Helped for various reasons by political leaders from neighboring countries, the RUF was not a typical guerilla force fighting to achieve a defined political purpose, or a separatist or reform movement. Its ideology remains a mystery as it was neither leftist nor rightist; it wasn't even nationalist. Rather, the movement evolved into a group of bandits whose leaders' sole purpose was to continue to pillage the diamond mines of Sierra Leone, which had come under their control. Prior to the RUF's eventual disintegration into a negligible political party, the organization's annual revenues from the sale of diamonds were estimated at $25–$125 million per year.[16]

The following case exemplifies how terrorist organizations use criminal methods in a systematic and substantial way to either finance their operations or enrich themselves while continuing to proclaim the virtues of their political cause.

The Revolutionary Armed Forces of Colombia (FARC)

The military wing of the Colombian Communist Party, known as the Revolutionary Armed Forces of Colombia (FARC), was established in 1964. There are other forces operating in Colombia with the avowed aim of overthrowing the government, but the FARC has been the largest, best organized, and most effective. The organization is said to have about 18,000 fighting members and to control almost 40% of the territory of the country, parts of which even the Colombian military dares not enter. The FARC engages in ambushes, mining, assassinations, kidnapping-for-ransom, extortion, protection rackets and, especially, in narco-terrorism. The FARC's annual revenues from narcotics are estimated at up to $400,000,000.

From a humble beginning dedicated to an egalitarian vision for the Colombian populace, the FARC has come a long way to unabashedly using criminal activities to amass fortunes. As ideological idealism lost out to the lure of money, the FARC has been trading in narcotics at an industrial level,

MAP 7–1   MAP OF SOUTH AMERICA

Source: The CIA World Factbook https://www.cia.gov/library/publications/the-world-factbook/
docs/refmaps.html

What Do YOU Think?

Imagine being a Colombian government official involved in combating the FARC narco-terrorists. How do you think you would feel putting your life, and the lives of your family, at risk by fighting such a large organization, knowing that its combatants are probably better trained, equipped, paid, and motivated than the government's forces? Or, if you were an 18-year-old thinking of joining your country's military forces, knowing that such an imbalance existed, would you decide to join?

---

complete with production plants and distribution channels. The organization levies taxes on local growers and collects protection money from others.

Necessity creates strange bedfellows. In this case, in addition to the expected alliances FARC has with similar leftist Colombian organizations, it has also established working arrangements with their ideological nemesis on the right, the drug lords. The situation has become bizarre: in areas in which the drug lords are strong, the FARC pays taxes to leave its drug and military operations uninterrupted. Conversely, in areas controlled by the FARC, drug lords continue their cultivation and distribution of narcotics without interference for an agreed upon "cut" to the FARC.[17]

The real irony is not so much the betrayal of idealism; it is how the money is actually used. For example, it is estimated that the FARC needs only 10% of its substantial revenues to finance its war chest. It, therefore, does not take a seasoned accountant to question the whereabouts of the rest of this treasure, especially as it has been accumulating year after year after year. The answer is that, like all good capitalists, the FARC leadership has been stashing these considerable amounts in the West—in the stock markets, in real-estate holdings, and in other profitable investments.[18]

Terrorist Organizations and Predatory War Economies

The FARC's practices constitute a pattern of what Napoleoni terms *predatory war economies*, referring to the ruin armed groups cause to the livelihood of the indigenous populations in the name of some cause. These strategies exist in other areas of the world as well. For example, the Basque ETA hid their criminal activities under the guise of a "revolutionary tax," which devastated the Basque economy.[19] Similarly, Yasser Arafat's Palestine Liberation Organization (PLO) was involved in various profitable criminal schemes while in Lebanon, activities that accrued billions of dollars to the organization. Napoleoni analogized the PLO's behavior in Lebanon to an "economic parasite," which depletes the host country of one resource after the other.

To grasp the magnitude of the funds available to some terrorist organizations and the challenge of attempting to starve them financially, it is worth

---

Did You Know?

Beginning in the late 1960s and gaining momentum in the 1970s, the PLO
and the PFLP perfected a scheme to

extort protection money from international airlines, which netted them millions of dollars each year.[20]

---

noting that, according to researcher Rachel Ehrenfeld, by the late 1990s the
PLO had accumulated $8 billion in a few Western accounts. In addition,
the PLO imposed a 5% "revolutionary tax" on the wages of all Palestinians
working in Arab countries. In 1999, the CIA estimated the PLO's assets from
this tax to be between $8 billion and $14 billion.[21]

Syrian officials stationed in Lebanon were also known to accumulate their
retirement nest eggs from the drug trade and other criminal acts, while promoting the interests of Hezbollah and Palestinian terrorists based in Lebanon.
What the poppy fields of the Bekaa Valley in eastern Lebanon failed to provide,
a substantial industry of smuggling and counterfeiting more than made up for.
Half a world away, Peruvian coca growers have been collaborating with the
Shining Path terrorist group, exporting narcotics worth $28 billion annually to
the United States alone and paying the Marxist group a substantial "protection" tax.[22] The syndrome is universal.

A CASE IN POINT: The Kurdistan Workers' Party

Established in November of 1978, the Kurdistan Workers' Party (PKK) platform
was to advance the cause of Kurdish independence in the context of a Marxist revolution. From its bases in southeastern Turkey, and supported by neighboring countries such as Syria and Iran, the group commenced a terrorist campaign against
Turkey that lasted about 15 years and cost the lives of over 30,000 people. Led by
the brutal Abdullah Ocalan, the PKK killed about 10,000 Kurds over the years, in
order to stifle any dissent from its own population. The PKK's declared goals were
neither clear nor credible to the Kurds themselves, who could never tell with certainty if the organization was pursuing Kurdish independence or promoting
Marxism. In 1999, Ocalan was captured and sentenced to death. Following an international outcry against the use of capital punishment, the Turkish authorities com-
muted the sentence to a life imprisonment. In 2000, the PKK renounced its quest for
a violent struggle for Kurdish independence.

In the course of its armed struggle, the PKK enjoyed substantial financial
assistance from Kurdish émigrés abroad. To finance its operations, the organization
used an international network of exiles to run a profitable crime enterprise, which
included smuggling and distributing narcotics in Europe. After its defeat, and with
its political struggle at a dead end, one would have expected the PKK to end its
involvement in crime. Instead, the criminal side of the PKK operation has never
ceased. "Money isn't everything," wrote Edmund Stockdale, "but it's a long way
ahead of what comes next."

Reflecting on the tendency of such revolutionaries to prefer riches to lofty ideals if given a choice, Walter Laqueur wondered, "what would have happened to Mao and his faithful if early during the *Long March* they had come across a gold mine—and the same applies to the other classic guerrilla movements."[23]

ISLAMIST GROUPS

Since the name of the game for any organization is survival—and terrorist organizations are not immune from this reality—Islamist groups have recognized that in order to survive they had to become financially independent. What better way to ensure a hefty flow of revenues than by turning to crime? In their view, the victims of the criminal acts are infidels, the enemy, and therefore values such as honesty and obedience to the law do not apply. As Abu Bakar Bashir, the head of the Jemaah Islamiah, al-Qaeda's affiliate in Southeast Asia, reasoned, "you can take their blood; then why not take their property?"[24]

Some Islamic authorities justify growing, manufacturing, and selling narcotics to infidels even though Islam forbids the use of drugs or alcohol. In fact, religious decrees, *fatwas*, have been issued in recent years by radical Islamist clerics permitting the narcotics industry to distribute its products in the West on the grounds that drugs help destroy Western societies. Paul L. Williams in his book *The Al Qaeda Connection* describes a Hezbollah fatwa that explicitly states, "We are making these drugs for Satan—Americans and Jews. If we cannot kill them with guns . . . we will kill them with drugs."[25] Another writer reports in *U.S. News and World Report* that the Taliban-linked narco-terrorist Baz Mohammad expressed the same sentiment, "selling heroin in the United States was a jihad, he said, because they were taking the Americans' money at the same time the heroin was killing them."[26] This attitude reminds one of the former CIA official Michael Scheuer, who warned of "the power of focused, principled hatred."[27]

Great as the need may be, converting terrorist cells to criminal ones is not simple. One way to begin is to emulate criminal gangs because both types of underground enterprises share the same basic requirements: cash, safe houses, weapons, false-documentation, means of transportation, and so on. In their quest for survival, the terrorists have proven themselves quick learners. In a

---

Robberies and the Bali Explosions

On the night of October 13, 2002, a series of explosions rocked the resort area of Bali, a coveted tourist spot in Indonesia. When the dust settled on the scene, nearly 200 people, mostly foreign tourists, were dead and scores of others were badly injured. Soon thereafter, authorities managed to establish the responsibility of Jemaah Islamiyah, an Islamist terrorist organization, for the crime. The group had financed the operation with a string of jewelry store robberies.[28]

The Islamist cell that blew up this train in Madrid, Spain, in 2004, gained the money for this operation from criminal activities

Source: Courtesy of AP Wide World Photos.

surprisingly short amount of time, Islamists worldwide became experts in the narcotics trade, in the art of smuggling and counterfeiting, in the finer points of armed robbery, and a battery of other unlawful moneymaking specialties. The strategy has worked remarkably well. For example, the Moroccan Islamist cell that carried out the Madrid train bombings of March 11, 2004, financed its operation by trafficking in hashish and Ecstasy.[29]

Napoleoni reports that the global narcotics trade is estimated at $300–$500 billion each year. Seventy to eighty percent of the narcotics trade in Europe—estimated at $50 billion a year—reaches the continent via Turkey. The contraband originates in the Middle East and Asia, especially in Afghanistan, is transferred through Turkey to the Muslim swaths throughout the Balkans, and is then dispersed throughout the rest of Europe. Each month, 4–6 metric tons of heroin are transferred from Turkey via the Balkans to Western Europe. In addition, billions of dollars are laundered in Balkan banks each year and, as legitimate money, help further finance Islamist terrorists.[30]

This glimpse into the magnitude of the criminal economy demonstrates vividly why Islamist terrorists have no shortage of money to sustain themselves and to conduct operations; the funds are either self-generated by illegal activities or provided by outside criminal as well as legal sources.

Hawala and *Zakat*: Why Financial Controls Hardly Work

Western attempts to fight terrorists and those who support them by blocking their financial lifeblood have been dealt a severe blow by a system Westerners know too little about, called *hawala*. This ancient method for transferring money without physically moving it has been in practice in Africa, Southeast Asia, and the Middle East for over a thousand years.

The technique is ingeniously effective. People wishing to remit funds from one location to others in a different country pay the sum to a *hawala* dealer at an exchange rate and a commission level lower than a bank's. At the other end, the recipients collect the amount paid on their behalf. All identities are kept secret and records are immediately destroyed, enabling this "honorary system" to work faster and more reliably than that of formal banks.

Historically, the reason for this method made sense. It enabled traders in the prebanking era to travel safely without cash, yet have money available for them upon reaching their destinations. In more modern times, migrants from South Asia, Africa, and the Middle East have made extensive use of this system to send money back home quickly and anonymously.

Understandably, such a reliable and secret system for transferring cash from one place to another has proven a huge bonanza for criminal networks and for terrorists. According to United Nations sources,[31] the *hawala* system moves about $200 billion a year, free of any governmental knowledge or interference, a phenomenon that frustrates law enforcement's attempts to stop the flow of money to terrorists more than is commonly understood.

Feeding the Islamists' use of *hawala* are funds obtained from almsgiving, *zakat* in Arabic. One of the five pillars of Islam, almsgiving requires Muslims to donate at least 2% of their personal wealth to charitable causes. Numerous charities have been established to help disseminate the accumulated amounts to the needy and other worthy causes. While most charities fulfill their humane mandates as required, others nurture an agenda of their own and funnel money to terrorists.

Law enforcement agencies the world over have focused their attention on this vulnerable area, but with limited success due to the enormous amounts *zakat* generates, which are then transferred using the *hawala* system. In certain Middle Eastern countries, *zakat* is automatically deducted from all business transactions. Given the huge amount of money in that region of the world, the total deductions translate into figures that are both fantastically large and untraceable, since all records are routinely destroyed. For example, the 6,000 members who compose the Saudi royal family are jointly worth an estimated $600 billion.[32] This means that the deductions for *zakat* for this group alone total $12 billion—money that ends up with charitable organizations. The challenges facing Western authorities struggling to stem the flow of money from those Islamic charities that support terrorist organizations are overwhelming, given the semi-regulated monetary systems of the Persian Gulf region.

The self-serving rhetoric that the West is making progress in fighting Islamist terrorists by going after their financial resources and those of their backers is counterproductive. That does not mean that we should discard all "traditional" methods and embrace every single option available in this war, but other strategies for confronting the terrorists should receive at least equal consideration, resources, and funding. Focusing on the money trail has hardly worked.

SUMMARY

In this chapter you have learned the following:

1. Terrorism is going through a new and dangerous metamorphosis.
2. Crime and terrorism have become indistinguishable.
3. Unprecedented amounts of illegal money are generated by this underworld economy each year, as high as $1.5 trillion!
4. Islamist terrorists thrive on this "new economy of terror" in their worldwide jihad.
5. Almsgiving and the *hawala* system generate and facilitate the transfer of huge amounts of untraceable money.
6. Consequently, Western attempts to dry up the Islamist terrorists' financial resources have generally been an exercise in futility.

💣💣💣

During the brutal civil war in Lebanon, one could hardly find more passionate hatred than that which existed between Yasser Arafat's al-Fatah, the largest of the PLO terrorist groups, and the Christian Phalanges, led by Bashir Gemayal. Yet, according to Napoleoni, in January 1975 they reached an agreement to work together to rob the British Bank of the Middle East in downtown Beirut.

Combined teams from each organization worked in tandem for a few days to seal off the area and to dig their way with picks and axes through the bank's walls until they reached the vault. Once there, they realized that cracking the vault itself was beyond their skills, and a team of experts from the Corsican Mafia was quickly contracted and flown into Beirut on a chartered plane. Expertise had its rewards and upon completing the job, the three groups split the loot—cash, jewelry, certificates of deposit, and gold. The Corsicans took their third back with them in the chartered plane, the Phalange used the windfall to buy arms, and Yasser Arafat chartered a plane, loaded it with the booty, and personally flew to Switzerland to invest the treasure in several financial institutions.[33]

💣💣💣

NOTES

1. The quote by Antonio Costa, head of the United Nations Office on Drugs and Crime, is found in David Kaplan, "Paying For Terror," *U.S. News and World Report*, Vol. 139, No. 21 (December 5, 2005), p. 42.

2. Credit for the term *the new world disorder* goes to Loretta Napoleoni, *Terror Incorporated: Tracing The Dollars Behind The Terror Networks* (New York: Seven Stories Press, 2005). The term *terror economic network* was also originated by her on page 189.

3. The data concerning the $1.5 trillion transacted annually, the equivalent of 5% of the world's gross domestic product, is found in Ibid., p. 234.

4. Napoleoni's contention that Western capitalism is unlikely to relinquish an annual injection of $1.5 trillion from the underground economy can be found in p. 235.

5. The sources of terror revenues are found in Alex Schmidt, "Links Between Terrorism And Drug Trafficking: A Case Of 'Narco Terrorism'? " *SafeDemocracy.Org* (January 27, 2005), http://english.safe-democracy.org/causes/links-between-terrorism-and-drug-trafficking-a-case-of-narcoterrorism.html (accessed October 18, 2006).

6. For more on the IRA's financial dealings, see, for example, Napoleoni, pp. 59–63, 192; and Jonathan R. White, *Terrorism: An Introduction*, 4th ed. (Belmont, CA: Wadsworth/Thomson Learning, 2002), p. 41.

7. For the origins of the term *narco-terrorism*, see, for example, Alex Schmidt, "Links Between Terrorism And Drug Trafficking: A Case Of 'Narco Terrorism'?"

8. The $12 billion sum mentioned with regard to the criminal activity in the Triple Border region is found in Napoleoni, p. 205.

9. More on the role of Iran and *Hezbollah* in the 1994 attack on the Jewish Community Center in Buenos Aires is found in MSNBC, "Breakthrough Made in '94 Argentina Bombing," November 9, 2005, in http://www.msnbc.msn.com/id/9983810/from/RL.5 (accessed July 27, 2006); Reuters, "Iran Linked to Buenos Aires Blast," May 5, 1998, at http://www.ict.org.il/spotlight/det.cfm?id=78 (accessed July 27, 2006); BBC "Iran Blamed for Argentine Bomb," November 6, 2003, at http://news.bbc.co.uk/2/hi/middle_east/3245641.stm (accessed July 27, 2006); and Ze'ev Schiff, "How Iran Planned the Buenos Aires Blast," Ha'aretz, July 27, 2006, at http://www.haaretz.com/hasen/pages/ShArt.jhtml?itemNo=273898&contrassID=2&subContrassID=1&sbSubContrassID=0 (accessed October 3, 2006).

10. For more on Dawood Ibrahim's involvement in the Bombay attacks see *U.S. News and World Report*, Vol. 139, No. 21, p. 48.

11. The information about the alliance between the Napoli-based branch of the Italian Mafia, the Neapolitan Camorran, and Islamist groups is found in Ibid., p. 46.

12. For information concerning the $500 billion that was transferred out of Russia during the 1990s, see Napoleoni, p. 232.

13. For the assertion regarding the level of corruption characterizing the Russian law enforcement establishment, see Walter Laqueur, *The New Terrorism: Fanaticism and the Arms of Mass Destruction* (New York: Oxford University Press, 1999), p. 222.

14. The description of the six largest criminal gangs in Moscow and the claim that of those, three are Chechen is advanced by Laqueur in Ibid., pp. 119–220.

15. More on the Chechen patriotism is found in Ibid., pp. 220–221.

16. For a discussion of the RUF, see Napoleoni, pp. 215–216.

17. See Laqueur (1999), p. 214, for the cooperation between the Colombian drug cartels and the FARC.

18. See Ibid., pp. 213–214, for the destination of the huge amount of revenues the FARC acquires annually.

19. For more about the devastating impact of the ETA on the Basque economy, see Napoleoni, pp. 66–69.

20. The protection money the Palestinian groups extorted from Western airlines is mentioned in Neil C. Livingstone and David Halevy, *Inside the PLO* (New York: William Morrow, 1990), pp. 186–187.

21. The assessment that by the late 1990s the PLO had $8 billion in Western banks and that it had accumulated assets worth $8 billion to $14 billion from its "revolutionary tax" can be found in Rachel Ehrenfeld, "Intifada Gives Cover to Arafat's Graft and Fraud," News World Communication, Inc., *Insight on the News*, Vol. 17, No. 26 (July 16, 2001), pp. 44–45.

22. The tax paid by Peruvian coca growers to the Shining Path organization is mentioned in Napoleoni, p. 57.

23. For the speculation about the future of Mao's band of revolutionaries had they encountered a gold mine during the Long March, see Laqueur (1999), p. 216.

24. The quote that if Muslims can take infidels' blood they should be able to take their money as well is in *U.S. News and World Report*, Vol. 139, No. 21, p. 44.

25. Hezbollah's "fatwa" is cited in Paul L. Williams, *The Al Qaeda Connection: International Terrorism, Organized Crime, and the Coming Apocalypse* (Amherst, New York: Prometheus Books, 2005), p. 57.

26. Baz Mohammad's boast is found in *U.S. News and World Report*, Vol. 139, No. 21, p. 52.

27. Scheuer's quote about the power of focused, principled hatred, is found in Anonymous, *Imperial Hubris: Why the West Is Losing the War on Terror* (Washington, DC: Brassey's, Inc., 2004), p. 1

28. For the method used by Jemaah Islamiyah to finance its Bali operation, *U.S. News and World Report*, pp. 42–44.

29. The way the Madrid bombers raised the funds needed for their operation is described in Ibid., Vol. 139, No. 21, p. 44.

30. The figure of $300–$500 billion for the global narcotics trade and the one attributed to Turkish criminal enterprises are cited in Napoleoni, pp. 233 and 207 respectively. That 4–6 tons of heroine flow into Europe via Turkey each month is found in p. 124.

31. The source of the figure of $200 billion for the annual transactions of the *hawala* industry is found in, United Nations, Security Council, "Letter Dated 19 September 2002 from the Chairman Of The Monitoring Group Established Pursuant To Resolution 1267 (1999) Addressed To The President Of The Security Council." Document Number: S/2002/1050/Corr.1.

32. For the figure of the total worth of the Saudi royal family, see David Pallister and Owen Bowcott, "Banks to Shut Doors on Saudi Royal Cash," *Guardian*, 17 July 2002, p. 17.

33. The combined operation to rob the British Bank of the Middle East in Beirut is described in Napoleoni, pp. 64–65.

NOWHERE TO HIDE

TERRORISM: A UNIVERSAL PLAGUE

The wounded American eagle on 9/11
Source: Courtesy of DePixion Features.

NOWHERE TO HIDE

TERRORISM: A UNIVERSAL PLAGUE

Games Nations Play

State and State-Backed Terrorism

The supreme excellence is to subdue the armies of your enemies without even having to fight them.

Sun Tzu

The people of the Soviet Union experienced a fear so stifling during Stalin's bloody purges that Westerners spared such incapacitating terror cannot possibly fully comprehend it. In a 1938 communist party meeting, at the height of the political repression, Stalin delivered a speech. Each time he paused, fearful delegates applauded him vigorously with a standing ovation. So pervasive was the panic in the hall that no one dared be the first to stop applauding, lest that person pay with his or her life for the offense. In a grotesque scene, the delegates, still on their feet, applauded enthusiastically for over ten minutes. The secret police monitoring the proceedings noted the first to eventually stop clapping and instantly labeled them potentially independent thinkers. The offenders were arrested and sent to concentration camps in Siberia.

To introduce a measure of sanity to subsequent meetings, Stalin would pause, await the mandatory applause, and hit a buzzer indicating to all that it was safe to stop applauding and to sit down.

The involvement of the state in terrorism primarily takes place at three levels: (1) the state terrorizes its own population; (2) it supports terrorist groups that operate against other states; and (3) it is directly involved in terrorism abroad.

TERRORISM AGAINST A STATE'S OWN POPULATION

The late movie director Stanley Kubrick said that "the great nations have always acted like gangsters, and the small nations like prostitutes." The study of state-terrorism, in both great and small nations, shows no such distinction, however. For all the talk about the threat the world currently faces from terrorist organizations, the cumulative damage, suffering, and casualties this type of terrorism has inflicted pales in comparison to that caused by internal state-terrorism. Over the last century, states have perfected the art of controlling their own populations by means of brutal repression to a degree that makes terrorist organizations look like bumbling amateurs.

The numbers of the casualties involved and the vicious nature of state-terrorism are incomprehensible to those who have never been exposed to it. Consider, for instance, the following comparison: in the ten years between 1968 and 1977, terrorist organizations worldwide caused 10,000 fatalities. Between the years 1976 and 1983 alone—the period known as the *Dirty War*—Argentina's military junta had 10,000 to 30,000 Argentineans killed!

Under the Thumb of Idi Amin

There are many types of dictatorships, representing a variety of ideologies, and all of them are invariably bad for their people. The effect of the dictatorship of Idi Amin, who ruled Uganda from 1971 to 1979, on the population of the country was no different.

Idi Amin came to power in 1971 in a military coup. Soon after taking over, Amin began showing the true color of his regime. The beginning of the reign of terror was indicative of things to come: death squads hunted down and murdered political opponents, members of the intelligentsia, and suspect military officers. Next, the government began to persecute, and then expel, rival Ugandan tribes. In 1972, Idi Amin went a step further and ordered the immediate expulsion of all the "Asians," that is, the community of British passport holders, mostly people of Indian origin, who had settled in Uganda. The move would prove catastrophic to Uganda's economy.

Although often depicted as a murderous buffoon in the West, he was responsible for the wholesale slaughter, it is believed, of 300,000 to 500,000 Ugandans. As Amin's paranoia grew, so did the volume of sadistic tortures and executions under his rule. Amin was known to feed prisoners to crocodiles and rumors abound that he forced prisoners to engage in cannibalism, which, some maintain, he himself personally practiced. In 1979, he fled to Saudi Arabia, where he died in exile in August 2003.[1]

Genocide and Mass Murder: Nazi Germany and the Soviet Union

Most of us know something about the internal terrorism in Nazi Germany and in the Soviet Union. However, it has taken decades to penetrate the shields both countries erected to hide their crimes and, therefore, for us to fully understand the horrors represented by the staggering numbers. Once Nazi Germany was defeated, many facts concerning the SS-run death camps and the Gestapo's crimes were well publicized, but exposing the full scope of the terrorism practiced by communist countries against their own populations remains an ongoing process. The Soviet Union, for example, sent between 40 and 50 million people to concentration camps in Siberia between 1917 and 1953. Of these, 15 to 25 million people died of starvation, disease, or execution. These figures exceed the estimated 10–12 million victims of the Nazi killing machine.[2]

Of course, the state-terrorism of Nazi Germany and the former Soviet Union are two of the most well known, but internal terrorism has been carried out not only by well-known culprits but also by numerous other countries—large and small.

The Three Faces of Internal Terrorism

Combs identifies three levels of state-terrorism.[3] In escalating order, each represents an increased form of violence against a helpless populace.

1. *Intimidation*: Here, a state frightens the opposition—even potential opposition—from engaging in any antigovernment activity. To accomplish this, the state exploits its monopoly over the means of communications and uses force to pressure the population into submission. For example, during the apartheid era in South Africa, blacks and their white supporters were subjected to a policy of persecution, arrest, torture, and execution. The white government's aim was to coerce the black majority into passive acquiescence to the racial policies of the regime.

2. *Forced Conversion*: States compel all citizens to change their political outlook; everyone's thinking must toe the government's line. This type of terrorism usually follows revolutions that trigger campaigns to radically change people's daily lives, patterns of behavior, and thinking. For example, since its establishment, North Korea (the Democratic People's Republic of Korea—DPRK) has been indoctrinating its population in the merits of communism and the threats allegedly posed by the outside world, especially the capitalist countries. Decades of arrests, torture, executions, and brainwashing have resulted in a disciplined society that is physically and ideologically within the grasp of the regime.

3. *Genocide*: This level denotes states' deliberate extermination of all undesirable ethnic or racial minorities within their country. The motives for such policies

range from ideological to religious. One example, out of too many, is that of the attempted genocide in the African country of Rwanda in 1994. In that year, long-simmering tensions and social divisions between the Hutu majority and the Tutsi minority erupted into a full-fledged effort to commit genocide. Within three months, Hutu military and militia forces aided by ordinary Hutu civilians engaged in an orgy of looting, rape, torture, and murder that left almost one million Tutsis dead.

What's in a Name?

Political scientists crunch and debate the fine points that differentiate *authoritarian* from *totalitarian* regimes. For our purposes, here is a quick rule of thumb: The difference lies in the level of control governments exercise over their respective populations. Authoritarian governments mistreat their people and pillage the country's resources and coffers. However, their attitude is one of "live and let live"; that is, no harm comes to those who do not challenge the government's looting and other abuses of the country or the selective murders it commits. Anastasio Somoza Debayle, the President of Nicaragua from 1967 to 1972 and from 1974 to 1979, headed such a classic authoritarian regime. Similarly, Fulgencio Batista, the strongman who ruled Cuba under one guise or another from 1933 to January 1959, was the embodiment of a corrupt authoritarian ruler.

In contrast, totalitarian regimes actively engage in changing the thinking and behavior of the entire population, bringing everybody in line with the government's policies. As the word suggests, they want total control over every facet of their society and will use any means to get it—even mass murder. For these governments, being tolerated is not enough; everybody must embrace the regime's philosophy. The secret police and networks of agents, informants, youth groups, mandatory workers' meetings for "education" purposes, the encouragement of children to spy and inform on family members, brutal penal systems, and concentration camps work in tandem to brainwash the population. Modern history is replete with examples of totalitarian regimes, from Saddam Hussein's Iraq to the Iranian theocracy to the Cuban communist dictatorship.

Getting Away With Murder

The principle in international relations that a state's sovereignty is so complete that whatever it does *inside* its borders is an internal matter goes a long way toward explaining state-terrorism. With the introduction in recent decades of international governmental organizations (IGOs), such as the United Nations, and non-governmental organizations (NGOs), such as Amnesty International, we have witnessed some reduction in this absolute state power and authority. This development notwithstanding, the principle that no entity transcends that of a sovereign state is still a dominant factor in international relations, which, with few exceptions, enables states to exercise domestic terrorism without fear of external reprisal.

The reason for the continued existence of this loophole is easy to understand; some states are concerned that if other nations are permitted to interfere in certain aspects of a country's behavior, the precedent might come back to haunt them. For example, in 1999 a debate raged over the possibility of armed intervention by the international community to stop what was being described as the "ethnic cleansing" of the Muslim population of Kosovo by Serbians. Russia and the People's Republic of China (PRC) spearheaded the resistance to the proposed intervention. Their rationale was the inalienable sovereign right of states, in that case Serbia, to enact domestic policies free of outside interference. It is plausible, however, that they opposed military intervention in Serbia because they feared that if interference in Serbia's domestic affairs was allowed, in the future similar steps might be taken over their respective policies in Chechnya and Tibet. Such concerns hinder concrete action against states that violate human rights.

The cynical reality is that for all the talk about intervention to stop internal terrorism, outside pressure reflects power relationships in the international arena, rather than clearly defined rules that apply equally to all nations. How else does one explain the long list of states committing acts of terror against their own populations without a word of protest from the international community? At best, economic sanctions or other diplomatic sanctions are imposed, not outright political or military confrontation. World attention to internal terrorism is hopelessly selective when it comes to identifying guilty countries. For example, when was the last time the international community considered taking action against China over its policies in Tibet, against Iran, Syria, and Turkey for their treatment of their Kurdish populations, or against Cuba for its domestic political repression? Albert Einstein's insight that "the world is a dangerous place to live in—not because of the people who are evil but because of the people who do not do anything about it" is still true.

Cambodia: A Case Study in Internal Terrorism

One of the worst instances of internal state-terrorism in the twentieth century was that inflicted by the communist party of Cambodia, the Khmer Rouge, from 1975 until its formal downfall in 1979 (officially, the party continued to

---

What Do YOU Think?

Why, in your opinion, was there such a universal outcry against the internal terrorism that accompanied apartheid in South Africa, but no equal world revulsion against other forms of internal terrorism stemming from ideological or religious motives, such as in Idi Amin's Uganda, Augusto Pinochet's Chile, or Saddam Hussein's Iraq?

Skeleton and bones of genocide victims in Cambodia
Source: Courtesy of National Geographic Image Collection.

exist until 1999). An incredible amount of killings and destruction took place in the course of those four years. Relative to the size of its population, just over 7 million, the Cambodian regime murdered more of its own people, an estimated 1,400,000 to 2,000,000 people, or about 20% of the population, than did Nazi Germany. The exact numbers are debatable and, probably, will never be known precisely.

Once in power, the Khmer Rouge, under the leadership of Pol Pot, implemented a monstrous and massive program to transform the nation into a "pure" agrarian society. To accomplish their vision, the Khmer Rouge literally emptied the country's cities of their inhabitants and forced the entire population into labor camps in the countryside. At the same time, they closed schools, hospitals, factories and banks, abolished the monetary system, seized private property, and outlawed religion. In the next four years, untold numbers of people starved to death. Capital punishment was widely used to punish even minor infractions. For instance, in an attempt to break up traditional family structures, the new rulers forbade communication among family members. Those caught breaking the rules were put to death instantly. Any person suspected of having been an intellectual, clergy, teacher, professional, or involved with the previous government was summarily executed.

Border conflicts with Vietnam resulted in a Vietnamese invasion in 1979 that toppled the regime. The Khmer Rouge retreated to the countryside and fought a guerrilla campaign for a few years. Pol Pot died of natural causes in

---

What Do YOU Think?

Some people in Russia and Georgia continue to admire the former dictator Joseph Stalin although the enormity of his crimes and the fact that he was responsible for the deaths of millions of innocent people is well known. How do you explain this phenomenon?

1998 and the Khmer Rouge officially disbanded a year later. (For a sense of what this episode in state-terrorism was like, I recommend that you watch the movie *The Killing Fields*.)

TERRORISM AGAINST OTHER STATES

When a country backs terrorists who operate against another country to "project its power into the territory of another without accepting responsibility,"[4] it is a form of state-terrorism. Numerous instances of such cases litter the history of recent decades, reminding us of the late Spanish philosopher José Ortega y Gasset's lament that violence—he did not mention terrorism explicitly but the meaning is unmistakable—is the rhetoric of our period.

Supporting terrorism against another state is a foreign policy strategy, generally practiced secretly. The goals of such a policy include the following:

1. Weakening the resolve of the opponent state to the point where its government complies with the political demands of the state supporting the use of terrorism.

2. Disheartening the targeted population by the hardships terrorism causes and the government's inability to end it so that the populace demands a change of the government, or a change in its policies, in ways the country supporting the use of terrorism desires.

3. Demoralizing a nation's resolve to the point where the country collapses in the face of the relentless terrorist onslaught.

The Soviet Union was a noted supporter of terrorism.[5] In the context of the Cold War, it provided, sometimes openly and on many occasions covertly, training and other logistical help for organizations whose potential the Soviet Union deemed beneficial to its standing in the world. To promote its international power and prestige, the Soviet Union proclaimed its "peace loving" nature as it supported "revolutionary" and "progressive" movements around the globe that were supposedly struggling against "Western imperialism." Some movements benefiting from Soviet support, from Latin America to Africa and the Middle East, used terrorism in pursuit of their own political objectives. Others, such as Fidel Castro in Cuba, came to enjoy Soviet support once they assumed power and introduced a reign of internal terrorism.

Only during the presidency of Mikhail Gorbachev (1985–1991) did the Soviet Union take stock of the cost effectiveness of this policy. The findings showed that no tangible benefits had resulted from the country's tacit involvement in terrorism, as the dismal results of the Soviet support for left-wing terrorist groups in Western Europe clearly indicated. These conclusions led to a significant decrease in Soviet support for terrorist organizations around the world, and training camps for foreign terrorists in the Soviet Union and its satellite countries were closed.

Types of State-Backed Terrorism

Combs uses the terms *sponsors* and *supporters* of terrorism to describe two distinct ways in which states back terrorism against other countries. When a state sponsors terrorism, it is intensively involved in helping a terrorist organization by financing it, participating in the organization's decision making, controlling its day-to-day operations, and so on. Supporting a terrorist organization is more limited in comparison. In such cases, the state may provide monetary support, permission to use its territory and political backing, but the terrorist organization maintains its political, operational, and decision-making autonomy. [6]

Paul Millar, a former counterterrorism official at the CIA, similarly distinguishes between states that closely *sponsor* terrorists and states that, by omission or passive winking, enable terrorists to function. He calls these states sponsors and enablers of terrorism, respectively. Regardless of the terminology, the state rendering the assistance uses terrorism to reap its fruits while, by virtue of not being directly involved, evading retribution from the target state.[7]

Hezbollah: A Case Study in State-Sponsored Terrorism

The relationship between Iran and the Lebanese terrorist group Hezbollah, which was established by Iran during the 1980s and which it has continued to cultivate, finance, train, equip, and support in all ways possible, is a good illustration of state-sponsored terrorism.

Hezbollah's operations are closely controlled by Iranian officials, who are involved in the minutest details of the organization's policies, decision making, budgetary allocations, and military operations. For reasons stemming from pan-Shi'i affinity through shared hostility to Israel to the quest for leadership in the Muslim world, thousands of Iranian Revolutionary Guards have been

stationed in the Bekaa Valley in eastern Lebanon. There, they have been training and directing Hezbollah fighters, especially during and after the organization's conflict with Israel in the summer of 2006, and lending their weight to the
Shi'i group.

Syria: A Case Study in State-Supported Terrorism

The best example of the relationship between a state and one or more terrorist
organizations it backs is Syria's role in recent decades in the Israeli–Palestinian
conflict. In spite of its repeated denials, Syria has been home to more than a dozen
Palestinian terrorist groups and their political and military leaders. Terrorist
organizations that reject the concept of peace with Israel, such as Hamas, Islamic
Jihad, and the Popular Front for the Liberation of Palestine are headquartered in
Damascus. Syria allows these groups to use its territory, coordinate policies, plan
attacks on Israel, raise funds, and so on, but its direct involvement in these particular terrorist groups' day-to-day operations is restricted. When pressed on
the issue, Syrian officials maintain that these organizations maintain only public
relations offices in Damascus. The facts are different.

Greece: A Case Study in Passively
Enabling Terrorism

Greece is an example of a player on the international scene that has found that a
passive attitude toward the use of terrorism has helped it over a long period. For
a few decades culminating in the Athens Olympic Games, antiterrorism security
in Greece was among the worst in Europe. Greece was the vulnerable link from
which several terrorist operations in Europe—such as the hijacking of the Air
France Flight 139 to Paris (which flew to Entebbe, Uganda) and the TWA Flight
847 to Rome (which landed in Beirut, Lebanon)—originated. Greece's attitude
toward terrorism and security has been noticeably better since 2004.

***

If "politics is a blood sport," as the Welsh politician Aneurin Bevan wrote about
politics in general, what words can adequately describe states' involvement in
international politics via terrorism? Each year the U.S. Department of State identifies countries it considers backers of terrorism. On the list of usual suspects are
Iran, Syria, Libya, Cuba, and North Korea. Each of these countries has accumulated a distinguished record that justifies this designation. For example, North
Korea has been directly involved in terrorism and has been known to harbor
Japanese terrorists; Cuba has done the same for Basque ETA fugitives.

    Some Arab and Muslim states' involvement either in anti-Israeli or in intra-
Arab terrorism is historically irrefutable. The pattern began as early as the 1970s

when certain Arab states were suspected of exploiting the diplomatic immunity of their mail to smuggle to Europe—via diplomatic pouches exempted from inspection—weapons and explosives to be used by Palestinians to attack Israeli and Jewish civilian facilities. To this day, the support rendered by certain Arab countries, such as Syria, for Palestinian groups that terrorize Israeli civilians has been immense. Sometimes this type of assistance is openly acknowledged, as in the case of Iraq under Saddam Hussein; more often, it is done covertly, as Saudi Arabia did by providing financial support to Hamas in the 1990s.

The Lure of Terrorism by Proxy

States conduct a careful cost–benefit calculation prior to backing terrorism against another country. According to Combs, some of the factors rendering such support appealing are [8]

1. *Low-cost, financially*: Offering support for terrorists does not come close to the huge costs associated with conventional warfare. In this regard, backing terrorism is a clearly superior, inexpensive foreign policy alternative. For example, Pakistan supports groups fighting in Kashmir, but the cost of engaging India conventionally would be enormously prohibitive.

2. *Low-cost, politically*: Members of the international community tend to look the other way, even when it is clear that a state supports acts of terrorism. Libya suffered no political costs for supporting the IRA and the German Red Army Faction (RAF) during the 1970s.

3. *High-yield, financially*: States can profit from selling military hardware and other supplies to terrorist organizations. They can also share in the profits from the criminal activities of terrorist organizations. Cuba's involvement with Latin-American narco-terrorism has helped the regime obtain desperately needed hard currency.

4. *High-yield, politically*: The strategy of terrorism by proxy can yield desirable political results for a negligible cost. For example, Syrian collaboration with Hezbollah resulted in driving the Israelis out of South Lebanon in May 2000. This development embarrassed Israel, bolstered Syria's prestige as a champion of the Arab cause, and signaled the Arab World that Syria was a power to be reckoned with.

DIRECT INVOLVEMENT IN TERRORISM ABROAD

States engage directly in terrorism in other countries to silence political opponents residing or functioning there and to clandestinely attack their enemies' interests in that country. The following exemplify this type of direct involvement by states in terrorism outside their borders.

Libya: A Case Study in a State's Direct Involvement in Terrorism Abroad

Libya provides several juicy examples from its involvement with terrorist activities in African political struggles through its attacks on political dissidents abroad to the notorious Lockerbie Bombing.

On December 21, 1988, Pan Am Flight 103 was cruising at 434 knots per hour over Scotland, carrying 243 passengers from 21 countries and a crew of 16. It was just before Christmas and many of the passengers were students returning from their fall semester studies abroad, business people, government officials, and others residing in, or visiting, the United States. At 7:02 p.m., just as the plane was flying over Scotland, an explosion inside the plane resulted in the deaths of everyone aboard. Small sections of the plane, debris, and body parts hit the ground over a corridor of 81 miles. Some hit a residential area in the Scottish village of Lockerbie, killing 11 locals as well.

A lengthy investigation established a Libyan connection to the crime. The inquiry narrowed down the Libyan suspects to two operatives: Abdelbast al Megrahi, a Libyan intelligence officer, and Amin Khalifa Fhimah, the station manager for the Libyan Arab Airlines in Malta. Although indictments were issued in 1991, Libya refused to cooperate or extradite the suspects, claiming a frame-up. Only in 1999, after years of United Nations sanctions, did Libya's ruler, Muammar Quadaffi, agree to extradite the two suspects to stand trial in Europe. Megrahi was found guilty in 2001 and sentenced to life in prison, while his co-defendant, Fhimah, was acquitted. Later, Libya would effect a financial settlement with the families of the victims in exchange for lifting of the sanctions.

Direct Terrorism Abroad and Type of Regime

It is naive to believe that a young Libyan agent could do this by himself. That Libya knew absolutely nothing about a complex plot involving planning, the use of technology, and smuggling of explosives by a lone, young agent takes quite a stretch of the imagination.

States using internal terrorism sometimes put the practice to good use against their enemies abroad as well. Those states enjoying efficient secret services manage to evade detection or use plausible deniability to distance themselves from the potentially embarrassing act. Some are caught red-handed, usually at the cost of a diplomatic slap of the wrist. The decisive factor for a state in embarking on this policy is the nature of the society and its type of government. Those with shaky records in the area of human rights and government succession find the pursuit of an illegal policy abroad a natural and complementary extension of their internal practices.

For countries used to brutally suppressing their own populations or to orchestrating terrorist operations against their enemies by proxy, the line is straight to directly using terrorism abroad, the distance short, and the temptation irresistible. In contrast, democracies rarely engage in terrorism in other countries' territory. However, not all countries are democratic. The implications are alarming for a future in which states will directly put in their resources for terrorist purposes. In the era of weapons of mass destruction, "every time history repeats itself, the price goes up" as the old saying goes.

The Poisoned Umbrella

In 1969, a Bulgarian intellectual, Georgi Markov, defected to the West. In London, he worked for the BBC and Radio Free Europe, broadcasting anticommunist propaganda to his Bulgarian compatriots. The communist authorities in Bulgaria decided to silence him. The "hit" was to be a joint operation between the Bulgarian secret service and the Soviet KGB.

Case of the Fooled Fiancé

Syria, a major exporter of terrorism as a strategy for furthering its foreign policy, has not only supported terrorists, it sometimes gets directly involved in the practice.

Ann-Marie Murphy was a 32-year-old Irish Catholic living in London. When she became pregnant, her Palestinian fiancé, Nizar Nawwaf al-Hindawi, suggested that they travel to the "Holy Land," where his family lived. She was thrilled, despite her fiancé's insistence that they travel separately. They would meet a couple of days later in Tel Aviv. Al-Hindawi surprised her with a new suitcase for her flight on El Al, the Israeli airline.

It was April 17, 1986. At Heathrow Airport, El Al security personnel noticed that the suitcase was inexplicably heavy; examination of the luggage turned up a false bottom containing ten pounds of Semtex plastic explosives, ready for automatic detonation once the plane was in the air. The plan was to blow up the airplane in midair, killing all 375 passengers on board, including Ann-Marie and the couple's unborn baby.

A rigorous investigation by Scotland Yard revealed that al-Hindawi had been recruited and trained by Syrian intelligence, and that the plot had been hatched at the highest echelons of the Syrian government, which also closely controlled every step of the process, from al-Hindawi's official Syrian passport that enabled him to visit England to his romantic relationship with Ann-Marie. A series of government officials assigned to the plot disguised him as an employee of Syria's national airline, gave him the sophisticated bomb, and supplied him with the false-bottomed suitcase. Once al-Hindawi realized that the plot failed, he fled to the Syrian embassy in London, where the Syrian ambassador, Loutof Haydar, arranged to hide him in a safe house in London.

In October 1986, a British court sentenced al Hindawi to 45 years in jail. Citing irrefutable evidence implicating Syrian officials in the crime, the British government broke off diplomatic relations with Syria and expelled its ambassador.[9]

On September 7, 1978, as he was waiting for a bus in London, Markov was "accidentally" poked in his right leg by a man carrying an umbrella. The man apologized and left. Later that evening, Markov developed a high fever and died three days later. An autopsy revealed the umbrella that stabbed him was actually a sophisticated device that injected him with the poison *ricin*.[10]

SUMMARY

In this chapter, you have learned the following:

1. States practice terrorism at three levels: by terrorizing the domestic population, by supporting terrorist organizations abroad, and by getting directly involved in terrorism outside their borders.
2. Historically, state-terrorism against its own population has been the most deadly.
3. The concept of "state sovereignty" helps explain domestic state-terrorism.
4. States back terrorism by sponsoring, supporting, and passively enabling the practice.
5. Direct state involvement in terrorism abroad tends to reflect a state's domestic practices and the nature of its regime.

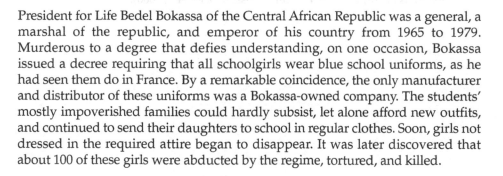

President for Life Bedel Bokassa of the Central African Republic was a general, a marshal of the republic, and emperor of his country from 1965 to 1979. Murderous to a degree that defies understanding, on one occasion, Bokassa issued a decree requiring that all schoolgirls wear blue school uniforms, as he had seen them do in France. By a remarkable coincidence, the only manufacturer and distributor of these uniforms was a Bokassa-owned company. The students' mostly impoverished families could hardly subsist, let alone afford new outfits, and continued to send their daughters to school in regular clothes. Soon, girls not dressed in the required attire began to disappear. It was later discovered that about 100 of these girls were abducted by the regime, tortured, and killed.

NOTES

1. Estimates of the number of victims under Amin's rule of terror vary. An account by the BBC, for example, puts the number at approximately 400,000. See http://news.bbc.co.uk/2/hi/africa/3155925.stm (accessed October 5, 2006).
2. For the numbers of killings carried out by Nazi Germany and the Soviet Union, see Cindy C. Combs, *Terrorism in the Twenty-First Century*, 3rd ed. (Upper Saddle River, NJ: Prentice Hall, 2003), p. 73.
3. The three types of internal terrorism appear in Ibid., pp. 72–73.
4. The quote about a country backing terrorists against another country to "project its power . . ." appears in Ray S. Cline and Yonah Alexander, *Terrorism as State-Sponsored Covert Warfare* (Fairfax, VA: Hero Books, 1986), p. 38.

5. See Claire Sterling, *The Terror Network: The Secret War of International Terrorism* (New York: Holt, Reinhart and Winston, 1981).

6. For Combs's conceptualization of "sponsors" and "supporters" of terrorism, see p. 81.

7. For Paul Millar's discussion of "supporters" and "enablers," see Paul R. Millar, *Terrorism and U.S. Foreign Policy* (Washington, DC: Brookings Institution Press, 2001), pp. 157–186.

8. The four types of calculations that render support for terrorist organizations appealing are discussed in Combs, p. 93.

9. An elaborate description of this episode involving official Syria can be found in Neil C. Livingstone and David Halevy, *Inside the PLO* (New York: William Morrow, 1990), pp. 143–144; Daniel Pipes, *National Interest*, Spring 1989, at http://www.danielpipes.org/article/1064 (accessed October 5, 2006).

10. For more on this episode, see the October 23, 2003, account by CNN, "Ricin and the Umbrella Murder," at http://www.cnn.com/2003/WORLD/europe/01/07/terror.poison.bulgarian/ (accessed October 5, 2006). See also the account by the BBC from January 8, 2003, "Flashback: Dissident's Poisoning," at http://news.bbc.co.uk/1/hi/uk/2636459.stm (accessed October 5, 2006).

CHAPTER

9

Horrors in our Backyard

Domestic Terrorism in the United States

The Biblical God, or Yahweh, created a single race in his own image—the White Race. . . . Only White People have souls.

The Christian Identity

On August 11, 1999, a white supremacist opened fire with a submachine gun on children attending summer camp at the North Valley Jewish Community Center in California. Five people were shot and wounded: the 68-year-old receptionist, a 16-year-old counselor and three boys ranging in ages from five to six. The perpetrator was Buford O'Neal Furrow, then 37, a member of the Aryan Nation and an adherent of the Christian Identity movement. A hard-core white supremacist, Furrow took it upon himself to attack nonwhites, especially Jews, as part of a holy racial war. Two days earlier, he had shot and killed a Filipino-American mailman because he was a particularly attractive target being both a federal employee and a nonwhite.

Although serving a life sentence without possibility of parole, Furrow's act of terrorism has not gone unnoticed. He has become an admired martyr-of-sorts for the bewildering array of American racist groups, who view him as a hero and a symbol of self-sacrifice on the altar of the white race's cause.

A GLANCE THROUGH THE REARVIEW MIRROR

U.S. history is plagued by a long record of terrorism. The country was established on the ruins of the defeated original inhabitants of the land, who were systematically deprived of and expelled from their land and eradicated by the newcomers either through outright national policies or by myriad state-tolerated or encouraged acts. This historical fact is matched in its barbarity only by the institutionalized slave trade. America's involvement in a system that kidnapped people from their villages and families, transported them across the ocean in conditions not fit for animals, and sold them into slavery—all the while viewing them as subhuman—has stained the foundations of a country otherwise so proud of its founding principles and moral heritage.

Smallpox-Infested Blankets?

During a 1763 American Indian uprising against the British in the Ohio Valley, the Delaware and Shawnee Indians laid siege to the British Fort Pitt, today's Pittsburgh. Evidence suggests that high-ranking British officers conspired to exterminate the rebellious Indians using biological terrorism: providing them blankets infected with smallpox. The act was apparently carried out as planned, but historians are divided over the issue. Some suggest that the Native Americans had already been infected by the plague inadvertently via their interactions with local whites who had been exposed to the disease.

A culture of officially sanctioned brutality and killing cannot be stopped quickly, and the precedent continued into the twentieth century. Acts of violence against workers attempting to unionize, for example, constitute just one infamous milestone in the American experience with state-tolerated, if not outright state-supported, terrorism. The magnitude of terrorism committed against Americans inside the United States will never be fully known because records have not been kept and because acts of terrorism appear in the records as "arsons," "homicides," and so on.[1]

John Brown

Born in 1800 to parents who raised him to fear God and hate slavery, John Brown pursued his life's mission with extreme, uncompromising determination. Between 1855 and his death in 1858, he engaged in a series of increasingly militant acts designed to prompt southern slaves to rebel and fight for their freedom. Conducting a mini-insurgency, his men raided targets associated with slavery, set facilities and houses on fire, and murdered people involved with slavery. Eventually, Brown miscalculated and attacked the United States' Armory at Harper Ferry, West Virginia. Following a bloody fight, Brown and some of his followers were captured by federal troops commanded by Robert E. Lee. He was hanged in Charleston, South Carolina, in December 1959. Brown's unflinching commitment to the cause of abolition and the stoic, unrepentant manner with which he went to the gallows earned him many admirers after his death and may have hastened the outbreak of the Civil War.

Types of Domestic Terrorism

If we exclude state-terrorism, the American experience contains several histori- cal types of terrorism. Robert Gurr, for example, classifies these types: vigilante, insurgent, and transnational. *Vigilante* denotes groups, such as the Ku Klux Klan, which try to preserve the status quo or turn the clock back to a past era perceived as more idyllic. *Insurgent* alludes to those attempting to overthrow the status quo, such as the terrorist group the Weather Underground, which was devoted to militantly advancing a new social order. *Transnational* refers to foreign nationals fighting for their cause in the United States, such as the Puerto Rican nationalists.[2]

Other scholars look at the same landscape, but perceive it differently. Pamela Griset and Sue Mahan, for example, classify domestic terrorism in the United States according to five different categories: *state sponsored*, *left wing*, *anarchists* (ecological terrorists), *white supremacists*, and *religious extremists*.[3]

Cherry-Picking Our Categories

Much has been written about modern American terrorism and its parallels with the European experience. As the French newspaper *Le Monde* put it, America has its demons and Europe has its ghosts. But the American experience is unique, and, for this reason, we have synthesized various scholars' approaches with a spin of our own to come up with the following four categories of domes- tic terrorism: *left wing, right wing, ecological,* and those using American soil to continue their struggle *on behalf of their country of origin.*

Left-Wing Terrorism

Largely a phenomenon of the past, this category of domestic terrorism sheds light on an important phase in the evolution of the American society. Hidden in the experience of left-wing terrorists is a lesson to be learned about terrorist groups at present. A variety of left-wing terrorist organizations made their name and spread their violent message throughout the United States in recent decades. We will examine this history by looking at two defunct organizations: the Weather Underground and the Black Panthers.

The Weather Underground

An offshoot of the leftist Students for a Democratic Society (SDS), the Weather Underground organization began in 1969 and died in the mid-1970s, with the conclusion of the Vietnam War. Mostly composed of young, probably idealistic, and certainly misguided people, the group drew its name from lyrics to a song written by a hero of the era, Bob Dylan, which went, "You don't need a weatherman to know which way the wind blows." Established as a protest movement against the Vietnam War, the Weather Underground grew by ambition and militancy into an action group. As it expanded, members of this "revolutionary organization of communist women and men" busily threw themselves into plotting the violent over-throw of the U.S. government with the naive enthusiasm of youth. Curiously, the majority of the organization's membership consisted of women, which makes one appreciate the wisdom of Mae West's reflection that when women go wrong, men go right after them.

   In the aftermath of a horrific accident in a Greenwich Village safe house that killed three amateur bomb-makers preparing an attack against U.S. military personnel, the organization began to falter. Although the group would conduct several bombing attacks on politically symbolic properties and landmarks in the United States, such as the Pentagon, police stations, and prisons, by the time the Vietnam War was over it lost its essential reason for being and dissolved.

The Black Panthers

Established in 1966 as the Black Panther Party for Self Defense, the organization was a militant political movement for promoting the cause of African-Americans. A product of the 1960s, the Black Panthers created a unique plat-form that used the Marxist rhetoric of "class struggle," mixed it with Maoist concepts, sprinkled-in aspects of black nationalism as popularized by Malcolm

---

What Do YOU Think?

American left-wing terrorist organizations often associated with radical African-American groups, with whom they attempted to coordinate both political agendas and some operations. Why, in your opinion, did members of these groups find it natural to develop such relationships?

X, added organizational elements of the Nation of Islam, and cooperated with some white revolutionary groups to come up with an operationally impossible "community self-help" doctrine.

The wave of violence that ensued resulted in bloody shoot-outs with law enforcement—the FBI was in hot pursuit of group members—and also in deadly clashes with ideologically opposed militant black groups and criminal gangs. Dozens of group members and law enforcement personnel were killed and injured in these violent confrontations. By the end of the 1970s, internal conflicts over doctrine, actions, and petty, inexplicable criminal acts effectively caused its downfall.[4]

M19CO—The Combined Task Force

Leftist terrorist groups in the United States sometimes coordinated with one another to carry out joint operations at opportune times. In one such case, the groups went as far as forming an official alliance, complete with a name. The organization was composed of elements of the Weather Underground, the Black Liberation Army, Black Panthers, and the Republic of New Africa (RNA). The name they chose for the new entity was particularly defiant: M19CO. May 19 was the birthday of both North Vietnam's leader Ho Chi Minh and the black leader Malcolm X; CO stood for "communist organization."

Not surprisingly, the new organization needed money for its planned attacks. On October 20, 1981, the joint task force carried out a bloody robbery of a Brink's armored van. They got away with $1.6 million, but not before killing a Brink's security guard and two police officers. After a series of raids and bombings of federal facilities and prisons, which were met with an energetic counter campaign, M19CO was dismantled and scores of its members were forced to go underground for many years.

RIGHT-WING TERRORISM

This type of domestic terrorism, potentially the most dangerous of all homegrown terrorism, includes religious and nonreligious racists. Other variations and combinations of right-wing terrorist groups exist as well. However, for our purposes, a discussion of religious and nonreligious but racist terrorist groups is sufficient to capture the essence of domestic right-wing terrorism.

A dizzying array of right-wing terrorist organizations structured along racial lines and organized according to pseudo-Christian tenets swamp the American hinterland. From American Christian Patriot movements to various paramilitary hate groups disguised as "militias" to an array of white supremacist groups awash with deep antigovernment suspicions, the organizing principles are similar. Whether the American Nazi Party, the Aryan Nation, The Order, Nordic Christianity (Odin), the World Church of the Creator, Posse Comitatus, or survivalists invariably they hold to the conviction that God created the world for whites only. Their ideology usually stresses (1) seething anti-Semitism whose theoretical underpinnings occasionally exceed even that of Nazi Germany, (2) fierce loathing and suspicion of the federal government, and (3) a virulent racist outlook. Terrorism expert Bruce Hoffman estimates followers of these militias and movements to number from 50,000 to millions![5]

Origins of the Name Ku Klux Klan

The name that has frightened and terrorized so many had its beginnings in an innocent prank. In December 1865, six bored southern veterans of the Civil War from Pulaski, Tennessee, created a social club, similar to a modern-day fraternity. Its fun-seeking founders resolved to invent ludicrous names for the new club and its various positions to ensure that it would not be taken seriously or confused with anything political. The result was indeed a bunch of nonsensical and comical names. To the Greek word *Kuklos*, from which the English word *circle* is derived, they added the word *clan*, but with the slight variation *Klan*. Hence the *Ku Klux Klan*. Delighted, they set out to add more ridiculous titles: the head of the association became the *Grand Cyclops*; his deputy, the *Grand Magi*; messengers were *Night Hawks*, and so on. Needing costumes, they came up with white sheets, masks, and funny tall hats. In one of those amazingly ironic twists of history, by the time the social club's founders realized they had created a monster, it was too late.[6]

The Christian Identity Movement

Anglo-Israelism was a concept turned into a movement during the Victorian era in England. Its major premise was that the British people, as well as some other northern Europeans, were the real descendents of the biblical Israelites and, therefore, the true chosen people. According to the Bible, their reasoning went, God had promised the Israelites would multiply as the stars in the sky and as grains of sand to eventually become a people that dominated much of the earth. One look at the status of the Jews easily showed that they were far from chosen and from world domination. Since God and the Bible don't lie, it followed, they said, that the real Jews were the descendants of the ten Jewish tribes exiled by the Assyrians at the end of the eighth century B.C., who found their way to and inhabited the British Isles. Significantly, this curious assertion was meant to justify nineteenth-century British imperialism, not to be anti-Semitic.

This changed in the middle of the twentieth century when a radical American racist, Wesley Swift, adopted the concept and gradually transformed it into an anti-Semitic, racist, and a loosely knit religious-extremist movement centered in churches throughout the United States. Today, it is a network of

The Alfred Murrah Federal Building in Oklahoma City after the 1995 bombing
Source: Courtesy of AP Wide World Photos.

believers that Armageddon will take place when Jesus' second coming ushers in a cosmic war between the white race and the forces of evil, meaning all the other races, headed by the Jews—the "children of Satan." Opponents of the Christian Identity Movement—white people of different religions, as well as homosexuals, blacks, Native Americans, and immigrants—are considered sub-human and are to be exterminated.

To prepare for this eventuality, believers, who tend to reside in rural areas, store weapons and undergo paramilitary training. Impatient for the arrival of the great racial showdown, and to prepare for it financially, some of those iden-tified as Christian Identity members have been implicated in acts of violence, robberies, and bombings. This informal network shows no sign of losing steam and its true believers remain a potent terrorist threat, biding their time in the margins of society, awaiting some political, economic, or security calamity to impact the American political landscape to unleash their holy war.

Posse Comitatus

Established in the late 1960s, the true originator of the movement is not known. With its center of gravity in the Midwest and Northwest of the United States, the Posse Comitatus is a loose network of like-minded people who share the same ideological tenets. Like the Christian Identity movement, it is not a clearly

What Do YOU Think?

What could happen in the United States that would culminate in replacing the existing political system with one dominated by right-wing racists and religious zealots? Is this scenario fantastically unrealistic or could it happen? Explain why.

structured, hierarchical organization. The name Posse Comitatus, or the "county's power," derives from the legal prohibition on using the military to enforce the law. Adherents believe that the highest form of government ends at the county level, and only the county's Sheriff may legally enforce the law within the county's jurisdiction. Members of this movement view state and federal governments and institutions with disdain and enmity. As is typical of American movements harboring hatred for the central government, Posse Comitatus is abuzz with conspiratorial theories and its members are infected with a virulent strain of racism. Although not explicitly a religious movement, those belonging to Posse Comitatus tend to be religious, and it is not always easy to differentiate from the followers of the Ku Klux Klan or Christian Identity.

Hatred of the government and loathing of all nonwhites is a common denominator of many such groups, but Posse Comitatus' ideological grievance against the federal government sets it apart from other white supremacist movements. Because its members maintain that the central government has no legal authority to enforce laws, those functioning on the government's behalf—for example, the Internal Revenue Service (IRS), the Federal Bureau of Investigation (FBI), the Alcohol, Tobacco and Firearms (ATF), judges, and state officials—are viewed as enemies. Not surprisingly, this racist attitude focuses on Jews; in particular, the ferocious conviction that Jews control the U.S. government. Hence their frequent use of the term Zionist Occupied Government (ZOG) to describe and explain everything they dislike about the country.

Posse Comitatus members frequently resort to tax protests, refuse to recognize U.S. currency because it is not backed by gold, and engage in various criminal activities, such as counterfeiting and shoot-outs with law enforcement personnel. Following bloody standoffs with authorities and due to the notoriety of their peculiar racist and antigovernmental attitudes, the popularity of the Posse Comitatus has been on the decline since the late 1980s. Efforts to resuscitate the movement in the late 1990s focused on racism, the dimension most likely to appeal to the maximum number of potential followers. However, by choosing a strategy centered on the lowest common denominator, racism, the movement deliberately sacrificed its unique ideological platform.

LEFT- AND RIGHT-WING TERRORISM TODAY

Historically, American left-wing terrorism differs from right-wing terrorism in that the former sought to improve the lot of mankind, whereas the latter have cared only about those who were like themselves. In addition, left-wing terrorism has all but disappeared from the American political scene and, by and large, has become a historical curiosity.

Right-wing terrorism, on the other hand, represents a potential danger, one that is awaiting the historical opportunity to exert its power. For the time being, the alert level is low. For example, Jonathan White asserts that the violent message of both types has been totally rejected by the American public and refers to terrorists from the left and the right as "small bands of social misfits who had very little impact on the political system."[7]

Testifying before a Congressional Committee on Intelligence in February 2005, FBI Director Robert S. Muller suggested that the white supremacists were an ongoing threat to government targets, Jewish establishments, and nonwhite ethnic groups. About the right-wing patriot movement, consisting of militias, tax protesters, and other antigovernment entities, he warned that it "remains a continued threat in America today."[8] In 1999, the FBI foiled seven right-wing terrorist plots. Two of them "were potentially large scale, high casualty attacks," according to the FBI.[9]

In a detailed study of terrorism in the United States, Professor Brent Smith established five criteria for analyzing the differences between left- and right-wing terrorism: *ideology, economic views, location, tactics,* and *target* selection. Smith found that leftists tend to believe in a socialist–Marxist economic agenda, live and function mainly in urban areas, organize their membership into cells, and use safe houses; they rob armored cars in order to fund their operations, and target government facilities and other symbols of capitalism.

In contrast, right-wing terrorists are driven by a religious ideology, are anticommunist, reside in rural areas, network nationally and live in compounds with like-minded people; they rob armored trucks to fund their operations and target law enforcement entities and personnel as well as racial and religious groups they perceive as the opposition.

Smith found other interesting distinctions. Left-wing terrorists are, on average, 35 years old, mostly male (73%) and minorities (71%), well–educated, with 54% holding college degrees, and are a vocational mix, but the majority are white-collar professionals. Right-wing terrorists' average age is almost 40, almost all are male (97%), only 12% have college degrees, and many are unemployed or self-employed and usually poor.[10]

Single Issue Causes: Antiabortion Movement

Since the 1973 Supreme Court decision, known as *Roe* v. *Wade,* which legalized abortion, a significant debate has split the American public. Pitted on each side of the divide are two camps popularly known as *pro-choice,* for those advocating the right of women to choose abortion, and *pro-life,* denoting those opposed to abortion. Fringe elements of the "pro-life" movement have conducted terrorist acts to advance this "single issue" cause. Groups such as the Army of God and the Lambs of God have been accused of bombing abortion clinics, assassination, arson, and invading clinics.

The decrease in the number of physical attacks on abortion clinics in recent years is believed to correlate to two legal developments: (1) the introduction and enforcement of the Freedom of Access to Clinic Entrances Act (FACE) of 1994 and (2) the application of the Racketeer Influenced and Corrupt Organizations (RICO) Act, a law originally designed to be used against organized crime, which has been used against leaders of various antiabortion movements, such as Operation Rescue.

ECOLOGICAL TERRORISM

Ecological terrorism is a type of "single issue" terrorism. There are two main types of domestic ecoterrorism: terrorism for the sake of preserving the environment and terrorism on behalf of animals. Although there are some exceptions, the mainstream of both types express reservations about inflicting direct violence or taking lives, and direct their attacks against property, not people. However, violent offshoots of these movements are less concerned about the sanctity of human life.

The Earth Liberation Front

The Earth Liberation Front (ELF) is the mid-1990s North American spin-off of a similar British movement named Earth First! According to its website, the ELF has no structure, is nonhierarchical, and functions without a centralized organization or leadership. It also has no organized, formal membership; individuals committed to the cause are contacted by someone familiar who offers them an opportunity to join in an operation on behalf of the cause on an *ad hoc* basis.[11]

The goal of the movement is to protect the earth by destroying the property of those who damage the earth: companies involved in logging, genetic engineering, energy, construction, motor vehicles, among others. Some activists in the movement harbor radical ideologies, such as anticapitalism, which go beyond protecting the environment. From 1998, when the ELF launched its violent campaign, to the present, adherents of the movement have caused tens of millions of dollars in damage to businesses they have attacked. No human life was lost in any of these assaults, however.

The Animal Liberation Front

The Animal Liberation Front (ALF) is the older sister of the ELF. While the movement boasts cells and activists in many countries, its operations in the United States commenced in circa 1980. Essentially, its mission is to protect animals from cruel and inhumane treatment, abuse stemming from painful or deadly research, and from being used for fur or food. Adherents have been pursuing this mission with great zeal, raiding farms, factories, research labs that experiment on animals, and slaughterhouses in order to free the animals or to secretly whisk them away for safekeeping at volunteers' houses. But ALF activists have taken their struggle one step too far, landing them in the realm of terrorism. For purposes of deterrence or as punishment, the ALF has engaged in acts of arson, vandalism, and attacks on such facilities and companies that ALF considers abusive to animals. The ALF's principles may honor the sanctity of life, but the movement has been undergoing a process of radicalization.

Like the ELF, the ALF is composed of a loose collection of grassroots activists and is not a formally structured organization. As the spokesperson for the group in England, Robin Webb, put it, "There is no hierarchy; there are no leaders. There is just a compulsion to follow [one's] heart in pursuit of justice. That is why the ALF cannot be smashed, it cannot be effectively infiltrated, it cannot be stopped." [12]

Some may find this activity noble. It was none other than Leonardo da Vinci who exclaimed, "The time will come when men such as I look upon the murder of animals as they now look upon the murder of men." But, as one would imagine, some who commit to a cause, any cause, may get swept up in the fervor and go beyond norms acceptable to the mainstream of their movements.

"Specieism"

The idea that all species inhabiting the earth are entitled to certain rights, just as humans are, became popular in the early 1970s. Thereafter, acceptance of the principle of some sort of a "moral equivalency" among the various species gained in popularity among animal rights activists. The theory of "specieism" is represented by three main competing approaches which are divided over the degree of rights animals should enjoy.

The Justice Department

As if the ALF's own radicalization over time was not enough, the unapologetically violent animal protection organization the Justice Department appeared on the American scene in 1993. Just like their comrades of the Animal Rights Militia (ARM) in the United Kingdom, this group has forsaken active persuasion in favor of outright violence. Members of the Justice Department have sent booby-trapped letters and packages to targeted individuals, firebombed facilities, and carried out other terrorist activities. Because of their similar ideological platform and the fact that key activists in the ALF appear to condone this violence either by their silence—refusing to condemn it—or by verbal nods of approval, authorities treat members of both groups as terrorists, and also have extended that designation to some followers of the animal protection movement in general. As John Lewis, the FBI's Deputy Assistant Director for Counterterrorism summed it up in May of 2005, "Violent animal rights extremists . . . pose one of the most serious terrorism threats to the nation."[13]

What Do YOU Think?

Some people sympathize with certain premises of the ecological terrorists, but not with their actions. Consider your own thinking about this issue; how would you react if you were approached by an acquaintance who suggested that you participate in an operation to help animals or to save a park?

Escalating Radicalism

Ecoterrorism in the United States is a growing problem. People devoted to the cause of helping the environment and all that share this earth have become increasingly violent in recent years. Although the concerns of the environmentalists and the animal rights activists seem to be different, there are similarities and the profile of individuals attracted to the two causes is similar as well.

Environmental terrorists isolate their campaign to damaging properties of entities they perceive as harming the environment. Animal liberation groups' crusades have taken a more violent direction. Pushed by smaller cadres of activists determined to pursue direct action, they do not shy from activities that might harm people. Due to the violent nature of their struggle, authorities have managed to curb these movements' activities quite considerably, but not completely.

The deliberate lack of a hierarchical structure all but guarantees that they can continue their violence by relying on grassroots sympathizers who can be counted on to step in and help when needed. According to authorities, the ELF and the ALF together have been involved in over 1,200 criminal incidents between 1990 and 2005, with hundreds of additional investigations still under way.[14]

TERRORISM ON BEHALF OF THE "OLD COUNTRY"

This type of terrorism consists of two categories: (1) Attacks on the United States within its own territory on behalf of a country of origin or for a cause affiliated with that country of origin. Reasons for taking the fight to American soil are usually rooted in perceived national, religious, or cultural grievances. The Arab-Muslim attacks on the United States on September 11, 2001, are an example of this kind. (2) Use of the United States' riches and freedoms to help the cause of terrorists in the old country. For example, certain Albanian-Americans engaged in raising funds and arranging for illegal armaments to be shipped to the Kosovo Liberation Army (KLA) fighting the Serbs during the 1990s, although in the West the KLA was considered a terrorist organization until 1999.

Frank Sinatra and the Pre-Israel Haganah

In the period preceding the establishment of the state of Israel, President Truman slapped an arms embargo on the warring parties in Palestine, a measure that affected mostly the Jewish community, which was fighting for its life. In March 1948, Frank Sinatra became a money runner for the Zionist cause by helping to smuggle the then significant sum of $1 million to help purchase arms for the pre-Israel Haganah organization, which the British authorities in Palestine considered an illegal militant entity.[15]

Fighting America on Its Own Soil

Several independence-seeking Puerto Rican organizations have used terrorism in recent decades to pursue their goal. Inside the continental United States, the most visible and violent was the Armed Forces of Puerto Rican National Liberation (FALN). Between 1974 and 1983, the organization conducted more than one hundred bombings throughout the United States, some of them deadly. Authorities eventually managed to dismantle the organization and 19 of its leaders were sentenced to lengthy prison sentences. Only in 1999, as an act of clemency prior to leaving office, President Clinton pardoned 16 of the imprisoned FALN members who had no blood on their hands on the condition that they renounce violence. All freed members had served 19 years by the time of their release.

Spraying Congress with Bullets

Yelling "Long live free Puerto Rico!" in Spanish, a hit-team of four Puerto Rican nationals opened fire on members of Congress on March 1, 1954. Led by Lolita Lebron, then 34 years old, the terrorists were protesting Puerto Ricans' commonwealth status. They fired 30 rounds at the lawmakers from the visitors' gallery, hitting five of the 240 congressmen in attendance. Republican representative Alvin Bentley was gravely wounded, but survived the attack. President Carter released the captured terrorists from jail in 1979.

As the FALN began to falter in the mid-1970s, one of its founders, Filiberto Ojeda Rios, renamed what was left of it in 1976. Now called the Macheteros, or "cane cutters," the organization's center of gravity was relocated to Puerto Rico, although it kept several cells across the United States as well. On the island, the Macheteros attacked U.S. military personnel, a Puerto Rican Air National Guard base, and local government equipment and infrastructure facilities. However, the organization carried out its most notorious terrorist act on American soil. In a well-publicized 1983 heist, the Macheteros robbed a Wells Fargo depot in Connecticut and got away with over seven million dollars. It took the FBI 23 years to catch Filiberto Ojeda Rios and kill him in a shootout in September 2005. As is occasionally the case, his killing evoked a wave of sympathy among Puerto Ricans that turned the terrorist into a martyr for the cause. The Macheteros presently boast hundreds of members and sympathizers.

Using American Soil to Further the Old Country's Cause

Recent decades have witnessed a considerable influx of immigrants from Muslim countries into the United States, "the best poor man's country in the world," in the words of William Allen. Pursuing the centuries-old tradition of seeking a better life, the "American Dream," the vast majority of American Muslims are loyal and law-abiding citizens; but disturbingly, not all.

In one of the best exposés of the growing threat posed by some extremist American Muslims, Steven Emerson compiled a chilling account of the inner workings of those using the opportunities that life in United States offers, in order to advance their pan-Islamic cause elsewhere in the world. Here we are not talking about Muslims arriving in the United States to attack America on its own soil as the perpetrators of 9/11 did. At the heart of this discussion are the multiple schemes to illegally use America's riches and freedoms to help terrorists back home, especially in the Middle East.

The Sting

Fund-raising is an important vehicle for helping the struggle of militant compatriots in other countries. Such organizations take advantage of unsuspecting, well-meaning Americans and manipulate them into donating money for purposes far removed from the donors' intentions. For example, major weekly magazines in the United States used to carry a paid advertisement for helping suffering children in the Holy Land. The advertiser, Holy Land Foundation, would later come under suspicion for being a front for Hamas and had allegedly funneled millions of dollars to the organization.[16]

According to Emerson's study, *American Jihad: The Terrorists Living Among Us,* Muslim terrorists take advantage of America in four ways.[17] First, the United States is fertile ground for *recruitment* because its religious laws, political traditions, and freedoms enable recruiters to function with ease. Second, *fund-raising* in the United States is an age-old, hallowed practice. Along with the permissible, those manipulating the American system add illegal activities, such as money laundering and other fiscal schemes, to finance terrorists abroad. Third, *networking* among Muslim groups, charities, and associations, some of which intentionally or innocently lend support to terrorist causes in the Middle East. While some Muslim networking in the United States is the result of a few bad apples occasionally infecting a few of the rest, this is not the case with Emerson's fourth factor: *direct organizing,* which includes the purposeful establishment of cells and offices in dozens of cities throughout the United States from which to manage illegal activities.

Most alarmingly, Emerson contends that since the late 1980s groups like Islamic Jihad, Hamas, Hezbollah, and others, which can all be bundled under the umbrella name *jihadists,* have established terrorist cells in almost every state in the United States, and in some states even more than one! In addition, there are dozens of other radical Islamist groups operating in this country.[18]

SUMMARY

In this chapter you have learned the following:

1. The United States has a long history of domestic terrorism that is not well recorded.

2. For purposes of this study, four types of terrorism were established: left wing, right wing, ecological, and those using American soil in the service of terrorism.

3. Left-wing terrorists tend to be young, well educated, professional, and adherents of Marxism.

4. Right-wing terrorists tend to be older, undereducated males, religious, advocates of capitalism, and poor.

5. Ecological terrorists are concerned mainly with the environment or animal rights.

6. Fighting the United States on American soil for independence has been associated with Puerto Rican terrorist groups.

7. Several terrorist groups around the world enjoy funds raised, usually illegally, by compatriots in the United States. In recent years this practice has been associated mostly with American Muslims.

💣💣💣

Dedicated to the mission of changing the status quo, members of the Weather Underground were amateur Marxist revolutionaries intent on tearing down the fabric of the American capitalistic society. Their premise was to rebuild it free of the shackles of the old notions about life. Challenging the bourgeois values with which they had been raised, these young men and women resorted to Marxist principles in trying to abolish expressions of what they considered the corrupt capitalistic and imperialistic society in which they lived, such as social classes, racial divides, and gender gaps. Defiantly, members of the Weather Underground used sex to shock society's norms.

Despite the righteous rhetoric about breaking sexual taboos and a new societal emphasis on the needs of the collective, in reality—with the exception of a few token female leaders—the organization was in fact run by men. Not only were men known to take sexual advantage of their female comrades, but in the name of female liberation they attacked the concept of monogamy, encouraged women to engage in homosexual sex, and practiced multiparticipant sex.

💣💣💣

NOTES

1. That cases of domestic terrorism were designated as "arson" or "homicide" is mentioned by Pamela L. Griset and Sue Mahan, *Terrorism in Perspective* (Thousand Oaks: Sage Publications, 2003), p. 85.

2. For the classification of domestic terrorism into the vigilante, insurgent, and transnational categories, see Ted Robert Gurr, "Political Terrorism in the United States: Historical Antecedents and Contemporary Trends," in Michael Stohl, ed., *The Politics of Terrorism*, 3rd ed. (New York: Marcel Dekker, Inc., 1988), pp. 549–578.

3. The classification according to state-sponsored, left wing, anarchists (ecological terrorists), white supremacists, and religious extremists is found in Griset and Mahan, pp. 85–86.

4. This Black Panthers organization should not be confused with a new group with a similar name that emerged two decades later. Having little in common with the leftist ideology of their predecessors, the newcomers are black vigilantes with an extreme anti-Semitic attitude.

5. The 50,000 to millions estimate of membership in the right-wing movements is found in Bruce Hoffman, *Inside Terrorism* (New York: Columbia University press, 1998), p. 107.

6. For the story behind the name Ku Klux Klan, see *Ku Klux Klan: A History of Racism and Violence*, 5th ed. (Montgomery, AL: Southern Poverty Law Center, 1997), p. 9.

7. The "social misfits" quote is found in Jonathan R. White, *Terrorism: An Introduction*, 4th ed. (Belmont, CA: Wadsworth/Thomson Learning, 2002), p. 206.

8. For the FBI's warning about the threat posed by the *patriot movement*, see "Testimony of Robert S. Mueller III, Director FBI, Before the Senate Committee on Intelligence of the United States Senate, February 16, 2005," at http://www.fbi.gov/congress/congress05/mueller021605.htm (accessed October 7, 2006).

9. The information concerning the right-wing terrorist attacks foiled by the FBI in 1999 is found in "2002 Congressional Testimony by Dale Watson, then Executive Assistant Director of the FBI's Counterterrorism/Counterintelligence Division before the *Senate Select Committee on Intelligence*," in http://www.fbi.gov/congress/congress02/watson020602.htm (accessed October 7, 2006).

10. The analysis of the left- and right-wing terrorists is found in Brent L. Smith, *Terrorism in America: Pipe Bombs and Pipe Dreams* (Albany, NY: State University of New York Press, 1994), pp. 31–52.

11. For the ELF's website concerning its structure, see http://www.earthliberationfront.com/index.htm (accessed October 7, 2006).

12. For Robin Webb's quote about the structure of the ALF, see "Staying on Target and Going the Distance: An Interview with U.K. A.L.F. Press Officer Robin Webb," *No Compromise*, issue 22, at http://www.nocompromise.org/issues/22robin.html (accessed October 7, 2006).

13. The observation by FBI's John Lewis about the dangers of the more extremist animal rights groups is in Terry Frieden, "FBI, ATF Address Domestic Terrorism," CNN, May 19, 2005, at http://www.cnn.com/2005/US/05/19/domestic.terrorism (accessed October 29, 2006).

14. The information about the damage inflicted by both the ELF and the ALF was provided by John Lewis, then the FBI's Deputy Assistant Director for
Counterterrorism, as reported by Terry Frieden, CNN, can be found in Ibid
(accessed October 7, 2006).

15. For more on Frank Sinatra's role in running money for the pre-Israel Haganah to
advance the cause he supported in that conflict, see Jennifer Siegel, "Sinatra Bio
Explores Icon's Jewish Connections," *All About Jewish Theater*, at
http://www.jewish-theatre.com/visitor/article_display.aspx?articleID=1458
(accessed October 7, 2006).

16. For the "Holy Land Foundation" serving as a possible front for Hamas, see Steven
Emerson, *American Jihad: The Terrorists Living Among Us* (New York: The Free
Press, 2002), p. 35.

17. For the contention about the multitude of Jihadist cells established throughout the
United States, see Ibid., pp. 31–41.

18. More on the existence of radical Islamist groups in the United States is found in
Ibid., pp. 152, 178–181.

10

The Struggle for the Soul of a Faith

The Islamic Dimension

Islam is not a religion of pacifists

Ayatollah Khomeini

❧❧❧

Twelve days after the September 11, 2001, attacks, an interfaith ceremony took place at Yankee Stadium in New York to help people come to grips with the disaster that had befallen their city. A Muslim chaplain with the New York Police Department, Imam Izak-El M. Pasha, was one of the speakers. In an emotional address, he agonized over the fact that "those who would dare do such dastardly acts claim our faith [Islam]."[1] A few weeks later, *Newsweek*'s Foreign Affairs Editor, Fareed Zakaria, himself a Muslim born in India, described a transformation taking place in Islam: "Islam is being taken over by a small poisonous element, people who advocate cruel attitudes toward women, education, the economy and modern life in general. I have seen this happen in India, where I grew up. The rich, colorful, pluralistic and easy going Islam of my youth has turned into a dour, puritanical faith, policed by petty theocrats and religious commissars."[2] Has Islam been "hijacked"?

❧❧❧

FROM ZENITH TO NADIR: A BRIEF HISTORY OF ISLAM

Islam was humanity's showcase for one thousand years, from approximately A.D. 700 to the Treaty of Karlowitz in 1699, which signaled the beginning of the decline of the Ottoman Empire, a period of time longer than the Roman era or the British Empire. It was responsible for some of the greatest scientific, philosophical, and artistic achievements up to that point in history. Islam's golden era represents one of the most influential civilizations prior to the current one, which we know as "Western Civilization," to which it was a major contributor. This enviable record reminds us never to confuse the current link between some radical Muslims and terrorism with the rich, tolerant, and dominant culture it once was and that it may become again.

The West, writes a leading historian of the Middle East, Professor Arthur Goldschmidt, Jr., owes much to Islam for providing the setting in which the classical knowledge of the ancients was bridged over to Europe and for the innovations and scientific breakthroughs created during the heyday of Islam. The list of accomplishments is long. It includes philosophy, medicine, mathematics, astronomy, engineering, optics, botany, chemistry, as well as major work in the fields of art and literature.[3] Contrast this peak of culture and advancement with Europe of that time, and the stark differences are telling. Baghdad, to use one example, was built in A.D. 762 as a planned city with wide boulevards, street lamps, and universities at the same time as many Europeans, drenched in superstition and ignorance, lived in crowded and dark dwellings.

Arabs and Muslims: Often the Same, but Not Always

It is easy for those unfamiliar with the intricacies of Islam and its history to become confused when trying to understand contemporary Arabs and Muslims. After all, Islam is embraced by many, but not all, Middle Easterners as well as by some societies, for example Pakistan and Indonesia, outside the Middle East. This has created a situation in which not all Muslims are Arab and not all Arabs are Muslims. Although often intertwined, the two are not the same. Global Islam emanates from the Arabs, and the crucial influence of Arabs and the Arabic language in the glorious "Islamic Civilization" is hard to exaggerate. Either because the language of the Koran was Arabic—as were the early elites of this civilization—or because Arabs provided the framework in which non-Arab minorities (such as Persians and Berbers) and non-Muslims (such as Jews and Zoroastrians) flourished, the prominent role Arabs and Arabic played in creating and perpetuating this civilization is unmistakable. To this day, despite Islam's geographic reach the Arab lands are the center of the Islamic world. Therefore, understanding the Arab factor in the recent outbreak of Islam-associated terrorism is a prerequisite for understanding the phenomenon.

Thirteen Centuries of Animosity

In Islam, a division of historical proportion took place in A.D 680. In that year, the Prophet Muhammad's grandson, Hussein, fell in battle against the Muslim caliph Yazid in Karbala, in what is today Iraq. A theological split erupted from that date on between the Sunnis, composing the vast majority of Muslims, and a small minority siding with the fallen Hussein, son of Ali and grandson of the Prophet himself. The latter have been known as belonging to the party, or Shi'i, of Ali. In the following thirteen centuries, what began as a theological divide would expand into an irreconcilable historical and political gulf.

Almost 90% of Muslims are Sunnis and they believe that any pious Muslim can be the caliph, the political, and military leader of the Muslim nation. But on matters of religious doctrine, the caliph must be guided by Islamic scholars. In contrast, the Shi'i adhere to the principle of the bloodline, that only descendents of the Prophet Muhammad can guide the Muslim community until that day when a Mahdi, a Messiah, reveals himself to lead humanity to a new dawn. According to Shi'i doctrine, such leaders, Imams, are divinely qualified to be both political and religious leaders.

There are many other differences, important enough for believers to be willing to die for the principles involved. In our context, you need to know that the Sunnis despise Shi'is as apostates and the latter, in turn, have no love lost for the Sunnis either; Shi'i history is a tale of thirteen centuries of persecution at the hands of the Sunni majority.

The Decline of Islam

The modern Middle East features an Islamic Civilization at its nadir. It is violent, poor, oppressive, backward, and angry.

The Islamic Middle East has been in steep decline for centuries; its past glory is hardly recognizable. Once, the Islamic Empire stretched from France to China and was at the global epicenter of progress and learning. Nowadays, Arab lands are divided among two-dozen countries and yesteryear's dominance has turned into weakness and humiliation. The Arab decline began in 1258 when the Mongols conquered and destroyed Baghdad, heralding the end of Arab grandeur. The Turks then took over the leadership of Islam from the Arabs and created a venerable Islamic empire of magnificent splendor. Unable to modernize and keep pace with European technological and administrative advances, the Ottoman Empire, as the Turkish realm came to be known, began its decline in the eighteenth century and formally expired at the end of World War I.

Dumbfounded at their predicament, many of Islam's adherents are full of anger. From Kashmir to the Philippines and Sudan, from Kosovo to the Palestinian territories and Iraq, from Egypt to Saudi Arabia and Iran, and from Indonesia to Western Europe—deep Muslim resentment is brewing. Anger combined with accusations—sometimes made at hysterical pitch—and violence is visited upon those viewed as "enemies" of Islam. Arabs and Islam are not synonymous, but it is impossible to diagnose the latter's present malady without grasping the modern ills of the former.

What Do YOU Think

Imagine that you are a young, educated Arab. As a religious person, you believe that God is responsible for everything and you reject explanations based on coincidence. As we all know, the sacred heartland of Islam—the area containing countries such as Saudi Arabia, Kuwait, and Iraq—is blessed with fantastic oil riches. You believe that it is no coincidence that, of the 200 or so countries in the world, gigantic oil reservoirs are located in the land of the believers. God obviously smiled on the believers and bestowed his blessings on them—on all of them—for a reason.

Yet, when you look at the condition of your fellow Arabs, the picture you see is infuriatingly gloomy. God provided generously for the entire Arab–Muslim community so that they could be prosperous, advanced, and powerful among the nations. Instead, Arabs are divided among countries that were artificially created by Western colonizers. Moreover, a few Arabs live in incredible luxury and spend their fortunes in the West while tens of millions of others live in abject poverty. God certainly did not create all of this wealth for the benefit of the few to squander, leaving the Arab masses undereducated and backward, oppressed by tyrannical regimes, fragmented and weak.

Along come charismatic religious leaders who are willing to sacrifice everything to rectify this situation. Their platform is straightforward: to redistribute the wealth more equally among all Arabs, to follow in God's path, and to unite under a powerful new caliphate, which will restore the Arabs' glory and perhaps even reclaim Islam's dominant position in the world.

Would you join this action-oriented movement, which you perceive is working for a noble cause, or would you reconcile yourself to the continued misery of the status quo?

ISLAM AND THE MODERN WORLD

In the years 2002 to 2004, a three-part report about the predicament of the Arab world, written by a battery of distinguished Arab intellectuals especially commissioned for this task, was presented to the United Nations Development Program.[4] Couched in conciliatory language, the report nonetheless offers scathing criticism of the status of present-day Arab social, economic, and political development. Some of the findings are worth special mention because the statistics on which they are based illustrate clearly the abyss in which the Arab world finds itself in comparison to other countries and regions of the world. This is important because the path to understanding what is happening with Islam requires a review of the troubles at its core—in the Arab lands.

The Arab writers of this report cited three factors as the main causes of the relative backwardness of Arab nations compared to other regions of the world: lack of freedom, lack of empowerment for women, and lack of knowledge. Two hundred and eighty million people were living in the Middle East in 2000, almost all Muslims, and, according to the report, about 65 million of them were illiterate and only 0.6% of the population had access to the Internet. Under the appropriate heading "Bridled Minds, Shackled Potential," the authors of the report maintain that "more than half of Arab women are still illiterate. . . . Society as a whole suffers when a huge proportion of its productive potential is stifled."[5]

In a subsequent report in 2003, the authors lament the fact that 25% of all college graduates throughout the Arab world emigrated in search of better opportunities abroad, resulting in a brain drain. Moreover, there were only 18 computers per thousand people compared to a global average of 78.3. A further illustration of the deeply rooted problems in the Arab Middle East is that over a period of five years, the number of books translated in the entire Arab world was one-fifth the number translated in Greece alone. Thus, less than one book was translated per one million Arabs compared with 920 per one million Spaniards, for example. Additional somber data portray an Arab world lagging behind in almost every important criterion. Research in advanced fields, such as information technology and molecular biology, is almost nonexistent. In the area of technological progress, a significant indicator is the number of patents registered by countries. Disturbingly, between 1980 and 1999–2000, only 434 new patents were registered in the entire Arab world. In contrast, during the same period, Israel registered 7,652 patents and South Korea 16,328.[6]

Modern Islam and Science

The lack of scientific progress is not limited to Arab countries and is evident in other Muslim societies as well. The following observation by Pervez Hoodbnoy, a Pakistani professor of nuclear physics, is noteworthy: "[Today] you seldom encounter a Muslim name in scientific journals. Muslim contributions to pure and applied science—measured in terms of discoveries, publications, patents and processes—are marginal. . . . The harsh truth is that science and Islam parted ways many centuries ago." As an example, he pointed to the status of education in Pakistan: "Pakistan's public universities are intellectual rubble, their degrees of little consequence. . . . Pakistanis have succeeded in registering only eight patents internationally in 57 years."[7]

In the 2004 report, the Arab experts bemoan what they consider an Arab world "caught between oppression at home and violations from abroad." Essentially, this report places much of the blame for the dismal Arab predicament on the political repression so rampant in Arab lands. The tyranny Arabs live under is conducive neither to free inquiry nor to free market economies and prosperity.[8]

If the findings of this distinguished panel are valid, and there seems to be no reason to doubt the data, it becomes easier to understand the connection between an angry Middle East and political violence. One important question the Reports do not answer is why now. As the widely read Arab columnist and general manager of the popular Al-Arabiya television channel, Abdulraham al Rashed wrote after the Beslan school massacre in Russia, "The Painful Truth: All the World Terrorists are Muslims!" He added, "Most perpetrators of suicide operations in buses, schools, and residential buildings around the world for the past 10 years have been Muslims."[9] Al Rashed and other Muslim intellectuals point to the fact that terrorism has become associated with Islam in recent decades, but their observation leaves us wondering about the *reasons* for this phenomenon. After all, people in the Middle East—as well as in many non-Muslim countries and regions—have been poor and repressed for centuries yet do not resort to terrorism!

MAP 10–1   THE MIDDLE EAST

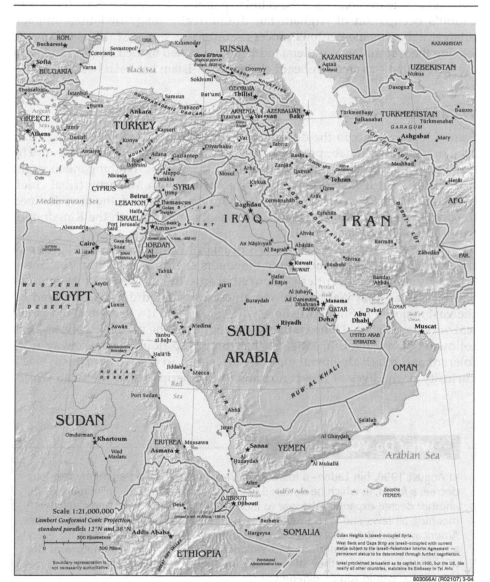

Source: U.S. Government Publication Access http://www.gl.iit.edu/govdocs/maps/Middle%20East1.gif

ISLAM AND TERRORISM

Modern Islamist terrorism is anchored in three factors which are at the bottom of this mystery. Each contributes in its own way to the gradual transformation of Islam into what many Westerners and others have come to view as a clear and present danger. The three are the spread of Wahhabism, the impact of the Iranian Revolution of 1979, and the advent of technology (e.g., the Internet, independent television channels, cellular phones). The war against the Soviet Union's occupation of Afghanistan dramatically magnified their impact. Interestingly, this momentous process caught numerous Muslims off-guard, leaving them straining to understand what happened to their religion and with the feeling that—as an often-heard cliché goes—Islam has been hijacked.

Wahhabism

Some 250 years ago, in the desert that is today Saudi Arabia, a young Arab scholar, Abd al-Wahhab, preached a particularly strict version of Islam. His doctrine was so draconian that he had to flee for his life. Nothing much might have come of it if not for an alliance he struck with a nearby tribal chief, Muhammad ibn Sa'ud, the ancestor of Abdul Aziz ibn Saud, the man destined to conquer almost all of the Arabian Peninsula and establish the Kingdom of Saudi Arabia after World War I.

The Sunnis constitute up to 90% of Islam; Wahhabism is a subgroup of the Sunni sect. So puritanical were the tenets of this new Islamic doctrine— which by the early twentieth century became the official state religion of Saudi Arabia—that Wahhabism remained an isolated dogma, shunned by the vast majority of Sunni Muslims, who considered it a primitive and fanatical version of Islam. Unhesitatingly, they ignored the savagely conservative followers of Wahhabism, satisfied that the group flourished far away from tolerant and relatively liberal mainstream Islam. To them, Wahhabism was a curiosity of the lives of desert nomads in the periphery of the Arab world.

What Do YOU Think?

In August 1996, bin Laden—a follower of Wahhabism—issued a lengthy religious decree, a *fatwa*, in which he declared war on the United States. In February 1998, another decree expanded the war to include "Jihad against Jews and Crusaders," meaning all Jews and Westerners in the world. In bin Laden's words, "to kill the Americans and their allies—civilians and military—is an individual duty for every Muslim . . ."[10] Have American and Western leaders grasped the nature of the threat correctly, or are they still not fully mobilized, asleep at the wheel? If the latter, what would you do differently?

This all changed when more oil than could be imagined was discovered in Saudi Arabia.

As if overnight, what was previously considered a primitive and unimportant doctrine became the state religion of a very affluent country zealously committed to exporting its brand of Islam to the rest of the world. After World War II, Saudi Arabia began sending tremendous amounts of money to Muslim communities all over the world. It is responsible for thousands of *madrassas*, religious schools, which teach almost exclusively the Koran and Arabic.

If you have traveled to Europe, for example, and have seen the sprawling new mosques throughout the continent with their beautiful minarets, chances are good that they were built with Saudi money. Similar mosques have been built the world over, also courtesy of Saudi Arabia. This global phenomenon has propelled what only a few decades ago had been a fundamentalist, largely ignored form of Islam, whose adherents sought to regress the faith back to its founding era, into a serious rival of the Islamic Sunni mainstream.

In the United States alone, up to 80% of all mosques are managed by Saudi-funded Wahhabi clerics, who by virtue of their position also get to set the political tone of their communities.[11]

Militant Fundamentalism   Since the United States has led the West in the war against those using or supporting terrorism, Wahhabism has received a fresh look and serious scrutiny as a potential contributor to terrorism. Because Osama bin Laden is from Saudi Arabia, as were 14 of the 19 September 11, 2001, hijackers, it is hard to ignore a link between Saudi Arabia's Wahhabism and the anti-Western onslaught of recent years. A study published by the American Center for Religious Freedom, affiliated with the Freedom House, analyzed the Saudi Arabian-generated religious literature disseminated to the twelve largest mosques in the United States. The following sampling of Wahhabi thought provides a clearer perspective on some aspects of present-day Wahhabism, which may contribute to radical Islamists stoking the fires of terrorism.[12]

- It is a religious obligation for Muslims to hate Christians and Jews.
- Befriending, helping, or taking part in the festivities of Christians and Jews is strictly forbidden.
- Treat democratic and hence un-Islamic societies with contempt.
- Believers who are in the United States for any reason should feel as if they are in hostile territory, and, therefore, should try to convert local nonbelievers, accumulate funds to be used later in jihad, or conclude their business as soon as possible and leave.
- Treat non-Wahhabi Muslims as infidels.

- Spill the blood of a Muslim who commits adultery and take his money.
- Kill anybody converting out of Islam.
- Veil and separate all Muslim women from men and bar them from certain vocations.

The pervasiveness of the phenomenon leads those wishing to understand Islam's current militancy to find a partial answer in the rise of Wahhabism. Its confrontational nature and the fact that it is associated with an exceptionally wealthy country dedicated with the utmost religious commitment to spreading the faith both in Muslim lands and beyond render this version of Islam a key component in the growing militancy of the faith. Nonetheless, it is important to keep in mind that there is a far more humane and tolerant side of Islam, one that is not reflected in *Wahhabism*.[13]

True Believers and Hatred

Murderous incitement causes homicidal results. Italian police recorded the reaction of the Egyptian terrorist Rabei Osman Sayed as he was watching the beheading of a civilian American captive in Iraq, Nicholas Berg, on the Internet. Sayed is recorded shouting with excitement as he watched, "Go to hell, enemy of God! Kill him! Kill him! Yes, like that! Cut his throat properly. Cut his head off! If I had been there, I would have burned him to make him feel what hell was like. Cut off his head! God is great! God is great!"[14]

The Iranian Revolution

In February 1979, the world was watching with concern the euphoria in Iran as the Shah's autocratic regime was deposed and replaced by a new theocratic one under the leadership of Ayatollah Ruhollah Khomeini. There were good reasons for the anxiety as future developments would prove. Over the next decades, Shi'i Iran would secure for itself the title of the most implacable foe of the West, especially Israel and the United States.

Dedicated to advancing the cause of Islam throughout the world, the Islamic Republic has become the most conspicuous supporter of terrorism in the world. Iran has followed two tracks to achieve this distinction:

1. Consistent sponsorship of political violence outside of its borders to advance its foreign policy goals.
2. Relentless generation of anti-Western sentiments among Muslims.

It has pursued both tracks with increasing messianic fervor.

Impact on Direct and Indirect Terrorism   No country has surpassed the Islamic Republic in the use of terrorism in recent decades. The following is a representative sample of the country's deep involvement in international terrorism:

1. In Lebanon, Iran has created, financed, and managed the terrorist group Hezbollah. Among other exploits, the group is believed to have carried out the Khobar Towers bombing in Saudi Arabia on behalf of Iran on June 25, 1996, in which 18 U.S. servicemen were killed and hundreds wounded.

2. The Islamic Republic has been in complete control of the Palestinian Islamic Jihad, financing it, influencing its day-to-day operations, and determining both its strategy and tactics.

3. Iran was also involved in anti-Israeli and anti-Jewish terrorism in Buenos Aires, Argentina, in the 1990s.[15]

A Seminar Tehran Style

The Islamic Republic of Iran has always proclaimed its intention to destroy Israel. To demonstrate the seriousness of its intentions, Iranian officials organized a "seminar" dealing with "wiping Israel off the face of the earth" in February of 2006, at the University of Tehran. The focus of the event was the recruitment of suicide bombers. One thousand people volunteered immediately to become suicide bombers; 50,000 others signed a document expressing their willingness in principle to volunteer for suicide operations when called upon in the future. The event was so successful that organizers expanded the list of potential targets to include American and British ones as well.[16]

Role in Inciting Anti-Western Sentiment   In Iran, more than 25 years after the revolution, staged demonstrations featuring agitated crowds chanting "Death to America!" take place weekly, usually after Friday prayers. The government-controlled media spreads the political tone and repeats the anti-Western, anti-Israeli mantra.

The Iranian policy to oppose all vestiges of Western influence in the Middle East is not restricted to that goal alone. Successive Iranian governments have expressed increasingly aggressive ambitions founded on years of growing success. Iran's harsh rhetoric and single-minded dedication has resulted in a wave of successive foreign policy triumphs that have become a growing inspiration for restive Muslim populations the world over. The Shi'i country's successes have created anxiety among influential Sunni countries in the Middle East, such as Egypt and Saudi Arabia, concerned with Iran's growing power and influence.

Iran as Potential Nuclear Threat   As Iran proceeds with its nuclear program, the Western world seems increasingly out of realistic options. The Islamic Republic has maintained steadfastly that its nuclear program is for peaceful purposes only, but for many in the international community, the issue is too crucial to take its leaders' words at face value. This is especially true since the tortuous cat-and-mouse lengthy interaction between the United Nations' International Atomic Energy Agency (IAEA) and Iran has been far from a confidence-building exercise. The frustrating process earned the Iranians much admiration for their bargaining skills and manipulative prowess among aficionados of the art of international negotiations. Inevitably, the experience gave rise to fears that the Iranian policy is based on the Shi'i practice of *takiyyah*, deception for the sake of preserving vital interests, while the country dashes ahead at full throttle to manufacture nuclear bombs.

In recent years, Iran has undergone an ominous change in its declared policy regarding the use of nuclear weapons. Whereas Ayatollah Khomeini opposed Iranian acquisition of such weapons, the country's ruling clerics have begun voicing opinions favoring them. In December of 2001, Iran's former president Ali Rafsanjani said, "If a day comes when the world of Islam is duly equipped with the arms Israel has in [its] possession, the strategy of colonialism would face a stalemate, because application of an atomic bomb would not leave anything in Israel but the same thing would just produce minor damages in the Muslim world."[17] There are other expressions of this paradigm change, which reverses the principled opposition to nuclear weapons and replaces it with approval of the benefits in, and justifications for, using the bomb. For example, Hajotal-Islam Mohsen Gharavian, an influential cleric seeking to become Iran's spiritual leader, voiced the following about playing the nuclear card: "When the world is armed with nuclear weapons, it is permissible to make use of these weapons in order to stand up against this threat."[18]

The Iranian nuclear potential poses a threat to Israel, Sunni Muslims, and the West. Iran's president Mahmoud Ahmadinejad's repeated assertions that Israel will be wiped off the face of the earth is one part of the threat. Second is the concern that an Iranian nuclear capability will force major regional Sunni Muslim countries, such as Egypt and Saudi Arabia, to engage in an arms race to ensure nuclear parity with Shi'i Iran, and, third, the fear that Iran's ballistic missiles will soon be able to hit not only Israel, but the European continent as well.

Iran as Agitator of Holy War   Iran's strategy seems to be working as it turns into a central driver of the forces energizing the Muslim world. Iran's Shi'i version of Islam, especially as practiced by the ruling theocracy, emphasizes martyrdom, suicide attacks, and the importance of jihad, or holy war. In the Middle East and elsewhere, Iran's determination, reach, and growing self-confidence threaten to galvanize Muslims into a furious anti-Western campaign against the infidels and Muslim regimes allied with them. One analyst summed up the Iranian role in the militant Islamic resurgence this way: "A renascent and ascendant Muslim world would first acquire nuclear weapons and thus attain parity of power with the West. Then it would annihilate Israel." The plan does not stop there; the author maintains that the combined forces of reawakened Islam "will proceed to assail the West, weaken it, and ultimately subdue it." He quotes Iran's President Ahmadinejad's boast that the result of his country's policies will be a world without a United States.[19]

Communication Technology

Arabs in the Middle East and much of the Muslim world have few freedoms, a limitation which nonetheless hardly slows the flow of information reaching them. Unfortunately, much of that information is biased. Middle Easterners and Muslims around the world get their information the new-fashion way—printed news, radio and television channels, the Internet, and cellular phones. The validity of the information notwithstanding—for biased news is processed as fact—the last decade has witnessed an explosion of new technologies for disseminating up-to-the-minute news using the latest in information technology and Western-style reporting.

The Means of Communication   Traditional means of communication, such as newspapers, magazines, and government-controlled television channels and movies, have been augmented in recent years with the newest delivery media, an improvement that has had a dramatic impact on the political climate in Muslim lands. Chief among these innovations are privately owned and uncensored television channels, the Internet, and cellular technologies. However, modernity's contribution has been a mixed blessing as technology facilitated the faster transmission of information aligned with extremists' perspectives to the Muslim masses, resulting in more radicalized audiences.

Independent Arab television channels, such as al Jazeera and al Arabiyyah, have had an earthquake-like impact on the politics of the Middle East. The newcomers' reporting style distinguishes itself with an unabashedly and unprecedented critical coverage of regional events, policies, and governments. Western-style programming with freethinking reporting accompanied by panel discussions and studio debates has been a successful formula and has earned independent channels huge Arab audiences, even among those residing outside the Middle East. For example, al Jazeera's immense popularity stems from a product whose content and presentation caters to, and reinforces, the belief system of the news channel's customer base. The channel's programming is said to center on Arab nationalism.[20]

An Alleged Bias   Some critics charge that this success has come at the cost of journalistic integrity at best, and of outright crowd-pleasing anti-Western bias at worst. The trappings of the broadcasts may be Western, but the content is alleged to be rabble-rousing incitement that has been altering the political map of the Middle East with a relentless and effective barrage of radical propaganda.

The Qatari-based independent television channel al Jazeera has been a particularly controversial disseminator of news and opinions. Despite al Jazeera's repeated denials, many in the West view it as the epitome of slanted, anti-Western reporting. For example, former Secretary of State Colin Powell charged that al Jazeera "takes every opportunity to slant the news and present it in the most outrageous way possible . . . for the purpose of inflaming the world and appealing to the basest instincts."[21] A Congressional report asserts that "*Al Jazeera* Western-style format is merely a cover for a reporting style that is slanted toward a popular pan-Arab, pan-Islamist viewpoint."[22] The noted Middle East expert Fouad Ajami charged that al Jazeera uses "broadcasters who play to an Arab gallery whose political bitterness they share—and feed."[23] It is important to keep in mind that al Jazeera has rejected such charges consistently and vigorously.

The Impact of the Internet and Cellular Technology   Although the Internet and cell phones are not as widely accessible as they are in other parts of the world, they have nonetheless had an impact similar to that of television on the political discourse of the Middle East. The unprecedented number of people with access to this technology can spread the word to others for whom the Internet is unavailable, ensuring that facts, rumors, and conspiratorial explanations swamp the Internet chat rooms. Similarly, cellular technology has augmented the expedited transmission of information. Moderate governments in the Middle East, which until recent years managed to control the content and mode of their populations' communications, have become increasingly helpless in their efforts to check the use of these technologies to prevent the growing popularity of political Islam and the further radicalization of Arab and Muslim public opinion. Those looking for the Internet and innovative information technology to be the medium for a progressive new moderate trend in the Middle East misread the current radical reality in the region.

Shrinking Distances and Infuriating Emotions

In the past, a Muslim learned of the plight of the Palestinians by reading a newspaper article, listening to the radio, or by watching the government-censored news on television. The time-delayed information and the controlled nature of the coverage would normally dull the intensity of the audience's reaction. This is no longer the case. Nowadays, new technology—be it private television channels, the Internet, or cellular communication—instantly conveys coverage that inflames feelings of affinity and rage even in far corners of the Muslim world. Twenty years ago a Muslim in Indonesia, instinctively pro-Palestinian by religious solidarity, would follow with some concern developments in the Arab–Israeli conflict based on information available through traditional means. Today, news concerning Palestinians can reach the same person instantly, even live. Enraging gory pictures and tendentious reporting of a story developing thousands of miles away often result in a personal feeling of injury and a new convert to the cause of radical Islam. Too often, technology is the fuel in the engine of Jihad.

The Afghanistan Catalyst

With powerful Islamic forces pushing a radical agenda with growing success, fate provided the spark that would escalate the rhetorical campaign to the level where shock troops physically took on the infidels. In turn, the heralded exploits of these Islamic fighters further inspired Muslim religious awakening and mounting hostility toward non-Muslims.

In a monumental historical blunder, the Soviet Union invaded Afghanistan in 1979 to prop up a friendly regime in the neighboring Muslim country. The move was meant to ensure that Afghanistan would not turn into an anti-Soviet outpost from which radical Islamic agitation could influence the Soviet Muslim minorities and threaten the country's stability. The brazen takeover of a Muslim country by a superpower—an atheistic one, at that—energized political Islam and generated a tidal wave of support for the Afghan resistance. As an enraged Muslim world united politically to foil the Soviet move into Afghanistan and to reverse its results, thousands of highly motivated young Muslims from all over the world flocked to Afghanistan to join the indigenous resistance. These were Mujahadeen, or "Holy Warriors," engaged in jihad. The United States jumped on the anti-Soviet bandwagon, determined to turn Afghanistan into the Soviet Union's Vietnam. Using Pakistan's intelligence services, the Americans sent substantial financial and military support to the Islamic insurgents. The insurgents' courage, religious zeal, and massive Muslim and American support proved too much for the Soviet Union. Acknowledging that the costly war was hopelessly unwinnable, the Soviet Union withdrew its forces in 1989. However, the Soviet capitulation proved more of a beginning than an end.

The Gift that Keeps Haunting

As part of the American assistance to the Mujahadeen during the Afghanistan war, the United States supplied the insurgents with about 2,000 shoulder-fired antiaircraft missiles, the lethal Stinger, to help them offset Soviet air supremacy. Nobody knows exactly how many of the missiles were used and how many remained in the fighters' hands. Fearing that Islamist terrorists might use the sophisticated weapon to down Western commercial airlines, the CIA initiated a buy-back program, offering $150,000 to $200,000 for each missile sold back to the United States. The results have been disappointing.

Switching Targets: From the USSR to the USA   The result of the Islamic victory in Afghanistan was electrifying. The fact that the outnumbered, poorly equipped but highly committed bands of "Holy Warriors" prevailed in a war against a superpower proved ideologically intoxicating. Later, when the Soviet Union imploded and collapsed, radical Islam unabashedly claimed credit for single-handedly vanquishing the mighty superpower itself. It was then that they turned their attention to that other hated superpower still waiting in the wings, the United States. Whatever goodwill Americans might have enjoyed

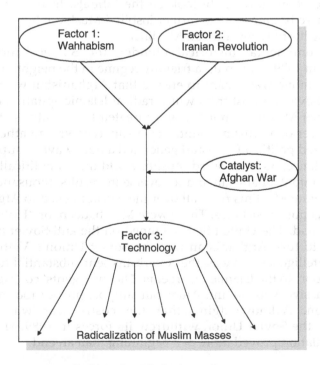

Factors contributing to the radicalization of Islam

with the jihadists for helping them in Afghanistan was quickly erased from memory; on the contrary, they now reasoned that if they could do away with one superpower, taking on the other superpower was likely to yield similar results. Thus, the residue of the war in Afghanistan became the catalyst that ignited the anti-Western passions of Muslims already inflamed by Wahhabism and the massive Iranian propaganda steamroller. Worldwide jihad was upgraded from the realm of charged words to that of direct violent action against the Western infidels, in particular, the United States.

WHAT DO ISLAMISTS WANT?

Because this chapter deals with the Islamic dimension of terrorism, by definition the discussion centers not on the pious majority but on the militants vying to lead Islam.

Radical Islam's grievances and demands are plentiful, but sorting out real from spurious, valid from propaganda, and the wishes of the many from those of the radical few is nearly impossible. Nevertheless, a consensus seems to exist among certain Muslim governments, Arab nationalists, Western academicians, security specialists, and connoisseurs of history that the goal of radical Islam is worldwide jihad. This growing realization has created serious doubts about the often-cited grievances of radical Islam.

Labels for this extremist Islamic movement vary. Be it political Islam, Islamo-Fascism, or Islamism, certain radical Muslims are on record as to their endgame.

1. They plan to topple all governments in the Middle East in order to create a united, wealthy, and powerful Islamic caliphate.

2. Next comes the destruction of Israel.

3. Then, they intend to recapture all areas of the world that were once under Muslim control.

4. Last, they wish to keep pushing the West until the whole globe falls under the dominance of Islam.

Fantastically ambitious perhaps, this plan is nevertheless deeply rooted in religious conviction and popularly supported by an enthusiastic grassroots Muslim constituency throughout the world. Current Middle Eastern governments are aware of the popular appeal and growing power of the Islamists, and some have been trying to appease the Islamists by appearing more pious and anti-Western than they really are. "It is a peculiarity of the Arab-Islamic political culture that a ruler's authoritarianism is more permissible than his identification with Western powers," observed Middle East expert Fouad Ajami.[24] How long these rulers can keep up the charade before the Islamist reality catches up and topples their regimes is open to conjecture.

The Lost Lands of Andalusia

Islamist terrorists' aspirations are more universal than is generally understood. For example, the goals of the Islamist Palestinian terrorist organization Hamas go beyond its conflict with Israel. In 2006, on the organization's website for children, Al Fatah, "The Conqueror," was the demand for the return of the Spanish city of Seville to the "lost paradise" of Andalusia, the part of Spain that was under Muslim control between 711 and 1492.[25] This and similar demands are supported by various *fatwas*, or religious decrees, stressing the imperative of reconquering all territories that used to be under Muslim control. Sheik Yousef Al-Qaradhawi, president of the International Association of Islamic Scholars, explicitly ruled, "Islam must return to Europe as the conqueror."[26]

Islamists feel aggrieved for myriad reasons. As the British *Daily Telegraph* summed up, the wars in Afghanistan and Iraq have now added "a new pebble to the mountain of grievances that militant fanatics have erected." Writing about the goal of the Islamists, the newspaper asserted that their "real project is the extension of the Islamic territory across the globe, and the establishment of a worldwide 'caliphate' founded in Shari'a law."[27] Examples of this thinking abound in statements by al-Qaeda leaders as well as other Islamists. Osama bin Laden's mentor, the Palestinian Abdullah Azzam, is famous for preaching Muslim world domination. His life, he once wrote, revolved around a single goal, namely the establishment of Allah's rule on earth and the restoration of the caliphate. Fazlur Rehman Khalil, an al-Qaeda leader, said, "Due to the blessings of *Jihad*, America's countdown has begun. It will declare defeat soon."[28] Al-Qaeda's spokesman Abu Gheith proclaimed, "We have the right to kill four million Americans—two million of them children—and to exile twice as many and wound and cripple hundreds of thousands. Furthermore, it is our right to fight them with chemical and biological weapons . . ." Sheik Nasir bin Hamed Al Fahd, a senior cleric from Saudi Arabia, issued a fatwa in May 2003 in which he sanctioned the use of nuclear weapons in order to kill up to ten million Americans. Hamas's Chief Khaled Mashal boasted that "Tomorrow, our nation will sit on the throne of the world. This is not a figment of the imagination, but a fact. Tomorrow we will lead the world, Allah willing." One Western writer described radical Islam this way, "totalitarian, aggressive, conquering, cocksure about its superiority and destiny to rule, intolerant, bristling with resentment, and only tenuously in touch with aspects of reality."[29]

Picking Versions

Many Muslims invoke peaceful quotes from the Koran to demonstrate the serene nature of Islam. Like the Old Testament, the Koran contains nonviolent sentences and passages as well as belligerent sentiments. In the case of the Koran, the reason is said to be rooted in the changing circumstances in the life of the Prophet Muhammad. When he began his ministry in Mecca, he was a pious, peaceful man who spent his time praying, fasting, and preaching. Later, after he was forced to flee to Medina and fend for himself and his followers by resorting to arms, some of his revelations became correspondingly violent.

What Do YOU Think?

If radicals seeking worldwide jihad dictate the political climate in the Muslim world, the tone of media coverage of events, the nature of grievances, and Islam's ultimate goals, to what extent can American political gestures, economic help, or changes in its Middle East policy help change Muslims' attitude toward the United States?

Expressions by radical Islamic elements do not represent the thinking of most Muslims. In fact, many Muslims are upset at the militant spirit overtaking their faith and portraying their religion as a bloodthirsty menace to the world. In the eloquent words of one Muslim expert, Waleed Ziad, "these groups [of Islamists] demonize not just the West, but mainstream Islamic culture and philosophy as well; they pose perhaps the greatest existential threat to 1400 years of Islamic tradition."[30]

Islamo-Fascism: The Rationale Behind the Term

In recent years, an increasing number of Western writers have taken to using the derogatory label *Islamo-fascists*, when discussing Islamists. Of all the disparaging words so readily available to writers, why choose this particular term *fascism*? The answer lies in the parallel that characterizes both radical Islam and fascism; that is, the mass mobilization and push for immediate action. Fascists see—and find—enemies from within and from without and they convince their societies to mobilize against that threat, increasingly heating up the rhetoric until they whip the population into a nationalistic frenzy. As people's passions against the enemy reach the boiling point, a feeling of urgency and great danger to the collective sweeps the nation. To put an end to the perceived threat, the manipulated, stirred-up masses demand immediate action. Invariably, the catharsis, or psychological outlet, comes in the form of an angry explosion of violence against the enemy, be it by repression, terrorism, or outright war against other countries. Fascism culminates in a violent eruption.

Radical Islam and International Law

Angry with the West and rejecting its religion, culture, and legacy, Islamists discard the international codes of war in their universal war of terrorism. From their vantage point, international law reflects arrangements initiated by, and beneficial to, the despised colonial aggressors. More important, these Western-generated laws are not in tandem with the only body of laws Islamists recognize, God's, as expressed in the Muslim religious code, the Shari'a. The latter views the conduct of hostilities in ways that are different from prevailing international norms and laws.

Scholars had begun to notice similarities between radical Islam and fascism decades before the issue came into vogue. For example, Princeton University professor, Manfred Halpern, explored the parallels as early as 1963. In a work about Islam destined to become a classic, he observed that "The neo-Islamic totalitarian movements are essentially fascist movements. They concentrate on mobilizing passion and violence to enlarge the power of their charismatic leader and the solidarity of their movement.... [and they] entirely deny individual and social freedom. [The neo-Islamic totalitarian movements] champion the values and emotions of a heroic past, but repress all free critical analysis of either past roots or present problems."[31] The Iranian intellectual Said Amir Arjomand added his own analysis of the direction of radical Islam following the Iranian Revolution of 1979. Writing from the safety of the United States, Arjomand noted that "Like the fascists, the Islamic militants are against liberal democracy.... [are] anti-bourgeois.... [and] anti-Marxist."[32]

The tendency demonstrated by radical Islam to egg on Muslims against threats, "insults," perceived dangers, and actual killings is strongly reminiscent of similar techniques used by fascists prior to World War II. The last video testament of an Islamist member of the suicide team that attacked the London transportation system on July 7, 2005, is one example. Mohammad

Scene of a 1996 Hamas bombing of an Israeli bus in Jerusalem
Source: Courtesy of AP Wide World Photos.

Sidique Khan justified his actions saying, "Your democratically elected governments continuously perpetrate atrocities against my people all over the world. And your support for them makes you directly responsible, just as I am directly responsible for protecting and avenging my Muslim brothers and sisters. . . . Until we feel security, you will be our targets. Until you stop the bombing, gassing, imprisonment and torture of my people, we'll not stop this fight. We are at war and I am a soldier."[33] Similarly, on March 3, 2006, a Muslim-American student at the University of North Carolina at Chapel Hill, Mohammed Reza Taheri-Azar, drove his sports utility vehicle into a crowded pedestrian area, hitting nine people on campus. Fortunately, all victims of the attack escaped serious injury. The would-be killer later explained that his motive was to "avenge the deaths of Muslims around the world."[34]

What brought young British Muslims to a state of mind that necessitated mass murder of civilians and why did a young Muslim in North Carolina decide that something had to be done to avenge Muslims now, and not before? Chechen Muslims suffered much worse atrocities at the hands of Stalin's Soviet Union during World War II than during the recent Chechen wars, yet there was no global Muslim effort to avenge their fate. Similarly, the consequences of the monumental defeat of the Palestinians by Israel in the 1948–1949 war far exceeded their present plight, yet Muslims the world over did not participate in terrorism to help the Palestinian cause. In Iraq, Saddam Hussein had murdered hundreds of thousands of Muslims, which is only a fraction of the human cost accrued by the U.S.-led war. India ruled Kashmir for decades, yet a bloody conflict erupted in the disputed region only recently. Each year, in Afghanistan, al-Qaeda was training numerous members for future action, which suggests that it is difficult to consider the American war against al-Qaeda and its Taliban host an unprovoked aggression. Muslims have been involved in conflicts all over the world in the modern era, yet they hardly resorted to terrorism in the past. It is conceivable that an artificially created atmosphere of great wrong and urgency—generated by Wahhabism, the impact of the Iranian Revolution of 1979, and the advent of technology—has recently swept through the Muslim world, engendering a burning desire to engage in a bloody conflict to protect a supposedly threatened Muslim collective languishing in grave and immediate danger.

What Do YOU Think?

Arabs have been angry with the West for its colonial past in the Middle East. Yet, the colonial era lasted, generally speaking, only a few decades. In the meantime, Arabs consider their own conquests and colonization of vast regions of the world, including in Europe, as their "golden era." How do you explain this paradox?

THE VIEW FROM THE WEST

The West is slowly awakening to the perceived danger posed by radical and politicized Islam. From the European perspective, decades of liberal and well-meaning policies which enabled Muslim immigration and integration into the Christian societies of Europe are being reciprocated with hatred, talk of taking over the continent via demographics, and terrorism. To many Europeans, the situation is incomprehensible because of the paradox that persecuted and impoverished people, who have been allowed into Europe from lands of tyranny and destitution, might attempt to turn their hosts' prosperous and tolerant societies into the ones from which they have just been lucky to flee. Ethnocentrism and strong faith can partially account for this occurrence, but they cannot explain the phenomenon in full. That some immigrants and their descendents hate the countries that provided them refuge and the opportunity for a better life and transfer their loyalty to a transnational religious ideology that has declared war on the West seems incredible to many Europeans.

Failed "isms" and Radical Islam

The roots of radical Islam in the Middle East can be found in part in the failed experiences of the region's inhabitants with alternative political systems. The Arabs have tried to borrow alien concepts with the hope that foreign political systems will speed up their modernization and help them reclaim the old era of glory. All these "isms" met with dismal results. Western-introduced nationalism fared as well as the Nasserism which succeeded it, only to be replaced by socialism that was later switched to capitalism and globalism—all in vain. Hence the attraction of the slogan for the latest alternative, the Islamists' cure-all silver bullet: "Islam is the solution."

Few Westerners concur with the long and growing list of grievances raised by Islamists. A celebrated counterargument comes from one of the most eminent experts on the Middle East, Professor Bernard Lewis, Professor Emeritus of Near Eastern Studies at Princeton University. In his article, "The Roots of Muslim Rage: Why So Many Muslims Deeply Resent the West, and Why Their Bitterness Will Not Easily Be Mollified,"[35] Lewis lists the possible reasons for the anti-Western, and especially anti-American, fury. He also scrutinizes each anti-Western allegation to establish its validity. His conclusions are informative. At bottom, he says, is the Islamic civilization's distress with its present inferiority to the West, represented chiefly by the United States, and Islam's attempt to regain its lost supremacy. Essentially, the Muslim looks at himself in the mirror, knows what his culture had been and becomes enraged at those cultures surpassing his own venerated traditions. According to Lewis, the grievances themselves are baseless charges, excuses, propaganda, and pretexts.

The West, contends Lewis, is accused of an array of wrongs: sexism, racism, imperialism, tyranny, and exploitation. Guilty as charged, admits Lewis,

Fanning the Flames: Caricatures and Mayhem

Non-Muslims can understand Islamic anger directed at Israel and occasionally empathize with anti-American sentiments as well. However, in 2006, Muslim extremists overplayed their hand when they took on the Danes. The origin of the spectacle was the September 30, 2005, publication in a Danish newspaper of 12 cartoons offensive to Islam, which were reprinted in October in a Norwegian newspaper. The small Muslim community in Denmark was unhappy but the incident might have been forgotten if not for a few Danish-Muslims who traveled to the Middle East to stoke the flames of anger at their adoptive country. Their efforts were greeted apathetically, until they presented the offensive materials to the Foreign Ministers of the Organization of the Islamic Conference (OIC) meeting in Mecca, Saudi Arabia. A few radical regimes, some of them infamous for the brutal treatment of Muslims in their own countries, pounced on the opportunity to undermine the appeal of the West among their own populations. Bloody riots erupted, as if spontaneously, throughout the Muslim world. For a few weeks, mobs attacked foreign embassies, burned facilities, kidnapped foreigners, and expressed their anger in various violent ways.

Stunned, the world took notice of this manipulated campaign and began to look at angry Islam through a fresh lens, questioning its positions, allegations, and true intentions in ways it had never before done. This was especially so in Europe, which "has awakened to the presence within its borders of a strand of politicized Islam, surely and un-reconciled to the demands of modern life," as one analyst put it.[36]

but as human beings, not as Westerners. Every civilization throughout history has been complicit in such sins, and the West has done no worse than others have, including the Arabs, the Mongols, and the Ottomans. In fact, the West has been a leader in recognizing these sins and trying to rectify them. Professor Lewis takes issue with such accusations to demonstrate the West's innocence of these charges. In his opinion, the problem is that Islam, accustomed to dominating much of the world since its inception, cannot reconcile itself to the "rise of the house of unbelief" and to the loss of what it considers its natural, God-given right to dominate the world to the "enemies of God."

Irrational Anti-Americanism

To demonstrate his point that Muslim revulsion directed at the United States is essentially illogical and unwarranted, Professor Lewis cites two examples: (1) In November, 1979, a Pakistani mob attacked the American embassy in Islamabad and burned it to the ground because an armed group of radical Saudi dissidents had taken over the Great Mosque in Mecca and were forcibly dislodged from it after heavy fighting. That the United States had nothing to do with the attack, which was carried out by Wahhabi religious extremists, was immaterial. (2) A decade later, Pakistani rioters attacked the United States Information Service building in Islamabad. This time, the motive was the publication of Salman Rushdie's book *The Satanic Verses* in the United States. That the book had been published in Britain five months earlier and that the author was Indian by birth, Muslim, and a British citizen did not seem to matter.

The Challenge of Orientalism

Many have disagreed with Lewis's main thrust, but none has articulated the difference of opinion more eloquently and forcefully than the Palestinian-American professor Edward Said. In his influential work *Orientalism*,[37] Said argues that most scholarly work about the Arab and Muslim worlds has been produced by biased Western scholars and Western-influenced elites of the indigenous societies. Consequently, the entire gamut of thinking and relating to the "East" has been romanticized and distorted over the generations in a way that made these societies appear weak and incapable in order to perpetuate Western imperialism and domination of these lands. Said labeled this phenomenon *Orientalism* and stated that "Orientalism is fundamentally a political doctrine willed over the Orient because the Orient was weaker than the West."[38]

Professor Said's conception of Orientalism has its supporters as well as its many detractors. The book criticizes Westerners whose understanding of the Orient, frame of reference, and ability to draw objective conclusions regarding Arabs and Muslims, according to Said, are inherently flawed. Because Said's work censures Western scholars, including Professor Bernard Lewis, the intellectual sparring that ensued has made for important and fascinating reading.

Poverty and Islamist Terrorism

Middle East expert Daniel Pipes examines the possibility that Islamist terrorism may be traced to poverty in the Middle East, the famous "poverty breeds terrorism" axiom.[39] His conclusions may seem counterintuitive and fly in the face of convention because Pipes disputes the assumption that some Muslims have turned to extremism and terror because of socioeconomic distress. His findings point to the opposite conclusion, that Muslim terrorists are usually well-educated individuals from the middle class of their societies, as were the 19 perpetrators of the September 11, 2001, attacks. Islamic terrorists typically are economically comfortable, maintains Pipes, because money, education, and privilege are actually the prerequisites to becoming a terrorist. In fact, terrorism is an alien phenomenon in the most impoverished Muslim countries; instead, the wealthier the society, the greater the likelihood that it will spawn terrorists. According to Pipes, the old story of "haves" and "have-nots" is reversed. The have-nots are regular, pious Muslims, whereas the haves are the ones among whom one finds the militants.

If valid, these findings have important ramifications. For example, Pipes's provocative study implies that investing substantial amounts of capital in the Palestinian economy with the hope of boosting the "peace process," guided by the assumption that a reduction in poverty will result in diminished terrorism, is misguided. In fact, claims the author, investing in the Middle East is bound to be counterproductive because "a prosperous enemy may simply be more capable of making war." He presents the following conclusions: (1) Prosperity cannot be looked to as a solution to militant Islam, (2) Westernization does not provide a solution either, as many Western-grown Islamists attest to, (3) Economic growth does not necessarily lead to improved relations with Muslim states.

In general, scholars tend to agree that Islamist terrorism is not the result of poverty. For example, Professor of Islamic Thought and Culture at the University of South California in Los Angeles, Timur Kuran, concurs that Islamic terrorism does not necessarily reflect poverty, also pointing to the comfortable backgrounds of the 19 perpetrators of the September 11 attacks. According to Professor Kuran, the Islamists reject modern Western capitalism because they consider it a corrupting, American-led system masquerading as globalism.[40] They may abhor modern capitalism but Islamists do not engage in terrorism because they are poor.

SPANISH INQUISITION OR PEACEFUL QUAKERS?

When discussing Islam, there is no one body that stands for all shapes and brands of the faith. We need to be cognizant of the fact that our focus tends to be limited to the headline-grabbing events of today, which may misrepresent the legacy of an entire civilization. Condemning today's Islam as a violent religion because of the terrorists who speak in its name makes as much sense as judging Christianity by the Spanish Inquisition. The struggle for Islam's soul is raging inside of Islam between the silent majority and the radicals, and its conclusion will decide the nature of the religion for a long time to come. As the rest of the world is holding its breath, the clock keeps ticking on this struggle for the soul of Islam.

SUMMARY

In this chapter, you have learned the following:

1. A splendid Islamic civilization existed for a thousand years.
2. In recent centuries, Islam has lost much of its influence and prestige.
3. Over the last half century, a political Islamic movement has been on the rise, increasingly mobilizing the Muslim masses.
4. Three main factors account for the Islamic awakening: Wahhabism, the Islamic Republic of Iran, and technology.
5. The war in Afghanistan served as the catalyst moving the rhetoric into the realm of action.
6. A growing body of evidence suggests that Islamists are bent on worldwide jihad.
7. The West is becoming increasingly uncomfortable about its future relations with Islam.
8. Islamist terrorism is probably not the result of poverty.

💣💣💣

Years ago, as a doctoral student, this writer enjoyed political discussions with Arab friends, who were also graduate students, in the many coffee-holes in and around campus. Whenever the conversation turned to the politics of the Middle East, the young Arab intellectuals would become agitated and angry. Their most bitter and often-cited complaint alleged a hypocritical U.S. policy of exalting democracy and human rights while in practice supporting oppressive pro-American Middle Eastern regimes. At the time, I found it difficult to reply with a winning answer. In 2003, at great cost, the United States did something about an Arab dictator, Saddam Hussein, and overthrew him in an attempt to usher in a new dawn of democracy and human rights in a major Arab country. Yet, instead of gratitude, Arab masses and their elites reacted with cynicism and antagonism toward the American intervention in the affairs of the Middle East.

The paradox was best explained by the eminent scholar Fouad Ajami, who wrote about the impossible American predicament in the Middle East in general, "Policy can never speak to wrath. Step into the thicket [get involved] and the foreign power is blamed for its reach. Step back [stay out of the region's affairs] and Pax Americana is charged with abdication and indifference."[41] In other words, when it comes to the Middle East, the United States is damned if it does and damned if it does not.

💣💣💣

NOTES

1. See "Remarks by Imam Izak-El Mu'eed Pasha," at http://www.belief.net/story/90/story_9016_1.html (accessed October 26, 2006).

2. See Fareed Zakaria, "Why Do They Hate Us? The Politics of Rage," *Newsweek*, Vol. 138, No. 16 (October 15, 2001), p. 32.

3. For more on the scientific and other advances in Islam during its heyday, see Arthur Goldschmidt, *A Concise History of the Middle East*, 7th ed. (Boulder, CO: Westview Press, 2002), pp. 111–118.

4. From Arab Human Development Report 2002, *Creating Opportunities for Future Generations*, United Nations Development Program (New York, NY: U.N. Publications, Room DC2-853), p. xx.

5. Ibid.

6. From Arab Human Development Report 2003, *Building a New Society*, United Nations Development Program. (New York, NY: U.N. Publications, Room DC2-853).

7. Professor Pervez Hoodbnoy's comments about the poor state of Pakistan's science education are quoted in Thomas Friedman, "Empty Pockets, Angry Minds," *New York Times*, February 22, 2006, p. A19.

8. From Arab Human Development Report 2004, *Towards Freedom in the Arab World*, United Nations Development Program (New York, NY: U.N. Publications, Room DC2-853), p. xx.

9. Abdulraham al Rashed is quoted in Associated Press, "Self-Criticism in Arab Media Follows School Siege," September 4, 2004, at http://www.msnbc.msn.com/id/5912071/ (accessed March 31, 2006).

10. Bin Laden's first declaration of war was issued on August 23, 1996, and the second on February 23, 1998. See Daniel Benjamin and Steve Simon, *The Age Of Sacred Terror* (New York: Random House, 2002), pp. 140–143 and 148–150.

11. For these estimates, see, for example, Susan Katz Keating, "The Wahhabi Fifth Column," FrontPageMagazine.com, December 30, 2002, at http://www.frontpage mag.com/Articles/ReadArticle.asp?ID = 5270 (accessed May 29, 2006). See also Stephen Schwartz, "Wahhabism and Islam in the U.S.: Two-Faced Policy Fosters Danger," Middle East Information Center, March 22, 2005, at http://www.middle eastinfo.org/forum/index.php?showtopic = 3752 (accessed May 29, 2006).

12. The Report by the *Center for Religious Freedom*, "Saudi Publications on Hate Ideology Invade American Mosques," can be retrieved at http://www.freedomhouse.org. In addition, see a related article by Hassan Fattah, "Don't Be Friends with Christians or Jews, Saudi Texts Say," *New York Times*, May 24, 2006, A10. For a critical perspective on this publication, consult Junaid M. Afeef, "Are American Mosques Promoting Hate Ideology?" February 4, 2005, at http://www.altmuslim.com/perm.php? id-1389_0_25_0_C37 (accessed May 29, 2006).

13. For a more balanced perspective on Islam, consult the websites of mainstream Islamic organizations, such as that of the Council of American Islamic Relations (CAIR) at http://www.cair-net.org.

14. Rabei Osman Sayed's reaction is quoted in Elaine Sciolino, "From Tapes, a Chilling Voice of Islamic Radicalism in Europe," *New York Times*, November 18, 2005, pp. A1, A10.

15. For details on the Iranian involvement in the Buenos Aires bombings, see Chapter 7 "Unholy Alliances: The Irresistible Lure of Money."

16. The information on the seminar held at the University of Tehran in February 2006 is cited by the Israeli daily *Ma'ariv*, February 19, 2006.

17. Ali Rafsanjani's calculation regarding a nuclear exchange with Israel is quoted in Daniel Pipes, "Iran's Final Solution Plan," *New York Sun*, November 11, 2005, p. 6.

18. Hajotal-Islam Mohsen Gharavian's ruling that permits the use of nuclear weapons is found in Yossi Melman, "Iranian Cleric: Use of Nuclear Arms Sometimes Permissible," in the Israeli newspaper *Ha'aretz*, February 19, 2006.

19. Iran's ambitions and the quote about its President, Mahmoud Ahmadinejad, are found in Daniel Jonah Goldhagen, "The New Threat: The Radical Politics of Islamic Fundamentalism, *The New Republic*, Vol. 234, No. 9 (March, 2006), pp. 15–27.

20. For example, the president of the Canadian Arab Federation is quoted as saying that Arab nationalism is at the heart of al Jazeera's programming. See Mark Bourrie, "Yes Means No for *al-Jazera* in Canada," July 23, 2004, at http://www. antiwar.com/ips/bourrie.php?articleid=3137 (accessed March 28, 2006).

21. Colin Powell is quoted in Daniel Pipes and Charlotte West, "Al-Jazeera in Al Canada?" at *FrontPageMagazine.com*, August 13, 2004, in http://www. danielpipes.org/article/2013 (accessed March 28, 2006).

22. For the Congressional report regarding al Jazeera, see CRS Report for Congress, "The *Al-Jazeera* News Network: Opportunity or Challenge for U.S. Foreign Policy in the Middle East?" Updated July 23, 2003, at http://fpc.state.gov/documents/ organization/23002.pdf, p. 3 (accessed March 28, 2006).

23. For Fouad Ajami's quote regarding al Jazeera, see "What the Muslim World is Watching," *New York Times Magazine* section, November 18, 2001, p. 148.

24. That it is preferable nowadays for an Arab ruler to be a tyrant than to appear pro-American is found in Fouad Ajami, "The Uneasy Imperium," in Hoge and Rose, eds., *How Did This Happen: Terrorism and the New World* (New York: Public Affairs Reports, 2001), p. 28.

25. On radical Islam's view on "Andalusia," see "Hamas Demands Return of Seville in Internet Children's Magazine," *The Spain Herald*, January 4, 2006.

26. The *fatwa* concerning the reconquest of Europe is found in Steven Stalinsky, "Sheikh Yousef Al-Qaradhawi in London to Establish 'The International Council of Muslim Clerics,' " in *MEMRI*, Special Report-No. 30, July 8, 2004, at http://memri.org/bin/articles.cgi?Page=archives&Area=sr&ID-SR3004 (accessed July 29, 2006).

27. For the *Daily Telegraph* quotes, see Daniel Pipes, "What Do the Terrorists Want?" *New York Sun*, July 26, 2005, p. 7.

28. Abdullah Azzam and Rehman Khalil are quoted in Ibid.

29. The quotes of al-Qaeda's Abu Gheith, the Saudi cleric Sheik Nasir bin Hamed Al Fahd, Hamas's Khaled Mashal and the concluding quote of the paragraph are found in Daniel Jonah Goldhagen, pp. 15–27.

30. The quote by Waleed Ziad is found in his critique of the Islamists in "Jihad's Fresh Face," *New York Times*, September 16, 2005.

31. Manfred Halpern's analysis is found in *The Politics of Social Change in the Middle East and North Africa* (Princeton, NJ: Princeton University Press, 1963), pp. 135–136.

32. See Arjomand's treatment of the meaning of the Iranian Revolution in Said Amir Arjomand, *The Turban For The Crown: The Islamic Revolution in Iran* (New York: Oxford University Press, 1988), pp. 204–205.

33. Khan's video, accompanied by a transcript, can be found at http://www.informationclearinghouse.info/article10079.htm (accessed March 14, 2006).

34. Mohammed Reza Taheri-Azar is quoted in Daniel Pipes, "The Quiet-Spoken Muslims Who Turn to Terror," *New York Sun*, March 14, 2006, p. 7.

35. Bernard Lewis' article is accessible at http://www.travelbrochuregraphics.com/extra/roots_of_muslim_rage.htm (accessed April 2, 2006).

36. The quote concerning the European awakening to the alien presence in their midst is in Fouad Ajami, "The Fire This Time," *U.S. News and World Report*, Vol. 140, No. 6 (February 20, 2006), p. 30.

37. Edward W. Said, *Orientalism* (New York: Vintage Books, 1994).

38. Professor Said's quote about Orientalism being a political doctrine is found in Ibid., p. 204.

39. For Daniel Pipes's article on poverty and terrorism in Islam, see Daniel Pipes, "God and Mammon: Does Poverty Cause Militant Islam?" in Martin, ed., *The New Era of Terrorism: Selected Readings* (Dominguez Hills, CA: Sage Publications, 2004), pp. 111–117.

40. Professor Kuran's article is found in Timur Kuran, "The Cultural Undertow of Muslim Economic Rage," *NationalReview.com*, December 12, 2001, at http://www.independent.org/newsroom/article.asp?id=401 (accessed July 29, 2006).

41. Fouad Ajami's quote regarding the American impossible position in the Middle East can be found at Fouad Ajami, "The Uneasy Imperium: Pax Americana in the Middle East," in Hoge and Rose, eds., p. 23.

CHAPTER

11

Rage and Lessons

September 11, 2001

Many Muslims who do not belong to bin Laden's terrorist network consider the United States on a moral par with Genghis Khan.

Michael Scott Doran, Middle East expert

❖❖❖

As the terrorists were flying the hijacked United Airlines Flight 175 toward New York City, one of the passengers, Peter Hanson, used his cell phone to contact his father, Lee. At 09:00, three minutes before the plane smashed into the World Trade Center, the son told his father, "It's getting bad, Dad—A stewardess was stabbed—They seem to have knives and mace. . . . It's getting very bad on the plane—Passengers are throwing up and getting sick . . . I think we are going down—I think they intend to go to Chicago or someplace and fly into a building—Don't worry, Dad—If it happens, it'll be very fast—My God, My God."[1]

❖❖❖

September 11, 2001, is a watershed in American and world history. The events and ramifications of that fateful day inflicted incalculable human, financial, and psychological pain on the United States. It also brought Americans back to reality by forcing them to acknowledge that a war had been declared on them, and that a "colossal failure of deterrence" had taken place.[2] The first step to understanding the horrific events of September 11, 2001, is to read

163

Did You know?

Western estimates of the number of terrorists al-Qaeda trained in its camps in Afghanistan between 1989 and 2001 range from 70,000 to 110,000. Only a few thousand of these trainees distinguished themselves sufficiently to be recruited as full-fledged members of al-Qaeda. The esteem in which members of the chosen elite were held enticed Islamists the world over.[3]

---

the official 9/11 Commission Report because it delineates the facts of that day in great and careful detail. Others have also contributed their perspectives, which complement the report and enhance our grasp of what happened on that day, the reasons behind the catastrophe, and how 9/11 has affected us since.

In this chapter, we will examine the events of September 11, 2001, outline the strategic thinking of their planners, provide two main perspectives on the meaning of those events, and conclude with an analysis of the impact of the attacks on U.S. foreign policy in the years that would follow.

SEPTEMBER 11, 2001: THE FACTS[4]

Four American passenger planes were hijacked on September 11, 2001, and deliberately crashed, killing all on board and thousands of people in the attacked World Trade Center and Pentagon. The shocking and traumatic events of that day officially inaugurated the American war against terrorists and those who support them.

American Airlines Flight 11

It was a beautiful Tuesday morning on the East Coast. American Airlines Flight 11, scheduled to fly from Boston's Logan Airport to Los Angeles, boarded its passengers between 06:45 A.M and 07:40 A.M. Among them were five Arab Muslims led by the leader of all the hijacking operations planned for that day, Mohammed Atta. The computerized prescreening system known as *Computer-Assisted Passenger Prescreening System* (CAPPS), which identifies passengers whose baggage should be checked with extra care, red-flagged three of the five members of the hijacking team. Although their checked-in bags were subject to extra attention, the individuals themselves at the security checkpoint did not receive special screening. With a crew of 11 and 81 passengers on board (including the hijackers), the Boeing 767 took off at 07:59 A.M.

The hijacking commenced at about 08:15 A.M. The terrorists seem to have used sharp objects, a mace-like irritant and the threat of a bomb to force their way into the cockpit and to push the passengers to the back of the plane. Within five minutes, two of the flight attendants began reporting the hijacking and providing details of what they knew to the airline. They reported that two flight attendants had been stabbed outside the cockpit and a passenger's throat had been slashed.

At 08:44, Betty Ong, one of the flight attendants updating the company's operations center was recorded saying, "Something is wrong. We are in a rapid descent . . . we are all over the place. . . . We are flying low. We are flying very, very low. We are flying way too low." A short time later she repeated, "Oh my God we are way too low." At 08:46:40, American Airlines Flight 11 smashed into the North Tower of the World Trade Center, killing everybody on board and many others in the building and its vicinity.

United Airlines Flight 175

The five-member terrorist team that commandeered United Airlines Flight 175, which also departed Boston's Logan Airport for Los Angeles, was led by Marwan al Shehhi. None of this team's members were selected by CAPPS for special scrutiny. They boarded the Boeing 767 between 07:23 A.M and 07:28 A.M. and the plane left the gate close to 08:00 A.M, as scheduled, and took off at 08:14 A.M. with 9 crewmembers and 57 passengers.

The terrorists' assault on the cockpit took place sometime between 08:42 and 08:46. Like the hijackers of Flight 11, they used knives, some sort of mace, and the threat of a bomb to overtake the cabin and push the passengers to the rear of the plane. At 08:52, a flight attendant notified a United Airlines official of the hijacking, telling him that both pilots were dead and that one flight attendant had been stabbed. Six minutes later, at 08:58, the plane changed direction and headed toward New York City.

At about the time that passenger Peter Hanson contacted his father, Lee, to tell him of the hijacking, another passenger, Brian Sweeney, managed to speak with his mother, Louise, and told her of the situation. In their separate locations, Mrs. Sweeney and Mr. Hanson turned on their television sets. At 09:03:11 both parents watched a live broadcast of United Airlines Flight 175 hitting the South Tower of the World Trade Center. Everybody on board perished instantly, as did many others in the building and the surrounding area.

American Airlines Flight 77

Dulles Airport is located in Virginia, not far from Washington DC. On the morning of September 11, a five-member terrorist team, among them the pilot Hani Hanjour checked in for their flight. Unlike the other groups, they boarded in ones and twos, and therefore were less conspicuous than a large group of foreigners might have been. Even so, they aroused suspicion. The CAPPS security system singled out three of the terrorists for extra scrutiny of their check-in luggage. There was some suspicion of the other two because of their documentation and

Hijacked United Airlines Flight 175 about
to hit the South Tower of the World Trade
Center on September 11, 2001
Source: Courtesy of AP Wide World
Photos.

difficulty with the language ; nevertheless, their bags were loaded onto the plane
when it became clear that the two had boarded. Interestingly, three of the five
hijackers set off the alarm when passing through the X-ray machine at the security checkpoint; yet they were allowed to proceed after being rescreened with a
hand-wand.

The Boeing 757 departed its gate at 08:09 A.M. and took off for Los
Angeles at 08:20 with a crew of 6 and with 58 passengers, among them three
11-year-olds on an educational trip. The takeover took place sometime
between 08:51 and 08:54. The hijackers used knives and box cutters, but
apparently did not use mace or the threat of a bomb. At 08:54, the plane
turned and headed back in a northeasterly direction. Within minutes, a
couple of passengers contacted family members to tell them what was
happening. At 09:16 and again a short time thereafter, passenger Barbara
Olson, wife of the Solicitor General of the United States, called her husband
from the hijacked plane and told him of the unfolding of events. During the
second call, Ted Olson disclosed to his wife the fate of the other two hijacked
planes. She remained calm. Descending sharply to 2,200 feet and only five
miles west-southwest of downtown Washington DC, the American Airlines
Flight 77 increased its speed to maximum and dove straight toward the
Pentagon. It hit the building at a speed of 530 miles per hour at exactly
09:37:46 A.M. Everybody on board died instantly; 125 military and civilian
Pentagon personnel perished.

United Airlines Flight 93

There were only four terrorists in the team slated to hijack United Airlines
Flight 93 from Newark, New Jersey, to San Francisco. The four checked in
between 07:03 and 07:39 A.M. One of the terrorists was flagged by the CAPPS
security system, but was allowed through after his bag was checked for explosives. At 08:42 A.M, the Boeing 757 took off after a critical delay of 25 minutes.
On board was a crew of 7 and 37 passengers.

The hijacking took place at about 09:28 A.M. approximately five minutes after the flight crew had been alerted to beware of cockpit intrusion, because by this time it was known that two aircraft had hit the World Trade Center. Wearing red bandanas, the terrorists used knives and the threat of a bomb to wrestle control of the plane. In the process, one passenger and a flight attendant apparently were gravely stabbed. The others were herded to the back of the plane. From their location in the rear, the two pilots and at least ten passengers contacted family members, friends, and colleagues to let them know of the hijacking. The 25-minute delay proved crucial since it allowed the trapped passengers to learn the fate of the other three hijacked planes and to realize that passive compliance was not an option.

The passengers voted to attack the cockpit and regain control of the plane. At 09:57, they stormed up the aisles toward the cockpit. One female passenger abruptly terminated her phone call, saying, "Everyone's running up to first class. I've got to go. Bye." The hijackers are believed to have locked themselves in the cockpit, trying to hold off the passengers. The struggle lasted about five minutes. A passenger was overheard to shout, "In the cockpit. If we don't we'll die!" As the passengers were about to force their way into the cockpit, the terrorists made a decision to crash the plane rather than allow themselves to be overwhelmed. Flying at 580 miles per hour, the plane nose-dived and slammed into an open field in Shanksville, Pennsylvania, about a 20-minute flight from Washington DC, killing everybody on board.

The terrorists' actual target in Washington DC will never be known with certainty. While the White House is a possibility, the Capitol Building is a more likely target. The bravery of the passengers and crew of United Airlines Flight 93 saved many in Washington DC on that morning. Their heroism has been immortalized in a couple of made-for-TV documentaries and in a Hollywood movie, *United 93*.

Permission to Engage

At approximately 10:10 A.M, Vice President Richard Cheney, who was located in the sheltered conference room in the White House, received authorization from President Bush to shoot down hijacked airplanes if necessary. A few minutes earlier, at 10:02 A.M., the first report reached those in the shelter of a hijacked plane headed toward Washington DC. This turned out to be United Airlines Flight 93. The Vice President, twice within a period of ten minutes, received permission from the President to shoot down hijacked planes, and conveyed the presidential authorization down the chain of command. When word reached them that Flight 93 went down in a field in Pennsylvania, they wondered whether the plane had been shot down by American interceptors authorized by the Vice President.[5]

***

September 11, 2001, has entered history books as the epitome of international terrorism and the event that made the global war against it both necessary and unavoidable. On that day, 2,986 people perished: 2,752 died in New York City, 189 in Washington DC, and 45 in Shanksville, Pennsylvania. Bin Laden summed up the events of that day, "The values of this Western civilization under the leadership of America have been destroyed. Those awesome symbolic towers that speak of liberty, human rights, and humanity have been destroyed. They have gone up in smoke. . . . I tell you, freedom and human rights in America are destroyed."[6] In the face of such lethal conviction, it is important to remember that he who cries loudest is not necessarily right. In the words of the Austrian author and playwright Arthur Schnitzler, "Martyrdom has always been a proof of the intensity, never of the correctness of a belief."

Impact of 9/11 on Muslims in America

Professor Shibley Telhami describes some of the pain and confusion that befell American Arabs and Muslims after the September 11 attacks. He forces readers to stop for a moment and acknowledge the predicament of pious and loyal American Arabs and Muslims, who had been conducting normal lives, raising families, working, and studying when 9/11 forced itself on their lives. As he points out, "Most Arabs in America are not Muslim, and most Muslims [in America] are not Arabs."[7] In fact, many Arab and Muslim Americans also lost loved ones and friends on 9/11. Following the attacks, one of this community's first proclamations was that bin Laden did not represent Islam and that his message of conflict between Islam and the West was unacceptable.[8]

OVERREACH? WISHFUL PLANNING MEETS REALITY

National Security Analyst James Robbins analyzed the strategic rationale behind al-Qaeda's decision to attack the United States. Robbins concluded that while the terrorist organization correctly anticipated an American attempt to retaliate severely for the attacks, it counted on several premises its leaders believed would allow them to emerge victorious. In reality, as far as the war and its immediate aftermath were concerned, almost all their assumptions turned out to be strategic miscalculations.[9]

Expectations

First, al-Qaeda's leadership assumed that the inhospitable terrain of Afghanistan would deter the conventional American war machine. The Afghans' successful war against the mighty Soviet military filled them with confidence that if the United States were to launch air strikes or initiate a massive ground operation in Afghanistan, they would defeat the Americans just as they had defeated the Soviet Union. Second, bin Laden and his organization expected the Taliban to continue to shelter them and to join forces with them to repel an American attack.

Third, at the highest echelons of the organization, planners assumed that Pakistan would rush to their aid should there be a war against the United States in Pakistan's own backyard. This had been Pakistan's policy during the Afghan war against the Soviet Union. Fourth, al-Qaeda anticipated that an immense American attack in Afghanistan would trigger a riotous reaction in the "Muslim street." This violent reaction, they hoped, would force Muslim countries to oppose the American offensive, come to the Islamists' aid, and deter non-Muslim countries from supporting the United States. "[The way] to make God laugh," mused Woody Allen in another context, "[is to] tell him your future plans."

The Outcome

Within a few months, it became clear that the 9/11 attacks failed to cause deep and lasting damage to the American economy. They also proved counterproductive in terms of affecting the American public's morale, as the attacks actually galvanized the American public against al-Qaeda. More important, almost every premise guiding the terrorists' 9/11 onslaught would prove wrong, at least in terms of the immediate war and the subsequent few years.

Instead of launching a conventional war against the Islamic forces in Afghanistan, the Americans surprised al-Qaeda and its Taliban allies. Rather than sending convoys of trucks to be ambushed, columns of tanks to prove useless at the slopes of mountains, and aimlessly carpet bombing mountain ridges—as had been the practice of the Soviet Union—the United States military did the unexpected and struck with ingenious creativity.

Instead of the Islamic forces fighting a guerilla war against a huge invading army, the United States engaged them asymmetrically; that is, the Americans engaged in a guerrilla war against the Islamic forces, who found themselves fighting as a stationary conventional military burdened with ineffective heavy military platforms, such as tanks and artillery. At the strategic level, the United States forged an alliance with indigenous segments of the population, mainly the Northern Alliance, who opposed the Taliban rule. Thousands of these fighters became a conventional infantry to take physical control of territory. Al-Qaeda and the Taliban were routed in short order, with the terrorist organization's top leadership lucky to escape alive.

Al-Qaeda Morphing

Two processes changed the nature of Islamist terrorism in the years following the September 11, 2001, attacks. First, the successful American war in Afghanistan and the ongoing international effort to obliterate Islamist terrorism have registered certain tangible results. Terrorist leaders have been killed, many more have been taken out of circulation, radical groups' chain of command has been disrupted, and the groups' operational effectiveness has been hindered.

(Continued)

Second, reacting to these setbacks, the Islamists abandoned the centralized structure that dominated the organization before 9/11 and fragmented into small groups without a hierarchical chain of command that leads directly to al-Qaeda. As a result, various radical groups all over the world that share the same ideological convictions formed their own cells and to the best of their abilities, began operating independently. Although loosely affiliated with al-Qaeda, they do not need specific instructions from bin Laden and his lieutenants because what needs to be done is clear to all. In essence, al-Qaeda has increasingly become more an inspiration than a structured organization involved in the details of operations. Even in its weakened state, however, al-Qaeda is still capable of orchestrating future mega attacks.

Al-Qaeda's expectation that the Taliban regime would support the organization to the end proved correct, but cost the Taliban control of Afghanistan and put its own leadership and many of its men on the run.

In what must have been a bitter surprise to al-Qaeda's leadership, Pakistan's General Pervez Musharraf made a strategic turnaround, abandoned al-Qaeda and joined ranks with the United States. Last, while 9/11 genuinely delighted numerous Muslims in all corners of the world, there was no widespread outpouring of fury in the "Muslim street" against the subsequent American offensive. The deliberate attempts to portray the American action as a war against Islam and a bloodletting of the Afghan population at a scale reminiscent of the Mongols' invasion of Muslim lands seven centuries before soon faltered as it became clear that the war was progressing with elegant ease and relatively little suffering to civilians.

In addition, the West and other non-Muslims actually rallied to the American cause. As Robbins described the reaction, "9/11 brought forth an outpouring of sympathy, and fostered a renewed respect for the United States. . . . [Bin Laden's brutality] reminded the civilized nations of the world what it means to be civilized."[10] Consequently, NATO members, as well as other countries, sent troops for Taliban-fighting missions to Afghanistan, and later for state-building missions as soon as it became feasible.

Did You Know?

In his State of The Union Address of January 29, 2002, President Bush labeled three countries, Iran, Iraq, and North Korea, as the "Axis of Evil." Most believe the phrase was used deliberately to mobilize the American public after 9/11 by reminding it of the World War II-era Axis powers of Germany, Italy, and Japan.

In addition to understanding al-Qaeda's operational thinking as it prepared for the September 11, 2001, strikes, we need to understand what causes motivated al-Qaeda to launch the attack in the first place and to consider whether it could have been avoided with a different American foreign policy.

PRELUDE TO DISASTER

The origins of the 9/11 attacks go back to the end of the Afghanistan war between the Soviet Union and its satellite regime and the Islamic forces. Once the war was over, there was no going back for this cadre of thousands of trained, experienced, and religiously committed fighters. There were other causes of Islam to fight for and the natural target was the leader of the West, the United States.

Beginning in 1988, zealots to the cause began to congregate around the Saudi multimillionaire of the Afghan war fame, Osama bin Laden. In turn, bin Laden would soon crystallize a name for the budding organization, *al-Qaeda*, "the base" in Arabic. While preparing—creating the infrastructure for the organization and spawning its international web—leaders of the organization studied the enemy's policies in the Middle East and drew lessons from them. Among these was the idea that the United States was a "paper tiger" that could be driven out of the Middle East and defeated with relative impunity.

The Ten Deadly Sins of Nondeterrence

The following milestones demonstrate an unmistakable pattern that influenced al-Qaeda's worldview in dramatic fashion and bolstered its leaders' conviction that they could take on the United States, and win:

1. *The Iranian hostage crisis*: On November 4, 1979, an Iranian mob led by students stormed and occupied the United States Embassy in Teheran. They captured 52 members of the staff and held them hostage for 444 days, instigating the first crisis between the new Islamic regime and the United States. With diplomacy proving futile, President Carter ordered a rescue operation. The mission, code-named "Eagle Claw," took place on the night of April 24, 1980, and ended disastrously. The failure was a bonanza for the revolutionary regime and helped it consolidate power as it demonstrated its ability to take on the United States and prevail. Iran released the hostages only when the Reagan administration took office.

2. *Bombing of the American embassy in Beirut*: On April 18, 1983, Shi'i terrorists, the precursor of present day's Hezbollah, blew up the American Embassy in Beirut, Lebanon, killing 63 people. The United States did nothing in response.

3. *Bombing of the Marine barracks*: On October 23, 1983, the same group used a suicide bomber driving a truck bomb to kill 241 Marines sleeping in their barracks near the Beirut International Airport. This time, the result was even more telling: after deciding not to retaliate, the Reagan administration made an about-face and pulled all of its forces out of Lebanon, leaving the radical Shi'i Muslims and their Iranian supporters the clear winners in that country. In the region, people took notice.

4. *Targeting GIs in Yemen*: On December 29, 1992, al-Qaeda carried out an attack on Gold Mihor Hotel in Aden, Yemen, where some 100 American soldiers were supposed to be staying. The bombing killed a few people, none Americans. The fortunate soldiers had been dispatched to Somalia two days before the attack. Again, there was no overt American reaction.

5. *Fleeing Mogadishu*: In December of 1992, the United States sent military forces to Somalia as part of an international relief effort (known as *Operation Restore Hope*) in the aftermath of deadly civil strife. Al-Qaeda became involved. Its members, opposed to the international presence in a Moslem country, provided Somali rebels with shoulder-held rocket-propelled grenades (RPGs) and training on how to use them. On the night between October 3rd and 4th, 1993, a particularly intense battle developed between mostly American Special Forces and the rebels under a local warlord. Eighteen soldiers lost their lives and the sight of American dead dragged through the dirt in Mogadishu proved too much for Americans to stomach. Within six months, the Clinton administration withdrew its forces from the country. Again, al-Qaeda's leadership did not fail to take notice.

6. *The first attack on the World Trade Center*: On February 26, 1993, Islamist terrorists loosely affiliated with al-Qaeda bombed the North Tower of the World Trade Center, killing six people, injuring about 1,000, and causing considerable damage to the building.[11] The United States treated this incident as a criminal justice issue and not a military act, and prosecuted several of the culprits in civilian courts. Stubbornly, al-Qaeda remained committed to completing this mission.

7. *Bombing American passenger planes*: In 1995, the Islamist terrorist Ramzi Yousef, who had a leading role in the 1993 bombing of the World Trade Center, was arrested in the Philippines. Authorities soon discovered that he was planning to hijack an American passenger plane and crash it into CIA headquarters in the Virginia suburbs of Washington DC. Yousef was also readying a plan to blow up 11 American passenger planes over the Pacific Ocean. This plot was aborted, but the seeds of the operational principle took deep root. In the interim, no significant security measures were introduced in the United States to protect the aviation industry from a similar attack in the future.

8. *The Khobar Towers attack*: On June 25, 1996, Muslim terrorists not associated with al-Qaeda bombed the Khobar Towers, a housing complex for American servicemen and women in Dhahran, Saudi Arabia, killing 19 and wounding hundreds. Although Shi'i Hezbollah terrorists were implicated, along with their handlers in Iran, the American response was muted. Worse, the United States reacted meekly to the Saudi policy of keeping the Americans at arms length from the investigation into the bombing. From then on al-Qaeda upped the ante substantially in a demonstration of its growing organizational and operational muscle and its decreasing concern for a crushing American counterstrike.

9. *Attack on American embassies in Africa*: On August 7, 1998, al-Qaeda executed complex, simultaneous attacks on the American embassies in the African capitals of Nairobi, Kenya, and Dar es Salaam, Tanzania. Of the 224 people killed, 12 were American; both embassies were destroyed.

The United States reacted with a barrage of Tomahawk missiles on six al-Qaeda camps in Afghanistan and on a pharmaceutical company in Sudan, al Shifa, which was suspected of manufacturing nerve gas for al-Qaeda. Casualties were relatively light, an estimated 30–40 members of al-Qaeda, but bin Laden himself was unharmed. The attack on the pharmaceutical company in Khartoum, Sudan, proved embarrassing. In the words of then Deputy National Security Advisor, James Steinberg, the retaliation was "of little benefit, [caused] lots of blowbacks against [a] bomb-happy U.S."[12] The limited American reaction to these bombings reinforced the organization's conviction about the American resolve and abilities.

10. *Suicide-bombing of* USS Cole: On October 12, 2000, al-Qaeda orchestrated an attack on an American military target, the *USS Cole*, which was laying anchor in the Yemeni port of Aden. Two suicide bombers using a boat-bomb approached the *Cole* and detonated themselves next to the vessel, killing 17 sailors, wounding 39, and causing massive damage to the craft. After this full-fledged al-Qaeda assault, there was no American retaliation at all.

A Missed Opportunity?

Zacarias Moussaoui, a French national of Moroccan extraction, is a member of al-Qaeda who came to the United States to perpetrate a terrorist attack. When he was undergoing flight training in Eagan, Minnesota, his erratic behavior aroused suspicion and the FBI was alerted. He was arrested on August 16, 2001, only weeks before the 9/11 attacks. Although labeled "The 20th Hijacker," Moussaoui was probably not a member of the 9/11 plot, but was training for a different terrorist attack involving an airplane. Nevertheless, he might have known the general outlines of the 9/11 plot and prevented the catastrophe had he chosen to share that information with the authorities. Upon his arrest, the FBI did not try to obtain a warrant to search his laptop computer because it assumed that a Foreign Intelligence Surveillance Act (FISA) judge would reject the request. We will never know what a judge would have permitted, but, by not trying to obtain permission, the authorities forfeited the possibility of discovering information about the brewing 9/11 conspiracy before it was unleashed.

He was convicted of conspiracy in the 9/11 terrorist attacks, and on May 3, 2006, a defiant Moussaoui was sentenced to life in prison without the possibility of parole.

This sequence of events suggests a complete breakdown of American deterrence and, as a consequence, the inevitable, almost fatalistic straight line leading to the 9/11 attacks. By that time, al-Qaeda's leadership had come to view Americans as cowards: "the American Army is going downhill in its morale. Its members are too cowardly and too fearful to meet the young people of Islam face to face," bin Laden asserted in 1999.[13] Al-Qaeda's leadership came to characterize the United States as weak, ineffective, and vulnerable.[14] It was time to strike at the heart of what Islamists called the "Zionist–Crusader alliance." At this point in the timeline, the planning and training for the big strike on American soil had already been well underway.

WHAT AL-QAEDA REALLY WANTS

Al-Qaeda's ideological platform is no secret, but there are two schools of thought about its true meaning.

Genuine Grievances, Rational Objectives

Michael Scheuer, the former CIA official entrusted with countering al-Qaeda, forcefully represents the first point of view.[15] Scheuer maintains that bin Laden is neither a crazed nihilist nor an irrational fanatic who has targeted the United States because he hates what America stands for. Instead, the bin Laden phenomenon should be viewed as part of a worldwide Muslim insurrection that represents quite a broad grassroots consensus among Muslims.

Rather than hating Americans for what they *are*, writes Scheuer, al-Qaeda hates Americans for what they *do*. Chief among the grievances cited are

- support for Israel
- desecration of the sacred lands of Islam by stationing troops in the Arabian Peninsula
- occupation of Afghanistan and Iraq
- support of countries fighting their Muslim minorities in places like Kashmir, Chechnya, and Xinjiang (in China)
- support for secular, oppressive Arab and Muslim regimes
- Artificially low oil prices, which al-Qaeda contends are the result of American pressure on oil-producing Muslim countries.

Scheuer supports this thesis by quoting bin Laden, "America will not be able to leave this ordeal unless it leaves the Arabian Peninsula, and stops its involvement in Palestine, and in all the Islamic world . . . they shall remain restless, shall not feel at ease, and shall not dream of security until they take their hands off our nation and stop their aggression against us and their support for our enemies."[16]

Legitimizing the Killing of Millions

Al-Qaeda spokespeople and supportive theologians have gone on record legitimizing attacks on the United States with weapons of mass destruction. Drawing on Islamic scripture and precedents, they laid the foundation for future strikes based on the principle of reciprocity for the alleged Western killing of up to 10 million Muslims, which, therefore, justified the killing of 4 million to 10 million Western civilians.[17]

Since the Muslim grievances are real and widely shared, the author recommends a reevaluation of the premises behind American policies to determine whether staying the course is in the best American national interest.[18]

World Domination

The second school of thought does not give much credence to al-Qaeda's grievances. They point to numerous statements by Islamic radicals, whose hatred for the United States is religiously based and thus can only be quenched with the mass conversion of all Americans. In their view, there can be no appeasement of, or genuine negotiations or lasting peace treaties with, Islamists. As two experts on national security wrote of the Islamic radicals' list of complaints, "their grievances are ill-posed, self-serving, and dysfunctional (as when Islamists blame the West and the United States for the plight of Islamic states in the Middle East)."[19]

On Negotiating with Islamists

L. Paul Bremer III, counterterrorism expert and head of the Coalition Provisional Authority in Iraq from May 1, 2003, to June 28, 2004, analyzed the options for countering terrorist organizations like al-Qaeda. He concluded that negotiating with this type of terrorists is probably impossible since "Such groups are not trying to start negotiations. . . . These men do not seek a seat at the table; they want to overturn the table and kill everybody at it."[20]

In 2002, a prominent al-Qaeda theologian and, at the time, an official spokesman, Sulaiman Abu Ghaith, penned an influential sermon entitled "Why We Fight America," in which he explained the reasons behind the

September 11, 2001, attacks. After rendering the common anti-American complaints, he added one breathtaking motive. Under the heading "The Entire Earth Must Be Subject to Islam," he explains that the Muslim nation "was created to stand at the center of leadership, at the center of hegemony and rule . . ."[21] Explaining the 9/11 attacks, bin Laden himself was quoted as saying, "It is the step necessary to prod the [Islamic nation] to embrace Jihad and the final conflict with world Infidelity. Here, we are in a world where cause and effect lose all meaning."[22] In a video released in December of 2001, bin Laden promised his audience, "God willing, the end of America is imminent."[23]

Expressions like these bolster the point of view that the notion of accommodating Islamists is a nonstarter since their actual agenda goes beyond resisting specific American policies and aims for eventual world domination. Anyone who believes that this eventuality is not necessarily bad should consider author Helen Macinnes's warning that "Men who use terrorism as a means to power, rule by terror once they are in power."

What Do YOU Think?

Al-Qaeda and all other radical Islamic groups consistently call for the destruction of Israel. Indeed, the American position as Israel's chief benefactor is one of the Islamists' often-expressed complaints against the United States. Some leading American academicians and security experts have begun to wonder whether Israel has not turned into an albatross around the American neck. In their view, the special relationship between the two countries does not serve the U.S. national interest well and only drags the country unnecessarily toward a collision with hundreds of millions of angry Muslims worldwide.

Consider what would happen within a decade if the United Sates were to abandon Israel to its fate. Which of the following scenarios do you consider most likely? If an outcome different from these two extremes is possible, what might that be?

1. Israel will be destroyed and afterwards the United States will enjoy good relations with the Arab and Muslim world. With Israel gone, radical Islam will stop attacking American interests, the Middle East will become more stable, and the United States will return to the good graces of the Arab and Muslim fold.

2. Without American support, Israel will eventually be obliterated and millions will die. Afterwards, a euphoric and vindicated militant Islam will emerge more emboldened than ever before. A radicalized Middle East will become a springboard for ever-fiercer attacks on the West. In the United States, a debate will rage over the question of "who lost Israel?" as the once most powerful and pro-American country in the Middle East will have been replaced by an anti-Western Islamic Palestine.

A Giant Awakened

As Aristophanes wrote, "The truth is forced upon us, very quickly, by a foe." The United States was indeed caught off guard and paid a dear price for it. Nevertheless, following the 9/11 assault, the United States rallied behind the Bush administration as the country mobilized for war. The American retaliation was to be particularly resolute: "We will not waver, we will not tire, we will not falter, and we will not fail," vowed President George W. Bush.[24] A counter policy quickly crystallized, anchored in two pillars, the legislative and the military.

Congress, with uncharacteristic deference and unanimity, on September 14, 2001, passed a Use-of-Force Joint Resolution giving the president what one scholar termed "a blank check . . . [demonstrating] Congress's responsiveness to the public and the willingness of the legislative branch to follow Bush wherever he might lead."[25] Militarily, the United States trounced the Taliban, decimated *al-Qaeda*, and forced its surviving members into hiding. An outpouring of international sympathy consolidated political support for the United States and facilitated an American-led global effort to fight terrorism.

Once the Bush administration designated Iran, Iraq, and North Korea as the "Axis of Evil," the American war was not going to stop in Afghanistan. The shock waves of September 11 created a sea change in American foreign policy. To prevent future 9/11s, the administration's thinking went, the United States needed to get physically involved in the Middle East to "dry the swamp" of anti-American Islamic agitation. The assumption was that creating a model secular democracy in the region would generate in the region a tidal wave of goodwill toward the United States and its values, resulting in a positive spillover effect throughout the Middle East. Thus did September 11, 2001, effect an assertive American posture that was quickly turning into a tsunami headed toward Iraq.

Summary

In this chapter, you have learned the following:

1. Reading the official 9/11 Commission Report is strongly recommended in order to understand the unfolding of events on 9/11.
2. September 11, 2001, inflicted great pain on the Arab and Muslim communities in the United States.
3. Al-Qaeda's leadership miscalculated the effectiveness of the American reaction to 9/11.
4. There are two perspectives on al-Qaeda's endgame: (1) that its complaints and goals are rational and merit American soul searching, and (2) that its declared grievances and goals are simply pretexts and it is actually committed to establishing a worldwide Islamic caliphate.

5. The attacks of September 11, 2001, changed American foreign policy and put it on the warpath against not only Afghanistan but also Iraq.

❀❀❀

The devastating attacks of 9/11 left New York City in shock, incapacitated to some degree and struggling to get back to normalcy. The *New York Times* made one of the most memorable contributions toward helping the city move on, make sense of the horror, and begin the slow recovery process. In a remarkable initiative, the newspaper published 2,400 short stories in the months that followed, in which it profiled individual victims who had perished in the World Trade Center. Half a dozen *New York Times* reporters assisted by over 100 staff members did not write short biographies or obituaries; instead, the stories they wrote captured personal, even intimate glimpses of the individuals whose lives were so abruptly and brutally cut short. The stories told of the humanity of the victims and their idiosyncrasies the way relatives and friends eulogize loved ones.

The monumental series earned high praise all over the world. Known as *Portraits of Grief*, it is considered one of the best attempts to commemorate the dead humanely to help soothe the traumas of those left behind.

❀❀❀

NOTES

1. The 9/11 Commission Report, *Final Report of the National Commission on Terrorist Attacks upon the United States*, Authorized Edition (New York: W.W. Norton & Company, 2004), p. 8. For an insightful critique of this report, see Richard A. Posner's assessment in "The 9/11 Report: A Dissent," the *New York Times Book Review*, August 29, 2004. An additional recommended definitive work of these attacks is found in Lawrence Wright, *The Looming Tower: Al-Qaeda and the Road to 9/11* (New York: Alfred A. Knopf, 2006).

2. The phrase "being brought back to reality" was coined by Alan J. Cigler, ed., *Perspectives On Terrorism: How 9/11 Changed U.S. Politics* (New York: Houghton Mifflin Company, 2002), p. 6. The idea that that day was "a failure of deterrence," is from Davis and Jenkins, *Deterrence and Influence in Counterterrorism: A Component in the War on al Qaeda* (Santa Monica, CA: Rand, 2002), p. 59.

3. Jessica Stern, *Why Religious Militants Kill: Terror in the Name of God* (New York: HarperCollins Publishers, Inc., 2003), p. 260.

4. The information about the four hijackings is based mainly on the 9/11 Commission Report.

5. Ibid., pp. 40–41.

6. Quoted in "Transcript of Bin Laden's October Interview," CNN.com/WORLD, February 5, 2002, http://archives.cnn.com/2002/WORLD/asiapcf/south/02/05/binladen.transcript/ (accessed on May 30, 2007).

7. Shibley Telhami, "Arab and Muslim America: A Snapshot," in Cigler, ed., pp. 12–13.

8. Ibid., p. 14.

9. James S. Robbins, "Bin Laden's War," in Russell D. Howard and Reid L. Sawyer, eds., *Terrorism and Counterterrorism: Understanding The New Security Environment* (Guilford, CT: McGraw-Hill/Dushkin, 2003), pp. 354–366.

10. Ibid., p. 360.

11. For an unusually insightful account of the 1993 World Trade Center bombing, see the version offered by the former detective in charge of antiterrorism intelligence for the Port Authority of New York and New Jersey, which also operated the World Trade Center: Peter Caram, *The 1993 World Trade Center Bombing: Foresight and Warning* (London: Janus Publishing Company, 2001).

12. Quoted in 9/11 Commission Report, p. 120.

13. "Wrath of God, Osama bin Laden Lashes Out Against the West," *Time*, January 11, 1999, as quoted in Davis and Jenkins, p. 26.

14. Quoted in Davis and Jenkins, p. 59.

15. See Anonymous, *Imperial Hubris: Why the West Is Losing the War on Terror* (Washington, DC: Brassey's, Inc., 2004)

16. Quoted in Ibid., p. 153.

17. See, for example, Sulaiman Abu Ghaith, "Why We Fight America," in Paul L. Williams, *The Al Qaeda Connection: International Terrorism, Organized Crime, and the Coming Apocalypse* (Amherst, New York: Prometheus Books, 2005), p. 21; Shaykh Nasir bin Hamid al Fahd, "A Treatise on the Legal Status of Using Weapons of Mass Destruction Against Infidels," as quoted in Anonymous, p. 156.

18. See Anonymous, pp. 252–259.

19. Davis and Jenkins, pp. 28–29.

20. L. Paul Bremer III, "A New Strategy for the New Face of Terrorism," in Gus Martin, ed., *The New Era of Terrorism: Selected Readings* (Dominguez Hills, CA: Sage Publications, 2004), p. 244.

21. Sulaiman Abu Ghaith is quoted in Williams, pp. 16–17.

22. Bin Laden is quoted in Daniel Benjamin and Steve Simon, *The Age of Sacred Terror* (New York: Random House, 2002), p. 158.

23. Ibid., p. 161.

24. President Bush's vow is quoted in Jeremy D. Meyer, *9–11: The Giant Awakens* (Belmont, CA: Wadsworth/Thomson Learning, 2003), p. 18. The subheading of this section, "A Giant Awakened," paraphrases the title of Meyer's book.

25. Ibid., p. 28.

CHAPTER

12

The Double-Edged Sword

The Media and Terrorism

Publicity is the oxygen of terrorism

Margaret Thatcher

💣💣💣

It was in line with the arrangement that had worked so well in the past. The leaders of the German Red Army Faction (RAF) were in jail in Germany and their followers called on their allies in the Marxist Popular Front for the Liberation of Palestine (PFLP) for help. On October 13, 1977, a four-member PFLP team hijacked Lufthansa Flight LH181 with 91 people aboard and demanded the release of the RAF leaders, or else. Early in the drama, the captain of the plane, Jurgen Schumann, managed to transmit information about the hijackers to the authorities. A radio station happened upon this information and put it on the air. When the hijackers discovered what the captain had done, they murdered him during a stopover in the Yemeni capital of Aden. Two days later, while the hijacked plane was on the tarmac in Mogadishu, Somalia, the West German antiterrorist unit GSG 9 effected a successful rescue operation. The commando team liberated the hostages and eliminated the terrorists, but the rescue came too late for captain Schumann, who paid with his life for the media indiscretion.

💣💣💣

A debate rages over the Western media's role in terrorism. On one side of the debate are those who view the media as consciously or inadvertently complicit

180

Did You Know?

Worldwide, 23 multinational corporations own over 80% of the global mass media. In the United States, the entire membership of the Board of Directors of the "big 10" media giants consists of just 118 people who, for the most part, also sit on one another's corporate boards! Think of the impact they can have on the direction media coverage takes on the war against terrorism.

in promoting terrorists' causes. Unimpressed, opponents reject this perspective with equal conviction.

"Terrorism is theater," is a frequently quoted phrase coined by terrorism expert Brian Jenkins.[1] Indeed, terrorists thrive on publicity and view media coverage of their actions and agenda as vital for achieving their strategic goals. In fact, some terrorist attacks have been specifically timed and choreographed to generate maximum exposure to the public.

"Death to Carter!"

In 1979, a frenzied mob acting with the blessing of the new Iranian government stormed the United States embassy in Teheran and took 52 Americans hostage in violation of international law. Skillfully staged for the media, the following 444 days saw daily "spontaneous" demonstrations by crowds shouting anti-American slogans. An eye witness recounted how locals congregating idly near the embassy suddenly came to life one day when they spotted a Canadian TV crew about to start shooting. People now looked angry and agitated, raising their fists in the air and burning American flags. Two minutes later, when the Canadian crew stopped shooting, the demonstration ended. However, when the Canadians needed another take, only in French this time, the crowd again leaped to its feet, this time "spontaneously" shouting, "Mort à Carter."[2]

Abetting this need for attention is the fact that the media are not always value-free, detached, and objective. The purpose of big business is to make money and since people are interested in terrorist incidents, the media satisfies the demand regardless of the wishes of government or the cost to the victims, as long as doing so ensures high ratings. As some scholars have noted "the mass media are large, profit seeking corporations, owned and controlled by wealthy people, heavily dependent on advertising for revenue."[3] Because few news items can rivet an audience as can a bloodcurdling incident of terrorism broadcast live, it may be naive to consider the coverage of terrorist incidents as agenda-free even in the freest of democracies.

What Do YOU Think?

A storm of controversy erupted in April 2003 when it was learned that CNN had withheld information about specific cases of killing and torture by the Iraqi regime prior to the Iraq war. CNN responded that exposing the cases would probably have resulted in the deaths of the witnesses. Critics, however, charged CNN with choosing presence in Baghdad and continued access to sources within the regime over the journalistic duty of reporting the facts regardless of the consequences. In your opinion, what course of action should CNN have followed?

COLLABORATORS OR SCAPEGOATS?

There are differing perspectives about the role of the media. We will examine two representative scholarly approaches, each illustrated with relevant examples in order to explain each point of view.[4]

Framing the Message

Robert Picard conceptualized four types of reporting:

1. The *information* tradition: Presents information factually and reliably.
2. The *sensationalist* tradition: Presents information in a style that gives rise to emotions—fear, anger, alarm, and so forth.
3. The *feature story* tradition: Presents information by focusing on one individual's saga, portraying him or her as a hero, villain, or victim in order to personalize the story; at times this focus is at the expense of a deeper coverage of the issues involved.
4. The *didactic* tradition: Presents information with the goal of educating the public; this potentially biased approach uses documentaries and other nontraditional means of reporting.[5]

What Do YOU Think?

What should the role of the media in a free society be at a time when the nation is engaged in a "war against terrorism"? If a "disconnect" exists between the government and the citizenry during such a war, should the media be blamed? Explain your position.

THE MEDIA: HANDMAIDENS OF TERRORISM

Bruce Hoffman's view is representative of those who view the media as beneficiaries of terrorist incidents and, therefore, as indirect promoters of the terrorists' agenda of gaining publicity for their struggle.[6] More important, however, Hoffman points out that regardless of this tendency by the media, research shows no evidence that the media coverage influences public opinion favorably toward the terrorists. The media do not serve the interests of terrorists deliberately; they do so for reasons of business—scenes of terrorists' actions attract viewers—and because it is technologically possible to do so.

The dramatic growth in the sensationalization of terrorist incidents by the media since the 1970s is attributed to three technical developments: (1) the portability of the mini–video camera, (2) the battery-powered video recorder that could be carried to remote areas, and (3) the satellite technology that makes instant transmission straight to the television sets throughout the world possible.[7]

The consequences were siginifcant because they laid the foundation for the nature of media coverage of terrorism for decades to come. Technology provided the ability to instantly transmit breaking news, but there is only so much "new" news that happens at any given time. What were commercial media to do to retain the maximum number of viewers, which they needed in order to recoup the cost of maintaining a broadcast crew on the scene? The solution arrived at was to keep the audience riveted to the ongoing saga by all means possible, including "human interest" stories focused on the unfolding personal agony of victims' families. As a result, instead of a hard-nosed examination of the important facts and an analysis of the broader context leading to the event, the media focus much of their coverage on secondary aspects.[8]

The need to engage the public at any cost at the expense of actual news has proven a bonanza for terrorists, whose goal is to have their message repeated to as many viewers as possible as often as possible. The result, concludes Hoffman, is that instead of a responsible approach to covering incidents of terrorism, the media have concentrated on the "trivial, the marginal and the irrelevant in the search for excitement. Colour photos, lurid images and sensational headlines splashed across the front pages of tabloids . . . an obssession with voyeuristic

Did You Know?

According to the former deputy of the Shabac, Israel's equivalent of the FBI, during the Palestinian first Intifadah (1987–1991), foreign correspondents used to instigate Palestinian violence against Israelis in order to obtain interesting footage of the conflict. The going rate was $50 for televised incidents of stone-throwing and $100 for staged attacks on Israelis with firebombs.[9]

detail now predominates . . . dictated by the same financial pressures and declining revenues that have ravaged network television news."[10]

Coverage Run Amok

To illustrate this point, Hoffman provides a convincing account of the media's behavior in the crisis that followed the hijacking of a TWA passenger plane to Beirut. While on route from Cairo to Rome, on June 14, 1985, TWA Flight 847 was hijacked by Shi'i terrorists from Lebanon, the predecessors of Hezbollah. When the hijacked plane landed in Beirut, Lebanon, the 39 hostages were whisked away to safe houses thoughout the city to prevent a rescue attempt. It soon became clear that the hijackers were part of a larger operation aimed at securing the release of hundreds of Shi'i combatants captured by Israel in exchange for the release of the hijacked TWA passengers.

A 17-day crisis ensued in which the media became willing participants in a staged drama. A fleet of media personnel descended on Beirut to cover the story, 85 of whom were members of the three major American television networks (ABC, CBS, and NBC). In an atmosphere of a media frenzy, the terror of the hostages and their families was turned into a circus that is cited to this day as an example of media irresponsibility.

During the crisis, it was evident that the media was making the terrorists seem sympathetic. From interviewing a weeping mother in the United States pleading with the administration to give the hostage-takers whatever they demanded so that her son would return safely to a reporter suggesting that all would be resolved if only the Israelis released the Shi'i fighters and the terrorists released their hostages, deliberately or inadvertendly the media helped promote the terrorists' agenda. This coverage tied the administration's hands and worked in favor of the terrorists. In some circles at the time, the networks were renamed *AMAL Broadcasting Company* (ABC) for the Shi'i group AMAL, and *Nabih Berry Company* (NBC), for their leader.

"Loose Lips Sink Ships"

So read a famous World War II poster. Something similar might apply to newspapers reporting on hijackings. One of the first stops the hijacked TWA plane made was the Algiers Airport in Algeria. Delta Force deployed to the scene to attempt a rescue. As if the hijackers were operating incommunicado, isloated from supporters who also followed the news, the New York Times published a story saying that the United States had sent a commando team to the Mediteranean to storm the hijacked plane. The newspaper identified the Delta Force by name and stated that the team had left its base in Fort Bragg that Saturday. This squandered the military option. Following the publication of this story, the hijackers left Algiers for Beirut, rendering the rescue virtually impossible.[11]

In his analysis of this episode, Hoffman highlights the following events:

1. In the days prior to cable news networks, the three American television networks broadcast almost 500 news segments concerning this hijacking, or 28.8 per day!
2. Fourteen out of 21 net minutes of nightly news focused on the hostage crisis.
3. To retain the public's attention to the story, a third of the coverage was devoted to "human interest" stories, including interviews with the hostages' understandably upset families, where their opinion about ways to resolve the crisis was asked for.

Reporters, rather than conveying the news, took it upon themselves to make news and to influence policymaking. This last observation is most telling. The media let itself be manipulated by media experts supporting the terrorists, who would meet daily to plan the following day's media campaign, including which of the American networks would get interviews and with whom. Since the objective was to influence American public opinion, media personnel who were not American or who were not television reporters were ignored by the terrorists. With the media providing the terrorists a wealth of exposure they probably had not dared expect, the result was that the U.S. government had no choice but to force its Israeli ally to capitulate to the terrorists' demands and release 756 imprisoned Shi'i fighters. Equating combatants with innocent airline passengers set a precedent that would haunt the West for years to come.

This was not an isolated episode. Another well-documented case often cited by those who are concerned about the media's coverage of terrorism is the audacious act of terrorism that took place right in the heart of Washington DC on a March day in 1977. A dozen Muslim terrorists calling themselves *Hanafi* stormed three buildings—the Islamic Center, the headquarters of the Jewish organization B'nai Brith, and the City Hall of the District of Columbia—near the White House and took 134 occupants hostage. Chief among the terrorists' demands were to stop showing a movie about the life of the Prophet Muhammad—an act of blasphemy in Islam—and to surrender to them the convicted murderers of the family of the terrorists' leader, Hamaas Abdul Khaalis, and their accomplices.

The following is a sample of what occurred during the 39-hour crisis:

1. The media ran live coverage flattering to the terrorists.
2. Reporters phoned the terrorists directly, tying up the lines and making it more difficult for police negotiators to communicate with the hostage takers.
3. Live television coverage enabled the terrorists to find out that a group of frightened civilians who had evaded them was hiding on another floor.
4. Reporters speculated on the air that boxes containing ammunition to be used in an assault on the terrorists were being lifted to one of the floors

---

What Do YOU Think?

As you reflect on the unfolding events in the Hanafi terrorist incident, what should the media have done in discharging their responsibilities covering this incident?

---

when in fact the boxes contained food. This information agitated the terrorists and intensified the crisis.

5. One reporter from the Associated Press asked the terrorist leader if he had given a deadline to authorities when in fact he hadn't.

6. Another reporter suggested to the leader, Khaalis, that the authorities were attempting to trick him. This prompted him to designate some hostages for execution in the event of a showdown.

7. A TV station in Washington aired a 40-second clip from the movie about the life of the Prophet Muhammad, which may have added fuel to the fire, since this was one of the terrorists' main grievances.

8. Another reporter asked the hostage takers, "How can you believe the police?" In the words of one analyst, "it was as if an alliance was formed between the terrorists and the media against the police." While authorities attempted to buy time with regard to the terrorists' demands to hand over to them the convicted killers of their leader's family, a reporter told the terrorists that one of the convicts was actually in Washington DC, thus undermining the police negotiators' credibility.[12]

The tense standoff ended after 39 hours, following mediation by the ambassadors of Egypt, Iran, and Pakistan. One man was killed and 12 were wounded in the episode.

THE MEDIA: IMPARTIAL CONVEYERS OF INFORMATION

Anecdotal evidence correlating the media to terrorism has its entertainment value—some cases make for fascinating reading—but serious research has found no evidence that the media promotes or advances the cause of terrorists by influencing the audience in their favor.

Opposing Hoffman's view, others see the media as conveyers of information simply trying to carry out their mandate on behalf of the public in spite of pressures from government and threats from terrorists. Moreover, the few juicy tales of media mishaps some analysts so delight in presenting, attest in fact, in their view, to the opposite conclusion. They point out that the huge volume of media work conducted ceaselessly, around the clock and around the world, provides only few examples of wrongdoing because the overwhelming majority of reporting is essentially fair and responsible. The very few slip-ups generate critics' attention because they are the exception to the rule and result in bad publicity that obscures the overall exemplary level of the media's performance. In addition, in an era dominated by the Internet, satellite TV, cable and network TV, and a host of print venues, it is unrealistic to think of information as concentrated in the hands of a few manipulative entities with an irresponsible agenda. What's more, there are a few bad apples in any industry.

Those who take the view that the media are professionals doing their best under challenging circumstances often cite their conscientious approach in reporting the takeover of the Iranian embassy in London in 1980 and the responsible policy of the editors of the *Washington Post* and the *New York Times* regarding the publication of the Unabomber's political manifesto.

Keeping the Lid On

Following the Iranian Revolution, six Arab–Iranian dissidents of the Mahealdin Al-Naser Martyr Group took over the Iranian embassy in London on May 5, 1980. The terrorists took 26 people hostage and threatened to kill them and blow up the embassy unless their demands were met. As a team of the famed British Special Air Service (SAS) commando unit prepared to storm the embassy, some media were kept updated by the authorities and advised of the impending rescue operation. Premature revelation of the imminent raid would have had disastrous consequences, but the media—despite the temptation to go live with the scoop—acted responsibly and did not broadcast the information. Even as the operation commenced and SAS commandos stormed the building in broad daylight with the cameras of both the BBC and ITN rolling, the media did not broadcast the unfolding drama. Instead, they waited until the operation was over and only then broadcast clips of the rescue effort. The raid was a spectacular success—five of the terrorists were killed, the sixth captured, and all the hostages were freed—partly due to the restraint of those in the media.[13]

Helping the Authorities

He was a lone terrorist whose deadly actions earned him a top spot on the FBI's "Most Wanted" list and a starring role in a decade-long manhunt for the person known as the *Unabomber*.

Theodore John Kaczynski was born in Chicago in 1942 and, early on, was considered both a prodigy and something of a social enigma. He entered Harvard at the age of 16 and majored in mathematics, the same subject in which, in 1967, he would earn a Ph.D. from the University of Michigan at Ann Arbor. Kaczynski taught mathematics at the University of California at Berkley from 1967 to 1969, when he resigned and dropped out of sight.

Mentally unbalanced but rational, Kaczynski developed an obsession with what he considered the global danger of technology. Living the life of a hermit in a cabin in the wilderness of Montana, the recluse unleashed a series of letter/package bombs from 1978 to 1996 by using the postal service. During those 18 years, Kaczynski killed three people and wounded 28 others.

He also tried and failed to blow up a passenger plane in 1979. Except for the attack on the commercial airliner, all of his bombs were sent to specific individuals—symbolic targets he believed were associated with technology. In 1995, he offered to voluntarily end his attacks if his 35,000-word essay (that became known as his "manifesto") was published in the *Washington Post* and the *New York Times*.

The policy of both major newspapers was not to succumb to terrorists' pressures and publicize their demands under duress, and the managements of both publications agonized over the issue for months. Federal authorities, including Attorney General Janet Reno, finally intervened and asked the newspapers to publish the document on the grounds (1) that its publication might save lives (2) and in the hope that if it was published, somebody would recognize the content and identify him. Both publishers acquiesced for the sake of public safety and published the document in full in September of 1995.

Theodore Kaczynski's younger brother, David, did, in fact, recognize the ideas in the manifesto and, in April 1996, turned his brother in. It was determined that Kaczynski was competent to stand trial, and a plea deal was arranged in which he was sentenced to spend the rest of his life in prison without the possibility of parole.

THE MEDIA: WALKING A TIGHTROPE

Aware of the possibility that when covering terrorism the media are damned if they do and damned if they don't, and with the profit factor notwithstanding, Raphael Perl suggests that we need to look at the relationship between the media and terrorism from three perspectives: (1) what terrorists want from the media; (2) what governments want from the media; and (3) what the media itself wants.[14]

Reporting the News: A Dangerous Trade

Members of the media often put their own well-being on the line as they perform their service to the public. The increasing indifference to the rule of law that characterizes many current conflicts has taken its toll on reporters as well. Reporters Without Borders, which tracks statistics on the number of journalists who have lost their lives in the line of duty, reports a growing trend that leaves little room for doubt about the danger reporters face: 25 were killed in 2002, 40 in 2003, 53 in 2004, and 63 in 2005. In Iraq, 71 reporters and dozens of other media employees were killed in approximately the first three years. In addition, in 2005, 119 reporters were imprisoned in countries around the globe.[15]

In thinking about the role the media play in covering terrorism, it is important to be mindful of their humanity and their mission and the fact that when covering conflicts, more often than not, they operate in hostile countries to the chagrin of the powers-that-be and at the mercy of warlords, thugs, and terrorists.

What Terrorists Want from the Media

Often, terrorists seek to manipulate the media in order to

- obtain *free publicity* for their cause, preferably *sympathetic coverage*;
- have the media report in a way that *projects legitimacy* for their cause and methods;
- *help legitimize their front organizations* by depicting them as independent entities, while these "charities," "clubs," "study centers," and "associations" continue to provide for their needs;
- cultivate good mutual relationships with the media in the hope that they will *share with them information* about the identity of hostages, as well as any information the media might have of plans by law enforcement; and
- *hurt the government* by exposing its inaptitude and spreading information that causes panic and damages the economy.

What Governments Want from the Media

Governments, too, seek to manipulate the media to further their cause. Essentially, they would like the media to

- *promote the government's perspective* about terrorist-related events;
- *portray the terrorists negatively;*
- provide to the government information that is not already available to it regarding terrorist incidents;
- help *lower tensions* in crisis situations;
- *avoid broadcasting "human interest" stories* that put pressure on the government to yield to terrorists' demands;
- *treat confidentially sensitive information,* such as planned rescue operations or the identity of hostages;
- *keep secret methods and techniques* used by the government even after a terrorist incident is over;
- *avoid being manipulated* by the terrorists or their supporters;
- *report favorably about the government* policies and conduct;
- *inform authorities about any planned terrorist actions* they may have become privy to; and
- *actively cooperate by deliberately disseminating misinformation* to mislead the terrorists.

In addition, the government would like to *distance the media from the terrorists* to prevent them from making their case to the public.

What the Media Wants

The media would like to remain professional and provide accurate information despite attempts by terrorists and governments to manipulate them. They also want to

- be the first to convey a breaking story;
- maximize the drama and timeline of the story;
- be safe from legal harassment, intimidation, and physical attack resulting from unfavorable coverage to either side;
- protect the public's right to access information from all parties; and
- help as much as possible without compromising professional and ethical responsibilities.

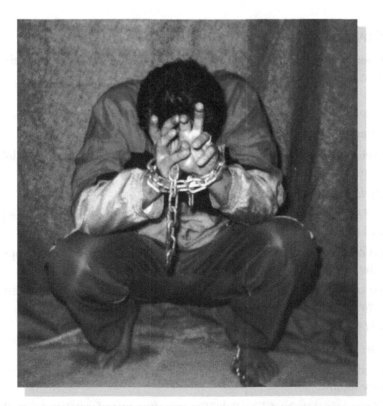

Kidnapped *Wall Street Journal* Reporter Daniel Pearl, Before Islamist Terrorists Murdered him in Pakistan in 2002
Source: Courtesy of AP Wide World Photos.

What Do YOU Think?

In an often-quoted assertion, former Israeli prime minister Benjamin Netanyahu wrote, "there is apparently a moment of truth in the life of many modern democracies when it is clear the unlimited defense of civil liberties has gone too far and impedes the protection of life and liberty, and governments decide to adopt active measures against the forces that menace their societies."[16] With the Patriot Act in mind, do you agree with Netanyahu that some democratic societies may reach a point where they have to curtail civil liberties, possibly including freedoms of the press, in order to increase their publics' safety?

THE MEDIA AND STATE-TERRORISM

When discussing the relationship between terrorism and the media, we intuitively tend to think of terrorist organizations' attempts to harness the media for their purposes. In fact, terrorists have been far more effective in using the media ruthlessly when they are in power and employ terrorism against their own populations—state-terrorism.

One author conceptualized the issue as "terrorism from below" and "terrorism from above." In the former, from the Armed Forces of National Liberation (FALN) in Colombia through the Irish IRA to the Palestinian Islamic Jihad, sub-state organizations try to use the media to promote their cause. In the latter, from Nazi Germany through the Soviet Union and Syria to North Korea—to name just a few such cases—undemocratic governments use the media relentlessly to indoctrinate the masses, control the flow of selective information, and perpetuate their own regimes.[17]

CONCLUSIONS

Scholars and experts go back decades to draw conclusions about the Western media's coverage of terrorism. However, simply scanning the media's involvement over the years is insufficient, because it is easy enough to find opinions and events to support one's exisiting points of view. Analysts may not deliberately set out to reinforce a given belief, but there have been so many cases of terrorism in modern history that it is easy to find examples that validate any presupposition. Thus, neither of the two mainstream perspectives provide a conclusive answer to the question regarding the role the media plays in relation to terrorism.

A Word of Caution: The First Amendment

While analyzing the conduct of the media in relation to terrorism, we cannot ignore the crucial role the First Amendment of the U.S. Constitution plays in the debate.

What Do YOU Think?

During a televised 1987 discussion among military top brass and the media icons Mike Wallace and Peter Jennings, the following interesting hypothetical was raised: During hostilites involving the United States, an American reporter is invited by the enemy to report on one of their units. While with that unit, the reporter realizes that an unsuspecting American force is heading straight into an ambush. Would he warn his countrymen? Both Wallace and Jennings agreed that their highest duty was to report the event, not to help fellow Americans.[18] Were they right? If so, why? If not, why not?

It is unrealistic and perhaps counterproductive to discuss the role of the media without understanding the broader context of freedom of expression in the United States. Ratified in 1791, the amendment concerns the freedom of religion, the press, and of expression. It reads,"Congress shall make no law respecting an establishment of religion, or prohibiting the free exercise thereof; or abridging the freedom of speech, or of the press; or the right of the people peaceably to assemble, and to petition the Government for a redress of grievances." This precious law looms high over any expectation that the media will limit their own responsibilities or allow themselves to be manipulated in any way so as to help an administration burdened with the needs *de joure* of a security crisis or a war.

A Lost "Fairness Doctrine"

U.S. News and World Report Editor-in-Chief Mortimer Zuckerman argues that in the past, the American public trusted the media because the perception was that the reporting was fair and represented the middle of the ideological divide on various issues. According to him, this confidence has eroded for a variety of reasons and today only 50% of the public express faith in the reporting of the major media.[19]

The dangerous ramifications of curtailing the media's freedoms because of current public safety concerns are hard to exaggerate. The nineteenth-century newsman Wilbur F. Storey tried to educate his contemporaries about the role of the media and the sanctity of freedom of expression, warning that "it is a newspaper's duty to print the news and raise hell." From this vantage point, imposing limitations on the freedom of speech as part of the war on terrorism may be the ominous first step on a slippery slope whose end cannot be foreseen.

SUMMARY

In this chapter, you have learned the following:

1. The Western media plays a crucial role in shaping the public's attitude toward the war against terrorists.

2. In the United States, free expression, including freedom of the press, is guaranteed by the First Amendment of the Constitution.

3. A debate exists over whether the media supports the war on terrorism or hinders it.

4. The paramount issue concerning the media's coverage of terrorism is the exact role the media is expected to play in this regard.

💣💣💣

On October 30, 1994, the BBC broadcast its "From Our Own Correspondent" program. It included a dispatch from a BBC reporter who described her feelings as the ailing Yasser Arafat was flown from his headquarters in the West Bank to Europe for medical treatment. For a news organization such as the BBC, which is presumed to be impartial in its reporting, the words were quite stunning: "When the helicopter carrying the frail old man rose from his ruined compound," recalled the BBC reporter, "I started to cry." Angry complaints from listeners protesting the biased, sentimental coverage forced the BBC's Governors' Program Complaints Committee to admit to "editorial misjudgment." The episode cast a worrisome shadow over the BBC's coverage of other terrorist-related aspects of its reporters' dispatches from the Middle East.[20]

💣💣💣

NOTES

1. Brian M. Jenkins, "International Terrorism: A New Mode Of Conflict," in David Carlton and Carlo Schaerf, ed., *International Terrorism and World Security* (New York: John Wiley and Sons, 1974), pp. 13–49. The quote is found on page 16.

2. The Teheran mob demonstrating outside the United States embassy is described in A. P. Schmid, "Terrorism and the Media: The Ethics of Publicity," in *Terrorism and Political Violence*, Vol. 1, No. 4 (October, 1989), pp. 539–565. The episode is mentioned on page 559, citing *Der Spiegel*, Vol. 33, No. 4 (December 3, 1979), p. 159.

3. The quote regarding the media as big business is found in Pamela L. Griset and Sue Mahan, *Terrorism in Perspective* (Thousand Oaks: Sage Publications, 2003), p. 134.

4. In addition to these two perspectives, there are other important schools of thought regarding the media. One influential school of thought is represented by

scholars who emphasize the control that corporations and the government exercise over the media. It is not covered in this chapter because our discussion of the media is narrowly focused on the issue of terrorism. For a sample of the school of thought which focuses on the control the corporate world yields over the media, see Edward S. Herman and Robert W. McChensey, *The Global Media: The New Missionaries of Gobal Capitalism* (Washington: Cassell, 1997); Todd Gitlin, *Media Unlimited: How the Torrent of Images and Sounds Overwhelms Our Lives* (New York: Metropolitan Books, 2001); and Michael Parenti, *Inventing the Politics of News Media Reality*, 2nd ed. (New York: St. Martin's Press, 1993).

5. The four traditions of reporting are found in Robert P. Picard, *Media Portrayals of Terrorism: Functions and Meaning of News Coverage* (Iowa: State University Press, 1993), p. 103.

6. For Hoffman's perspective on the media, see Bruce Hoffman, *Inside Terrorism* (New York: Columbia University press, 1998), pp. 131–155.

7. Grant Wardlaw, *Political Terrorism: Theory, Tactics, and Counter-measures* (Cambridge, MA: Cambridge University Press, 1990), p. 80.

8. Hoffman's explanation of the advantage the soft type of television coverage has accorded terrorists is found on pages 138–142.

9. The Israeli assertion that foreign media occasionally paid Palestinians to foment violence is found in Raphael Cohen-Almagor, "The Terrorists' Best Ally: Media Coverage of Terror." This chapter from a future book can be found at http://www.inter-disciplinary.net/ati/violence/v5/almagor%20paper.pdf.

10. For Hoffman's quote regarding the results the advent of technology has had on the type of coverage the media provides, see Ibid., p. 141.

11. The story of the media alerting the world to the secret arrival of Delta Force can be found in Bernard Gwertzman, "U.S. said to send commando squad," *New York Times*, June 16, 1985, pp. 1, 11.

12. On the media's dangerous mischief during the standoff with the *Hanafis*, see Raphael Cohen-Almagor. This chapter from a future book can be found at http://www.inter-disciplinary.net/ati/violence/v5/almagor%20paper.pdf.

13. For more of the Media's role in the SAS rescue operation, see Ibid.

14. The discussion regarding what terrorists and governments want from the media and what the media itself desires can be found in Raphael F. Perl, "Terrorism, The Media, And The Government: Perspectives, Trends, and Options for Policymakers," in Griset and Mahan, pp. 143–149.

15. For the website of *Reporters Without Borders*, see http://www.rsf.org/rubrique.php3?id_rubrique=20. The statistics concerning the number of media casualties in the Iraq war can be found in Marc Santora and Bill Carter, "War in Iraq Becomes the Deadliest Assignment for Journalism in Modern Times," *New York Times*, May 30, 2006, p. A10.

16. Benjamin Netanyahu's quote is found in *Fighting Terrorism: How Democracies can Defeat Domestic and International Terrorists* (New York: Farrar Straus Giroux, 1995), p. 33.

17. More on the discussion of "terrorism from above or below" can be found in Joseph S. Tuman, *Communicating Terror: The Rhetorical Dimensions of Terrorism* (Thousand Oaks: CA: Sage Publications, Inc., 2003), pp. 120–129.

18. The roundtable discussion involving the media and the generals is described in Stuart Taylor, Jr., "Legal Affairs: The Media, The Military, and Striking the Right Balance," in Alan J. Cigler, ed., *Perspectives On Terrorism: How 9/11 Changed U.S. Politics* (New York: Houghton Mifflin Company, 2002), p. 22.

19. The discussion of the "fairness doctrine" is found in Mortimer Zuckerman, "A House Divided," in *U.S. News and World Report*, Vol. 140, No. 6 (February 20, 2006), p. 72.

20. See *Reuters*, November 26, 2005, for the story of the weeping BBC correspondent.

13

The Femme Fatale

Women and Terrorism

Well behaved women rarely make history.

A bumper sticker

❦❦❦

The young woman's name was Thenmuli Rajaratnam, but she was better known as *Dhanu*. On May 21, 1991, she approached the former Indian prime minister Rajiv Gandhi, who was campaigning for upcoming parliamentary elections. After putting a garland around his neck, she knelt at his feet in a gesture of respect, and instantly detonated the bomb she was carrying on her body, killing herself, Gandhi, and 16 others.

The island of Sri Lanka, formerly known as Ceylon, is located south of India. The composition of the population is 75% Buddhist-Sinhalese, 12% Hindu-Tamils, and 8% Muslim-Arabs. Since 1975, in a separatist struggle, the Tamils have engaged in a bloody terrorist campaign against the Buddhist majority. In 1987, the then Indian prime minister Rajiv Gandhi sent troops to Sri Lanka in an attempt to end the campaign; they were met with resistance from the Tamils' terrorist group the Liberation Tigers of Tamil Elam (LTTE). In 1991, fearing that Gandhi might be reelected and would again send troops to Sri Lanka, the LTTE dispatched the young suicide-bomber.

❦❦❦

Two factors influence women to join terrorist groups in addition to ideological or nationalist motives. Both are personal. The first has to do with individual victimization. Numerous case studies demonstrate a correlation between personal injury inflicted on a woman, such as abuse, rape, or torture and her decision to turn to political violence. In addition, the death or arrest of a family member by security forces or any traumatic event that causes a woman to feel the need to reclaim her dignity or to help others within the collective escape a similar fate may drive her to violent action. Dhanu is said to have suffered from such a personal trauma.

The second factor is a romantic connection. More than formal explanations would make us believe, a relationship with a male terrorist is often responsible for a woman turning to terrorism. It is impossible to know what would have become of Gudrun Ensslin, the capable organizer and one-time declared pacifist, had she not become the girlfriend of Andreas Baader and helped him form what became the Baader–Meinhoff terrorist organization.[1]

In a general comment about women's struggles in a man's world, not in relation to the subject of terrorism, Charlotte Whitton, the Canadian politician and feminist, suggested that "Whatever women do they must do twice as well as men do to be thought half as good. Luckily, this is not too difficult." In reality, although women have been assuming increasingly prominent roles in social causes in general, full equality with men has not been achieved. However, as women began to fill active leadership roles in various social organizations, almost inevitably there was a spillover effect into terrorism. This new sense of assertiveness varies greatly by society, culture, and ideology; but the unprecedented trend is unmistakable. Gloria Steinem once quipped that "a woman without a man is like a fish without a bicycle," and throughout the globe women terrorists have repeatedly demonstrated that they are as capable as men are and just as deadly. In fact, those expecting greater gentility, compassion, and reason from women terrorists are gravely mistaken. Laqueur goes as far as suggesting that "women terrorists are more fanatical and have a greater capacity for suffering. Their motivation is predominantly emotional and can not be shaken through intellectual argument."[2]

WOMEN AND TERRORISM: LEVELS OF INVOLVEMENT

Analyzing the role of women in terrorism, Griset and Mahan established a classification based on four types. Any case of terrorism anywhere in the world that involves women falls into one of these four categories:[3]

1. *Sympathizers*: These women enable the men to go about their terrorist operations by taking care of the mundane chores, like cooking, sewing, and providing for the needs of the men. At this level of involvement, women also support the effort by providing safe houses, moving money, and smuggling war materiel.

2. *Spies*: These women are even more actively involved in terrorism. They act as spies, collect intelligence, and serve as messengers. Like sympathizers, they are inconspicuous, but provide the infrastructure the terrorist organization will need in the future: apartments to be used as safe houses and jobs that might be of value to the organization, such as in banks or the government. These missions are more dangerous and require a higher level of commitment than those performed by sympathizers. However, like them, women spies have no political ambitions and see themselves as supporters of the cause, while they await their return to their traditional roles in society.

3. *Warriors*: Women in this category participate in actual combat fighting side by side with the men. They are fiercely committed to the cause and fight with arms and bombs, risking life, limb, and liberty. However, they are not the decision makers, and there is no explicit program for their status in society once victory is achieved.

4. *Leaders*: These women attain dominant positions in their organizations and are central figures in shaping ideology, creating strategies, planning, and sometimes personally leading operations. By virtue of their position, stature, and abilities, female terrorist leaders do not see themselves going back to women's traditional roles in society after the hostilities are over. Instead, they envision a future in which women's status and function within their respective societies will be dramatically altered.

The First Palestinian Female Suicide-Bomber

It was January 27, 2002. The female paramedic driving an Islamic Red Crescent ambulance was waved through by security into downtown Jerusalem. There, the divorced 27-year-old Wafa Idris got out of the car, walked to a busy street and blew herself up, killing an 81-year-old Israeli who stood next to her in the street and wounding over 100 bystanders. As the first Palestinian female suicide-bomber, Idris became an instant heroine in the Arab world. Within Palestinian society, her act bestowed a level of unprecedented stardom on her: she was proclaimed a role model for Palestinian feminism and was glorified with parades, concerts, and other official programs in her honor.

The Russian revolutionary, Sergei Nechaev (1847–1882), was a radical who believed in pursuing revolution by any means, including violence. He advocated that all revolutionaries forsake their earthly identities and passions and devote their lives to only one purpose: the revolution. Writing about the role of women in promoting revolution, this theoretician categorized them as[4]

1. "Empty-headed, senseless, and sullen women," who may be useful for the revolution, and, if they are in positions of wealth or influence, ought to be exploited by every possible means to advance the cause.

2. Women who are sympathetic to the revolution, talented, and devoted but not yet completely committed to the cause. Such women, he said, were not to be trusted, just manipulated, used—knowingly or otherwise—and compromised so that they would never be able to quit the struggle and join mainstream society again.

3. Women who are absolutely and completely dedicated to the cause, proven revolutionary comrades, the "precious treasure without whose help [the revolution] could never succeed."

TYPES OF TERRORIST GROUPS AND WOMEN'S ROLES

Important differences exist among women who join leftist, rightist, separatist/nationalist, or religious terrorist organizations. While devotion to the respective cause is usually a common feature, the concerns and aspirations of women terrorists vary widely. Chief among these differences is the vision the women have for what the role of women will be in the society that will emerge after the war.

Left-Wing

Left-wing female terrorists are driven by the desire to change society so that a fairer and more equitable social order will replace the existing one and accord women their full rights. This ideal may sound utopian but many women with such aspirations have actually fought, suffered, and even died for this goal during the last century. By far, left-wing terrorist groups feature women in roles that go beyond mere combatants to include leaders and policymakers. Recent history is strewn with cases in which women have secured prominent positions in such organizations, from Baader–Meinhoff in Germany through the Marxist FARC in Colombia to the various left-leaning Puerto Rican liberation groups.

Bernardine Dohrn, Weather Woman

A leader and often spokesperson for the Weather Underground leftist terrorist group of the 1960s, Dohrn was a flamboyant revolutionary. Having declared war on the U.S. government and engaged in bombings and other illegal activities, she reached the pinnacle of her radical career when she was placed on the FBI's list of the Ten Most-Wanted Fugitives in the United States. She married a fellow Weather Underground leader, Bill Ayers, and together they spent a decade underground until they turned themselves in to authorities in 1981. In recent years, Dohrn has been an associate professor of law at Northwestern University.

What Do YOU Think?

The French actress Brigitte Bardot said in a context unrelated to terrorism, "Women get more unhappy the more they try to liberate themselves." Can you think of historical examples in which the struggle and sacrifice of female members of leftist terrorist organizations yielded a change in society that resulted in an improved status for women?

As ideologues, women find left-wing organizations better suited to their vision of bringing about a sea change in society in ways that will alter the status of women and promote gender equality. This long-range goal, for a movement seeking to take society and change it radically, is significant in explaining the consistently high percentage of female members, usually around 50%, that characterize such groups. For example, about half of the M-19 terrorists who took over Colombia's Palace of Justice on November 6, 1985, were women, who also distinguished themselves in the subsequent battle with the government forces. Similarly, an estimated 30% to 50% of Nepal's Maoist insurgents are females.[5]

Some leftist female terrorists have gained universal recognition for their leadership positions and exploits. Among the most famous is Ulrike Meinhoff of the West German Baader–Meinhoff terrorist group. The fact that the group became identified by her name speaks volumes of her prominence and influence within the group. Similarly dominant was Augusta Guzman, the wife of the founder of the Shining Path in Peru, Abimael Guzman. Using her innate ability to connect to poor people and organizational skills, the charismatic Augusta Guzman was the true driving force behind the Shining Path. In Nicaragua, Dora Maria Tellez Arguello was a senior *Sandanista* and the second in command when her group overran Nicaragua's National Palace in Managua in August 1979. "Commander Parvati," as she is known, is the most senior leader of Nepal's Maoist insurgency.

The "Most Feared Female Terrorist in the World"

The name Fusako Shigenobu once spread terror in people's hearts. Married to a cofounder of the communist terrorist group, the Japanese Red Army (JRA), Shigenobu gradually wrestled away leadership of the organization and headed it ruthlessly during some of its most violent years. The ideological premise of the JRA was the overthrow of the Japanese government and promotion of a worldwide communist revolution.

The group's crowning achievement under Shigenobu's command was probably the May 1972 attack on the Tel Aviv Airport. Working on behalf of the Palestinian Popular Front for the Liberation of Palestine (PFLP), three JRA members arrived on a flight to Israel, retrieved their weapons from their luggage, and began shooting and tossing grenades at the crowd. Twenty-six people were killed and 80 wounded in the attack, most of them Puerto Rican church members on a pilgrimage to the Holy Land. This murderous attack by the JRA was but one in a string of acts of terrorism the world over.

Infamy comes with a cost, and Shigenou spent the next 20 years on the run, hiding mostly in Lebanon, Syria, and North Korea. She was arrested in Japan in 2000 and sentenced in February 2006 to 20 years in jail.

Right-Wing

Right-wing terrorist organizations are conservative in nature, averse by definition to change, and wishing to protect the status quo, including women's traditional roles in society. Such logic is not conducive to nurturing female leaders in right-wing terrorist organizations. As a rule, domestic terrorist movements, such as the Aryan Nation, the Ku Klux Klan, the World Church of the Creator, and the many "patriot" organizations have female members, but no women in their leadership hierarchy.

Women belonging to right-wing terrorist groups tend to accept secondary roles in these conservative groups that wish to turn back the clock to times they consider more idyllic—times when the notion of a woman leader was an oxymoron. Consequently, even today female members seem to find satisfaction in assuming a secondary role, participating as supportive spouses, mothers, and so on. Perhaps the reason for these women's willingness to take a back seat in the struggle has to do with the nature of their cause and their reasons for involvement. Instead of being motivated by universal or gender-related issues, these women are motivated by the desire to advance the cause of their own racial or religious groups.

Few and Far Between

There are few recognizable women associated with the extreme right. One exception is Rachel Pendergraft, a recruiter, operations coordinator, and spokesperson for the Ku Klux Klan at the national level. She is also the second highest-ranked official of that racist organization. Jessica Edwards is the "Secretary" of the Texas arm of the White Knights of the Ku Klux Klan, but as the wife of Steven Edwards, the Grand Dragon of the organization, one wonders whether her rank is entirely based on merit. Lisa Turner, follower of the racist World Church of the Creator, is a prolific writer and founder of women-focused websites. She has never achieved national recognition or prominence within her own movement. One is hard-pressed to identify other genuine female leaders in the ranks of right-wing domestic terrorist organizations.

They cheerlead husbands and sons, sew the robes and other regalia, attend meetings, and are hard-core believers, but women terrorists on the right of the political spectrum are not leaders. Those in positions of influence in their organizations are usually so few that, compared to their counterparts on the left or in single-issue groups, they are but exceptions to the rule. This is so despite the fact that 25% of the membership in these organizations is women.[6]

Women and Crime

The new hydra created by intertwining terrorism and crime has brought to the forefront the question of women's role in violent organizations of both kinds. Researcher and author Alison Jamieson compared the status and function of women in the Italian Mafia with those of female members of the Marxist Red Brigades.[7]

Left-wing women terrorists strive for a new social order that will, among other goals, provide equality for women. This goal was paramount for female members of the Red Brigades. In contrast, Italian women whose male relatives are members of the Mafia may be fanatically inclined to support their men in every way possible, but are relegated to the role of the "little woman" at home. Although some Mafia women have begun to assume direct operational roles in recent years, they are still not part of the organization's power structure. These findings suggest that women associated with the Mafia have more in common with women belonging to right-wing terrorist organizations than with those of the leftist Red Brigades.

National Liberation Movements

National liberation movements tend to assign their female members traditional roles befitting their societies' conservative nature, although there are exceptions. One can speculate that the struggle against the occupying foreign power entails a rejection of the culture and values it has imposed on the society and a desire to return to the way things were prior to colonization. Naturally, women's traditional roles in those societies were subservient and submissive. Therefore, female terrorists in national movements replace the desire to address global issues, or the struggle for a more just future for women in their societies, with the collective goal of helping to liberate society in general.

Terror in the Russian Skies

It was frightfully easy for the two women to bribe their way onto two separate flights on that fateful Wednesday, August 25, 2004. One Chechen woman, Satsita Dzhebirkhanova, boarded the Siberia Airlines Flight 1047. Her partner on the mission, Amanta Yagayeva, boarded the Volga-Avia Flight 1303. Both women were Chechen nationalists on a suicide mission, and the two planes exploded in midair at about the same time, killing all 89 people aboard both planes.

The subsequent investigation uncovered the gruesome facts concerning the criminal state of Russian law enforcement. Each woman got through security without being checked by bribing local airport officials. How much did it cost to have security personnel not bother with their IDs and whisk them through? The equivalent of $170 for one, and $30 for the other.[8]

An additional explanation for the significant number of women in national liberation terrorist organizations is related to the abuse and torture, sometimes sexual, of women by members of the occupying power. Female victims of such crimes sometimes substitute thoughts of romance, love, marriage, and motherhood with a total dedication to becoming the "mother" of society at large, on behalf of all suffering and persecuted members of their nation.

This syndrome is especially true in some third-world societies, such as Sri Lanka, Kashmir, and the Ache region of Indonesia, in which women compose 50% of the membership of the terrorist organizations, an unusually high number for such conservative societies. Regarding female victims of rape as tarnished forever is so widespread in some conservative cultures that these unfortunate women lose all hope of ever marrying or having families of their own. Scorned for having disgraced their families, isolated from their familiar social circles, and out of options for constructive, fruitful lives, some women seek purpose by devoting themselves to a greater cause, and try to salvage some of their dignity and reputation by self-sacrifice for the good of their societies. Frequently, the outlet for the pain leads from the initial shame, toward feelings of rage, then to the need for revenge, and eventually to the arms of those who can help them exact justice—the terrorist organizations. Once recruited, charismatic handlers find these traumatized women easy to persuade to volunteer for suicide missions and terminate their lives in the service of the nation while taking revenge against the enemy. This may provide a partial explanation as to why the ranks of LTTE suicide-bombers in Sri Lanka and of the Kurdish PKK have swelled with a significant number of women. According to Harvard terrorism expert Jessica Stern, women have been responsible for over a third of the suicide-bombings carried out by the LTTE in Sri Lanka and for two-thirds of those committed by the PKK.[9] This extraordinary representation in certain national liberation movements highlights women's notable absence from leadership positions in these organizations.

A word of caution: Fascinating theories, even if valid to an extent, must not blind us to the fact that, in the words of Sigmund Freud, "sometimes a cigar is just a cigar." Many times women join nationalist or separatist terrorist organizations not because of personal abuse or sexual traumas but because they are part of a society that fights for its independence.

Religious Terrorist Organizations

Religious terrorist organizations accept female members, but not in leadership positions. Across the board, women members of religious terrorist organizations have no aspiration to assume such roles, nor are they permitted to do so. Yet, terrorist leaders of all religious stripes and persuasions seem able to find religious justification for women to become combatants and sometimes suicide-bombers. Religious motivation drives women to join terrorist organizations; the organizations, in turn, find women operationally useful in the struggle and embrace their participation.

Female Members of the IRA during the Funeral for a Fellow Female Member
Source: Courtesy of Getty Images Inc. - Hulton Archive Photos.

Religions in general are averse to the idea of women leaders. They embrace the enrollment of women into the ranks in a variety of roles because their involvement offers the organization tempting operational opportunities, but relinquishing control over policymaking or operations to women, or even sharing such influential positions with them, is usually out of the question for religious terrorist organizations. This holds true of American religious extremists, Japanese followers of Aum Shinrikyo, and Sikh militants in Punjab, India.

Female Terrorists and Islam

Given the conservative nature of Muslim societies, religious authorities once frowned on the idea of women engaging in violent acts, especially if there were enough men to fill the ranks. However, this has changed in recent years along with the growing militancy of radical Islam and as operational needs particularly suited to women soon found religious justification. Bin Laden, for example, extolling the merits of the fighting Muslim woman, proclaimed, "You are the ones who have incited and motivated . . . the men who fight the jihad in Palestine, Lebanon, Afghanistan, and Chechnya. You are the ones who brought forth the band of heroes in the New York and Washington conquests ... we will not forget the heroism of the Muslim Palestinian woman in the sacred land and her great stands that many men could not equal. . . . She has even offered and sacrificed herself to join the convoy of martyrs . . ."[10]

From Drugs and a Motorcycle Gang to Suicide-Bombing

As a young Roman Catholic woman, Muriel Degauque of Belgium was a rebel—a known drug-user and a member of a local motorcycle club. After marrying an Algerian man who introduced her to Islam, she became increasingly devoted to her new faith, even adopting the head-to-toe chador that left only her eyes showing. This pattern has become quite familiar to Europeans in recent years, as some women alienated from their own societies and in search of spiritual meaning have converted to Islam. For their part, Islamist terrorists have not been waiting passively for new female converts. According to France's antiterrorism investigating judge, these terror networks have been actively recruiting female Caucasian converts, who are valuable to the organization since they do not raise suspicion among Westerners.

Muriel Degauque's journey ended in the Iraqi city of Baquba. She and her husband had secretly joined Abu Musab al-Zarqawi's terrorist network in Iraq, and on November 9, 2005, she detonated the explosive vest she was wearing near an American patrol, wounding one American soldier and killing herself. She is believed to be the first European-Muslim woman to carry out a suicide attack.[11]

Several religious decrees, *fatwas*, issued in recent years urge and extol the role Muslim women should play alongside their male counterparts in various struggles involving Muslims. In 2001, the High Islamic Council in Saudi Arabia issued a *fatwa* that called on Muslim women to martyr themselves in the fight against Israel. In the earlier phases of the conflict, Palestinian women who supported or carried out terrorist attacks against Israelis did so on nationalist rather than religious grounds. However, the new wind of religious extremism blowing through the Middle East has increasingly swept through the Palestinian territories as well, compelling even conservative religious Palestinian terrorist groups such as Hamas to embrace an active combat role for women and encourage them to carry out suicide-bombings. The enthusiastic energy generated by women's participation in "martyrdom" operations gained too much momentum for the Muslim clergy to resist. Prudently reconciling itself with the facts on the ground, religion yielded to demand and allowed women to join terrorist operations.

The Husband and Wife Team

On November 9, 2005, three Jordanian hotels in the capital, Amman, were simultaneously attacked by suicide-bombers. Fifty-eight people were killed in the attacks, including members of a Muslim Palestinian family who were celebrating a wedding. Jordanian authorities were quick to piece together the details of the attack and to arrest one Iraqi woman, Sajida Mubarak Atrous al-Rishawai, as an accomplice. A vigorous interrogation established that the perpetrators were Iraqi members of the Abu Musabal-Zarqawi terrorist network who had infiltrated Jordan to carry out the murderous operation. The captured female terrorist admitted to being a

(Continued)

suicide-bomber working in tandem with her husband. Their assignment was to enter the crowded Radisson SAS Hotel and, simultaneously, blow themselves up. While her husband succeeded in setting off his explosives, her explosive belt failed to detonate and she was forced to flee.[12]

Jordan is a staunch American ally, but the majority of its population is not. Hordes of reporters descended on the Kingdom to take the pulse of the people's attitude toward terrorism now that the strategy had been used against fellow Sunni Muslims. They found a population divided, with many angry with the terrorists not so much because they bombed civilians, but due to their target—Arab Muslims rather than Americans or Israelis.

Blackmailed into Terrorism?   Generally, Muslim women's eagerness to take part in violent operations, including terrorism, is undeniable. Yet, in recent years, Israeli authorities have charged that not all of these women were volunteers but rather that some were pressured into agreeing to carry out terrorist attacks and suicide operations.

Israel may have its own agenda in charging that certain Palestinian female suicide-bombers were extorted to carry out their missions and did so against their will. On the other hand, the hard-earned expertise of Israeli intelligence in matters of terrorism cannot be rejected out-of-hand either. The Israelis blame Palestinian leaders for systematically taking advantage of women's personal, emotional, or social vulnerabilities to force them into committing acts of terrorism. Women who have disappointed their families by not marrying or giving birth to children or who have been discovered having extramarital affairs may be coerced into rehabilitating themselves and their families' honor in their conservative society through self-sacrifice on the altar of the collective. Some female suicide-bombers, goes the charge, are recruited by preying on the strong emotional distress of such stigmatized women.[13]

One example cited is of a 20-year-old woman from Bethlehem in the West Bank, who was blackmailed by Fatah into carrying out a suicide mission when her involvement in an illicit affair was discovered. In this particular case, her family managed to whisk her away into hiding and saved her life, but Israeli intelligence maintains that this type of extortion is typical and frequent.

They also point to other examples: The first Palestinian female suicide-bomber, the 28-year-old Wafa Idris, was divorced because she could not have children. Another Palestinian woman, Abir Hamdan, was killed when her explosives detonated prematurely on her way to carry out a suicide-bombing on August 31, 2001. She had fallen into disgrace for having affairs with several men. Similarly, Iman Masha, a mother of two whose husband was suspected of collaborating with Israel, attempted to plant a bomb in the Central Bus Station in Tel Aviv on August 3, 2001, in an attempt to clear her family's name. These examples remind us that there may sometimes lurk a disturbing side to women's participation in terrorism that is not visible to the public, a phenomenon that may not be exclusive to the Palestinian society.

TABLE 13–1   WOMEN'S POSITIONS IN TERRORIST ORGANIZATIONS

Type of Group	Membership	Prominent Leadership Role
Left-wing	✓	✓
Right-wing	✓	-
Nationalist/separatist	✓	-
Religious	✓	-

THE VALUE OF WOMEN TERRORISTS

Despite changing attitudes toward women, they are still often regarded as the tender, motherly, and nourishing sex, while men are still thought of as the dangerous war makers, the violent killers. Given these attitudes, terrorist organizations have sought to capitalize on such misperceptions and outwit the defenses erected by their enemies by employing women. Some of these women have demonstrated remarkable skills in carrying out their missions. "Women who seek to be equal with men lack ambition," commented the late counterculture guru Timothy Leary. Indeed, when allowed, female terrorists have been as capable of planning and commanding missions as any man, to say the least.

Professor Karla Cunningham suggested four reasons women become prized members of terrorist organizations:[14]

1. Women are perceived as nonthreatening and thus are scrutinized less carefully than men, which helps women terrorists pass through checkpoints with relative ease or penetrate protected facilities without raising the suspicion men would. During Algeria's War of Independence against France in the 1950s and 1960s, women of the National Liberation Front (FLN) played key roles in smuggling war materials past unsuspecting guards.

2. Searching women thoroughly poses logistical problems since soldiers and security personnel are usually young men. In addition to the problems with physical searches this implies, it is not easy for young men to interrogate a woman using the same harsh techniques—suspicion and bluntness—that characterize their dealings with other men. Furthermore, in certain Muslim societies it is forbidden for men to search a woman. As Ralph Waldo Emerson observed, "a woman's strength is the irresistible might of weakness."

3. It is difficult for male law enforcement personnel to search pregnant women, yet the very changes in a woman's body during pregnancy enables them to conceal contraband on their persons.

> ### What Do YOU Think?
>
> In your opinion, are Western counterterrorism authorities ready to deal with attacks committed by female terrorists, such as women operating on behalf of al-Qaeda? Explain.

4. Convention holds women to be victims of violence, not its perpetrators. As a result, law enforcement personnel tend to pay less attention to women, providing female terrorists with an excellent opportunity to succeed under conditions impossible for men.

SUMMARY

In this chapter, you have learned the following:

1. Women tend to join terrorist organizations after experiencing personal trauma.
2. Women involved in terrorism may be classified as sympathizers, spies, warriors, and leaders.
3. Left-wing terrorist organizations tend to provide their female members leadership opportunities.
4. Terrorist organizations value female members because they provide the group with greater operational flexibility.

💣💣💣

The big intersection near the French Hill neighborhood in Jerusalem is a major bus hub and one can always find travelers standing at their respective stations waiting for their buses. For this reason, the site has had its share of terrorist attacks. As a result, authorities in Jerusalem fenced off the area, forcing all would-be passengers to enter the area through a checkpoint manned by two border police. During rush hour on a sunny September 22, 2004, the policemen noticed a veiled Muslim woman approaching the bus stops. They walked toward her just before she entered the cordoned-off area and asked for her credentials. The woman immediately blew herself up, killing the 19- and 20-year-old policemen. However, because she was stopped a distance from the waiting passengers, the lives of the many civilians were spared.[15] The Fatah's al-Aqsa Martyrs' Brigades of Yasser Arafat claimed responsibility for the attack and threatened that many more female suicide-bombers were at the ready for similar operations.

Life continues. The following morning two other young border police were sent to guard the bus station. Put yourself in the new cops' shoes: What would you do if you saw a Muslim woman approaching the bus station? She might be a suicide-bomber and if you shoot her, you would save many lives, but what if she were an innocent woman just trying to catch a bus? You have a few seconds to decide—what would you do?

NOTES

1. For an excellent discussion of women who become terrorists because of their love of a man, see Robin Morgan, "Token Terrorist: The Demon Lover's Woman," in Pamela L. Griset and Sue Mahan, *Terrorism in Perspective* (Thousand Oaks: Sage Publications, 2003), pp. 167–181.

2. Walter Laqueur, *The New Terrorism: Fanaticism and the Arms of Mass Destruction* (New York: Oxford University Press, 1999), pp. 38–39.

3. The four types of women's involvement in terrorism are described in Griset and Mahan, pp. 158–161.

4. For Nechaev's own views, see Sergei Nechaev, "The Revolutionary's Attitude toward Society," *Catechism of a Revolutionary,*" at http://www.geocities.com/satanicreds/revolut.html (accessed October 13, 2006).

5. The data on female membership in Nepal's Maoist insurgency can be found in Doualy Xaykaothao, "Nepal Maoist Leader: Women Driving Movement," in National Public Radio (NPR), May 5, 2006, at http://www.npr.org/templates/story/story.php?storyId=5387419 (accessed October 13, 2006).

6. The data concerning right-wing female membership can be found in Carla J. Cunningham, "Cross Regional Trends in Female Terrorism," in Gus Martin, ed., *The New Era of Terrorism: Selected Readings* (Dominguez Hills, CA: Sage Publications, 2004), p. 95.

7. Jamieson's discussion of women Mafiosi appears in Alison Jamieson, "MAFIOSI AND TERRORISTS: Italian Women in Violent Organizations," *SAIS Review*, Vol. 20, No. 2 (Summer–Fall, 2000), pp. 51–64.

8. See Peter Baker and Susan Glasser, "Russian Plane Bombers Exploited Corrupt System," *Washington Post Foreign Service*, September 18, 2004, A01, on the tragedy of the two doomed Russian passenger planes.

9. Jessica Stern, *Why Religious Militants Kill: Terror in the Name of God* (New York: HarperCollins Publishers, Inc., 2003), p. 52.

10. Bin Laden is quoted in *Anonymous, Imperial Hubris: Why the West Is Losing the War on Terror* (Washington, DC: Brassey's, Inc., 2004), p. 133.

11. See Craig Smith, "Raised Catholic in Belgium, She Died a Muslim Bomber," *New York Times*, Tuesday, December 6, 2005, for more about Muriel Degauque, the suicide-bomber from Belgium.

12. For more on the Iraqi husband and wife suicide team sent on a mission to Jordan, see Michael Slackman and Mona El-Naggar, "Amman Bombs Churned Local Emotions," *New York Times*, Thursday, November 17, 2005.

13. Examples of the Israeli contention that certain Palestinian female terrorists have been blackmailed into carrying out missions are found in Israeli Ministry of Foreign Affairs, "Blackmailing Young Women into Suicide Terrorism," under, "Terrorism: Terror Since 2000," in http://www.mfa.gov.il/MFA/Government/ Communiques/2003/Blackmailing%20Young%20Women%20into%20Suicide% 20Terrorism%20- (accessed March 10, 2006).

14. Karla J. Cunningham, "Cross-Regional Trends in Female Terrorism," in Martin, ed., pp. 90–111.

15. For Fatah's claim of responsibility for the attack on the Jerusalem bus-stop area, see Israel Ministry of Foreign Affairs website: http://www.mfa.gov.il, or via its direct link to the episode in http://www.mfa.gov.il/MFA/MFAArchive/ 2000_2009/ 2004/9/Behind+the+Headlines-+Suicide+bombing+in+Jerusalem+ 22-Sep-2004.htm.

PART IV

JUST A QUESTION OF TIME

Depiction of a biological attack on a city
Source: Courtesy of Photo Researchers, Inc.

JUST A QUESTION
OF TIME

14

Weapons of Mass Destruction

I know not with what weapons World War III will be fought, but World War IV will be fought with sticks and stones.

Albert Einstein

❧❧❧

With methodic cruelty that boggles the mind, a secret scientific Japanese military group began operating in occupied Manchuria, in northern China, in 1937. It later expanded operations to the rest of the occupied country. Code-named Unit 731, it was the only military unit in the world to conduct wide-scale biological experiments and actual biological warfare even before World War II. The exploits of this unit were horrific. It produced biological agents, such as bubonic plague, smallpox, and typhus, and, believing the Chinese were "subhuman," dropped fleas infected with these organisms over Chinese cities. Masquerading as medical care providers, members of the unit injected unsuspecting Chinese with a variety of other diseases, in the name of scientific experimentation as well as a form of biological warfare. The cruelty and the human cost were breathtaking. More than 10,000 people—including, after the outbreak of World War II, Korean and Russian POWs—were sadistically murdered in the secret facilities in Manchuria. The overall number of people who perished at the hands of Unit 731 between 1938 and 1945 is estimated at 300,000.[1] After World War II, the United States, then engaged in the Cold War with the Soviet Union, realized the potential of these experiments and struck a deal with the Japanese officers of the unit—the worst perpetrators—offering them immunity in return for the data the unit had collected. Decades passed before survivors and sympathizers

---

Did You Know?

By the year 2000, there were 20,000–   military- and civilian-separated pluto-
30,000 nuclear weapons worldwide.[2] In   nium and over 1,700 tons of highly
addition, there were about 450 tons of   enriched uranium.[3]

---

began to unravel the cover-up. By then, the guilty parties had already gotten
away with mass murder.

❖❖❖

Terrorism has been around from time immemorial, yet, despite the individual
and communal tragedies, with the exception of the immediate victims and their
loved ones, life and progress continued as if nothing had happened. These
days, it is different. Humanity is staring into the abyss of weapons of mass
destruction (WMD) and the potential annihilation of people on a magnitude
that defies historical precedent. Until now, states had a monopoly on weapons
of mass destruction, and, perhaps as a result, over the last century humankind
has managed to control itself and, with a few well-documented exceptions,
refrained from opening the Pandora's Box of nuclear, biological, and chemical
weapons. Recent technological developments coupled with changes in the
international arena now threaten to change all this. The catalyst for converting
the potential into actuality is rooted in terrorism.

"Mass destruction" can be the result of different types of attacks: those we
traditionally think of—nuclear, radioactive, biological, chemical, and cyber-
warfare—as well as such things as using a fuel-loaded passenger plane as a
missile. In our context, the review of weapons of mass destruction focuses on
the big unconventional five: nuclear, radiological, biological, chemical, and
cyber.

THE PERIL AT THE DOOR: NUCLEAR NIGHTMARES

Terrorists can obtain a nuclear weapon in one of the four ways: (1) *manufacturing*
it themselves, (2) *receiving* it from a state, (3) *stealing* it, and (4) *buying* it or its
components. Once in possession of nuclear weapons, it is probable that terrorists
will use them either to inflict mass casualties on a target society or to threaten a
government with such a weapon to force policy concessions.[4]

1. Manufacturing a nuclear bomb is easier than you might expect. If terrorists can obtain the necessary fissile material, building a bomb is surprisingly easy. However, even if they succeed, there are the challenges of

either shipping the device to the target site undetected, which would require defeating every safeguard in the process, or, barring that, constructing the nuclear device inside the target city itself, which would avoid the dangerous phase of smuggling the device into the city. In practice, building a nuclear weapon on enemy soil is a tasking process that requires smuggling the materials, components, and technical personnel into the city without exposing the plot. Still, at least in theory it is doable.

2. Receiving nuclear weapons from a sympathetic country is the easiest way for a terrorist organization to obtain such devices. Motives ranging from ideology to religious affinity to countering common enemies can tempt states to share their nuclear arsenal with terrorist organizations friendly to them.

A CASE IN POINT

Imagine, for example, that Iran succeeds in developing a nuclear weapons program and then provides one or more of these weapons to a terrorist organization such as Hezbollah or Islamic Jihad, which, in turn, attacks a major Israeli or Western city. Conceivably, Iran could deny all knowledge of, or responsibility for, the attack at the same time as it reaped the benefits of its policy.

3. Stealing a nuclear weapon is another plausible scenario. Terrorists or mercenaries might raid a facility in which nuclear weapons are stored and steal one or more nuclear bombs. Possessing these weapons is a significant achievement for the terrorist organization; however, they still must face the challenges of smuggling the weapon into the target area and finding competent personnel to prepare and activate it.

4. Terrorists buying nuclear weapons is another possible scenario. North Korea, for example, has conducted a nuclear policy in defiance of the international community's attempts to have the country rein in or relinquish its nuclear program. With North Korea's history of chronic poverty, shortages, and need for hard cash on the one hand and, on the other, its unyielding resolve to pursue its desired policies despite international pressures and threats, it is not inconceivable that for the right amount, the country would sell nuclear weapons, or essential components, to bidders willing to pay a high-enough price.

In addition, in the aftermath of the collapse of communism in the Soviet Union, there have been numerous allegations of nuclear theft by criminal elements. For example, the international community was abuzz in 1997 when the Russian general Alexander Lebed announced that amidst the chaos that accompanied the disintegration of the Soviet Union, more than 100 nuclear suitcases were unaccounted for in the Russian arsenal. Lebed, who had been President Boris Yeltsin's

National Security Adviser and later a presidential candidate, raised great alarm when he said on CBS's *60 Minutes,* "I don't know their [the nuclear weapons'] location. I don't know whether they have been destroyed or whether they are stored or whether they have been sold or stolen, I don't know."[5] Confusion over the validity of the claim reigned in the months and years to follow. Backpedaling, Russian officials denied the story and General Lebed recanted his assertion, but, later, suggested that even if the nukes were missing, they did not pose substantial danger.[6] Assuming some of the allegations are true, and Russia managed to safeguard 99% of its nuclear arsenal, there would still be dozens of nuclear weapons unaccounted for out of thousands of weapons.[7]

Al-Qaeda's Interest in Building a Nuclear Bomb

In November 2001, al-Qaeda and its Taliban allies were fleeing their strongholds in Afghanistan. Within days, partially burned al-Qaeda documents concerning nuclear weapons were retrieved from one of the organization's houses in Kabul. Some of the documents contained instructions for processing plutonium to set off a nuclear explosion. CNN, which was involved in finding the documents, retained experts to study them. Two months of intensive analysis established that "the *al Qaeda* terrorist organization was building a serious weapons program with a heavy emphasis on developing a nuclear device."[8] The principle that a terrorist organization might construct a nuclear device is not a figment of the imagination.

How Serious is the Nuclear Threat?

The magnitude of the threat nuclear terrorism poses can be judged by the terrorists' willingness to launch a nuclear strike and their ability to do so.

Nuclear Proliferation for Profit

By the time the Pakistani government could no longer deny the charges and launched an investigation, it was too late. The father of Pakistan's nuclear program Dr. Abdul Qadeer Khan, best known as A. Q. Khan, had caused irreparable damage. After years of denial, Dr. Khan confessed his role in providing classified nuclear information and technology to several countries between 1989 and 2000. The international network Dr. Khan had put in place smuggled nuclear expertise and components in a for-profit conspiracy stretching from south Asia through Europe to the Middle East. Among the beneficiaries were Libya, North Korea, and Iran, when the latter's nuclear program was still in its infancy.

Following the revelations, Dr. Khan was put under house arrest, but charges were never brought against him and President Musharraf has granted him a pardon. Perhaps due to suspicions that top Pakistani officials were also involved and because of Dr. Khan's huge popularity in Pakistan, nothing more was done.

Intentions—Explicit Yearnings

The main threat of nuclear terrorism nowadays stems from al-Qaeda and its loose confederation affiliates. As we have seen, some radical Islamist groups have explicitly expressed their intention and justification for a nuclear strike against those they consider enemies of Islam: the West, particularly the United States, and Israel. They specifically designate civilians and children as legitimate targets based, allegedly, on the Koran's teachings and historical precedents. These extremists reason that since the United States has used nuclear weapons against enemy cities, it is permissible to attack American cities in kind because Islam is at war with the West.[9] The Saudi cleric Shaykh Nasir bin Hamid al-Fahd has said, "Some brothers have totaled the number of Muslims killed directly or indirectly by their weapons and come up with a figure of nearly 10 million,[10] implying that killing this number of Americans would be justifiable.

According to Michael Scheuer, the former CIA analyst on the team hunting for Osama bin Laden, the evolution of al-Qaeda's declarations is particularly ominous because it reflects a series of actions that Islamic law mandates before there can be a major attack. First, you must warn your enemy of the imminent danger heading its way. Second, your enemy must have the opportunity to convert to Islam and save itself from the inevitable.

Having issued several warnings that major attacks on American soil are in advanced stages of preparation and offering the American people the chance to convert to Islam, bin Laden went further than the obligatory requirements and addressed the American public directly. He urged the American people to use the democratic system to force their government to change its foreign policies, cautioning that absent such a change all Americans would become targets since they failed to exercise their free choice. Scheuer speculates that the warning was intended more for al-Qaeda's pan-Islamic audience than for American ears. By legitimizing a particularly devastating attack on the United States by pointing out that al-Qaeda has done everything required by Islamic law—to warn the enemy and have it repent—but to no avail, bin Laden has been preparing the Muslim masses for the inevitable.[11] It is important not to underestimate humankind's capacity to rationalize the unthinkable in the name of "justice" or self-serving visions for a better future regardless of the human toll involved.

Not Just al-Qaeda

Iranian President Mahmoud Ahmadinejad is reported to have promised a "world without America," adding that such a goal is "attainable, and surely can be achieved."[12] Furthermore, Hassan Abbassi, a senior adviser to Ahmadinejad, said, "We have a strategy drawn up for the destruction of the Anglo-Saxon civilization. We must make use of everything we have at hand to strike at this front by means of our suicide operations or by means of our missiles.[13]

Did You Know?

Approximately 6 million big commercial containers arrive in ships at American ports each year. Only 2% to 5% of these containers are checked. If terrorists intend to explode a nuclear bomb in an American city, the ability to smuggle it into a city-harbor and detonate it there would not be a prohibitive challenge.[14]

Capabilities—The Wild Card Factor

We know from numerous sources that al-Qaeda has been trying very hard to obtain nuclear weapons by any means possible: building them, receiving them from a country that already has them, stealing ready-made nuclear bombs or fissile material, and buying the weapons on the black market. Years of rumors and alarms have left authorities guessing whether al-Qaeda has accomplished this ambition. Speculations abound, but nobody knows with certainty what the Islamist organization's capabilities are.

In the most optimistic corner of the debate is the argument that because no nuclear attack has taken place, al-Qaeda (as well as similar groups) does not yet have the capability to unleash this kind of catastrophe. In the other corner is the school that maintains that it is only a question of time before such an attack occurs. Writer Paul L. Williams represents this view: "US, Saudi, Pakistani, Russian, Israeli, and British intelligence sources have confirmed that *al Qaeda* possesses a small arsenal of tactical nuclear weapons—weapons that are being prepared for the 'American Hiroshima.'"[15] The former general in charge of strategic weapons at the Pentagon, Eugene Habiger, has said that a major nuclear attack on American soil is "not a matter of if, but when."[16] If Habiger is correct and if intentions plus capability spell a certain nuclear attack by terrorists, the equation suggests that we are frighteningly close to some sort of nuclear attack.

QUESTIONING TRADITIONAL THINKING ABOUT WMD

In recent decades, much has been written about the threat of nuclear weapons falling into the hands of terrorists and many argued the unlikelihood, if not the impossibility, of such a result. Professor Cindy Combs believes that changing circumstances have shattered such premises and therefore the old model is no longer applicable.[17] She points to two basic assumptions that she argues are no longer valid: the notion that the cost of engaging in nuclear terrorism is *financially* too high and *politically* too prohibitive for terrorists.

I. Prohibitive Financial Costs

Traditional thinking posits that the financial costs of obtaining nuclear weapons are just too high for nonstate actors, such as terrorist organizations. This premise may no longer be valid because of the following reasons:

1. The alleged theft from the nuclear arsenal of the former Soviet Union may have provided the materiel.
2. Nuclear know-how, data, and components were illegally sold by the Pakistani scientist, A. Q. Khan to various international entities.
3. Present computers have the modeling and calculating power that in the past only classified supercomputers could provide.
4. Nuclear suitcases or "backpacks" have allegedly made it to the black market.
5. Nuclear waste materials that can be used for making "dirty bombs" can be obtained with relative ease from poorly guarded nuclear plants and military installations.
6. An organization like al-Qaeda may have hundreds of millions of dollars at its disposal, which can be used for this purpose.

II. Prohibitive Political Costs

Traditional thinking holds that terrorists are, essentially, rational actors; therefore, they would refrain from escalating to nuclear terrorism because it would expose them, and their sponsoring nations, to counterattack. For example, if Iran were to provide Hezbollah with nuclear weapons with which to attack Israel, Israel might react with a nuclear attack on Iran.

This premise may no longer be valid because

1. Rationality itself may be suspect in the era of religious terrorism replete with suicide-bombers, martyrs, and the adulation of collective self-sacrifice. To stay with the example of Israel, imagine a situation in which the Libyan government decides to sacrifice its population of about 5.5 million by attacking Israel directly or via proxy with nuclear weapons. A decision based on "martyrdom" defies logic, as the West understands it, and defeats policies based on deterrence.
2. Self-sufficient organizations such as al-Qaeda do not need a sponsoring country to carry out a nuclear attack; therefore, against whom would the attacked country direct its nuclear retribution?

A Case in Point: South Africa's Nuclear Program

South Africa's covert nuclear program is an important testament to how easy it is to manufacture not just a single bomb, but also an entire nuclear weapons program. After it was shut down in 1989, shocking details emerged about the secret program by which South Africa had developed its entire project, with only a few dozen people actually building the weapons (the remaining participants were administrative staff and security personnel), on a total cost of $200 million. It would have cost far less had South Africa been able to purchase the needed uranium rather than having to develop it itself. The current cost of developing an entire program for terrorists who manage to obtain the highly enriched uranium would be significantly lower.[18] Thus, the amount of money needed to produce or buy nuclear weapons is not a deterrent. The ramifications are alarming: al-Qaeda's annual operating budget for the year 1990 is estimated at $200 million, sufficient to build or buy such weapons.[19]

Too Late to Turn Back the Clock

Three global developments have intensified the danger of nuclear terrorism: the proliferation of countries working on nuclear programs; the growth in the number of commercial nuclear reactors and available fissionable materials; and the black market's prowess in overcoming some countries' safeguards.

1. Eight countries are known to possess, or are strongly suspected of having, nuclear weapons programs; among them are India, Israel, North Korea, and Pakistan. At least 28 other countries have at one point or another attempted to develop such programs. Altogether, there are 32 countries with 3,200 tons of fissile material, from which 240,000 nuclear weapons can be produced.[20]

2. The mushrooming number of nuclear reactors, which produce spent-fuel waste from which the plutonium used to manufacture nuclear bombs is made, is also an acute problem, and materials needed to build a "dirty bomb" can increasingly be obtained from hospitals and industrial sites using nuclear materials.

3. The increasing ability of criminals to steal, extort, or buy nuclear weapons or equipment that they then sell to interested buyers is another cause of concern. One telling example, although not directly related to WMD, was discovered by Russian authorities in 1997. A commander of the Russian Pacific Fleet, Admiral Igor Khmelnov, secretly sold 64 ships, including two aircraft carriers, to foreign buyers! Khmelnov would decommission ships, declare them scrap metal and sell them for absurd amounts and outright bribes.[21]

Did You Know?

Here is a quick summary of what it takes to build a nuclear bomb: When the nucleus of an atom splits, a huge amount of energy is released. To sustain a chain reaction that will generate the energy required to produce a nuclear explosion, scientists use one of two types of fissile materials: either uranium-235 or plutonium-239. Years of intensive work can yield 35 pounds of uranium-235 or 9 pounds of plutonium-239, just enough for one nuclear bomb. Since the amount of time it takes to create enough material from scratch is considerable, it is obviously far easier if the material can be stolen or purchased. With the fissile materials available, all that is needed are three or four individuals with expertise in physics, chemistry, metallurgy, and electricity to put together a crude nuclear bomb.[22]

The genie is out of the bottle, and some may agree with the *British Army Journal*'s advice to its readers: "The best defense against the atom bomb is not to be there when it goes off."

AN INVISIBLE KILLER: THE RADIOACTIVE MENACE

The principle behind radioactive terrorism is the contamination of the affected area in ways that will hurt living things, poison the environment, and spread panic among the public. One effective way to employ radioactive terrorism is with a "dirty bomb," which does not cause a nuclear explosion but spreads harmful radioactive materials. A "dirty bomb" can be made with fissionable materials such as plutonium and spent nuclear reactor fuel, but it can also be built with nonfissionable radioactive materials, which are easier to find. For example, cesium-137 and other elements may be found in less-guarded sites, such as hospitals and industrial locations.

Did You Know?

There are three types of radiation hazards: external radiation exposure, external contamination, and internal contamination. *External radiation* results from exposure to radiation. Regardless of the severity of the injury, the exposed person does not become radioactive and poses no threat to other people. *External contamination* occurs when an individual touches radioactive material, be it in the form of powder, liquid, or airborne particles. That person becomes contaminated and must be isolated to prevent the spread of contamination. The third type, *internal contamination*, occurs when an individual ingests or inhales radioactive particles, or absorbs them through the skin or an open wound.

> **Did You Know?**
>
> Movies and thrillers notwithstanding, radioactive materials do not glow. They also have no special characteristics that distinguish them from nonradioactive materials.[23]

To build a dirty bomb, a minute quantity of radioactive material is placed around a conventional explosive, such as dynamite, in a small container, bottle, or shoebox. The subsequent explosion spreads the radioactive material in the environment, killing and contaminating. Technically, therefore, "dirty bombs" do not actually belong in the category of "weapons of mass destruction" because instead of exploding and registering a huge toll on human life, they spread poisonous contamination, killing few but frightening many. On the other hand, Professor Allison defines a "dirty bomb" as a "weapon of mass disruption," for its impact on the daily life of the people in the targeted area and the cost of decontamination.[24] Now you understand why the literature about "dirty bombs" contains the expression *radiological dispersion device*, or RDD, for such weapons.

American intelligence estimates that al-Qaeda has accelerated its quest for radioactive capabilities.[25] This makes sense because it is far easier to build a "dirty bomb" than a nuclear one.

A "Dirty Bomb" in a Moscow Park

The only known case involving a "dirty bomb" took place in Moscow in December 1995, during the first Chechen war. That incident, in the form of a warning only, never materialized into an actual radioactive attack but was real enough to leave disturbing aftershocks. During the war, an anonymous phone call to Moscow authorities guided local officials to a location in Moscow's Ismailovsky Park, where they found a 30-pound charge containing a mixture of the radioactive (but not fissile) material cesium 137 wrapped around conventional explosives, half buried in the ground. Although a radioactive attack never occurred, the threat of a future one was made real. The implied message was clear: this was just a sample of a larger quantity the Chechens might possess and activate in a future attack.[26]

According to the U.S. General Accounting Office, in the years 1955–1977 thousands of kilograms of fissile nuclear materials went missing. While much of the discrepancy may be attributed to accounting practices,[27] it makes sense to assume that some of it may really have disappeared. If this uncertainty exists in the United States, where such materials are relatively well guarded and accounting practices are relatively good, we can only imagine what might happen in other countries, such as in the former Soviet Union, where safeguards are chronically less stringent.

Firefighters check for radiation during a mock dirty bomb attack in Seattle, 2003
Source: Courtesy of Corbis/Reuters America LLC.

What can terrorists wreak with this windfall? By using aerosols for pre-cise dispersion of radioactive materials, or spreading it around wildly via a conventional explosion, or sabotaging one of the existing 434 nuclear plants, terrorists can succeed in 1) poisoning and harming people near the site of the radioactive attack, causing instant death or serious health hazards to sur-vivors and in some instances affecting future generations as well; and 2) contaminating the grounds and infrastructure of the attacked area, rendering it uninhabitable and useless for many years to come.[28] Inflicting widespread panic and disrupting people's regular routines and commerce can be as efficient a terrorist tactic as killing a large number of people. This renders radioactive terrorism relatively simple, inexpensive, and productive.

What Do YOU Think?

Since the relative ease of building or obtaining nuclear and radioactive weapons poses an acute danger in terms of terrorists' *capabilities*, would you invest in real estate in a major American city, such as New York City? Would you feel comfort-able working or studying there?

THE POOR MAN'S NUKE: BIOLOGICAL DANGERS

"The one that frightens me to death, perhaps even more so than tactical nuclear weapons, and the one we have the least capability against, is biological weapons," admitted the then U.S. chief of staff, Colin Powell, in 1993.[29] Powell's concerns were well founded. According to terrorism expert Walter Laqueur, biological weapons can be manufactured with relative ease, are difficult to detect and to protect against, can be produced inexpensively, are capable of causing mass casualties, and are liable to inflict substantial damage on the economy of the attacked society.[30] As we shall see, not all experts agree with this opinion and the actual degree of ease is a subject of considerable debate.

About 60 known microorganisms can cause great harm to humans. They are commonly classified into five groups: bacteria, viruses, fungi, rickettsiae, and protozoa. In terms of "mass destruction," these biological microorganisms are generally considered more deadly than chemical agents are, but less fatal than nuclear weapons. By way of illustration, 10 grams of anthrax are as toxic to humans as 1,000 kilograms of the chemical agent sarin! Compounding the problem of bioterrorism is the length of time needed to distinguish between a natural outbreak of a disease and a deliberate attack.[31]

An Ominous Diagnosis

Natural or manmade, the prospects for authorities coping efficiently with a biological catastrophe are not encouraging. In May of 2006, Secretary of the Department of Health and Human Services, Michael Leavitt, cautioned that "We don't know what a pandemic would look like. We don't know when it will come. But we do know we're overdue and unprepared."[32]

As mentioned above, experts disagree on the ease with which biological weapons can be produced. On the one hand are those who compare the difficulty level to that of an undergraduate biology student with a budget of only a few thousand dollars brewing beer in a garage or a home kitchen. On the other, those disputing this assumption maintain that manufacturing biological weapons is a more challenging process that requires a graduate-level science student, if not an entire team of experts, with a professional lab and a budget in the millions of dollars.[33] Either way, a terrorist organization with modest means that can afford the services of a few scientists will find the challenge of building biological weapons far from insurmountable. Insofar as states producing biological weapons are concerned, the issue is not the degree of technical difficulty but the political and ethical ramifications involved.

Biological Warfare in History

The ancients understood the awesome power of biological warfare. They may not have understood the concept of germs and the exact physiological processes by which their enemies died, but they knew enough about the basic methods needed to effectively replicate such attacks. For example: [34]

- In the sixth century B.C., the Assyrian army poisoned enemy wells using biological agents.
- Later, the Persians, Greeks, and Romans were not shy about using animal cadavers to contaminate their enemies' water sources.
- In A.D. 1155, Frederick Barbarossa, a Holy Roman Emperor, dumped bodies of dead soldiers into his enemies' drinking water to contaminate it.
- Nearly 150 years later, Mongols besieging the Crimean fortress of Caffa catapulted infected human cadavers into the fortress. The disease forced the population to capitulate.
- During World War I, Germany allegedly engaged in biological warfare in parts of Russia, Romania, and Italy in an attempt to kill the opposing armies' livestock. Simultaneously, Germany activated a secret cell in Maryland to infect horses and mules destined for the war effort in Europe with anthrax.[35]

Using germs as part of a war effort is not new, but the scientific lethality of modern biological warfare and terrorism is. This kind of development might have been on President Kennedy's mind when he warned with eloquent foresight that there was "too much point to the wisecrack that life is extinct on other planets because their scientists were more advanced than ours."

Did You Know?

In 1999, Department of Defense officials conducted a secret experiment to find out how difficult it would be for terrorists to build a biological weapons factory from readily available commercial sources. The project was codenamed *Bacchus*, an allusion to the Greek god of fermentation, a necessary phase in the development of germ weapons. In just one year, using equipment openly purchased from department stores and other companies, the team produced biological weapons. The lesson was disturbing. With a budget of only $1.6 million, knowledgeable terrorists could purchase components and build biological weapons without arousing the authorities' suspicion.[36]

Deadly Biological Agents

Among microorganisms, bacteria and viruses are the best known to laypeople. The difference between the two is significant. Bacteria are hundreds of times larger than viruses, or as Judith Miller puts it, "If bacteria were the size of cars or minivans, viruses would be the size of cell phones."[37] Bacteria that can be used as biological weapons include agents such as those causing anthrax, plague, and tularemia. The problem for terrorists when using biological agents as weapons is that a healthy dose of antibiotics can protect or cure those attacked. Enter the viral weapon. Although viral diseases are susceptible to prevention through vaccination, because of viruses' far smaller size, simplistic structure, and the way they attach themselves to host cells, they are more deadly than bacteria. Influenza, smallpox, and Ebola are among the best-known lethal diseases caused by viruses.

There are, of course, other types of microorganisms, but in terms of rates of dissemination and mortality, the concern is mainly with the so-called "Category A" biological agents. Members of this group share a remarkable ease of *dispersion* and degree of *lethality*. For example:

- *Botulinum* toxin (secreted by a bacterium), the most deadly agent known, is 10,000 times more deadly than a cobra's poison.
- The death rate of the *Zaire Ebola* (caused by a virus) is up to 90%.
- *Bubonic plague* (caused by a bacteria), which is one of half a dozen varieties of plague, has a mortality rate of up to 75%.
- *Smallpox* (caused by a virus) kills up to 30% of people infected.
- *Anthrax* (a bacteria) is often deadly when absorbed via inhalation.
- *Marburg* (a virus) is extremely deadly and there is no cure for those infected.

The Threat at Our Doorstep

The temptation of military leaders throughout history to weaponize these microorganisms for purposes of deterrence or for offensive military options has been as high as that of modern-day terrorists. In November 2005, Interpol Secretary General Ronald K. Noble warned of the international community's poor state of readiness to cope with the results of a bioterrorist attack: "Al Qaeda's global network, its desire to do the unthinkable and the evidence collected about its bioterrorist ambitions ominously portend a clear and present danger of the highest order that *al* Qaeda will perpetrate a biological terrorist attack." Jackie Selebi, president of Interpol, registered a similar alarm, cautioning that a bioterrorism attack "is not [a question of] 'if' but 'when.' " Advising that the threat is acute and imminent, he added, "We need to be ready today, not tomorrow."[38]

Not everybody agrees with such dire predictions. A small but forceful school of thought views bioterrorism as an inflated threat. Milton Leitenberg, a prominent biological weapons expert, maintains that the threat of bioterrorism "has been systematically and deliberately exaggerated," by lumping together

---

Did You Know?

Anthrax has been in the news in recent years, especially in the weeks and months following the attacks of September 11, 2001, when envelopes containing it were mailed to various individuals. As a result, five people died and there was considerable panic among the public. In general, anthrax can penetrate the human body in three ways:

1. Through cuts or abrasions in the skin, which has a mortality rate of up to 20%.
2. Infecting the intestines, caused by eating contaminated meat, which has a death rate of up to 60%.

3. Inhalation of the bacteria, which has a death rate of up to 80%.

Fortunately, if applied in time, antibiotics can cure those infected with anthrax. It is important to know that anthrax is not contagious and affects only those directly exposed to it. According to some sources, a Soviet defector revealed that in 1988 the Soviet Union armed its SS-18 intercontinental ballistic missiles targeting New York City, Washington DC, Chicago, Los Angeles, Seattle, and so on with anthrax.[39]

---

states' capabilities with those of terrorist organizations, thereby leading to the wrong conclusions. Moreover, "an edifice of institutes, programs, and publicists with a vested interest in hyping the bioterror threat has grown, funded by the government and by foundations."[40]

Defending Against the Threat

With indications of al-Qaeda and its affiliated networks showing interest in biological warfare increasing, the good news is that weaponizing microorganisms and deploying them effectively is not easy for several reasons.

- Biological agents behave unpredictably and can react in unplanned ways. They might even infect the terrorists themselves.
- Biological agents depend on variables that cannot be controlled, such as heat, cold, sun, wind direction, the lifespan of the germs, and so on.

In addition, bioterrorists need to worry about delivery systems—the microorganisms may not survive the journey to the target—and about preventive measures—such as vaccines, protective gear, gas masks, and postattack treatment with effective antibiotics—the attacked party may employ. Nevertheless, according to Joshua Lederberg, a Nobel Prize winner in generic structure and function in microorganisms, at present there is no technical solution against biological weapons, only an ethical one.[41] Relying on the ethical judgment of terrorists is not a realistic course of action, and, as the former president of the American Association for the Advancement of Science, Elvin Stackman, cautioned, "Science cannot stop while ethics catches up." This leaves governments with only two options: *deterrence* and *active defense*.

"Ethnic Cleansing" with a Biological Twist

One of the drawbacks of bioterrorism from the point of view of the terrorist is that the organisms cannot distinguish between Catholic and Protestant, Caucasians and Africans, Arab and Israeli. It was hoped, therefore, that terrorists would refrain from launching a biological attack because they might harm members of their own group in the process. This hope was dashed when British scientists disclosed that biological weapons that can distinguish between ethnic and racial groups would soon become available. By being able to identify minute genetic and cellular differences, weapons containing microorganisms that can detect differences in DNA could soon be in the hands of racists and terrorists, who will be able to unleash tailor-made biological attacks without fear of harming their own group.[42]

Deterrence is based on rationality—the terrorists' understanding that if attacked, the assaulted society will retaliate with its own devastating weapons. However, when countering bioterrorism the problem with deterrence is obvious: where to find the attacker's address. For example, if al-Qaeda uses bioterrorism against the United States, against whom will the American decision makers retaliate? Which Muslim societies with millions of innocent men, women, and children are to be annihilated by the reprisal, and why? Unless the responsibility of a sponsoring state can be clearly established, deterrence does not seem to be a practical strategy for stopping bioterrorists.

The alternative, active defense, has its own limitations. Western democratic societies, especially the United States, are too open and liberal to enact policies that hermetically close the borders to potential terrorists. What's more, successfully defending at the borders is a fantasy. Consider the following example: In an age of suicide terrorism, how can immigration officials detect terrorists who had deliberately infected themselves with a deadly strain of microorganism? Nowadays, a terrorist can travel to any spot on the globe within two-dozen hours or so, while the incubation period of certain lethal diseases is in the weeks! With over 140 million travelers entering the United States each year and with the incubation period of smallpox, for example, averaging 12 days, is there a realistic way to actively defend against suicidal bioterrorists?

Three problems hamper efforts to prevent terrorists from obtaining biological weapons:

1. *Dual-usage.* Factories that manufacture agricultural products, fertilizers, herbicides, medicines, and baby food can easily turn their machinery into equipment producing biological weapons. It is exceedingly difficult for

Did You Know?

In 1999, the United Sates established the Biological Preparedness and Response Program (BPRP), which is under the umbrella of the Centers for Disease Control and Prevention, to prepare for a future bioterrorist event. For the specific purpose of countering outbreaks of diseases, for example, the BPRP created the National Pharmaceutical Stockpile of various drugs and antibiotics. It also watches systematically for outbreaks, conducts research, and helps local governments to improve their own capabilities to respond rapidly to potential disasters.

intelligence agencies to determine with certainty what exactly the suspect night shift is producing in such a plant. If decision makers order an attack on the plant, they are certain to be blamed for an inexcusable assault on an innocent factory that turns out medicine for its needy population. If they do nothing, and biological terrorists strike, these same decision makers will be taken to task for gambling with the lives of their citizenry by choosing to err on the side of danger.

2. *Initially, only small amounts of deadly cultures are needed* to build biological weapons; this makes active defense a Sisyphean endeavor. Hundreds of collections of deadly organisms are available through natural outbreaks or in secret military labs around the world. Praying that they will not fall into terrorists' hands is hardly an "active defense."

3. *Constant innovations in biotechnology* ensure that defensive catch-up efforts—one scientist referred to them as "a biological defensive arms race"[43]—in the form of immunizations and early detection equipment will fall short of the ever-evolving needs.

What Do YOU Think?

In 1972, a Muslim pilgrim from Yugoslavia traveled to Mecca and returned to Yugoslavia via Iraq, where, unbeknownst to him, he had contracted smallpox. By the time the communist regime of Yugoslavia realized it had a huge problem, the sick man had already spread the disease to all who had been exposed to him. Communist regimes can carry out policies that free societies cannot. Yugoslavia in 1972 was no different and it quickly quarantined 10,000 people suspected of being infected in schools, hotels, and apartment buildings surrounded by armed soldiers and barbed wire. It also vaccinated 18 million people.

By 9/11—almost 30 years later—the United States, with a population of just fewer than 300 million, had only 15 million vaccines for smallpox at its disposal. Speculate what realistic options the United States would have and what its actual policy would have been if faced with an outbreak of smallpox.

THE GRIM PAST AND A SCARY FUTURE: THE CHEMICAL THREAT

Chemical weapons are a chief pillar in the array of unconventional weapons we classify as weapons of mass destruction because they not only are among the deadliest, they also are the easiest and least expensive to manufacture. Consequently, it is believed that a graduate student in chemistry could pull off such an attack, especially since the ingredients needed are widely available due to their widespread commercial use in such things as medicines, cleaning agents, herbicides, and insecticides.[44]

A CASE IN POINT: Terrorizing With Cyanide

As a junior leader of Hamas, Abbas al-Sayed had a prolific, if relatively short, run as a mastermind of terrorist operations and suicide bombings. Among his successes was the dispatch of a suicide bomber to the Park Hotel in Netanya, Israel, on March 27, 2002, which killed 30 mostly elderly revelers sitting down for their Passover meal. Following his capture, al-Sayed revealed that he had been planning a chemical attack on other locations in Israel. Al-Sayed's cousin, a pharmacist, purchased for him four kilograms of cyanide in Jordan. The plan was to mix the cyanide with oil and apply the concoction to various public places throughout Israel, causing mass poisoning.[45]

Chemical Warfare in History

Like biological weapons, chemical weapons have been used generously throughout history. Conflicts in India witnessed "toxic fumes" as far back in history as 2000 B.C., and in circa 400 B.C., the Spartans burned wood drenched with sulfur under a besieged city's walls to choke its defenders. This humble beginning gradually outdid itself in future years. German troops mastered the field use of noxious fumes to attack enemy formations in 1591 and, in the nineteenth century, British scientists perfected some of the worst modern chemical agents, such as mustard gas.[46] The real turning point came in 1915, during World War I, when all technical, political, and ethical inhibitions against the use of chemical weapons were dropped. Desperate to force a breakthrough in the stalemated trench warfare, the Germans surprised the Allies by shelling their lines with chlorine gas, killing 5,000 soldiers. The Allies retaliated, five months after being caught completely unprepared for a chemical attack, with a similar attack on the—amazingly—utterly surprised Germans, and inflicted similar horrific losses. With modern chemical warfare in its infancy, these and later chemical assaults during World War I proved a strategic failure despite the large number—at least 500,000—of casualties suffered by all sides.

When Italy invaded and occupied Ethiopia in 1936, it too used toxic gases, which were responsible for one-third of the Ethiopian casualties. During the Iraq–Iran war between 1980 and 1988, Iraq repeatedly used chemical weapons to block successive counterattacks by Iranian human waves. Saddam Hussein's regime used chemicals on its Kurdish population several times, the most notorious being the 1988 attack in Halabjah, in which at least 5,000 men, women, and children were killed.[47]

Did You Know?

It has been a mystery for decades. Germany resorted to chemical warfare in World War I. Yet, despite its leadership in the field of toxic gasses and demonstrated ruthlessness, Nazi Germany did not use chemical weapons against opposing armies even as it was losing the titanic struggle of World War II. Refraining from using chemical gasses against the Allies was clearly not for moral reasons; Germany had no compunction about using poisonous gasses in death camps to murder millions of "undesirable" civilians in their own country, as well as in territories under their control.

Professor Walter Laqueur provides a multifaceted explanation for this puzzle. In the early stages of World War II, Germany was winning and its troops were moving rapidly forward, occupying enemy countries with relative ease. Deploying chemical weapons in these circumstances would not have served any purpose. By the time the fortunes of war changed and Germany found itself on the defensive and in retreat, the Allies enjoyed such overwhelming air superiority that Germany feared that launching chemical attacks would result in much harsher retaliation by the Allies against German urban centers.

Another interesting speculation concerns Adolph Hitler himself. During his service on the Western Front during World War I, he was injured in an Allied chemical attack and is said to have developed a personal revulsion toward this type of weapon. In addition, although Germany had developed the most lethal poisonous gasses in the world by the late 1930s, including tabun, sarin, and other sophisticated nerve gasses, its leaders were deterred by the erroneous assumption that the Allies were in possession of similar chemical weapons. Interestingly, the allies had no such weapons and when their troops landed in Normandy on D-Day, they were not even equipped with gas masks.

Laqueur maintains that, had the Germans resorted to chemical warfare during World War II, the course of the war would not have changed much. Victory might have been somewhat delayed, but the United States would have used its nuclear bombs against Germany and the war would still have ended with Germany's defeat.[48]

Deadly Chemical Agents

Five types of chemical agents constitute the typical chemical terrorism threat:
Each type has a particular physical state, a unique means of delivery, and its
own route by which it infects the body.

1. *Blister* agents, which burn eyes, lungs, and areas of the skin with which
   they come in contact. They can be weaponized in the form of vapors,
   aerosols, or liquids. Mustard gas is an example of a blister agent.
2. *Blood* agents, which are dispersed as a vapor, prevent the body from
   using oxygen at the cellular level. Cyanide is an example of a blood
   agent.
3. *Choking* agents, such as chlorine and phosgene, affect the lungs, causing
   the "choking" effect. That 80% of the casualties of chemical attacks during
   World War I were victims of choking gasses is testimony to their deadli-
   ness. Chocking agents are dispensed as vapor.
4. *Incapacitating* agents are usually nonlethal; they disable their victims for
   hours or days by affecting the central nervous system. They are dispensed
   as aerosols or liquids. LSD is a well-known example of an incapacitating
   agent.
5. *Nerve* agents are the most fatal chemical agents. There are two major categories of nerve agents: G-agents and V-agents. Both are released as
   vapors, aerosols, or liquids to quickly disable the body's ability to transmit nerve impulses. Due to their high mortality rate, nerve agents have
   become the chemical weapon of choice in the arsenals of certain countries.
   Sarin and tabun belong to this category.[49]

A CASE IN POINT: A Day of Horrors in Oklahoma City

April 19, 1995, dawned as another calm morning in Oklahoma City. The tranquility
of that morning was shattered when a Gulf War veteran named Timothy McVeigh
detonated a truck bomb packed with 5,000 pounds of chemicals: a fertilizer known
as ammonium nitrate mixed with fuel used for auto racing, nitro methane, to
demolish the Alfred P. Murrah Federal Building. A total of 167 people were killed.
The lesson of this painful episode is unnerving—obtaining the materials needed
for the attack, putting the bomb together, and executing the plot is easy—and
serves as a warning that similar bombings could occur in the United States. Six billion pounds of explosives are used each year in the United Sates alone, 80% of
which are composed of the same materials McVeigh used in Oklahoma City. The
fact that the materials are so readily available makes it clear that the problem of
defending citizens against similar acts of terrorism is not susceptible to easy solutions in a democracy.

Planning and Carrying Out a Chemical Attack

Of the many chemical toxins that can be weaponized, how are terrorists to determine which to use? There are several criteria. The attackers need to decide (1) the level of *lethality* they wish to achieve; (2) the *route* through which the agent is to penetrate and affect the individuals targeted; (3) the *speed of action* of the chemical agents—that is, how quickly the poison will affect the body; (4) the *stability* of the chemical weapons from the point of view of storage and activation; (5) the *persistence of* the chemical—that is, how long the chemical continues to affect the environment once released; and (6) the *toxicity* of the chemical weapon, which will affect the quantity needed to obtain the desired effect.[50]

These considerations lead to three steps terrorists attempting to weaponize chemical agents must follow:

1. They need to select and apply chemical additives to stabilize the chemical agents so they can function as planned at the right time and in the chosen location.

2. They need to design and build the weapon itself so that it will disperse the chemicals at the time of the attack.

3. The most risky and complicated phase of the entire operation—they need to fill the weapon with the chemical agents, store it safely until it is time to move it, and securely transport it to the site where it is to be detonated.[51]

Chemical weapons may be the easiest and most inexpensive WMD to construct, but the many variables involved in activating them successfully depend on so many things over which the terrorists have little control that these weapons are also the most unreliable and erratic. Therefore, even if the terrorists' planning is flawless, the assembly of the weapon careful, and transportation of the charge to the site of the attack problem-free, success is not guaranteed. By the time the terrorists complete their activities, the behavior of the chemical agents depends on various meteorological and ground conditions, as delineated by bio-chemical terrorism expert Michael Moodie:[52]

1. *Air temperature*: High temperature tends to evaporate the chemical particles faster than planned.

2. *Ground temperature*: Dictates how long the attacked area will remain contaminated.

What Do YOU Think?

If you were planning a chemical attack in a major American city, knowing that the device must be portable enough to be carried to the site by a person or two and so powerful as to cause mass casualties, what *type of target* would you select?

3. *Exposure to sun*: Contributes an element of unpredictability to the effects of the chemical attack.

4. *Humidity*: Intense humidity enlarges the size of the particles disseminated by aerosol, thus making the results of the attack unpredictable.

5. *Precipitation*: Heavy rain dilutes chemical agents whereas light rain can spread them to a larger area than planned.

6. *Wind speed and direction*: High winds disperse chemical agents farther, but are likely to dilute the concentration and thus reduce the attack's lethality.

7. *Soil condition*: The degree of penetration into the ground is important to the success of a chemical attack. For example, when the agents are absorbed into the ground, the level of contamination is reduced.

8. *Nature of attacked site*: If a chemical attack takes place in an open space, the concentration is reduced and so is the toxicity of the attack. On the other hand, a closed space is likely to result in a more lethal outcome.

A CASE IN POINT: Aum Shinrikyo

Scholars often mention the Japanese terrorist group Aum Shinrikyo as an example of how difficult it is for a terrorist group to carry out a successful act of chemical terrorism. Enjoying a budget in the hundreds of millions of dollars and the services of top-notch scientists, the group carried out a sarin chemical attack on the city of Matsumoto on June 27, 1994. Yet, the sarin released from a converted refrigerator truck killed only seven people in a city of 300,000, demonstrating how the ease of putting together a chemical weapon is somewhat negated by the unpredictability of the chemical agents' behavior.[53]

Defending Against the Threat

As noted, the advantages of chemical terrorism—the relative simplicity and the very low cost of building a chemical weapon—also make it difficult for those trying to defend against this type of attack.

1. *Dual use*: Just as with biological terrorism, factories may use their machinery, raw materials, and personnel to manufacture chemical weapons. Authorities and law enforcement agencies trying to prevent chemical attacks are confronted with the dilemma of striking at the suspect factories and being accused of destroying a plant producing baby-formula, or refraining from taking preemptive action and potentially facing a chemical attack.

A CASE IN POINT: A Janus-Faced Factory

The human toll was devastating. Al-Qaeda's simultaneous truck bomb attacks on the American embassies in Dar es Salaam, Tanzania, and Nairobi, Kenya, on August 7, 1998, killed 220 people—including 12 Americans—and wounded 4,000 more. The Clinton administration decided that it had to respond militarily, but against what targets? It was felt that attacking only al-Qaeda's training camps in Afghanistan was not enough, so an additional target was selected, the pharmaceutical company al Shifa in Khartoum, Sudan, which was suspected of working clandestinely for bin Laden to manufacture a chemical needed for production of the VX nerve gas. On the night of August 20, 1998, 17 Tomahawk missiles rained down on the pharmaceutical company and demolished it, killing and injuring local people. An outraged Sudanese government denied the American allegations that the al Shifa company was somehow involved in manufacturing contraband chemicals for al-Qaeda and insisted that the only products manufactured by the company were medicines. Unable to prove otherwise, the United States came under fierce criticism worldwide in the aftermath of the controversial bombing. It is left to be seen if a future American administration would carry out a preemptive military strike under similarly obscure circumstances.

2. *Readily available materials*: Chemicals are used for two types of attacks: (1) to disperse toxins in a target area, and (2) to create a conventional blast. Because the chemicals (pesticides, herbicides, pharmaceuticals products, cleaning materials, fertilizers, and so on) needed for an attack are widely used, terrorists can obtain large quantities with relative ease.

A CASE IN POINT: The Ease of Obtaining Chlorine

Chlorine, a chemical substance that can be used in a chemical attack, is widespread and used regularly for commercial purposes. Millions of tons of chlorine are manufactured each year and sold to any purchaser. How can law enforcement keep track and protect against those purchasing this compound to perpetrate a chemical attack?

3. *Attractive targets in free societies*: Terrorists can appear smart, resourceful, and tough because they can choose any public location or gathering for their attack. It is impossible for democracies to hermetically protect each school, supermarket, train, bus, apartment building, water source, and pedestrian sidewalk against a terrorist outrage. This vulnerability may be too enticing for terrorists, who, in the words of Oscar Wilde, may be able to "resist everything except temptation."

A CASE IN POINT: Vulnerable Chemical Facilities

Terrorists do not need to purchase, assemble, and smuggle a chemical weapon. They can use chemicals stored in various installations in the target society to produce the results of a chemical attack by sabotaging one or more of them. Currently, there are 15,000 refineries, factories, and other installations in the United States that use potentially dangerous chemicals to manufacture fertilizers, paints, and other industrial products. If attacked by terrorists, about one hundred of these factories pose great potential danger to over one million residents living nearby. As a Congressional Research Service cautioned, "These plants are the equivalent of weapons of mass destruction prepositioned in some of the most congested parts of our country."[54]

State-sponsored terrorism adds a significant hurdle to authorities' efforts to foil chemical terrorism. There are at least 18 countries either with declared chemical warfare programs or with suspected production and stockpiling programs.[55] The presence of countries such as Iran, Syria, and North Korea on the list of countries with alleged chemical warfare capabilities adds a disturbing multiplier to the dangers of chemical terrorism.

VIRTUAL TO REALITY: CYBER-TERRORISM

"If the human race wants to go to Hell in a basket, technology can help it get there by jet," lamented biology professor Charles M. Allen. Cyber-terrorism is a shining representative of this warning. Since there is no one internationally recognized definition of cyber-terrorism,[56] understanding the concept and its dangers is left to common sense. It may help to think of cyber-terrorism as a surprise attack via the Internet or other computer technologies to undermine a country's electronic and physical infrastructure, as cyber-terrorism expert Dan Verton suggests.[57] The public in many societies has yet to internalize and come to terms with the extraordinary cost in lives and treasure that cyber-terrorism can inflict. We know that terrorism wears many guises but the bottom line is that it's always about frightening the many—by suggestions of violence, outright killing, and disruption—to force policy changes on the government. Although a devastating cyber-terrorism attack has not yet taken place, neither had hijacked airplanes flown into skyscrapers prior to September 11, 2001. Just imagine the devastating consequences of a massive cyber-terrorism attack that leaves a modern society with no water, sewerage facilities, electricity, phones, cell phones, televison, radio, traffic lights, functioning fire fighting equipment, trains, subways, hospitals, and so on. Other prime targets are information databases and decision systems, such as medical records, logistical data, disaster plans, personal information, blueprints of buildings, criminal histories, and financial reports.[58]

Electronics drive almost everything in industrialized societies and computers manage electronics. Consequently, those controlling the computers determine how the society functions. In the context of terrorism, our enormous dependence on computers presents a potential vulnerability of the greatest magnitude. Without electricity, almost everything would come to a halt, and electricity is generated in power plants and then distributed with the help of computers through vast geographic areas. Can you imagine the country with its electronic networks down? Moreover, industry in general could not function without computers. Consider how the functions of design, purchasing, inventory control, maintenance, manufacturing, sales, billing, shipping, and so on would be handled if computers were down for a long period of time. Hospitals, those mini-cities, would almost be at a standstill without computers, as would universities, banks, the stock markets, and airports. And we have not even mentioned the military.

It is obvious that cyber-space attacks could cripple the economy and cause tremendous losses, perhaps in the trillions of dollars, but losses will not be monetary only. Take aviation, for example. Five thousand passenger planes are in American skies at any given time in the course of an average workday. Imagine the catastrophic results if air traffic computers were suddenly immobilized and telecommunications severed. Thousands of planes would be left to fend for themselves in mid-air, with no guidance, fuel running short, blind, and incommunicado. Too fantastic a scenario? Not if you consider the fact that 50,000 computer viruses have been developed so far and 400 are active at any given time![59] Even if we limit our concerns to the financial realm, trillions of e-business dollars are on the line, since the Internet is based on easy access. Thus, protecting against potential cyber-terrorism is a national security issue of the first degree.

Verton points out a significant curiosity that turns traditional thinking about national security on its head. Normally, we expect the government to safeguard our security, as it has done for over two centuries. However, today over 85% of the nation's most important computer networks and physical infrastructure are owned by private companies.[61] In terms of cyber-terrorism, then, who is in charge of protecting this vulnerable behemoth?

Moreover, by posting such things as floor plans and structural information on the Internet for potential enemies to see, Americans tend to expose

---

What Do YOU Think?

Does hacking into a company's website to deface and mess up the site constitute cyber-terrorism?

Did You Know?

Cyber-attacks have been increasing at a rapid pace worldwide. In the first six months of 2002, for example, cyber-attacks grew at an annual rate of 64%. More than one million attempted cyber-attacks took place during that period, of which 180,000 were successful.[60]

---

the weaknesses and vulnerabilities of buildings, bridges, and infrastructure. Using a memorable metaphor, Verton cautions against such cavalier attitudes: "Terror is like a shark in the ocean that must constantly move in order to breathe—a top-feeder that strikes without warning from the murky depths below. It never stops searching for wounded or vulnerable prey . . ."[62]

Changing patterns of thought is not easy, even in the post-9/11 world. Traditionally, a cyber-attack is seen as simple hacking into governmental computers or malevolently disruptive but limited mischief. "Cybotage," as the standalone threat has come to be known, is a weapon of *mass disruption* more than it is a weapon of mass destruction.[63] A much more probable scenario, contends Verton, is one in which a cyber-attack is part of an integrated overall terrorist assault. Acceptance of such an idea, however, may require a paradigm shift in the way we think of cyber-terrorism. For example, it is possible to imagine a scenario in which a three-phased terrorist operation—the simultaneous (1) hacking and incapacitating of the software running the distribution of electricity to a major region of the country, (2) launching of a conventional terrorist attack to destroy the control site from which the flow of electricity is regulated, and (3) infecting of the area with a biological agent such as anthrax to prevent repair efforts for a very long

---

Did You Know?

Two important exercises were conducted by authorities and the private sector to simulate the impact of a natural disaster and/or a conventional terrorist assault combined with a cyber-attack. The first, code-named *Black Ice*, took place in November of 2000, in preparation for the 2002 Winter Olympics in Utah. The second simulation, Blue Cascades, was conducted in June of 2002. The findings vividly demonstrated the spillover paralysis that cyber-attacks on the computer networks managing a region's vital systems can cause if accompanied by a natural disaster or a terrorist attack. The most important effect was the spreading catastrophic shutdowns of essential telecommunications and power systems.[64]

time—occurred. The consequences would be catastrophic and the damage to the economy would be astronomical.

Perpetrators and Means

The centrality of information technology to all facets of modern life, especially in industrialized societies, dictates that "information warfare" is not a monopoly of individuals or terrorists. States are in the game as well. We know that countries such as the United Sates, Russia, China, France, India, and Israel[65] have weaponized information warfare, meaning that they have developed the ability to use information systems to disrupt and damage the military and economic infrastructures of their enemies. In this context, however, we are not concerned with states' preparations for future conflicts but with the possibility of states with information warfare capabilities sharing their knowledge with terrorist organizations that will do their bidding for them. If we omit the state, the focus is on individual hackers, terrorist organizations, and a combination of hackers and terrorists:

Individual hackers: There have been numerous cases in recent years of individual hackers penetrating governmental and corporate computer systems worldwide for purposes ranging from curiosity to political protest. Sometimes, these individuals have been part of loosely organized hacker groups, at other times, members of a political movement.

Terrorist organizations: Some terrorist groups are capable of disrupting a target society's electronic and physical infrastructure; others are in the process of attempting to acquire this capability.

Combination of hackers and terrorists: Terrorist organizations with the desire, but not the capability, to engage in cyber-terrorism may hire the expertise. Out-of-work Russian information technology experts, for example, may be amenable, just as their counterparts with bio-chemical expertise were, to tempting financial offers from terrorists.

Information warfare expert Gregory Rattray identifies three methods by which information systems can be attacked: mechanical, electromagnetic, and digital. *Mechanical* attacks occur when control sites are bombed, fiberglass wires are cut, and equipment is damaged. *Electromagnetic* terrorism entails the jamming of electronic transmission systems or damaging them with directed-energy weapons. *Digital-terrorism* is the partial or total incapacitation of information networks by corrupting dada and stealing information.[66]

The United States has become increasingly aware of the threat of cyber-terrorism. Starting in 1995, a series of mechanisms and directives have been enacted to safeguard against physical and cyber-threats, or an "electronic Pearl Harbor" as some have come to call this alarming prospect. In addition, experts agree that the complex nature of the cyber-threat is unique and unprecedented, which renders efforts to effectively defend a free society next to impossible for the foreseeable future.

SUMMARY

In this chapter, you have learned the following:

1. *Radioactive* weapons and *cyber*-warfare have been added in recent years to the traditional list of weapons of mass destruction: nuclear, biological, and chemical.

2. It is far easier to produce a radioactive weapon, commonly known as a *dirty bomb*, than a full-fledged nuclear weapon.

3. Biological and chemical warfare have been around for millennia.

4. Chemical weapons are easier and less expensive to come by, but more difficult to control than nuclear and biological weapons.

5. Terrorists have become less inhibited about inflicting large-scale casualties using WMD.

6. The prospect of state sponsorship of terrorist organizations is particularly disturbing in an era inundated with weapons of mass destruction.

❡❡❡

Visualize the unthinkable. In order to see for yourself the impact of a 10-kiloton nuclear explosion, visit the following website and plug in a zip code of your choice. The impact of toying with the "Blast Maps" link on this website can be as educational as reading a river of alarming words: http://www.nuclearterrorism.org.[67]

❡❡❡

NOTES

1. You can read more about Unit 731 in Anita McNaught, "Unit 731: Japan's Biological Force," in *BBC News World Edition*, February 1, 2002, at http://news.bbc.co.uk/2/hi/programmes/correspondent/1796044.stm (accessed May 30, 2006). See also, Walter Laqueur, *The New Terrorism: Fanaticism and the Arms of Mass Destruction* (New York: Oxford University Press, 1999), p. 61.

2. For the number of nuclear weapons, see the Natural Resources Defense Council (NRDC) estimate in "Table of Global Nuclear Weapons Stockpiles, 1945–2002," at http://www.nrdc.org/nuclear/nudb/datab19.ASP (accessed May 23, 2006); Matthew Bunn and George Bunn, "Nuclear Theft and Sabotage: Priorities For Reducing New Threats," *IAEA Bulletin*, Vol. 43, No. 4 (December, 2001), p. 21.

3. The tonnage of highly enriched fissile materials is in Ibid.

4. Part of the discussion concerning the methods by which terrorists can come to possess nuclear weapons and the purpose for their use is found in Friedrich Steinhausler, "What It Takes to Become a Nuclear Terrorist," in Gus Martin, ed.,

The New Era of Terrorism: Selected Readings (Dominguez Hills, CA: Sage Publications, 2004), pp. 130–132.

5. General Lebed's alarming interview in "60 Minutes," can be found in Richard Miniter, "Baggage Claim: The Myth of 'suitcase nukes,'" *WSJ.com*, October 31, 2005, at http://www.opinionjournal.com/extra/?id=110007478 (accessed October 19, 2006).

6. Read more on the issue of the alleged missing nuclear suitcases in Nikolai Sokov and William C. Potter, "'Suitcase Nukes': A Reassessment," Center for Nonproliferation Studies (CNS), September 23, 2002, at http://cns.miis.edu/pubs/week/020923.htm (accessed October 27, 2006).

7. For more on the threat posed if Russian nuclear weapons are missing, see, for example, Rensselar W. Lee and James L. Ford, "Nuclear Smuggling," in Maryann Cusimano Love, ed., *Beyond Sovereignty: Issues for a Global Agenda*, 2nd ed. (Belmont, CA: Thomson/Wadsworth, 2003), pp. 219–244; Graham Allison, *Nuclear Terrorism: The Ultimate Preventable Catastrophe* (New York: Henry Holt and Company, 2004), pp. 68–74.

8. For al-Qaeda's interest in nuclear capability, see Mike Boettcher and Ingrid Arensen, "Story: Al Qaeda Documents Outline Serious Weapons Program," *CNN.com*, January 25, 2002, at http://www.isis-online.org/publications/terrorism/cnnstory.html (accessed October 19, 2006).

9. The logic guiding Islamists' thinking about a nuclear attack on the United States may be found in Paul L. Williams, *The Al Qaeda Connection: International Terrorism, Organized Crime, and the Coming Apocalypse* (Amherst, New York: Prometheus Books, 2005), p. 38.

10. The Saudi cleric's number of 10 million is quoted in Anonymous, *Imperial Hubris: Why the West Is Losing the War on Terror* (Washington, DC: Brassey's, Inc., 2004), p. 156.

11. Bin Laden's preparation of Muslim public opinion for a particularly devastating attack on the United States is found in Ibid., pp. 152–158.

12. Ahmadinejad's boast is quoted in "Ending Iran's Genocidal Threat," Foundation for the Defense of Democracies, at http://www.defenddemocracy.org/programs/programs_show.htm?doc_id=324706 (accessed October 19, 2006).

13. Abbassi is quoted in Testimony of R. James Woolsey, "Iran: Tehran's Nuclear Recklessness and the U.S. Response," Committee on the Present Danger, November 15, 2005, at http://www.fightingterror.org/views/woolsey_15Nov2005.cfm (accessed October 19, 2006).

14. The number of containers and the search rate is found in Steinhausler, p. 131.

15. Williams's assertion that some countries believe that al-Qaeda possesses tactical nuclear bombs is found in p. 192.

16. General Habiger's contention that a nuclear attack on American soil is just a matter of when, not if, is found in Bill Keller, "Nuclear Nightmares," *New York Times Magazine* section, May 26, 2002.

17. The reasons the old pattern of thinking is no longer relevant are found in Cindy C. Combs, *Terrorism in the Twenty-First Century*, 4th ed. (Upper Saddle River, NJ: Prentice Hall, 2006), pp. 283–284. Some of the explanations and examples accompanying this section are this author's.

18. For more on the South African nuclear program, see Jessica Stern, "Getting and Using the Weapons," in Russell D. Howard and Reid L. Sawyer, eds., *Terrorism and*

Counterterrorism: Understanding The New Security Environment (Guilford, CT: McGraw-Hill/Dushkin, 2003), pp. 164–166.

19. Al-Qaeda's annual budget figure is cited in Allison, p. 24.

20. The number of countries possessing enough materials to make 240,000 nuclear weapons is cited in Ibid., p. 222.

21. For more on Admiral Khmelnov's antics, see Ibid., p. 70.

22. Laypeople wishing to learn more about the basics involved with nuclear weapons can consult Ibid., pp. 221–225; and Stern, p. 164.

23. That radioactive materials do not glow is mentioned in Paul M. Maniscalco and Hank T. Christen, *Understanding Terrorism and Managing the Consequences* (Upper Saddle River, NJ: Prentice Hall, 2002), p. 208.

24. Allison's description is found in p. 230.

25. That al-Qaeda has accelerated its quest for radioactive material is found in Jim Walsh, "America at War: Weapons of Mass Destruction," *washingtonpost.com*, December 5, 2001, at http://www.washingtonpost.com/wp-srv/liveonline/01/politics/walsh120501.htm (accessed June 6, 2006).

26. The Chechens' demonstration of their radioactive capabilities is described in Walter Laqueur, "Weapons of Mass Destruction," in Pamela L. Griset and Sue Mahan, eds., *Terrorism in Perspective* (Thousand Oaks: Sage Publications, 2003), p. 252.

27. The *General Accounting Office*'s finding is cited in Stern, p. 162. See also Steinhausler, p. 126.

28. The objectives for a radioactive attack are mentioned in Steinhausler, p. 125.

29. Powell is quoted in Laqueur (1999), p. 63.

30. These advantages of biological weapons are delineated in Ibid., p. 65.

31. The five categories of microorganisms and the discussion of their lethality appears in "Biological Weapons: What's What," United Nations Office on Drugs and Crime, June 1, 2006, at http://www.unodc.org/unodc/terrorism_weapons_mass_destruction_page005.html (accessed October 20, 2006). The problem with distinguishing between biological warfare and a natural disease can be found in "Terrorism and Weapons of Mass Destruction," United Nations Office on Drugs and Crime, June 1, 2006, at http://www.unodc.org/unodc/terrorism_weapons_mass_destruction_page002. html (accessed October 20, 2006).

32. Michael Leavitt is quoted in Katherine Hobson, "Are We Ready? A Large-Scale Disaster Like a Pandemic Flu or Terrorist Attack Could Overwhelm the Nation's Healthcare Providers," *U.S. News & World Report*, Vol. 140, No. 16 (May 1, 2006), p. 58.

33. The debate over the requirements for germ warfare is described in Laqueur (1999), p. 65.

34. The list of incidents is from Charles Stewart and Paul M. Maniscalco, "Weapons of Mass Effect: Biological Terrorism," in Maniscalco and Christen, eds., pp. 145–146.

35. The World War I historical anecdotes are from Laqueur (1999), p. 61.

36. For operation *Bacchus*, see Judith Miller, Stephen Engelberg, and William Broad, *Germs: Biological Weapons and America's Secret War* (New York: Simon & Schuster, 2001), pp. 296–299.

37. Miller's description of the difference between bacteria and viruses is found in Ibid., p. 43.

38. Interpol's assessment of the imminence of bioterrorist attacks appears in "Interpol Warns of Bioterrorism," *Jerusalem Post*, November 21, 2005.

39. For the arming of some Soviet ICBMs with anthrax, see "Biological Weapons: What's What," United Nations Office on Drugs and Crime, June 1, 2006, at http://www.unodc.org/unodc/terrorism_weapons_mass_destruction_page005.html (accessed October 20, 2006).

40. Milton Leitenberg is quoted in Ben Bain and Joseph Cirincione, "Exaggerating the Threat of Bioterrorism," March 16, 2006, at http://www.carnegieendowment.org/publications/index.cfm?fa=view&id=18135&prog=zgp&proj=znpp (accessed June 6, 2006); and Milton Leitenberg, "Bioterrorism Threat is All About Hype," *Los Angeles Times*, February 20, 2006.

41. The list of bioweapons' drawbacks, as well as the words attributed to Dr. Lederberg, is cited by Laqueur (1999), p. 69.

42. For customized bioterrorism, see "Terrorism and Weapons of Mass Destruction," United Nations Office on Drugs and Crime, June 1, 2006, at http://www.unodc.org/unodc/terrorism_weapons_mass_destruction_page002.html (accessed October 20, 2006).

43. The expression *defensive arms race* was coined by Christopher Chyba, "Toward Biology Security," in Howard and Sawyer, eds., p. 181.

44. The relative ease of manufacturing chemical poisons is described in Laqueur (1999), p. 57.

45. The Hamas plan to use cyanide against Israelis is described in Anat Aharonson, "New Information from the Verdict . . ." *Ma'ariv*, January 11, 2005.

46. The development of chemical warfare up to World War I is described in Michael L. Moodie, "The Chemical Weapon Threat," in Howard and Sawyer, eds., pp. 184–185.

47. The description of the development of chemical warfare from World War I on is available in Laqueur (1999), pp. 56–59.

48. See Laqueur (1999), pp. 57–58, for the reasons Nazi Germany did not use chemical warfare during World War II.

49. The five categories of chemical agents are mentioned in Gordon Burck, "Biological, Chemical and Toxin Warfare Agents," in Susan Wright, ed., *Preventing a Biological Arms Race* (Cambridge, MA: The MIT Press, 1990), pp. 352–367.

50. The criteria used to determine which agents to deploy in a chemical attack are found in Moodie, pp. 185–187.

51. The three steps involved in weaponizing chemical weapons are outlined in Ibid., p. 189.

52. The eight factors influencing the behavior of chemical agents are delineated in Ibid., pp. 189–191.

53. For information concerning Aum Shinrikyo's unsuccessful attack on Matsumoto, see Kyle B. Olson, "Aum Shinrikyo: Once and Future Threat," at http://www.cdc.gov/ncidod/eid/vol5no4/olson.htm (accessed June 5, 2006); Vernon Loeb, "Making Chemical Weapons Is No Easy Task," *Washington Post*, http://www.geocities.com/Area51/Shadowlands/6583/project347.html (accessed June 5, 2006).

54. The danger constituted by the American chemical infrastructure and the quote are from Angie C. Marek, "The Toxic Politics of Chemicals," *U.S. News & World Report*, Vol. 140, No. 3 (January 23, 2006), p. 32.

55. The list of 18 countries is available at Moodie, p. 194.

56. For the view that there is no universally accepted definition of cyber-terrorism, see, for example, Richard Love, "The Cyberthreat Continuum," in Love, ed., p. 205.

57. How to think of a cyber-terrorism attack is suggested in Dan Verton, *Black Ice: The Invisible Threat of Cyber-Terrorism* (New York: McGraw-Hill, 2003), p. xx.

58. For examples of databases and decision systems, see Maniscalco and Christen, p. 192.

59. The number of computer virus attacks is cited in Verton, p. ix.

60. The statistics concerning successful cyber-attacks are cited in Love, p. 195.

61. That 85% of the American infrastructure is owned by the private sector is cited in Verton, p. 22.

62. For the analogy of terrorists behaving like sharks, see Ibid., p. xxiii.

63. Of "Cybotage" as a weapon of "mass disruption," see Gregory J. Rattray, "The Cyberterrorism Threat," in *Terrorism and Counterterrorism*, in Howard and Sawyer, eds., pp. 223–224.

64. For the Black Ice and Blue Cascades exercises, see Verton, pp. 17–22.

65. The list of countries known to have weaponized information technology can be found in Ibid., p. xxiv.

66. The three methods by which information systems can be attacked, appear in Rattray, pp. 227–230.

67. The website http://www.nuclearterrorism.org is run by the Belfer Center for Science and International Affairs (BCSIA). Mentioned in this publication by permission of BCSIA's Director, Dr. Graham Allison.

PART V

FIGHTING BACK

THE LIMITS OF POWER

The conspiracy trial of Sheik Omar Abdel-Rahman, the "Blind Sheik"
Source: Courtesy of AP Wide World Photos.

FIGHTING BACK

THE LIMITS OF POWER

15

Counterterrorism on the Domestic Front

The Sisyphean Burden

The Government has a responsibility to protect our citizens, and that starts with homeland security.

President George W. Bush

❦❦❦

Defending citizens in a free society against terrorism is not simple. Consider, for example, "the most dangerous two miles in America." It is a stretch of highway in New Jersey connecting Newark's Liberty International Airport with Port Elizabeth to the east. Dozens of vulnerable industrial sites—chlorine gas processing plants, rail lines, oil storage tanks, pipelines, and refineries—dot the area and pose a deadly threat to the 12 million people living within a 14-mile radius. Making matters worse, the corridor that connects the "most dangerous two miles" to the Bayway Refinery complex at Linden—a few miles to the south—is the aptly named *chemical alley*. Serving the industrial needs of northern New Jersey are giant 90-ton railroad tankers carrying fuel, ammonia, chlorine, and other chemicals. Some of these materials are so lethal that one ruptured tank can "liquefy the lungs of people 25 miles

247

away."[1] A web of lightly guarded secondary railroads that thread their way through residential neighborhoods carries the tankers to their destinations. Sometimes, the railroads serve as temporary storage facilities for tankers full of chemicals. "We often give our enemies the means of our own destruction," wrote Aesop some 2,500 years ago. If you have ever traveled on the New Jersey Turnpike, you probably saw these black-steel tankers moving, or parked, only a few dozen yards from this major highway—a prime target for terrorists. Repeated public investigations arrive at the same conclusion: effectively safeguarding the existing transportation and physical infrastructure in chemical alley and the most dangerous two miles at current budgetary and personnel levels is beyond the authorities' capabilities. Perhaps future policy changes and rerouting the paths the chemicals travel and how they are dispersed will alleviate the problem, but, at present, defending against a catastrophic terrorist attack in northern New Jersey is a challenge with no satisfactory solution.[2]

💣💣💣

PREVENTING DOMESTIC TERRORISM: AN ISSUE OF LAW ENFORCEMENT OR WARFARE?

Most scholars and experts on terrorism agree that the big dilemma in domestic counterterrorism is whether it is an issue of criminal justice or of war. The difference is more than semantic. If authorities treat terrorism in the same way as they fight crime, the emphasis is on evidence, trial, and punishment. In the words of one analyst, a law enforcement approach in a democracy like the United States means that such things as coercion and violence by the state are exceptions and require special justification.[3]

The ramifications of a crime prevention approach could be overwhelming, if you consider that a typical single terrorist attack requires a support network of some 30 to 50 individuals who provide financing, recruitment, intelligence, indoctrination, reconnaissance, explosives and weapons expertise, transportation, public relations, and so on. If authorities treat a terrorist incident as a criminal investigation, it could be a logistical nightmare. They would have to issue warrants against hundreds of individuals in order to narrow the list to the 30 to 50 accomplices involved in each single case.

On the other hand, if authorities approached terrorism prevention as they would a war, methods and procedures that could not be used in domestic crime prevention would be allowed. The premise is that in war violence is the rule.[4]

To illustrate the quandary more vividly, fighting terrorism as if it were warfare opens a Pandora's box of controversial issues. Think of how assassinations, military tribunals, alliances with pro-American tyrants, and adherence to the Geneva Conventions in a war in which the enemy does not fight according

---

What Do YOU Think?

In 2006, some senior British police officials advocated dealing with potential terrorists in the same way they managed sex offenders, by putting less emphasis on enforcement and more on working with constituencies in the relevant communities to generate cooperation and prevent crime.[5] Do you agree with this approach when it comes to preventing terrorism?

---

to these rules—would rattle the American political landscape. Nevertheless, it is important not to lose sight of the fact that in order to be effective even a criminal approach necessitates, in the words of terrorism expert Bruce Hoffman, "nasty and brutish means."[6]

In Search of a New Paradigm

According to Paul Bremer III, at least two of the three premises that guided American counterterrorism policy until recently are no longer relevant when dealing with Middle Eastern and Islamic terrorism.[7] The three premises are (1) offering no concessions to terrorists, (2) handling terrorists as criminals, and (3) punishing countries that support terrorism. In fact, Islamist terrorism has rendered all three irrelevant for the following reasons: First, affiliates of al-Qaeda are not interested in negotiation and compromise. Since they believe their mandate is divine, the give-and-take required for successful negotiations cannot exist and the United States could never agree to the terrorists' absolute demands. Second, bringing terrorists to justice is a nonstarter when dealing with individuals who relish death and martyrdom and, therefore, would not be deterred by jail. Last, punishing states supporting terrorism is not easily done. For example, Iran has been sponsoring terrorism for decades with impunity, as has Syria. For these reasons, the old model of countering terrorism simply does not work well anymore.

This tension between the restraints of law and the desire to behave as if in a war is at the heart of the challenge of fighting terrorism because it threatens a free society's legalistic view of conflict management. Totalitarian regimes suffer few such gut-wrenching dilemmas. On the other hand, the United States must choose, when combating terrorism on its own soil, between approaching the issue as a criminal justice problem, for example, investigations, arrests, and punishments, or as a national security problem, that is, militarily. In recent years, the United States has used a combination of crime prevention techniques and warfare to prevent terrorism, amidst great legal and moral controversies and with debatable degrees of success.

PREVENTION AND DEFENSE

The United States reacted to the September 11, 2001, attacks by applying a mixture of deterrence, prevention, and defense, which constitute the essence of America's post-9/11 domestic strategy for protecting the nation. This strategy rested on four pillars: (1) the Department of Homeland Security (DHS), (2) the Patriot Act, (3) revitalizing and improving the intelligence community, and (4) increasing protection of potentially vulnerable sites.

Department of Homeland Security

The Homeland Security Act of November 2002 established a superstructure that, after a few early tries, by January 2003 morphed into what we know today as the Department of Homeland Security.[8] If, as the Arab proverb holds, an army of sheep led by a lion will always defeat an army of lions led by a sheep, the DHS's unofficial goal is to mold an antiterrorist army of lions that will be led by a lion. Officially, the department's mission is to unify the national effort to defend the country against the threat of terrorism. More specifically, among the DHS's stated strategic goals are to

- *Be aware* of potential threats and vulnerabilities.
- *Prevent* these threats.
- *Protect* the nation and its infrastructure from terrorism, natural disasters, and other emergencies.
- *Respond* to such dangers by assuming a leadership position.
- *Lead* national, state, local, and private recovery efforts following terrorist acts or natural disasters.
- *Serve* the public good in the areas of trade, travel, and immigration.

With a total workforce exceeding 180,000, the DHS has merged 22 federal agencies and now coordinates the efforts of 87,000 different governmental jurisdictions at the federal, state, and local levels in an effort to defend the nation. The magnitude of the task is breathtaking. There are 361 ports, more than 100 nuclear power plants, 300 oil refineries, 450 major airports, 10,000 highway and railroad bridges, tens of thousands of miles of electric power lines, and thousands of industrial facilities in the United States.[9] In addition—and this is an important omission in the literature on terrorism—are the territories that the United States has an obligation to protect, including Guam, the Virgin Islands, American Samoa, Midway Islands, and Wake Island, in some of which the United States has strategic naval installations.

Department of Homeland Security Organization Chart

July 2006

Department of Homeland Security Organization chart

Did You Know?

The American public seems aware of the enormity of the terrorism challenge and somewhat skeptical about the government's ability to protect it effectively. For example, in a poll conducted in July of 2005, when asked if they feared that they, or someone in their family, would become a victim of terrorism, the responses reflected this uncertainty: 14% said they were "very worried," 33% answered they were "somewhat worried."[10]

The Patriot Act

Perhaps no measure taken after 9/11 has created so much controversy as the Patriot Act. During the 1990s, as fear of terrorism grew after the first terrorist attack on the World Trade Center in New York City in 1993 and the Oklahoma City bombing of 1995, Congress passed new antiterrorist legislation, known as the Anti-Terrorism Act of 1996. The September 11 attacks, however, raised concerns that the existing laws were too weak to protect the nation effectively, and many felt a need for new laws to further empower the executive branch. In October 2001, a new body of laws were enacted by Congress and signed by President George W. Bush. The name and stated goal of the act is Uniting and Strengthening of America by Providing Appropriate Tools Required to Intercept and Obstruct Terrorism, commonly known by the acronym USA PATRIOT Act or simply Patriot Act. Essentially, the act expands the government's authority far beyond the previous limits on investigating terror-related threats, searching premises, conducting surveillance, detaining suspects, and examining suspicious activities in areas such as immigration and banking.

The Patriot Act provoked a storm of protests from individuals and groups concerned about what they believe are dangers the act poses to civil liberties. Many Americans, including some state and city governments, find the idea that the federal government can enact legislation that restricts traditional American freedoms, such as freedom of speech, the press, and the right to privacy, unacceptable and unconstitutional. (In the next chapter, some of these issues will be elaborated on in more detail.)

A CASE IN POINT: Detentions Based on Ethnic Profiling

Lessening the traditional criteria for detaining suspects resulted in "ethnic profiling." Approximately 5,000 young men, mostly Muslim, were held for questioning after the attacks of 9/11; by the end of 2001, nearly 1,200 were detained for continued interrogation. Specific charges were never filed against the majority of the detainees, and civil rights groups, such as the American Civil Liberties Union (ACLU) and Amnesty International, have criticized the detentions as violations of the detainees' civil liberties.

President George W. Bush, surrounded by lawmakers and Cabinet members, signs the HR 3199, USA PATRIOT and Terrorism Prevention Reauthorization Act of 2005
Source: Courtesy of Getty Images.

Intelligence

The third pillar on which American counterterrorism efforts rest is intelligence. After 9/11, the intelligence community was criticized for failing to prevent the calamities of that day despite its enormous annual budget of $30 billion.[11] In the investigations that followed the events of that day, critics demanded an explanation of that failure as well as assurances that the flaws would be rectified. As the Arab proverb goes, "Success has many fathers but failure is an orphan."

Diverting Blame   Following terrorist attacks, it is customary for some to point an accusatory finger at intelligence professionals for failing to sound the alarm. On the other hand, sometimes the intelligence community does issue alerts, only to see other branches of government and sometimes the country's elites failing to use the information to adequately amplify the alarm and enact appropriate policies. For example, the Bipartisan Hart-Rudman Commission on National Security in the 21st Century issued the following warning as early as 1999: "America will become increasingly vulnerable to hostile attack on our homeland. . . . Americans will likely die on

American soil, possibly in large numbers."[12] These prophetic words were mostly ignored by the administration and the media. Too often, government's inaction leaves the intelligence community exposed to criticism for the results, even when the intelligence agencies discharged their responsibilities competently and to the best of their abilities.

In the aftermath of 9/11, even as spymasters, uniformed intelligence professionals, and politicians generally declined to own up to the intelligence failure, a good number of reasons for it soon emerged. The following were among the almost universally acknowledged problems:

1. *Configuration*: Some of the intelligence community's flaws were *structural* and *procedural* in nature, which resulted in the fragmentation of the intelligence-gathering and assessment organizations and the failure to efficiently share information and coordinate operations. The primary goal in creating the Department of Homeland Security was to address such problems.

2. *Post–Cold War reductions*: With the Cold War over, many looked for a "peace dividend," the savings expected from reducing defense budgets, now that there no longer was a communist threat. The intelligence community underwent reductions in personnel and budget allocations that affected its ability to perform at peak levels.

3. *Replacement of humans with technology*: This weakness is historical in nature. The increasing reliance in recent decades on signal intelligence (SIGINT) at the expense of human intelligence (HUMINT) has proven ineffective in the war on terrorism. Where dependence on technological methods such as electronic eavesdropping may have worked well in the framework of a conventional conflict, such as the Cold War, SIGINT has proven grossly inadequate for penetrating the clan- and family-based cells characterizing Islamist terrorist groups. Consequently, following 9/11 the United States began the arduous and years-long rebuilding of its HUMINT capabilities in hostile lands.

4. *The sleaze effect*: In 1995, the Clinton administration issued a set of guidelines that forbade American intelligence officers from recruiting individuals with checkered pasts, such as those who were previously involved in terrorism. In the years following 9/11, a consensus within the Bush administration deemed this political obstacle to be a major impediment to efficient intelligence work. After all, they argued, those functioning in the shadowy world of spies and terrorists could hardly be confused with Mother Theresa. Frequently, they are petty thieves, thugs, or killers who spy on their own countries for a foreign country and, at times, even betray their families and friends, usually for money. From this perspective, the argument contends, the 1995 directive was bad for HUMINT collection and pulled the rug out from under case managers trying to

recruit informants in the back alleys of the Gaza Strip, Bogotá, Tehran, and New York City.[13]

5. *Linguists*: Americans in general do not speak foreign languages. Making matters worse, a critical shortage of interpreters and native speakers of languages such as Arabic, Farsi, and Urdu, which are of vital importance to a country in a war against Islamist terrorists, had been allowed to exist.[14]

6. *Wrong academic emphasis*: American academic institutions teaching political science tend to focus on *theory*, such as power and decision making, rather than *regional expertise,* such as the study of South Asia or the Middle East. Consequently, graduates do not understand the "real" world and are inadequately prepared for intelligence work, which requires familiarity with foreign locations.[15]

7. *Deliberate "noise"*: Terrorists can overwhelm intelligence organizations by bombarding them with so much information that the agencies cannot deal effectively with the quantity of incoming intelligence data. Capable terrorist organizations assume that, inevitably, a certain amount of information will be intercepted by their enemies. To counter this possibility, terrorists can flood the Internet and other communications media with a high volume of gibberish, known as "noise," to confuse intelligence services, distract their attention from actual plans, and manipulate them to waste time and invest resources in wild goose chases.

A Race against Time Understanding what has gone wrong with American intelligence is quite easy; fixing it is much more challenging. However, the rehabilitation work required to reposition the American intelligence community at the global cutting edge of professionalism began in the late 1990s and accelerated after the war on terrorists began in earnest following 9/11. It will

---

What Do YOU Think?

Foreigners with only a vague understanding of the Freedom of Information Act (FOIA) may be afraid to work for an American intelligence agency, lest information concerning their identity and activities might somehow be made public by a bureaucrat, and fall in the hands of their enemies. Put yourself in the shoes of a foreigner approached by an American intelligence officer who tries to recruit you to work for the United States. Being intelligent and well read, you know that the Act exists, but do not know its exclusions and exemptions. Would you agree to work for the United States if you believed that information about your activities might not be kept absolutely secret and might someday be released, jeopardizing your life and the lives of your family members?

take precious years to rebuild collapsed intelligence networks and to recruit and train intelligence operatives and spies all over the world. However, there are no other options. As one expert reminds us, unlike most other fields, when counterterrorism bats .900, it can mean a catastrophe.[16]

Defending Potential Targets

The problem the United States faces in defending an almost infinite number of potential targets is exacerbated by the ruthlessness of the terrorists, which makes even schools or hospitals attractive objectives.

A CASE IN POINT: A Surprise Package

To get a feeling of the enormity of the complex task of protecting the United States against terrorism, consider the issue of commercial shipping. Half of all American imports arrive into the country by ships carrying huge, 40-foot long containers. Up to 7 million containers enter the United States each year; the uncertainty of what they might contain poses a severe potential danger to the nation.[17] Brought to American shores from all over the world, each of these behemoths might contain a nuclear weapon or a "dirty bomb." Yet, economic pressures, the logistics of delivery, and other practical considerations dictate that only 5% of these containers are actually inspected, woefully short for effective control. Regulations require advance confirmation of the origins of the containers and the identity of the shippers, but in practice containers can pass through several suspect ports around the globe before arriving to the United States. The corruption and criminality in certain locations cast serious doubts that the containers' manifests match their actual contents. Present paperwork requirements, the minute percentage of containers inspected, and inadequate detection technology make smuggling a weapon of mass destruction into an American port city like Los Angeles or New York far from impossible.

Professor Combs conceptualizes three types of defenses: physical, operational, and personnel. While each is important in its own right, they are not mutually exclusive and are frequently used in conjunction with each other.[18]

Physical Security The purpose of physical security is to bolster the defenses of a potential terrorist target. The practice, known as "target hardening," entails one or more protective measures, such as erecting concrete barriers around public buildings, surrounding sites with regular police barricades, keeping all access to and from buildings locked at all times, magnetic ID nametags, bomb scanners, and so on.

Hardened Targets: Cost-Benefit Analysis

The notion of physical security as a major strategy for countering terrorism makes good common sense. Or does it? In a provocative work, James Stinson argues that hardening potential targets has not proven effective and terrorists historically have been highly successful in attacking well-fortified targets. According to Stinson, terrorists successfully attacked targets that were not defended at all 100% of the time and succeeded 85% of the time against the best-defended targets—a difference of only 15%! Stinson does not argue against hardening potential targets; rather, he argues for investing resources in actively preventive strategies, such as intelligence and interdiction of terrorists to complement static defense of potential targets.[19]

Operational Security   Used to curtail terrorists' ability to gather the information needed to plan and carry out an attack on a particular site, "operational security" is, in the words of Combs, "denial of opportunity." The principle behind this method of defense is straightforward: terrorists usually stake out a potential target to gather information on its procedures, personnel, safety measures, and so on, sometimes for a very long time. Alertness to strangers keeping watch on a premise, asking questions, and showing interest in its security operations can foil or divert a terrorist attack.

A CASE IN POINT: Al-Qaeda's Surveillance of U.S. Financial Institutions

The plot was in the making for years, until the 2004 arrest in England of four British citizens who were followers of al-Qaeda. Information discovered in Pakistan established that the four had been part of a conspiracy to attack major financial institutions, such as the New York Stock Exchange, on the East Coast of the United States. Between August 2000 and April 2001, they staked out the Prudential high-rise office building in Newark, New Jersey, methodically taking notes of the number of people going in and out of the building each day, the staff's routines, and security arrangements. They photographed the site as well as adjacent buildings and befriended the building maintenance staff and local shopkeepers. One of the things they concluded as a result of this surveillance was that while it would be difficult to park a truck bomb near the building, a limousine containing explosives could pull up curbside without arousing suspicion and be detonated, potentially bringing down the building and killing everybody inside. The four never aroused suspicion and the plot was still being hatched in April 2004, when the would-be terrorists were arrested in England.

Personnel Security   The threat of terrorism to individuals has been on the rise. Nowadays, one need not be an important diplomat or an industry tycoon to be a potential target. Simply by being an American, a Westerner, an "infidel," or an influential capitalist, a person may become a target of terrorists.

Personnel security is that relatively new and growing approach to training select individuals—government officials, business executives, and other individuals—who either travel frequently, do business in lands where terrorists are known to have a presence, or have personal backgrounds that might make them potential targets. The premise is to increase the probability these individuals will survive terrorist attacks, ambushes, kidnapping attempts, and so on. They are taught to keep a low profile, not to flaunt their nationality or uniqueness, and how to "escape drive." More and more American organizations, corporations, and universities simulate terrorist attacks and train their personnel in ways to survive such situations.

A Sign of the Times

As the threat of terrorism has increased in the United States, as well as globally the private sector has taken notice. Businesses devoted exclusively to antiterrorism personal protection training have mushroomed around the country. For hefty fees, individuals can enroll in schools that teach them to shoot, resist abductions, to arrange for forged credentials when traveling overseas to conceal their true nationality, and, generally, to survive terrorist attacks. Some corporations hire these training companies to conduct seminars and provide instruction to top executives whose position or travel may put them at risk.

A Case Study: Airport Security

There is hardly a better example than airport security to demonstrate how difficult it is to counter terrorism. As September 11, 2001, vividly brought home, terrorists can harm airline passengers at many stages in the process beginning with the travelers' arrival at the airport and culminating with their arrival at the airport of their destination. A brief review of some of the dangers associated with flying sheds light on the anxieties and dilemmas counterterrorism officials must confront.

The following five types of terrorist attacks that have occurred, either in an airport or in midair, represent a much wider variety of threats to the flying public:

1. *Shooting or bombing passengers as they arrive at the terminal.* In a simultaneous operation on December 27, 1985, Palestinian terrorists attacked the El Al Israeli airline check-in counters at the Rome and Vienna airports, killing 18 people and wounding 140 passengers.

2. *Shooting or bombing passengers as they wait to board the airplane.* On August 7, 1982, two terrorists belonging to the Armenian Secret Army for the Liberation of Armenia (ASALA) opened fire on passengers crowding a

waiting room at the Esenboga Airport in Ankara, Turkey. Nine passengers were killed and 82 injured.

3. *Hijacking and bombings (including suicide missions), using weapons smuggled aboard*: On November 24, 1985, terrorists belonging to Abu Nidal's renegade Palestinian group hijacked Egypt Air Flight 648 from Athens to Cairo carrying a total of 98 passengers and crew. After a bloody standoff at the airport in Malta, an Egyptian commando force effected a rescue operation that resulted in 57 dead, most of whom were passengers.

4. *Planting a barometrically triggered bomb, which would explode in midair, in a commercial package in the cargo hull under the passenger cabin.* A bomb planted on Swissair Flight 330 from Zurich to Tel Aviv exploded on February 21, 1970, killing all 38 passengers and 9 crewmembers. The terrorists used a barometric device that was automatically activated at a certain altitude.

5. *Shooting down a passenger plane with shoulder-held or antiaircraft missiles as it takes off and is most vulnerable.* On November 28, 2002, terrorists believed to be members of al-Qaeda attacked an Israeli Arkia chartered aircraft carrying 261 vacationers returning from Kenya, just as the plane cleared the runway near Mombassa and began its ascent. The terrorists fired two Soviet-era Strella ground-to-air portable missiles, but missed the left wing of the plane by only a few feet.

A CASE IN POINT: The "Shoe Bomber"

Richard Reid, a convert to Islam and an affiliate of al-Qaeda, tried to blow up American Airlines Flight 63 while en route from Paris to Miami on December 22, 2001. Two hundred people were spared because Reid smuggled explosives on board by hiding them in his shoes, but had trouble igniting them, which allowed other passengers to notice his unusual behavior and subdue him.

These five are a sample of the most common types of attacks; other possible threats to airport and airline industry security include

- Attacks on passengers as they land, deplane, await their luggage, or are about to exit the terminal.
- Suicide attacks from an especially outfitted private plane on a passenger aircraft.
- Attacks by terrorists who use stolen airport personnel ID tags to gain access to passenger aircraft.

- Attacks by "screeners" of passengers and baggage, "the foxes guarding the chickens," as one writer put it, referring to the fact that occasionally individuals with criminal backgrounds have been hired to these positions.[20]
- Attacks that result from lapses by airport security personnel who may be underequipped, undertrained, and undermotivated.

With large vulnerable crowds congregating at airports or jammed into thin tubes between heaven and earth, the stakes are high and the challenge of protecting them great.

A CASE IN POINT: Securing Airline Safety

The Israeli national airline, El Al, is known for having the epitome of airline security. The following measures provide an eye-opening glimpse into the unique world of an efficient airline security system:

- Covert, armed security officers roam the terminal, watching the human traffic.
- Passengers must check-in three hours prior to departure so that a thorough security check can be done.
- Complete screening of all passengers, including an oral interview with each and an examination of every passenger's check-in and carry-on luggage and bags using state-of-the-art explosive detection equipment.
- Shipper verification of each commercial package or box before it goes into the cargo hull.
- Neutralization of barometrically triggered charges by putting all commercial cargo through decompression chambers.
- Several undercover air marshals fly on each flight.
- No flights into or out of airports deemed insecure.
- Planes equipped with antimissile technology.
- All baggage reconciled against passengers to prevent unaccompanied luggage from being placed on a plane.

A NEVER-ENDING WAR

Counterterrorism is a war, but not the kind of war that has a beginning and an end. Americans are not accustomed to this type of protracted conflict; they typically think wars are fierce, but of limited duration and end in overwhelming victories. Because indecisive conclusions or perceived losses, such as in Vietnam, leave a bitter taste, and since the war against terrorism is unlikely to end with the tangible collapse of an easily identifiable enemy, the danger exists that the endless shadowy war against the terrorists will eventually meet with public impatience and apathy. Former CIA official Paul Pillar expressed this understanding best, when he likened counterterrorism to the fight against communicable diseases. Thinking of counterterrorism this way helps explain that the battle ahead will entail victories as well as setbacks as authorities struggle with various threats around the world. In Pillar's words, "terrorism cannot be 'defeated'—only reduced, attenuated, and to some degree controlled."[21] Therefore, expectations should be realistic: "Terrorism happens. It should never be accepted, but it should always be expected."[22]

SUMMARY

In this chapter, you have learned the following:

1. Protecting the United States against terrorism on its own soil is exceptionally difficult because of its freedoms, size, and extensive international commerce.

2. Domestic counterterrorism efforts in a democratic society are mired in the debate over whether the proper approach is one of law enforcement or military.

3. American counterterrorism strategies on the domestic front rest on four pillars:

   A. Establishing the Department of Homeland Security to coordinate and lead the effort.

   B. Enacting legislation, known as the Patriot Act, which gives more power to the federal government, in particular the executive branch of government.

   C. Rehabilitating the country's intelligence capabilities.

   D. "Hardening" potential targets.

4. The "war on terrorism" assumes that protecting the homeland is a protracted undertaking with no discernible end for many years to come.

💣💣💣

When Germany was divided between the communist East and the capitalist West, a tale has it that an East German man would ride his bicycle each morning across the border into the West, carrying a different package each time. Suspecting that he was smuggling contraband into the West, the East German guards checked the man and his packages thoroughly, always finding nothing. After years of searching in vain, but certain that the cyclist was up to something, curiosity got the better of the guards and they promised they would allow him to continue to do what he did with impunity if only he told them his secret. The man relented and told them the truth with a smile: each morning, he smuggled a stolen bicycle into the West. This man was only a thief; nowadays, a similar case might involve a terrorist. Security may check the packages of the delivery person, but the vehicle itself may be rigged as a truck bomb. Routine is security's worst enemy and what meets the eye is often an illusion.

💣💣💣

NOTES

1. "Liquefy the lungs of people 25 miles away" is found in Ron Marsico and Alexander Lane, "Terrorist Targets Sit in State's Rail Yards," *Star Ledger*, July 25, 2005.

2. More information regarding the dangers industrial chemicals pose to northern New Jersey can be found in David Kocieniewski, "Facing the City, Potential Targets Rely on a Patchwork of Security," in the *New York Times*, May 9, 2005, at http://www.nytimes.com/2005/05/09/nyregion/09homeland.html?ex=1273291 200&en=b3a933ec6ddf6c89&ei=5089 (accessed June 15, 2006); Marsico and Lane, "Terrorist Targets Sit in State's Rail Yards."

3. That criminal justice renders violence by the state the exception and in need of special justification is found in Andrew Hurrell, "There Are No Rules (George W. Bush): International Order After September 11," in Gus Martin, ed., *The New Era of Terrorism: Selected Readings* (Dominguez Hills, CA: Sage Publications, 2004), p. 210.

4. That in war, violence by the state is the rule is found in Hurrell, p. 210.

5. The idea of managing terrorism suspects in the same way as sex offenders can be found in Royston Martis, "Potential Terrorists Should Be Diverted and Not Criminalized," *Jane's*, June 22, 2006.

6. Hoffman's remark that the war against terrorism is a "nasty and brutish" endeavor is found in Bruce Hoffman, "A Nasty Business," in Martin, ed. p. 226.

7. For the irrelevance of the previous model for countering terrorism, see L. Paul Bremer III, "A New Strategy for the New Face of Terrorism," in Martin, ed., p. 244.

8. The following information, including the organizational chart, is available on the DHS website, at http://www.dhs.gov.

9. The figures for the number of ports is found in Scott Gourley, "Inside Job: US Seeks Solutions for its Security Jigsaw," *Jane's*, March 3, 2006. For the additional data in this paragraph, see Daniel Gouré, "Homeland Security," in Audrey Kurth Cronin and James M. Ludes, eds., *Attacking Terrorism: Elements of a Grand Strategy* (Washington, DC: Georgetown University Press, 2004), p. 277.

10. The poll measuring the level of confidence Americans have that government will protect them from terrorism appears in http://www.albany.edu/sourcebook/pdf/ t2292005. pdf (accessed June 22, 2006).

11. The figure of $30 billion as the annual budget of the American intelligence community is found in Richard Betts, "Intelligence Test: The Limits of Prevention," in James F. Hoge, Jr. and Gideon Rose, eds., *How Did This Happen: Terrorism and the New World* (New York: Public Affairs Reports, 2001), p. 145.

12. The United States Commission on Security/21st Century, "Major Themes And Implications," September 15, 1999, "Conclusions" section, article 1, at http://www.au.af.mil/au/awc/awcgate/nssg/nwc.pdf (accessed October 27, 2006).

13. To read more about the problem of working with dubious characters, see Bremer III, p. 245.

14. The intelligence community's shortage of linguists is found in Betts, p. 161.

15. The training of American university graduates is mentioned in Ibid., p. 161.

16. The idea of batting .900 is found in Ibid., p. 161.

17. For the figure of 7 million shipping containers, see Joe Charlaff, "Shipping Containers: The Next Port of Call for Terrorism?" *Jane's*, April 21, 2006.

18. The three types of defense are discussed in Cindy C. Combs, *Terrorism in the Twenty-First Century*, 3rd ed. (Upper Saddle River, NJ: Prentice Hall, 2003) , pp. 241–243.

19. Stinson's work is cited in Jonathan R. White, *Terrorism: An Introduction*, 4th ed. (Belmont, CA: Wadsworth/Thomson Learning, 2002), pp. 280–282.

20. The comparison with "the foxes guarding the chickens" was originally used in this context by Kathleen M. Sweet in one of the best books available on the legal aspects of air travel security, *Aviation and Airport Security: Terrorism and Safety Concerns* (Upper Saddle River, NJ: Pearson/Prentice Hall, 2004), p. 178.

21. That terrorism cannot be defeated, only reduced, comes from Paul R. Pillar, "Lessons and Futures," in Griset and Mahan, eds., *Terrorism in Perspective* (Thousand Oaks: Sage Publications, 2003), p. 218.

22. For the assertion that terrorism should be expected, see Ibid.

16

Counterterrorism on the Domestic Front

Legal and Moral Dilemmas

They that can give up essential liberty to obtain a little temporary safety deserve neither liberty nor safety.

Benjamin Franklin

In the first four months following the September 11 attacks, 98% of the official business of the House of Representatives and 97% of the Senate's had to do with terrorism. Whereas Congress proposed some 1,300 resolutions, bills, and amendments in its entire history, in these four months alone Congress proposed 450 counterterrorism measures. At the same time, President George W. Bush issued 12 executive orders and ten presidential proclamations related mostly to domestic antiterrorism measures. The shared common denominator was an alleged trend toward intrusion into constitutionally guaranteed civil liberties.[1]

AT WHAT PRICE LIBERTY?

Defending the nation is an imperative few would deny, but the means used to accomplish the task are at the heart of a debate that has been raging in the United States since September 11, 2001. Its essence concerns the need to reconcile the conflict between safeguarding the people's well-being and property on the one hand and preserving their civil liberties on the other.

At a time when civilians are deliberately targeted and prisoners of war tortured and beheaded by terrorists, the debate in the United States involves wise and honorable people on both sides of the divide over issues that are not trivial. The different perspectives are best understood by reviewing an example of each. One school of thought advocates adjusting the laws to reflect the new security reality after September 11; the other school is alarmed by the possible harm tinkering with freedoms could inflict on both civil liberties and human rights.

Urgent Risks Require Urgent Measures

Stuart Taylor, Jr., an expert on constitutional and international law, maintains that the type of war the United States currently faces is unprecedented because the enemy is an "army" of martyrdom-seeking Islamist fanatics who have publicly expressed their desire to attack civilians with weapons of mass destruction.[2] Therefore, he advocates a nontraditional approach in order to appropriately protect the nation, citing the American historical experience that when "dangers increase, liberties shrink." Taylor's point of departure is that the terrorist threat necessitates a reevaluation of the principles of civil liberties insofar as they restrict the government's ability to protect the homeland adequately. Specifically, he recommends that Congress pass laws that will enable the executive branch to discharge its mandate more effectively without judicial restrictions. Moreover, Taylor holds that new legislation that improves the nation's security will ultimately enhance liberties by setting reasonable limits on the power of the executive, which will ensure that government adheres to laws considered more practical and relevant. According to Taylor, it is preferable to adjust the rules and stop terrorism than to adhere to rigid laws

---

What Do YOU Think?

Do you agree with the maxim "extraordinary circumstances require extraordinary measures," as it applies to the war against terrorists and their supporters? Given the terrorists' disregard for international law as well as their ruthlessness, how should a democratic society prosecute a war when confronting an enemy whose fighting methods are incompatible with international law?

What Do YOU Think?

What would your reaction be to a new federal law mandating that to increase domestic security, each American citizen carry a national identification card at all times? Explain your position.

---

and suffer the consequences, because "preventing terrorist mass murder is the best way of avoiding a panicky stampede into truly oppressive police stateism, in which measures now unthinkable could suddenly become unstoppable."

Taylor quotes former law professor and later judge of the U.S. Court of Appeals for the Seventh Circuit, Richard A. Posner, "The safer the nation feels the more weight judges will be willing to give to the liberty interest." Taylor's opinion is that present laws enable authorities to deal with drug dealers and robbers but not with the most important threat facing the American public today because civil libertarians have "underestimated the need for broader investigative powers and exaggerated the danger to our fundamental liberties." Taylor contends that the only practical methods authorities can use to counter terrorists are to infiltrate their groups with covert agents, conduct surveillance and searches, and use detention and interrogation of those detained. Except for infiltration, existing laws are too restrictive for these methods to be effective. He quotes Lawrence H. Tribe of the Harvard Law School, who asserts that "The old adage in that it is better to free 100 guilty men than to imprison one innocent describes a calculus that our Constitution—which is no suicide pact—does not impose on government when the 100 who are freed belong to terrorist cells that slaughter innocent civilians. . . ."[3]

On Preventive Detentions

Taylor finds the concept of preventive detention potentially worthwhile. Dissecting the government's options in cases involving strong suspicion of future involvement in terrorism, he points out four possible courses of action and the results he foresees: (1) Leave suspects alone and unmonitored and one day they might commit a terrorist act of mass murder, (2) Put suspects under surveillance and tail them until they give the agents the slip and disappear, (3) Prosecute suspects with little concrete evidence, and risk almost certain acquittal, (4) Preventive detention.[4]

Fear of a "Counterterrorist Spiral"[5]

Laura K. Donohue, Fellow at the Center for Constitutional Law at Stanford Law School, offers a timely representation of the ideas of those who are uneasy with any increase in the executive branch's power, which they believe may lead to an erosion in the basic rights of individuals. Since terrorists use the freedom of an open society to facilitate their acts, the instinctive backlash is to close the society, contends Donohue. This tendency, she writes, creates problems in two areas: the *civil liberties of citizens* and the *human rights of noncitizens*. The first, readily understood in a democratic society, results from the possible conflict between the new security measures and citizens' constitutional rights.

The second type of danger derives from the very nature of major terrorist incidents, which carry the potential to provoke violations of the human rights of noncitizens who share ethnic, religious, or ideological characteristics with the perpetrators. Civil liberties and human rights are not synonyms. The former denotes the rights guaranteed to citizens of a particular country by that country's laws and institutions. In the United States, they include such things as freedom of speech and freedom of religion. The latter alludes to norms that are recognized as inalienable to every human being regardless of nationality, such as the right not to be discriminated against because of color, race, religion, or sex, the right to life, and the right not to be subject to cruel or inhuman treatment.

Donohue carefully examines both sides of the debate and points to the three specific measures introduced after September 11 which she finds violate civil liberties and human rights (in addition, she finds them generally ill-advised). The three are (1) detention and interrogation, (2) military tribunals, and (3) the death penalty.

1. *Detentions and interrogations*: In the aftermath of the September 11 attacks, authorities launched an unprecedented campaign to identify potential terrorists or their affiliates in order to prevent future attacks. Due to the broad parameters of the new antiterrorism legislation, individuals whom, in the past, the government could not even touch because all law enforcement had on them was a mere unsubstantiated suspicion became official targets for investigation and detention. For example, lists were created of young Muslim males who entered the country after January of 2000 and students visiting from Muslim countries in more than 200 universities.

   The measures did not stop there. Five thousand people were questioned and 1,200 detained. Immigration judges were overruled, noncitizens were held indefinitely, and the authorities monitored communications between detainees and their attorneys. In retrospect, we know that only a handful of these individuals were considered material witnesses and that authorities violated the universal human right against discrimination due to ethnicity or religion.

2. *Military tribunals*: On November 13, 2001, President Bush issued an order allowing the detention and prosecution of noncitizen suspected terrorists by military tribunals outside of the United States. The new rules allowed relaxed standards of evidence, secret proceedings, and a death penalty by

a two-thirds vote and without any right of appeal. In her analysis of this order, Donohue points out the following:

- The President has no authority to introduce military tribunals. The historical precedents often mentioned stem from Congressional, not presidential, authority.
- U.S. criminal courts are up to the task, as the high conviction rates in the various terrorism cases brought before them proves.
- The nature of the post–9/11 tough, new immigration laws infringes on certain individuals' basic human rights.
- The very existence of military tribunals indicates an interest in a higher rate of convictions rather than in justice.
- Due to the charged climate generated by terrorism, using ordinary criminal courts helps ensure that reason prevails, and facts, not emotions, lead to conclusions.
- Military tribunals are frowned on internationally, encourage other countries to use similar methods to advance dubious policies, and unnecessarily harm America's reputation.

3. *The death penalty*: Donohue outlines three arguments against capital punishment in cases related to terrorism:

- Numerous studies in traditional criminal cases indicate that the death penalty is not an effective deterrence. Moreover, in cases of terrorism, executing a terrorist may turn the person into a martyr and a role model for a new wave of terrorists.
- Execution, obviously, is irreversible. If a mistake is made, nothing can rectify the mistake and bring the person back to life.
- Most democracies have abolished capital punishment. Use of the death penalty puts the United States in an awkward position, out of sync with the progressive international community.

Did You Know?

Revelations that the U.S. government used a domestic surveillance program, which critics charge is illegal, to secure dozens of convictions of suspected al-Qaeda members may result in the convictions being overturned across the board. Based on a legal concept known as "the fruit of the poisonous tree," evidence found through illegal means may not be used to convict a defendant. Following the exposure of this surveillance program, lawyers for the convicted have been gearing up to challenge the convictions on the grounds that the clues which led authorities to their clients' arrests had been obtained illegally, therefore, tainting the judicial process and manipulating the system to secure convictions unlawfully. If the legal challenge proves successful, it will inflict a serious blow to some of the government's most coveted court victories in the war on terrorists.[6]

In Professor Donohue's view, by tipping the scale in the delicate balance between security and freedom too far in favor of security, the United States will emerge a loser—and not just at home. Internationally, such practices as secret proceedings, military tribunals, capital punishment, and violations of rights and freedoms will create a groundswell of animosity toward the United Sates, antagonize people and elites the world over, and give rise to great cynicism about American stated goals of promoting democracy, liberty, and human rights.

THE DEBATE GOES ON

The points of view represented by Taylor and Donohue illustrate a wider societal rift, not simply a disagreement between two schools of thought in an isolated academic ivory tower. Neither do the lines drawn in the sand mark a simplistic division between conservatives on the one side and liberals on the other; or one in which military and security personnel square off against a supposed leftist intelligentsia. Rather, it is a cultural divide characterized by individual reflection and moral standing on the issue. For example, former CIA Director William Webster cautioned against overreacting to domestic terrorism threats lest rights and liberties were lost in the process.[7]

Legal Questions

Similarly, legal authorities, journalists, and academicians one might expect would be associated with the liberal side of such a debate have defended certain tougher legal measures to counter domestic terrorism. For example, Judge Richard Posner dismisses the approach that seeks to subordinate the war on terrorism to the loss of civil liberties. Quoting Supreme Court Justice Robert Jackson's famous observation that "the Bill of Rights should not be made into a suicide pact," Posner maintains that fighting terrorists requires police measures *and* military force, which, he says, means "our civil liberties will be curtailed. They *should* be curtailed, to the extent that the benefits in greater security outweigh the costs in reduced liberty." The law is not an absolute, a divine gift, or a mandarin mystery, writes Posner, but a human creation intended to promote social welfare. It follows that laws should be changed to reflect the people's security needs until the threat to their lives and property is over.[8]

As the "war on terrorism" appears to be ongoing with no end in sight, there is no clear, decisive resolution for the "security versus liberties" quandary. The standing on the issue becomes a function of time, place, and circumstance. Jeremy D. Mayer, a professor of public policy, attempted to reconcile the two perspectives by synthesizing the controversy this way:[9] The most important obligations of government are to provide for the common defense, ensure domestic tranquility, promote the general welfare, and then to secure the blessings of liberty. Safeguarding the citizenry is an idea older than the Constitution itself. Mayer concedes that during emergencies the courts have interpreted constitutional safeguards more flexibly, based on the nature of the emergency. For example, the Constitution limits authorities' ability to arrest and search suspects to cases in which there is "probable cause" only. Once circumstances change, however, so does the way in which the Constitution is interpreted. Thus, searching a pilot of Middle Eastern descent prior to 9/11 without "probable cause" was unthinkable. After 9/11, searching such a pilot became acceptable as "probable cause." "The Constitution did not change," writes Mayer, "what changed was the nature of the threat." He allows that historically there is room for concern over civil liberties during times of war and crises, but that concern has to be balanced by the imperative of public safety, best articulated by *Time* essayist Lance Morrow: "A rattlesnake loose in the living room tends to end any discussion of animal rights."[10] Still, in the conflict between the opposing forces pulling in the opposite directions of defense and liberty, we need to be wary that Congress and the executive branches are susceptible to popular pressures and public polls. Fortunately, opined two other legal scholars, "No other branch of our government is as qualified to draw lines between the rights of individuals and those of society as the Supreme Court of the United States. The legislative and executive branches yield all too easily to the politically expedient and the popular." Only the Court can reliably "draw a line based on constitutional common sense."[11]

Interrogating Suspected Terrorists and the Fifth Amendment

The Fifth Amendment to the U.S. Constitution contains the famous clause that an individual "shall not be compelled in any criminal case to be a witness against himself." This, according to Stuart Taylor, Jr., means that the Fifth Amendment guarantees that suspects may not be forced to testify against themselves. However, authorities have the right to interrogate a suspect without Miranda warnings, reject requests for a lawyer, and extract answers vigorously because suspects have the right not to incriminate themselves, but have no constitutional right not to incriminate others![12]

Moral Dictates

The question is not restricted to legal issues alone; *moral* issues are also a prominent piece in this intellectual puzzle. A helpful way to think about morality in the war against terrorists is to apply Professor Manuel G. Valasquez's "ethical approach" concept to our discussion of combating terrorism on American soil.[13] In general, excluding the religious dimension, the concept of "ethics" boils down to three things:

1. *Utilitarianism*: If resources are finite, how useful will a particular solution be in satisfying the needs of the maximum number of people?
2. *Morality*: Rights and responsibilities must be applied equally to each individual according to universal moral standards, such as the right not to be discriminated against because of color, race, religion, or sex and the responsibility to adhere to the law.

A Case in Point: Renditions—Moral or Not?

A secret CIA program for fighting terrorism became public knowledge in 2006. Referred to as "renditions," this global CIA-sponsored operation apprehended individuals with suspected ties to terrorism and secretly whisked them away to countries in the Middle East and Eastern Europe for interrogation under torture. Legal aspects notwithstanding, the morality of the policy can be ascertained by answering Valazquez's three questions. After we ask ourselves the second question, the issue is settled. It is obvious that the program violated the suspects' universal rights not to be subject to cruel and inhumane treatment. Hence, the program was morally wrong.

3. *Justice*: The societal criteria that determine how benefits and burdens, such as social security benefits and property taxes, are distributed among members of the community.

Valazquez suggests three questions decision makers should ask themselves when considering the moral implications of their decisions. These are applicable to enacting counterterrorism measures as well:

1. Will the choice maximize social benefits and minimize social injuries?
2. Is the choice compatible with the universal rights of the people it will affect?
3. Will the choice result in a just distribution of benefits and burdens?

PROTECTION OR ABUSE?

The U.S. Patriot Act, rushed through Congress in the wake of 9/11, consists of more than 1,000 antiterrorism measures. In the years since, clandestine initiatives aimed at enhancing the nation's security, albeit controversial in many respects, were implemented in the United States and abroad. Whenever such initiatives are exposed, they raise questions among concerned citizenry because they frequently involve domestic "spying programs." While there have been controversial undertakings at the international level, the following is a sample of some of the controversial secret *domestic* programs.[14]

- The domestic "data mining" program of the National Security Agency (NSA). NSA, which legally eavesdrops on global communications, has been monitoring the phone calls and e-mails of thousands of Americans without obtaining warrants in search of terrorism leads.
- The FBI launched secret investigations into groups of animal rights, environmental, and anti–Iraq war activists after September 11. It even conducted surveillance of Roman Catholic clerics who were peace activists.
- The FBI considerably expanded its scrutiny of "national security letters," a term that actually covers phone records, e-mails, and financial transactions.

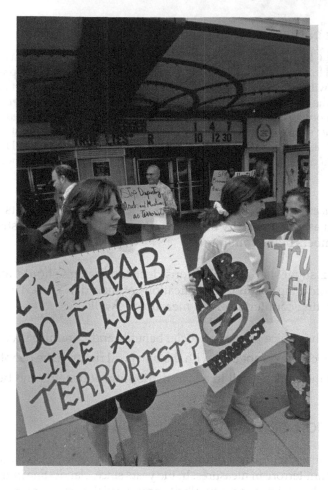

Arab-Americans protest equating Arabs with terrorists
Source: Courtesy of PhotoEdit Inc.

The figure reportedly shot up from a few, rare cases to 30,000 per year—all without the benefit of court review.

- Department of Defense officials have been accumulating a database of anti–Iraq war and anti–military recruitment protesters.

- The New York Police Department planted undercover officers in antiwar rallies.

Officials have defended such programs vigorously, contending that the charges are exaggerated and that in the antiterrorism war, Americans "want the president to err on the side of safety."[15] Many disagree. Senators, Congress people, members of the judiciary, academicians, media personalities, and a multitude of concerned citizens have rejected these programs, worried that

---

What Do YOU Think?

Under what conditions, if any, would you justify government efforts to institute tough security measures to safeguard the well-being of the American people if doing so entails curtailment of certain civil rights? Explain why.

---

they violate the various rights and civil liberties guaranteed in the Constitution and law, and will lead the U.S. law down the infamous "slippery slope." The dispute is intense and not going away anytime soon.

Assassinations: A Case Study

The issue of assassinations of terrorist leaders and operators provides a classic example of the hard choices and limitations facing authorities struggling to nip terrorism in the bud. At the core of the issue are international law and U.S. federal law. Attorney Daniel B. Pickard examined the legality of assassinations.[16] Because most readers are not expected to be of the "esquire" persuasion and thus in need of a deep and lengthy analysis of legal precedents and dissenting opinions, his study provides a succinct overview of the essence of the law in this regard.

International law forbids assassinations. However, according to Pickard, even though it is somewhat counterintuitive, it can be argued that international law allows for exceptions in cases involving terrorism. What may make assassination in the context of counterterrorism permissible is the body of international law which views such action as legally justified when it can be deemed self-defense. The argument goes that in the modern era terrorists can be viewed as yesteryears' pirates—*hostes humani generis*—common enemies of humankind, and treated accordingly. The author cautions that this opinion while plausible is not universally accepted.

U.S. law concerning assassinations may come as a surprise to many who are under the impression that assassinations are forbidden. For telling reasons, it does not forbid assassinations. President Ford issued Executive Order 12333 in 1976 that barred all government employees or agents from engaging in assassinations or from being involved in such activities. Significantly, however, Congress has never enacted its own specific legislation to forbid assassinations, a failure that speaks volumes about an implicit leeway deliberately left to a president, who could withdraw the Executive Order banning assassinations and use this policy in the future as he or she thought fit.

This situation, argues Pickard, leaves the option of assassinating terrorists arguably legal and subject only to a cost–benefit analysis of the practical implications of such actions. On the benefit side of the equation, assassinations may prevent a future catastrophe, entail fewer casualties than a widespread conventional attack would, target specific guilty parties, disrupt terrorist

What Do YOU Think?

Having read about the legality and wisdom of assassinating terrorists, what do you think about the American government using every opportunity it has to expedite the meeting of terrorist leaders and their maker whenever an opportunity presents itself? Why?

plans, and avoid situations in which captured terrorists become magnets for further attacks aimed at releasing them. On the liabilities side of the spreadsheet in this cost–benefit calculation is the argument that assassinations of influential terrorists may result in the targeting of American leaders for assassination, and that it is unbecoming for a great democracy such as the United States to stoop to the level of terrorists and emulate the repugnant practices assassination operations entail.

SUMMARY

In this chapter, you have learned the following:

1. In fighting terrorism in the domestic arena, it is difficult to reconcile the quest for increased security with the imperative of preserving civil liberties.
2. The dilemma is heightened by the temptations the terrorists' illegal methods pose to authorities' restraints.
3. Some argue that in the era of weapons of mass destruction, curtailing certain freedoms is inevitable in order to safeguard the majority of other rights and liberties.
4. Others contend that curtailing freedoms—as in the case of detentions, military tribunals, and the death penalty—will not increase security and will lead to ever-greater diminution of rights, the so-called slippery slope.
5. Controversial secret spying programs by the American government have further stoked the flames of the debate.
6. Both international and U.S. laws do not necessarily preclude the use of assassination of important terrorists as part of the war against terrorists and their supporters.

💣💣💣

The dispute over the balance between increasing security and violating civil liberties is fierce and angry. Even measures that at first glance appear sensible and beyond question are subject to heated controversy and plausible counterarguments. For example, in March 2005, the New York City Police Department reacted to threats of terrorism in the city's transportation venues by screening the personal possessions of randomly selected individuals entering the subway system. This security measure appeared perfectly reasonable to many, but it was immediately challenged in court. On August 4, 2005, five subway riders in New York City, along with the New York Civil Liberties Union (NYCLU), an affiliate of the American Civil Liberties Union (ACLU), sued the New York Police Department.

To some people's astonishment, when examined, the opposite perspective makes sense too. According to the plaintiffs, the NYPD had violated the Fourth Amendment rights of the commuters by randomly searching them although there was no suspicion that those selected had done anything wrong. Terming the search policy "unprecedented, unlawful and ineffective," the plaintiffs objected to searching millions of innocent people, a practice which was also bound to lead to "impermissible racial profiling." Moreover, according to the lawsuit, the NYPD's policy made no sense since the searches were not conducted at all subway entrances, police gave advance notice of those stations where searches would take place, allowed those refusing to be searched to simply walk away from the station, and did not target specific individuals exhibiting suspicious behavior. In short, the policy was useless for preventing terrorism while infringing on individuals' civil liberties unnecessarily.[17] This legal challenge is still pending in the courts.

💣💣💣

NOTES

1. The figures on the unusual flurry of antiterrorism legislation are in Laura K. Donohue, "Fear Itself: Counterterrorism, Individual Rights, and U.S. Foreign Relations Post 9–11," in Russell D. Howard and Reid L. Sawyer, eds., *Terrorism and Counterterrorism: Understanding The New Security Environment* (Guilford, CT: McGraw-Hill/Dushkin, 2003), p. 275.

2. The article by Stuart Taylor, Jr., advocating recalibration of the balance between security and freedoms is found in Stuart Taylor, Jr., "Right, Liberties, and Security: Recalibrating the Balance After September 11," in Gus Martin, ed., *The New Era of Terrorism: Selected Readings* (Dominguez Hills, CA: Sage Publications, 2004), pp. 218–225.

3. The adage may be found in Ibid., p. 225.

4. Taylor's argument in favor of preventive detentions is in Ibid., p. 224.

5. See Donohue's discussion in Howard and Sawyer, eds., pp. 275–300.

6. For more on the legal challenge stemming from the secret eavesdropping program, see Eric Lichtblau and James Risen, "Defense Lawyers in Terror Cases Plan Challenges Over Spy Efforts," *New York Times*, December 28, 2005.

7. For the citation of William Webster, see Jonathan R. White, *Terrorism: An Introduction*, 4th ed. (Belmont, CA: Wadsworth/Thomson Learning, 2002), p. 276.

8. Posner's views are found in Richard A. Posner, "Security Versus Civil Liberties," in Alan J. Cigler, ed., *Perspectives On Terrorism: How 9/11 Changed U.S. Politics* (New York: Houghton Mifflin Company, 2002), pp. 59–62.

9. Jeremy D. Meyer, *9–11: The Giant Awakens* (Belmont, CA: Wadsworth/Thomson Learning, 2003), pp. 38–39.

10. Lance Morrow is quoted in Ibid., p. 39.

11. The two legal experts cited in the discussion about the reliability of the Supreme Court are Henry J. Abraham and Barbara A. Perry, *Freedom and the Court: Civil Rights and Liberties in the United States*, 7th ed. (New York: Oxford University Press, 1998), pp. 217 and 220, respectively.

12. For the discussion on the Fifth Amendment, see Taylor, pp. 222–223.

13. The discussion about ethical approaches is found in Manuel G. Valasquez, *Business Ethics*, 5th ed. (Upper Saddle River, NJ: Prentice Hall, 2002).

14. The spying programs are mentioned in David Kaplan, "The Eyes Have It," *U.S. News & World Report*, Vol. 140, No. 1 (January 9, 2006), pp. 21–23.

15. For the assertion that Americans prefer the president to "err on the side of safety," see Ibid., p. 22.

16. Daniel B. Pickard, "Legalizing Assassinations? Terrorism, the Central Intelligence Agency, and International Law," in Howard and Sawyer, eds., pp. 518–542.

17. For more on the lawsuit against the NYPD, see http://www.nyclu.org/mta_searches_suit_pr_080405.html (accessed July 5, 2006).

THE FUTURE

Terrorism posing a threat to the whole world
Source: Courtesy of Creative Eye/MIRA.com.

PART VI

THE FUTURE

17

An Outlook of Discontent

What the Future Holds

The wave of the future is not the conquest of the world by a single dogmatic creed but the liberation of the diverse energies of free nations and free men.

John F. Kennedy

🔥●🔥●🔥

The Doomsday Clock is a tangible illustration of the degree of danger humankind faces from a nuclear holocaust. Created by the *Bulletin of the Atomic Scientists* in 1947, the minute hand of this "clock" changes periodically to indicate how far humanity is from "midnight," the metaphoric eruption of a nuclear devastation. Over the years, the time on this symbolic clock moved from seven minutes to midnight at the beginning of the Cold War in 1947 to three minutes in 1949 after the Soviet Union exploded its first nuclear device, to two minutes in 1953 when both countries armed themselves with thermonuclear weapons. The Doomsday Clock also reflects tension and conflict, the addition of new countries with nuclear capabilities to the nuclear club, nuclear disarmament treaties, the collapse of the Soviet Union—and the fear that event triggered about the safety of its nuclear arsenal—and the reports that terrorists have been trying to acquire nuclear devices with the intention of using them. All together, the clock has been changed 19 times—during periods of promise, backwards, and during periods of tensions or negative developments, forward, closer to midnight. In 2007, the clock moved to five minutes to midnight. Paul Williams, describing the danger of nuclear terrorism the Doomsday Clock reflects, put it this way, "Millions of Americans may be living on borrowed time."[1]

💣 💣 💣

"The afternoon knows what the morning never suspected," says a Swedish proverb, and it is not unique. The folklore of many cultures is laden with warnings against the folly of making predictions and engaging in prophecy. The perils of doing so are abundantly illustrated by the prophecies of many noted scholars and experts over the last 20 years that downplayed the threat of terrorism as "exaggerated," or believed that social deterrence would some-how curb future terrorism. It must be conceded that nobody knew better.

Who could, decades ago, imagine a phenomenon like al-Qaeda, foresee narcoterrorism in Latin America and the emergence of organizations such as Hezbollah, or predict the almost total disappearance of left-wing terrorism in Europe? Nothing rivals the wisdom of hindsight. Perhaps terrorism in the Middle East could have been foreseen and the experts not so readily exonerated. There is a good reason for the saying that nobody has ever lost money betting *against* peace in the Middle East. However, in general, although it is usually futile to predict the future without the help of a crystal ball, we have now reached the point in our saga of having to do just that. As the great inventor Charles F. Kettering explained, "My interest is in the future because I am going to spend the rest of my life there."

FIGHTING TERRORISM IN A WORLD IN TRANSITION

Understanding future trends in terrorism requires an awareness of general developments and trends in international relations. In recent years, three particularly influential works speculate about the future: Francis Fukuyama's *The End of History and the Last Man*, Samuel Huntington's *The Clash of Civilization and the Remaking of World Order*, and Benjamin Barber's *Jihad vs. McWorld: How Globalism and Tribalism are Reshaping the World*. To help us make educated guesses about the future, we will first consider these authors' thinking on the subject.

Francis Fukuyama's *The End of History and the Last Man*, published in 1992,[2] was an optimistic analysis of world affairs. Fukuyama's central premise is that the great clash of ideas over the best way to organize societies ended with the collapse of communism and victory of liberal democracy. The "motor of history," as Fukuyama conceptualized the process, rests on two factors: (1) humankind's relentless drive to better itself through a "rational economic process," and (2) individuals' ceaseless "struggle for recognition," which requires liberty and freedoms. Both these quests can be best satisfied within the framework of liberal democracy. According to Fukuyama, the end of the Cold War proved the triumph of democracy and finally settled the issue of how best to organize society. If only he was right.

Fukuyama's rosy analysis was based on assumptions that were not borne out. It did not—and certainly could not—predict the resurgence of Islam, and, although Fukuyama assumed that radical Islam would not pose a threat to liberal democracy, his analysis fell short of understanding the magnitude of the threat liberal democracy itself posed to radical Islam! The events of 9/11 and the genuine glee with which these acts were greeted among Muslim audiences antagonistic to the West revealed the gap between his theory and reality. In this sense, "the end of history" concept appears premature, to say the least, and not very helpful when it comes to predicting the future of the war on terrorists.

Benjamin Barber's Jihad vs. McWorld[3] foretells a less cheerful world predicament. The present is dominated by the two conflicting forces of globalism and jihad. The first force, globalism, describes the worldwide integration of markets and cultures by a ruthless, all-gobbling, and amok-running capitalism—bureaucratic, heartless, undemocratic, and terrifying to those wishing to preserve their unique values and way of life. As Barber puts it, this future is one of "shimmering pastels, a busy portrait of onrushing economic, technological, and ecological forces that demand integration and uniformity and that mesmerize peoples everywhere with fast music, fast computers, and fast food . . . one McWorld tied together by communications, information, entertainment, and commerce."[4]

The second force, jihad, represents retribalism, reduction of societies to tribes, clans, and nuclear groups, which are in conflict with all other ethnic or religious groups. According to Barber, this force is about "retribalization of large swaths of humankind by war and bloodshed: a threatened balkanization of nation-states in which culture is pitted against culture, people against people, tribe against tribe, a Jihad in the name of a hundred narrowly conceived faiths against every kind of interdependence . . . against technology, against pop culture, and against integrated markets; against modernity itself."[5] Thus, the world is torn between the conflicting pulls of "parochial hatreds vs. universalizing markets."[6]

Both forces are by nature and definition undemocratic. "Their common thread is indifference to civil liberty. Jihad forges communities of blood rooted in exclusion and hatred, communities that slight democracy in favor of tyrannical paternalism . . . McWorld forges global markets rooted in consumption and profit, leaving to an untrustworthy . . . invisible hand issues of public interest and common good that once might have been nurtured by democratic citizenries and their watchful governments."[7] Implicit in Barber's view is the opinion that the current war against terrorism is, in effect, a conflict with the forces of retribalism. Nevertheless, Barber is guardedly optimistic that democracy may prevail, against all odds, and will still be with us in the foreseeable future in spite of terrorism.

Huntington, too, envisions a future that has already begun to unfold. In his view, American and Western powers in general have already begun their relative descent compared to ascending new centers of power. Worse than the traditional indices of decline, such as demographics and economics, are problems of "moral decline, cultural suicide, and political disunity in the West."[8] This decline confirms the perceptions held by Asians and Muslims of their moral

What Do YOU Think?

Which of the three perspectives—Fukuyama's, Barbour's, Huntington's—is most compatible with the realities of the war against terrorism, in your opinion? Explain the reasons for your choice.

superiority over the West. Yet, Western civilization is unique; it alone invented pluralism, individualism, and modernity—which made it possible for the West to spread its values and characteristics throughout the globe. Therefore, the main task of the West, according to Huntington, is not to "reshape other civilizations in the image of the West," but to "preserve, protect, and renew the unique qualities of Western civilizations."[9] Short of a future war between civilizations, most likely pitting Muslims against non-Muslims, Huntington foresees a future in which the West will "recognize that Western intervention in the affairs of other civilizations is probably the single most dangerous source of instability and potential global conflict in a multicivilizational world."[10]

Huntington's counsel to retreat into relative isolationism and prepare for a future in which the United States will likely lose its dominant position in the world implies one of two things for the war against terrorism: Either continued brazen terrorism against a timid West or an isolationist West neutralizing the terrorists' motivation to attack it further. Reading between the lines of Huntington's idea of the future in terms of fighting terrorism, the implication is that a restricted, passive Western approach will leave the initiative in the hands of others. Take, for example, the notion that it is inadvisable to intervene in Muslim lands to proactively challenge the terrorists and attempt to reverse the indigenous populations' seething anti-Western sentiment. The inference: radical Islamists will determine whether to leave the West alone or to expand their agenda and press on with a ceaseless campaign of terrorism until the West succumbs.

THE MOST CLEAR AND PRESENT DANGER

"Just the facts Ma'am." We have now reached the point where lessons must be drawn, assumptions made, and conclusions derived. Proper academic discourse dictates that all aspects are covered methodically and analyzed objectively, allowing the facts to lead to the conclusions.

When a college student hesitates before taking a flight to Los Angeles or Amsterdam, if a professional couple wonders about the wisdom of living in Washington DC, and when a shopkeeper in London thinks twice before taking a subway, it is not because of the Colombian FARC, the Kurdish PKK, Sri Lanka's LTTE, or the Puerto Rican Macheteros. Internationally, and certainly in the United States, people's fear of terrorism is almost exclusively related to attacks by radical Islamists. Likewise, when discussing disturbing scenarios of future unconventional terrorism, the focus of most concerns is radical Islam. The stakes are too high to overlook these facts because one wishes it were not so or by using subjective reasoning.

There are two approaches to dealing with the threat of Islamist terrorism. One advocates accommodating Muslims' grievances by changing those American and Western policies Muslims consider antagonistic to their causes. The other approach promotes a proactive all-out mobilization to fight the war, which it believes has been imposed on the United States and the West.

Real Issues, Concrete Grievances

There is hardly a more knowledgeable and eloquent representation of the first perspective than that of the former CIA official Michael Scheuer. His analysis finds al-Qaeda's political agenda to be a faithful embodiment of the thinking and wishes of many ordinary and moderate Muslims angry at American foreign policies affecting Muslim interests. They "just don't get it," warns Scheuer about those who view bin Laden as a madman and radical Islam as an infectious disease. We must acknowledge, he urges, that al-Qaeda's voiced grievances reflect those within the mainstream of current Islam, especially with regard to American foreign policy. Specifically, the United States supports Israel against the Palestinians, has stationed troops on sacred Arabian soil, occupies Afghanistan and Iraq, supports China, India, and Russia in their struggles against Muslim minorities within their countries, forces oil-producing Arab countries to keep the price of oil artificially low, and backs and sustains corrupt and tyrannical Muslim regimes around the world. Bin Laden simply articulates widespread feelings of frustration and anger, reminding fellow Muslims of their duties in this regard.[11]

A CASE IN POINT: Al-Qaeda's Perspective

Al-Qaeda explained some of the Muslim grievances this way, "In the UN law against Islam, independence is forbidden to Muslims: independence is permissible for East Timor [where Roman Catholics are the vast majority], but taboo for Kashmir; independence is permissible for Christian Georgia, but taboo for Chechnya; independence is permissible for Crusader Croatia, but taboo for Bosnia."[12]

Many experts and academicians second Scheuer's opinion. For example, Professor Robert Pape agrees that Muslim anti-Americanism does not stem from hatred of American values of democracy and free markets. Instead, he argues, "American military policies, not revulsion against Western political and economic values, are driving anti-Americanism among Muslims."[13] This school of thought has been gaining acceptance in proportion to the increase in the threat of terrorism, as people in the United States and the West have asked themselves more and more "Why us?" or "Why do they hate us so much?"

Internal Dynamics within Islam

According to this widely held view, it is not Western policies, but processes taking place inside of Islam that are responsible for the surge of terrorism associated with Muslim radicals. For example, Steven Simon, former senior director of the National Security Council, argues that "the prominent role of clerics in shaping public opinion offers yet more obstacles. The people who represent the greatest threat of terrorist action against the United States follow the preaching of *Salafi* clerics—Muslim equivalent of Christian fundamentalists . . . their underlying assumption is that jihad . . . against non-Muslims is fundamentally valid and that Islamic governments that do not enforce *Sharia* must be opposed."[14] In other words, regardless of what the West does, internal dynamics within Islam determine the agenda and control the valve of anger and hatred, and therefore it is, for the most part, out of the West's control.

As we have seen in Chapter 10, it is easy to pinpoint examples of factors and developments in Muslim countries that perpetuate the misery and the consequent anger to which they give rise: a demographic explosion, economic sluggishness, political despotism, and a struggle for hegemony over the interpretation of the faith. These troubles will not disappear any time soon and are likely to continue to fuel the fury against the West, especially the United States, turning Western policies in the Middle East and elsewhere into a pretext that can be used by radical Muslims to advance their agenda. Between the inflow of petrodollars, the rise of Wahabism, and the emergence of extremist Muslim regimes in Iran and elsewhere, the anti-Western conditioning of Muslim people has reached a level that defies conventional reasoning and renders compromises over substantive issues a nonstarter. As Paul Bremer III explains, "Such groups are not trying to start negotiations. They make no negotiable 'demands' that the West can comply with to forestall further attacks."[15]

Same Hatreds, New Reasons

Angry rhetoric emanating from the Middle East in the twenty-first century projects an image of great injury caused by unfair Western policies. The implied solution appears to be simple: Address the anti-Arab and anti-Muslim roots of the fury and relationships between the people of the region and the West would become amicable. One must go back half a century to realize how naive this idea is.

During the 1950s, in the midst of the Cold War, the West was obsessed with efforts to stop a potential Soviet thrust south into the Middle East. To prevent this, and as part of its global containment policy, the United States and Britain engaged in several attempts to unify the Arabs in anticommunist alliances, a feat accomplished with other countries around the world. The West offered defense alliances, weapons, and support to entice the Arab nations to come on board. Students of history may recall the failed attempts of the 1951 Middle East Treaty Organization (METO), which turned into the Middle East Defense Organization (MEDO), the Northern Tier of 1954, and the Baghdad Pact of 1955. All of these efforts failed miserably. Moreover, an unprecedented wave of anti-Western hatred and violent rejection of the principle of an alliance with the West swept through the Middle East, orchestrated by Egypt. For example, when attempts to form the Baghdad Pact were underway, an explosion of anti-Western bitterness and hatred sent crowds all over the Middle East into the streets, forcing the regimes that were contemplating joining the alliance to reject it. Analysts studying current events, who assume that particular Western policies are to blame for the resentment against the West, would do well to remember that long before the United States became a strategic Israeli ally—prior to Kashmir, Chechnya, and before the resurgence of Islam—Middle Easterners had already violently rejected Western attempts to provide help, money, armaments, training, and offers for alliances.

Making Sense of Complex Alternatives

"To deny the specific virulence of Islamic terrorism in our time is self-deception, an exercise in political—or ecumenical—correctness," writes Walter Laqueur.[16] It is safe to conclude that Muslim extremists have been fishing in troubled waters, exploiting current weaknesses in their societies to incite a jihadist agenda. Advocates of an active Western stand against radical Islam imagine that if the West concedes to Islamic radicals' demands in order to accommodate them, the following developments will subsequently take place: Israel will disappear, all pro-Western, moderate Arab regimes will be toppled, and a new Islamist pan-Arab—perhaps pan-Islamic—empire will emerge in the Middle East and beyond. Using the oil wealth, weapons of mass destruction this new political entity will surely possess, demographics rivaling Europe's, and an indoctrinated and committed population, the new caliphate will not rest on its laurels and leave the infidels' Dar al Harb, the House of War, alone. Listening to the radicals' pronunciations about world jihad and of a future in which Islam will rule the world, these analysts are skeptical that there can ever be peaceful coexistence. In their opinion, chances are that a regional triumph for radical Islam will whet its appetite to implement its religious imperatives globally. Therefore, they believe that it behooves the West, especially the United States, to confront Islamist terrorism in an uncompromising war until the enemy is vanquished.

To quote Middle East expert Fouad Ajami, "Pax Americana is there to stay in the oil lands and in Israeli Palestinian matters. No large-scale retreat from those zones of American primacy can be contemplated. American hegemony is sure to hold—and so, too, the resistance to it . . . friends and sympathizers of terror will pass themselves off as constitutionalists and men and women of 'civil society.' They will find shelter behind pluralist norms while aiding and abetting the forces of terror."[17] If that is the case, then American interests in the Middle East are too entrenched and important to simply leave the region to appease terrorists. This, in turn, means that the threat of Islamist terrorism is here to stay.

A CASE IN POINT: East is East and West is West

A comprehensive survey by the Pew Attitudes Project for 2006 established a disturbing gap between the perception Muslims have about non-Muslims and vice versa. More than four years after 9/11, the majority of Muslims refused to believe that Arabs carried out the attacks. This can be attributed to the nature of the media providing information in Muslim countries, but that 56% of British Muslims, 46% of French Muslims, and 44% of German Muslims do not believe that the perpetrators of 9/11 were Arabs is astounding.[18]

INTERNATIONAL TERRORISM AND THE FUTURE OF HUMAN RIGHTS

The increased threat of terrorism and the accelerated war against its practitioners is likely to have ramifications on the global campaign for enhancing human rights. The 1990s may have been the pinnacle of the international movement to improve human rights conditions around the world; the 9/11 attacks, some fear, might turn back the clock on this effort.

Professor of human rights policy, Michael Ignatieff, observed the early changes 9/11 wrought,[19] and points out, for example, that attention to China's oppression of the inhabitants of the Xinjiang region has been reduced since the Chinese government became an ally in the war against users of terrorism. In Germany, when Chancellor Gerhard Schroder learned of evidence allegedly tying al-Qaeda to the Chechen fighters, he suggested a fresh look at the Russian war effort, despite the huge loss of life and misery the Russian war effort was inflicting on Chechnya. Australia invoked the threat of terrorism to detain Afghans seeking refuge. Egypt was let off the hook, in terms of its human rights record, when it signed on as an ally in the war against the terrorists. This situation reverses the process of growing awareness of human rights issues warns Ignatieff, and "may permanently demote human rights in the hierarchy of America's foreign policy priorities."[20]

This forecast may be true of some governments, but not all. Years after the war against the terrorists became a top priority, it is evident that many European governments, especially in northern Europe, continue to place the same emphasis on human rights as before in places ranging, for example, from Sudan through the Palestinian territories to the American detention center at Guantanamo, Cuba. In addition, at the grassroots level, the effort to ensure universal human rights does not appear to have lost any steam at all, despite the tension created by the unique circumstances of a war against terrorists on the one hand and the imperative of human rights on the other.

What Do YOU Think?

A terrorist plans to blow up a bus carrying mainly schoolchildren. She adds bolts and nails to the bomb to ensure greater carnage, and verifies that the bomb will go off when the bus is full to capacity. The woman succeeds, killing 14 children and maiming two-dozen others. Later, authorities arrest her and she is sentenced to death. What might the pros and cons of a death penalty in this case be? Include the international ramifications as well.

The concern that the era of human rights is fast approaching its end appears, therefore, to be premature. Comforting examples of continued emphasis on human rights—a phenomenon that infuriates a great many people who are uncomfortable with the attention paid to the rights of *terrorism suspects*—abound. Nonetheless, and regardless of the current trend, a severe challenge to the commitment to human rights may arise in the future if terrorists succeed in obtaining and using weapons of mass destruction, killing or harming large numbers of people. The scale of such an event could change the international agenda and refocus priorities in a way detrimental to the preservation of the sanctity of human rights everywhere.

Safeguarding an Accused Terrorist's Human Rights: A Case Study

Marwan Barghouti was a top Palestinian leader during the round of violence that erupted between Israelis and Palestinians in September of 2000. In January, 2002, he was personally involved in a special operation in which he dispatched an attacker to open fire on celebrants at a Bat Mitzvah, the Jewish confirmation party for a 12-year-old girl, in the Israeli town of Hadera.[21] As planned, the terrorist walked in and began shooting. A personal video recorder, which happened to be rolling at the time, captured the scene that later would be broadcast around the world: the food on the tables, the dancing 12-year-olds, and then the pandemonium as the shooting began. Six people were killed and 26 others wounded before the gunman was stopped.

Barghouti was arrested on April 14, 2002, and put on trial in Israel. Concerned for the accused, human rights activists flocked to Israel to ensure that Barghouti's rights were not violated. Reporters, family members, representatives of the European Parliament, and members of human rights groups attended the court's proceedings. In Europe, the Governing Council of the Inter-Parliamentary Union voted to appoint a special human rights representative to monitor Barghouti's trial to verify that his rights were upheld.

For his involvement in this and 36 other terrorist operations, in which more than 26 Israeli civilians were killed, Barghouti was sentenced to life in prison. The European human rights monitor filed a report faulting the Israeli judicial system on several grounds. Among them were the following: (1) Instead of being informed of the charges against him at the time of his arrest (in the West Bank, by Israeli special forces), Mr. Barghouti was notified of the charges only at the end of the day when he was handed over to the police, (2) The Israeli deputy minister of homeland security had said, "Barghouti thoroughly deserves death," and the Israeli attorney general had called Barghouti "a terrorist," thus, presumably, prejudicing the proceedings, (3) The nature of the restrictions placed on Barghouti's lawyers' ability to meet with him.[22]

In this case, the international community's commitment to protecting a suspected terrorist's rights was demonstrated vividly. On the other hand, it is not known how many, if any, of the dignitaries and human rights advocates visited with the families of the dead and injured girls, a paradox that demonstrates the controversies and dilemmas often associated with protecting terrorists' human rights.

FUTURE SCENARIOS AND RECOMMENDATIONS

Because, as commentator George Will wrote, "The future has a way of arriving unannounced," it makes sense to try to prepare for it. It is customary, therefore, for scholars and experts to bestow advice on how to manage future policy in the era of terrorism. A few seem ready to give up in exasperation at the forgiving attitude Western elites exhibit toward terrorism: "We live in a doomed continent of ostriches," complained the social commentator Michelle Malkin. Other writers, such as terrorism expert Bruce Hoffman, observed even before 9/11 that "until recently people underestimated the magnitude of the problem [of terrorism]." Today, the enormity of the terrorism challenge dictates "nothing less than a sea change in our thinking about terrorism and the policies required to counter it."[23] However, even with the best of intentions, what is to be done?

The following is a review of five perspectives on the future, a summary that hardly does justice to the voluminous body of work generated on the subject.

The "Grand Strategy"

Audrey Kurth Cronin, a specialist on terrorism, advocates a "grand strategy" against terrorism. She supports a counterterrorism policy that mixes a "negative" strategy of arrests and killing of terrorists with a "positive" strategy of foreign aid and promotion of human rights—to separate the terrorists from their audiences.[24]

The Changing Face of International Conflict

Professor Steve Smith offers the following observations: States are no longer the main "actors" in international relations; "identity" politics has become more important than the traditional organizing principles of international relations,

The Earth as a bomb with a lit fuse about to explode
Source: Courtesy of Images.com.

such as security, economics, or political interests. Future conflict will be one of asymmetrical warfare; "virtual war," meaning victories in the area of propaganda and ideas, will gain in importance. It will become increasingly difficult to use military force to attain political objectives; the meaning of "victory" will become evermore vague and difficult to define. Globalization and liberal democracy are not a universal inevitability; negotiating with non-Westerners, whose worldviews and priorities are different, is likely to be more complicated in the future. Lastly, "you are either with me or against me" type of thinking will not work well in a future dominated by a need to forge alliances with non-Western cultures.[25]

Nuclear Terrorism as First Priority

Professor Graham Allison, of the Kennedy School of Government, warns that preventing nuclear terrorism must be an "absolute national priority." He suggests fighting a strategically focused war on terrorism, complementing that war with "a humble foreign policy" because, "in an era when America's share of world power has never been greater, its international standing has fallen to the lowest point in modern history." Allison recommends building elaborate alliances against nuclear terrorism, improving intelligence, and applying a multilayered defense.[26]

Multipronged Approach

Paul Pillar, former deputy director for intelligence at the CIA, offers a list of recommendations for fighting terrorists that includes the following: (1) Policy makers should always take the counterterrorism implications of their decisions into account; (2) they must develop a greater awareness of the entire gamut of terrorism threats; (3) terrorist infrastructures worldwide must be disrupted; (4) all methods possible must be used to counter terrorism—no one particular method should be relied on; (5) policy makers must devise a variety of policies to meet different terrorist threats; (6) they must maintain proper, updated, and fair lists of suspects; (7) the United States must work in tandem with its allies; and (8) it must "give peace a chance."[27]

Protect the Home Front

Finally, we end with a sample of the recommendations made by the 9/11 Commission in its report, most of which relate to security arrangements, particularly those concerning travel. The report calls for better screening at the borders; tightening immigration laws and enforcing them better; focusing greater attention on aviation and transportation security without impacting civil liberties; and not neglecting the role of the private sector.[28]

The British philosopher Edmund Burke wrote, "You can not plan the future by the past." His words ring particularly true in an era in which terrorists have their eyes on weapons of mass destruction. There is no historical precedent to this type of conflict and should terrorists obtain such weapons the result could be catastrophic. Avoiding this requires responsible men and women of foresight and goodwill to come together to stop the threat before it is too late. Instead, today, empty declarations are routinely recycled by world leaders, and the elites in the West seem more occupied with squabbling and finger-pointing than with leading the campaign to unify the West to prevent the potential for a future calamity.

Did You Know?

With the debatable exception of Libya, no state sponsor of international terrorism, which the United States had placed on the State Department's list of countries that support terrorism, has ever changed its behavior, in spite of pressures and sanctions.

SUMMARY

In this chapter, you have learned the following:

1. Fukuyama, Huntington, and Barber reach conclusions that differ significantly in their degree of optimism about the future.
2. Radical Islam poses the most serious threat of terrorism.
3. One school of thought advocates trying to accommodate Muslim grievances; the other urges full-scale confrontation to eliminate the danger.
4. While some fear that the war against perpetrators of terrorism will be detrimental to universal human rights, it appears that, to date, that concern has not yet materialized in any substantial way.
5. As many scenarios about the future of terrorism have been offered as recommendations for coping with the problem.

Military historian Martin van Creveld foresees a future in which states will crumble, and instead of conventional militaries, gangs and other small-scale formations motivated mainly by fanatic ideologies, greed, and survival will be fighting under the leadership of charismatic leaders. This process will lead to the blurring of the difference between combatants and civilians, "front" and "rear," and the distinction between war and crime. Battles will become increasingly barbarous, and there will be no protection for POWs. Classic "strategy" will become an anachronism and "bases" will be replaced by hideouts and shelters. Sophisticated weapon systems and uniforms will disappear and warfare will become a mixture of gang warfare and SWAT teams.[29] This vision has begun to manifest itself throughout some swaths of the globe, as in western Africa and northern Pakistan. It is quite possible that terrorism is well on its way to morphing again, becoming the new mainstream strategy for conflict in certain areas of the world.

NOTES

1. Read more about the Doomsday Clock in Paul L. Williams, *The Al Qaeda Connection: International Terrorism, Organized Crime, and the Coming Apocalypse* (Amherst, New York: Prometheus Books, 2005), p. 205.
2. See Francis Fukuyama, *The End of History and the Last Man* (New York: The Free Press, 1992).
3. Benjamin R. Barber, *Jihad vs. McWorld* (New York: Times Books, 1995).

4. Ibid., p. 4.

5. Ibid.

6. Ibid.

7. Ibid., pp. 4–5.

8. Samuel P. Huntington, *The Clash of Civilizations and the Remaking of World Order* (New York: Simon & Schuster, 2003), p. 304.

9. The recommendation to focus on preserving Western civilization is found in Ibid., p. 311.

10. Huntington's advice not to get involved in the affairs of other civilizations is found in Ibid., p. 312.

11. For Michael Scheuer's perspective, see Anonymous, *Imperial Hubris: Why the West Is Losing the War on Terror* (Washington, DC: Brassey's, Inc., 2004), pp. 241, 261–263.

12. The Muslim grievances quoted are found in Ibid., p. 13.

13. Robert Pape's assertion about the reaction to American foreign policies is found in Robert A. Pape, *Dying To Win: The Strategic Logic of Suicide Terrorism* (New York: Random House, 2005), p. 243.

14. Simon's assessment of anti-Western attitudes is found in Steven Simon, "The New Terrorism: Securing the Nation Against a Messianic Foe," in Gus Martin, ed., *The New Era of Terrorism: Selected Readings* (Dominguez Hills, CA: Sage Publications, 2004), p. 170.

15. Bremer's remark concerning the futility of negotiating with Islamists is found in L. Paul Bremer III, "A New Strategy for the New Face of Terrorism," in Martin, ed., p. 244.

16. Walter Laqueur, *The New Terrorism: Fanaticism and the Arms of Mass Destruction* (New York: Oxford University Press, 1999), p. 277.

17. Fouad Ajami, "The Uneasy Imperium: Pax Americana in the Middle East," in James F. Hoge, Jr. and Gideon Rose, eds., *How Did This Happen: Terrorism and the New World* (New York: Public Affairs Reports, 2001), p. 29.

18. For the Pew poll, see http://pewglobal.org/reports/display.php?ReportID=253 (accessed July 12, 2006).

19. Michael Ignatieff, "Is the Human Rights Era Ending?" in Alan J. Cigler, ed., *Perspectives On Terrorism: How 9/11 Changed U.S. Politics* (New York: Houghton Mifflin Company, 2002), pp. 103–106.

20. For the quote, see Ibid., pp. 103–106.

21. More on Barghouti's role in the attack is found in the Israeli newspaper *Yediot Ahronot*, January 20, 2002, which euphemistically describes Barghouti as "giving his blessing" in advance of the attack.

22. The monitor's report is found in http://www.ipu.org/hr-e/174/report.htm (accessed November 3, 2006).

23. Hoffman's remark concerning the need for a sea change in our thinking about terrorism is in Bruce Hoffman, *Inside Terrorism* (New York: Columbia University press, 1998), p. 212.

24. Cronin's comments are found in Audrey Kurth Cronin, "Toward an Effective Grand Strategy," in Audrey Kurth Cronin and James M. Ludes, eds., *Attacking*

Terrorism: Elements of a Grand Strategy (Washington, DC: Georgetown University Press, 2004), p. 298.

25. Steve Smith, "The End of the Unipolar Moment? September 11 and the Future of World Order," in Martin, ed., pp. 261–262.

26. Professor Allison's recommendations can be found in Graham Allison, *Nuclear Terrorism: The Ultimate Preventable Catastrophe* (New York: Henry Holt and Company, 2004), pp. 177–202.

27. See Paul R. Pillar, "Lessons and Futures," in Griset and Mahan, eds., *Terrorism in Perspective* (Thousand Oaks: Sage Publications, 2003), pp. 297–302.

28. The 9/11 Commission Report, *Final Report of the National Commission on Terrorist Attacks Upon the United States*, Authorized Edition (New York: W.W. Norton & Company, 2004), pp. 383–398.

29. Van Creveld's views on the future of conflict are in Martin van Creveld, "The Transformation of War," in Richard W. Mansbach and Edward Rhodes, eds., *Global Politics in a Changing World* (Boston, MA: Houghton Mifflin Company, 2003), pp. 35–45.

Bibliography

BOOKS

Abraham, Henry J. and Barbara A. Perry. *Freedom and the Court: Civil Rights and Liberties in the United States*, 7th ed. New York: Oxford University Press, 1998.

Allison, Graham. *Nuclear Terrorism: The Ultimate Preventable Catastrophe*. New York: Henry Holt and Company, 2004.

Anonymous. *Imperial Hubris: Why the West Is Losing the War on Terror*. Washington, DC: Brassey's, Inc., 2004.

Arjomand, Said Amir. *The Turban for The Crown: The Islamic Revolution in Iran*. New York: Oxford University Press, 1988.

Barber, Benjamin R. *Jihad vs. McWorld*. New York: Times Books, 1995.

Barkun, Michael. *A Culture of Conspiracy: Apocalyptic Visions in Contemporary America*. Berkeley, CA: University of California Press, 2003.

Benjamin, Daniel and Steve Simon. *The Age of Sacred Terror*. New York: Random House, 2002.

Caram, Peter. *The 1993 World Trade Center Bombing: Foresight and Warning*. London: Janus Publishing Company, 2001.

Carlton, David and Carlo Schaerf, eds. *International Terrorism and World Security*. New York: John Wiley and Sons, 1974.

Cigler, Alan J., ed. *Perspectives on Terrorism: How 9/11 Changed U.S. Politics*. New York: Houghton Mifflin Company, 2002.

Cline, Ray S. and Yonah Alexander. *Terrorism as State-Sponsored Covert Warfare*. Fairfax, VA: Hero Books, 1986.

Combs, Cindy C. *Terrorism in the Twenty-First Century*, 3rd ed. Upper Saddle River, NJ: Prentice Hall, 2003.

Combs, Cindy C. *Terrorism in the Twenty-First Century*, 4th ed. Upper Saddle River, NJ: Prentice Hall, 2006.

Cronin, Audrey Kurth and James M. Ludes, eds. *Attacking Terrorism: Elements of a Grand Strategy*. Washington, DC: Georgetown University Press, 2004.

Davis, Paul K. and Brian Michael Jenkins. *Deterrence and Influence in Counterterrorism: A Component in the War on al Qaeda*. Santa Monica, CA: Rand, 2002.

Emerson, Steven. *American Jihad: The Terrorists Living among Us*. New York: The Free Press, 2002.

Fukuyama, Francis. *The End of History and the Last Man*. New York: The Free Press, 1992.

Gitlin, Todd. *Media Unlimited: How the Torrent of Images and Sounds Overwhelms Our Lives*. New York: Metropolitan Books, 2001.

Goldschmidt, Arthur. *A Concise History of the Middle East*, 7th ed. Boulder, CO: Westview Press, 2002.

Griset, Pamela L. and Sue Mahan. *Terrorism in Perspective*. Thousand Oaks: Sage Publications, 2003.

Hacker, Frederick J. *Crusaders, Criminals, Crazies: Terror and Terrorism in Our Time*. New York: W.W. Norton & Company, Inc., 1976.

Halpern, Manfred. *The Politics of Social Change in the Middle East and North Africa*. Princeton, NJ: Princeton University Press, 1963.

Herman, Edward S. and Robert W. McChensey. *The Global Media: The New Missionaries of Global Capitalism*. Washington: Cassell, 1997.

Hoffman, Bruce. *Inside Terrorism*. New York: Columbia University Press, 1998.

Hoge, Jr., James F. and Gideon Rose, eds. *How Did This Happen: Terrorism and the New World*. New York: Public Affairs Reports, 2001.

Howard, Russell D. and Reid L. Sawyer, eds. *Terrorism and Counterterrorism: Understanding the New Security Environment*. Guilford, CT: McGraw-Hill/Dushkin, 2003.

Huntington, Samuel P. *The Clash of Civilizations and the Remaking of World Order*. New York: Simon & Schuster, 2003.

Kegley, Jr., Charles W., ed. *The New Global Terrorism: Characteristics, Causes, Controls*. Upper Saddle River, NJ: Prentice Hall, 2003.

Laqueur, Walter. *Terrorism*. Boston, MA: Little, Brown and Company, 1977.

Laqueur, Walter, ed. *The Terrorism Reader: A Historical Anthology*. Philadelphia, PA: Temple University Press, 1978.

Laqueur, Walter. *The New Terrorism: Fanaticism and the Arms of Mass Destruction*. New York: Oxford University Press, 1999.

Livingstone, Neil C. and David Halevy. *Inside the PLO*. New York: William Morrow, 1990.

Love, Maryann Cusimano, ed. *Beyond Sovereignty: Issues for a Global Agenda*, 2nd ed. Belmont, CA: Thomson/Wadsworth, 2003.

Lustick, Ian S. *For the Land and the Lord: Jewish Fundamentalism in Israel*. New York: Council on Foreign Relations, 1988.

Maniscalco, Paul M. and Hank T. Christen. *Understanding Terrorism and Managing the Consequences*. Upper Saddle River, NJ: Prentice Hall, 2002.

Mansbach, Richard W. and Edward Rhodes, eds. *Global Politics in a Changing World: A Reader*, 2nd ed. New York: Houghton Mifflin Company, 2003.

Martin, Gus, ed. *The New Era of Terrorism: Selected Readings*. Dominguez Hills, CA: Sage Publications, 2004.

Meyer, Jeremy D. *9–11: The Giant Awakens*. Belmont, CA: Wadsworth/Thomson Learning, 2003.

Millar, Paul R. *Terrorism and U.S. Foreign Policy*. Washington, DC: Brookings Institution Press, 2001.

Miller, Judith, Stephen Engelberg, and William Broad. *Germs: Biological Weapons and America's Secret War*. New York: Simon & Schuster, 2001.

Napoleoni, Loretta. *Terror Incorporated: Tracing the Dollars Behind the Terror Networks*. New York: Seven Stories Press, 2005.

Netanyahu, Benjamin. *Fighting Terrorism: How Democracies Can Defeat Domestic and International Terrorists*. New York: Farrar Straus Giroux, 1995.

O'Ballance, Edgar. *Language of Violence: The Blood Politics of Terrorism*. San Rafael, CA: Presidio Press, 1979.

Palmer, R. R. *The Age of the Democratic Revolution*, Vol. 2: *The Struggle*. Princeton, NJ: Princeton University Press, 1964.

Pape, Robert A. *Dying to Win: The Strategic Logic of Suicide Terrorism*. New York: Random House, 2005.

Parenti, Michael. *Inventing the Politics of News Media Reality*, 2nd ed. New York: St. Martin's Press, 1993.

Picard, Robert P. *Media Portrayals of Terrorism: Functions and Meaning of News Coverage*. Iowa: State University Press, 1993.

Pious, Richard M. *The War on Terrorism and the Rule of Law*. Los Angeles, CA: Roxbury Publishing Co., 2006.

Reich, Walter, ed. *Origins of Terrorism: Psychologies, Ideologies, Theologies, States and Mind*. Washington, DC: Woodrow Wilson Center Press, 1990.

Said, Edward W. *Orientalism*. New York: Vintage Books, 1994.

Schmidt, Alex P. and Albert J. Jongman. *Political Terrorism: A New Guide to Actors, Authors, Concepts, Data Bases, Theories, and Literature*. New Brunswick: Transaction Books, 1988.

Simonsen, Clifford E. and Jeremy R. Spindlove. *Terrorism Today: The Past, The Players, The Future*, 2nd ed. Upper Saddle River, NJ: Prentice Hall, 2004.

Smith, Brent L. *Terrorism in America: Pipe Bombs and Pipe Dreams*. Albany, NY: State University of New York Press, 1994.

Sprinzak, Ehud. *The Ascendance of Israel's Radical Right*. New York: Oxford University Press, 1991.

Sterling, Claire. *The Terror Network: The Secret War of International Terrorism*. New York: Holt, Reinhart and Winston, 1981.

Stern, Jessica. *Why Religious Militants Kill: Terror in the Name of God*. New York: HarperCollins Publishers, Inc., 2003.

Stohl, Michael, ed. *The Politics of Terrorism*. New York: Marcel Dekker, Inc., 1979.

Stohl, Michael, ed. *The Politics of Terrorism*, 3rd ed. New York: Marcel Dekker, Inc., 1988.

Sweet, Kathleen M. *Aviation and Airport Security: Terrorism and Safety Concerns*. Upper Saddle River, NJ: Pearson/Prentice Hall, 2004.

Taheri, Amir. *Holy Terror: Inside the World of Islamic Terrorism*. Bethesda, MD: Adler and Adler Publishers, 1987.

The 9/11 Commission Report, *Final Report of the National Commission on Terrorist Attacks upon the United States*, Authorized Edition. New York: W.W. Norton & Company, 2004.

Tuman, Joseph S. *Communicating Terror: The Rhetorical Dimensions of Terrorism*. Thousand Oaks, CA: Sage Publications, Inc., 2003.

Valasquez, Manuel G. *Business Ethics*, 5th ed. Upper Saddle River, NJ: Prentice Hall, 2002.

Verton, Dan. *Black Ice: The Invisible Threat of Cyber-Terrorism*. New York: McGraw-Hill, 2003.

Wardlaw, Grant. *Political Terrorism: Theory, Tactics, and Counter-measures*. Cambridge, MA: Cambridge University Press, 1990.

White, Jonathan R. *Terrorism: An Introduction*, 4th ed. Belmont, CA: Wadsworth/Thomson Learning, 2002.

Williams, Paul L. *The Al Qaeda Connection: International Terrorism, Organized Crime, and the Coming Apocalypse.* Amherst, NY: Prometheus Books, 2005.

Wright, Lawrence. *The Looming Tower: Al-Qaeda and the Road to 9/11.* New York: Alfred A. Knopf, 2006.

Wright, Susan, ed. *Preventing a Biological Arms Race.* Cambridge, MA: The MIT Press, 1990.

ARTICLES IN EDITED BOOKS

"The Terror of the Nightrider," in *Ku Klux Klan: A History of Racism and Violence.* 5th ed. Montgomery, AL: Southern Poverty Law Center, 1997.

Ajami, Fouad. "The Uneasy Imperium," in Hoge, Jr. and Rose, eds., pp. 15–30.

Ash, Timothy Garton. "Is There a Good Terrorist?" in Kegley, Jr., ed., pp. 60–70.

Bandura, Albert. "Mechanisms of Moral Disengagement," in Reich, ed., pp. 161–191.

Betts, Richard. "Intelligence Test: The Limits of Prevention," in Hoge, Jr. and Rose, eds., pp. 145–161.

Bremer III, L. Paul. "A New Strategy for the New Face of Terrorism," in Martin, ed., pp. 243–248.

Burck, Gordon. "Biological, Chemical and Toxin Warfare Agents," in Wright, ed., pp. 352–367.

Chyba, Christopher. "Toward Biology Security," in Howard and Sawyer, eds., pp. 174–184.

Cooper, H. H. A. "Terrorism: The Problem of Definition Revisited," in Martin, ed., pp. 55–63.

Corrado, Raymond R. "Ethnic and Student Terrorism in Western Europe," in Stohl, ed., pp. 191–257.

Crenshaw, Martha. "The Logic of Terrorism: Terrorist Behavior as a Product of Strategic Choice," in Reich, ed., pp. 7–24.

Crenshaw, Martha. "The Causes of Terrorism," in Kegley, Jr., ed., pp. 92–105.

Cronin, Audrey Kurth. "Toward an Effective Grand Strategy," in Cronin and Ludes, eds., pp. 285–299.

Cunningham, Karla J. "Cross-Regional Trends in Female Terrorism," in Martin, ed., pp. 90–111.

Donohue, Laura K. "Fear Itself: Counterterrorism, Individual Rights, and U.S. Foreign Relations Post 9–11," in Howard and Sawyer, eds., pp. 275–300.

Gouré, Daniel. "Homeland Security," in Cronin and Ludes, eds., pp. 261–284.

Gurr, Ted Robert. "Political Terrorism in the United States: Historical Antecedents and Contemporary Trends," in Stohl, ed., pp. 549–578.

Hoffman, Bruce. "A Nasty Business," in Martin, ed., pp. 226–230.

Hoffman, Bruce. "Defining Terrorism," in Howard and Sawyer, eds., pp. 3–24.

Hurrell, Andrew. "There Are No Rules (George W. Bush): International Order After September 11," in Martin, ed., pp. 205–218.

Ignatieff, Michael. "Is the Human Rights Era Ending?" in Cigler, ed., pp. 103–106.

Jenkins, Brian M. "International Terrorism: A New Mode of Conflict," in Carlton and Schaerf, eds., pp. 13–49.

Jurgenmeyer, Mark. "The Religious Roots of Contemporary Terrorism," in Kegley, Jr., ed., pp. 185–193.

Laqueur, Walter. "Left, Right, and Beyond: The Changing Face of Terror," in Hoge, Jr. and Rose, eds., pp. 71–82.

Laqueur, Walter. "Weapons of Mass Destruction," in Griset and Mahan, eds., pp. 239–253.

Lee, Rensselar W. and Ford, James L. "Nuclear Smuggling," in Love, ed., pp. 219–244.

Love, Richard. "The Cyberthreat Continuum," in Love, ed., pp. 195–217.

Moodie, Michael L. "The Chemical Weapon Threat," in Howard and Sawyer, eds., pp. 184–203.

Morgan, Robin. "Token Terrorist: The Demon Lover's Woman," in Griset and Mahan, eds., pp. 167–181.

Perl, Raphael F. "Terrorism, the Media, and the Government: Perspectives, Trends, and Options for Policymakers," in Griset and Mahan, eds., pp. 143–149.

Pickard, Daniel B. "Legalizing Assassinations? Terrorism, the Central Intelligence Agency, and International Law," in Howard and Sawyer, eds., pp. 518–542.

Pillar, Paul R. "Lessons and Futures," in Griset and Mahan, eds., pp. 295–302.

Pipes, Daniel. "God and Mammon: Does Poverty Cause Militant Islam?" in Martin, ed., pp. 111–117.

Posner, Richard A. "Security versus Civil Liberties," in Cigler, ed., pp. 59–62.

Post, Jerrold. "Terrorist Psycho-Logic: Terrorist Behavior as a Product of Psychological Forces," in Reich, ed., pp. 25–40.

Rattray, Gregory J. "The Cyberterrorism Threat," in Howard and Sawyer, eds., pp. 221–245.

Reich, Walter. "Understanding Terrorist Behavior: The Limits and Opportunities of Psychological Inquiry," in Reich, ed., pp. 261–279.

Robbins, James S. "Bin Laden's War," in Howard and Sawyer, eds., pp. 354–366.

Simon, Steven. "The New Terrorism: Securing the Nation against a Messianic Foe," in Martin, ed., pp. 167–174.

Smith, Steve. "The End of the Unipolar Moment? September 11 and the Future of World Order," in Martin, ed., pp. 257–265.

Steinhausler, Friedrich. "What It Takes to Become a Nuclear Terrorist," in Martin, ed., pp. 125–134.

Stern, Jessica. "Getting and Using the Weapons," in Howard and Sawyer, eds., pp. 158–174.

Stewart, Charles and Maniscalco, Paul M. "Weapons of Mass Effect: Biological Terrorism," in Maniscalco and Christen, eds., pp. 143–186.

Taylor, Jr., Stuart. "Legal Affairs: The Media, the Military, and Striking the Right Balance," in Cigler, ed., pp. 20–23.

Taylor, Jr., Stuart. "Right, Liberties, and Security: Recalibrating the Balance after September 11," in Martin, ed., pp. 218–225.

Telhami, Shibley. "Arab and Muslim America: A Snapshot," in Cigler, ed., pp. 12–16.

van Creveld, Martin. "The Transformation of War," in Mansbach and Rhodes, eds., pp. 35–45.

JOURNAL AND POPULAR MAGAZINE ARTICLES

Ajami, Fouad. "The Fire This Time." *U.S. News & World Report*, Vol. 140, No. 6 (February 20, 2006).

Bunn, Matthew and Bunn, George. "Nuclear Theft and Sabotage: Priorities for Reducing New Threats." *IAEA Bulletin*, Vol. 43, No. 4 (December, 2001).

Ehrenfeld, Rachel. "Intifada Gives Cover to Arafat's Graft and Fraud." News World Communication, Inc., *Insight on the News*, Vol. 17, No. 26 (July 16, 2001).

Goldhagen, Daniel Jonah. "The New Threat: The Radical Politics of Islamic Fundamentalism." *The New Republic*, Vol. 234, No. 9 (March, 2006).

Hobson, Katherine. "Are We Ready? A Large-Scale Disaster Like a Pandemic Flu or Terrorist Attack Could Overwhelm the Nation's Healthcare Providers." *U.S. News & World Report*, Vol. 140, No. 16 (May 1, 2006).

Jamieson, Alison. "Mafiosi and Terrorists: Italian Women in Violent Organizations." *SAIS Review*, Vol. 20, No. 2 (Summer–Fall, 2000).

Kaplan, David E. "A Godfather's Lethal Mix of Business and Politics." *U.S. News & World Report*, Vol. 139, No. 21 (December 5, 2005).

Kaplan, David. "Paying for Terror." *U.S. News & World Report*, Vol. 139, No. 21 (December 5, 2005).

Kaplan, David. "The Eyes Have It." *U.S. News & World Report*, Vol. 140, No. 1 (January 9, 2006).

Marek, Angie C. "The Toxic Politics of Chemicals." *U.S. News & World Report*, Vol. 140, No. 3 (January 23, 2006).

Rapaport, David C. "Fear and Trembling: Terrorism in Three Religious Traditions." *American Political Science Review*, Vol. 78, No. 3 (September, 1984).

Schmid, A.P. "Terrorism and the Media: The Ethics of Publicity." *Terrorism and Political Violence*, Vol. 1, No. 4 (October, 1989).

Zakaria, Fareed. "Why Do They Hate Us? The Politics of Rage." *Newsweek*, Vol. 138, No. 16 (October 15, 2001).

Zuckerman, Mortimer. "A House Divided." in *U.S. News & World Report*, Vol. 140, No. 6 (February 20, 2006).

NEWSPAPERS AND OTHER DAILY PUBLICATIONS

"Hamas Demands Return of Seville in Internet Children's Magazine." *The Spain Herald*, January 4, 2006.

"Interpol Warns of Bioterrorism." *Jerusalem Post*, November 21, 2005.

"Jihad's Fresh Face." *New York Times*, September 16, 2005.

"What the Muslim World Is Watching." *New York Times Magazine*, November 18, 2001.

"Wrath of God, Osama bin Laden Lashes Out against the West." *Time*, January 11, 1999.

Aharonson, Anat. "New Information from the Verdict . . ." *Ma'ariv*, January 11, 2005.

Baker, Peter and Susan Glasser. "Russian Plane Bombers Exploited Corrupt System." *Washington Post Foreign Service*, September 18, 2004.

Bortin, Meg. "Poll Finds Discord between Muslims and Western Worlds." *New York Times*, June 2006.

Charlaff, Joe. "Shipping Containers: The Next Port of Call for Terrorism?" *Jane's*, April 21, 2006.

Dobbs, Michael. "Myths over Attacks on U.S. Swirl through Islamic World—Many Rumors Lay Blame on an Israeli Conspiracy." *Washington Post*, October 13, 2001.

Fattah, Hassan. "Don't Be Friends with Christians or Jews, Saudi Texts Say." *New York Times*, May 24, 2006.

Friedman, Thomas. "Empty Pockets, Angry Minds." *New York Times*, February 22, 2006.

Fritsch, Peter. "With Pakistan's Schools in Tatters, Madrasahs Spawn Young Warrior." *Wall Street Journal*, October 2, 2001.

Gourley, Scott. "Inside Job: US Seeks Solutions for Its Security Jigsaw." *Jane's*, March 3, 2006.

Gwertzman, Bernard. "U.S. Said to Send Commando Squad." *New York Times*, June 16, 1985.

Hanson, Victor David. "Enough Is Enough." *Washington Times*, July 22, 2005.

Keller, Bill. "Nuclear Nightmares." *New York Times Magazine* section, May 26, 2002.

Milton, Leitenberg, Milton."Bioterrorism Threat is All About Hype," *Los Angeles Times*, February 20, 2006.

Lichtblau, Eric and James Risen. "Defense Lawyers in Terror Cases Plan Challenges over Spy Efforts." *New York Times*, December 28, 2005.

Ma'ariv, February 19, 2006.

Marsico, Ron and Alexander Lane. "Terrorist Targets Sit in State's Rail Yards." *Star Ledger*, July 25, 2005.

Martis, Royston. "Potential Terrorists Should Be Diverted and Not Criminalized." *Jane's*, June 22, 2006.

Melman, Yossi. "Iranian Cleric: Use of Nuclear Arms Sometimes Permissible." *Ha'aretz*, February 19, 2006.

Pallister, David and Owen Bowcott. "Banks to Shut Doors on Saudi Royal Cash." *Guardian*, July 17, 2002.

Pipes, Daniel. "Iran's Final Solution Plan." *New York Sun*, November 11, 2005.

Pipes, Daniel. "What Do the Terrorists Want?" *New York Sun*, July 26, 2005.

Pipes, Daniel. "The Quiet-Spoken Muslims Who Turn to Terror." *New York Sun*, March 14, 2006.

Reuters, November 26, 2005.

Santora, Marc and Bill Carter. "War in Iraq Becomes the Deadliest Assignment for Journalism in Modern Times." *New York Times*, May 30, 2006.

Sciolino, Elaine. "From Tapes, a Chilling Voice of Islamic Radicalism in Europe." *New York Times*, November 18, 2005.

Slackman, Michael and Mona El-Naggar. "Amman Bombs Churned Local Emotions." *New York Times*, November 17, 2005.

Smith, Craig. "Raised Catholic in Belgium, She Died a Muslim Bomber." *New York Times*, December 6, 2005.

Yediot Ahronot, January 20, 2002.

INTERNET SOURCES AND WEBSITES

"2002 Congressional Testimony by Dale Watson, the then Executive Assistant Director of the FBI's Counterterrorism/Counterintelligence Division before the *Senate Select Committee on Intelligence*." http://www.fbi.gov/congress/congress02/watson020602.htm (accessed October 7, 2006).

"Arafat's Speech to the United Nations (13 November 1974)." http://electronicintifada.net/bytopic/historicalspeeches/305.shtml (accessed July 18, 2006).

"Breakthrough Made in '94 Argentina Bombing." *MSNBC*, November 9, 2005, http://www.msnbc.msn.com/id/9983810/from/RL.5 (accessed July 27, 2006).

"Chechen Guerrilla Leader Calls Russians 'Terrorists.' " ABC News (July 29, 2005), http://abcnews.go.com/Nightline/International/story?id=990187&page=1 (accessed July 18, 2006).

"Dictator Idi Amin Dies." *BBC News*, August 16, 2003http://news.bbc.co.uk/2/hi/africa/3155925.stm (accessed October 5, 2006).

"Ending Iran's Genocidal Threat." Foundation for the Defense of Democracies, http://www.defenddemocracy.org/programs/programs_show.htm?doc_id=324706 (accessed October 19, 2006).

"NYCLU Sues City Over Subway Bag Search Policy." http://www.nyclu.org/mta_searches_suit_pr_080405.html (accessed July 5, 2006).

"Remarks by Imam Izak-El Mu'eed Pasha." http://www.belief.net/story/90/story_9016_1.html (accessed October 26, 2006).

"Sourcebook of Criminal Justice Statistics Online." February 29, 2005, http://www.albany.edu/sourcebook/pdf/t2292005.pdf (accessed June 22, 2006).

"Staying on Target and Going the Distance: An Interview with U.K. A.L.F. Press Officer Robin Webb," *No Compromise*, issue 22, http://www.nocompromise.org/issues/22robin.html (accessed October 7, 2006).

"Testimony of Robert S. Mueller III, Director FBI, Before the Senate Committee on Intelligence of the United States Senate." February 16, 2005, http://www.fbi.gov/congress/congress05/mueller021605.htm (accessed October 7, 2006).

"Transcript of Bin Laden's October Interview," CNN.com/WORLD, February 5, 2002, http://archives.cnn.com/2002/WORLD/asiapcf/south/02/05/binladen.transcript/ (accessed on May 30, 2007).

Afeef, Junaid M. "Are American Mosques Promoting Hate Ideology?" February 4, 2005, http://www.altmuslim.com/perm.php?id=1389_0_25_0_C37 (accessed May 29, 2006).

Associated Press, "Self-Criticism in Arab Media Follows School Siege." September 4, 2004, http://www.msnbc.msn.com/id/5912071/ (accessed March 31, 2006).

Bain, Ben and Joseph Cirincione. "Exaggerating the Threat of Bioterrorism." March 16, 2006, http://www.carnegieendowment.org/publications/index.cfm?fa=view&id=18135&prog=zgp&proj=znpp (accessed June 6, 2006).

BBC, "Iran Blamed for Argentine Bomb," November 6, 2003, at http://news.bbc.co.uk/2/hi/middle_east/3245641.stm (accessed July 27, 2006).

BBC, "Flashback: Dissident's Poisoning," January 8, 2003, at http://news.bbc.co.uk/1/hi/uk/2636459.stm (accessed October 5, 2006).

Belfer Center for Science and International Affairs (BCSIA) can be accessed at http://www.nuclearterrorism.org.

Boettcher, Mike and Ingrid Arensen. "Story: Al Qaeda Documents Outline Serious Weapons Program." *CNN.com*, January 25, 2002, http://www.isis-online.org/publications/terrorism/cnnstory.html (accessed October 19, 2006).

Bourrie, Mark. "Yes Means No for *al-Jazera* in Canada." July 23, 2004, http://www.antiwar.com/ips/bourrie.php?articleid=3137 (accessed March 28, 2006).

Center for Religious Freedom, "Saudi Publications on Hate Ideology Invade American Mosques," can be accessed at http://www.freedomhouse.org.

CNN, "Ricin and the Umbrella Murder," http://www.cnn.com/2003/WORLD/europe/01/07/terror.poison.bulgarian/ (accessed October 5, 2006).

Cohen-Almagor, Raphael. "The Terrorists' Best Ally: Media Coverage of Terror." http://www.inter-disciplinary.net/ati/violence/v5/almagor%20paper.pdf (accessed February 12, 2007).

Council of American Islamic Relations (CAIR), can be accessed at http://www.cair-net.org.

CRS Report for Congress, "The *Al-Jazeera* News Network: Opportunity or Challenge for U.S. Foreign Policy in the Middle East?" Updated July 23, 2003, http://fpc.state.gov/documents/organization/23002.pdf (accessed March 28, 2006).

David Halevy, Neil C. Livingstone, and Daniel Pipes. *National Interest*, Spring 1989, http://www.danielpipes.org/article/1064 (accessed October 5, 2006).

Department of Homeland Security (DHS) can be accessed at http://www.dhs.gov.

Earth Liberation Front. "Information about ELF." http://www.earthliberationfront.com/index.htm (accessed October 7, 2006).

Frieden, Terry. "FBI, ATF Address Domestic Terrorism." CNN, May 19, 2005, http://www.cnn.com/2005/US/05/19/domestic.terrorism (accessed October 29, 2006).

Pew Global Attitudes Project. "The Great Divide: How Westerners and Muslims View Each Other." June 22, 2006, http://pewglobal.org/reports/display.php?ReportID=253 (accessed July 12, 2006).

Information Clearing House. "We are at War . . . I am a soldier." http://www.informationclearinghouse.info/article10079.htm (accessed March 14, 2006).

Israeli Ministry of Foreign Affairs can be accessed at http://www.mfa.gov.il/MFA/MFAArchive/2000_2009/2004/9/Behind+the+Headlines+Suicide+bombing+in+Jerusalem+22-Sep-2004.htm.

Israeli Ministry of Foreign Affairs. "Blackmailing Young Women into Suicide Terrorism,"under, "Terrorism: Terror Since 2000." http://www.mfa.gov.il/MFA/Government/Communiques/2003/Blackmailing%20Young%20Women%20into%20Suicide%20Terrorism%20- (accessed March 10, 2006).

Jim Walsh. "America at War: Weapons of Mass Destruction." *washingtonpost.com*, December 5, 2001, http://www.washingtonpost.com/wp-srv/liveonline/01/politics/walsh120501.htm (accessed June 6, 2006).

Keating, Susan Katz. "The Wahhabi Fifth Column." *FrontPageMagazine.com*, December 30, 2002, http://www.frontpagemag.com/Articles/ReadArticle.asp?ID=5270 (accessed May 29, 2006).

Kocieniewski, David. "Facing the City, Potential Targets Rely on a Patchwork of Security." *New York Times*, May 9, 2005, http://www.nytimes.com/2005/05/09/nyregion/09homeland.html?ex=1273291200&en=b3a933ec6ddf6c89&ei=5089 (accessed June 15, 2006).

Kuran, Timur. "The Cultural Undertow of Muslim Economic Rage." *NationalReview.co*, December 12, 2001, http://www.independent.org/newsroom/article.asp?id=401 (accessed July 29, 2006).

Lewis, Bernard. "The Roots of Muslim Rage." *The Atlanticonline*, September, 1990, http://www.travelbrochuregraphics.com/extra/roots_of_muslim_rage.htm (accessed April 2, 2006).

Loeb, Vernon. "Making Chemical Weapons Is No Easy Task." *Washington Post*, http://www.geocities.com/Area51/Shadowlands/6583/project347.html (accessed June 5, 2006).

McNaught, Anita. "Unit 731: Japan's Biological Force." *BBC News World Edition*, February 1, 2002, http://news.bbc.co.uk/2/hi/programmes/correspondent/1796044.stm (accessed May 30, 2006).

Miniter, Richard. "Baggage Claim: The Myth of 'Suitcase Nukes.'" *WSJ.com*, October 31, 2005, http://www.opinionjournal.com/extra/?id=110007478 (accessed October 19, 2006).

Natural Resources Defense Council (NRDC), "Table of Global Nuclear Weapons Stockpiles, 1945–2002." http://www.nrdc.org/nuclear/nudb/datab19.ASP (accessed May 23, 2006).

Nechaev, Sergei. "The Revolutionary's Attitude toward Society." *Catechism of a Revolutionary*, http://www.geocities.com/satanicreds/revolut.html (accessed October 13, 2006).

Olson, Kyle B. "Aum Shinrikyo: Once and Future Threat." http://www.cdc.gov/ncidod/eid/vol5no4/olson.htm (accessed June 5, 2006).

Pipes, Daniel and Charlotte West. "Al-Jazeera in Al Canada?" *FrontPageMagazine.com*, August 13, 2004, http://www.danielpipes.org/article/2013 (accessed March 28, 2006).

Pew Global Attitudes Project. "The Great Divide: How Westerners and Muslims View Each Other." June 22, 2006, http://pewglobal.org/reports/display.php?ReportID=253 (accessed July 12, 2006).

Reporters Without Borders can be accessed at http://www.rsf.org/rubrique.php3?id_rubrique=20.

Reuters, "Iran Linked to Buenos Aires Blast." May 5, 1998, http://www.ict.org.il/spotlight/det.cfm?id=78 (accessed July 27, 2006).

Schiff, Ze'ev. "How Iran Planned the Buenos Aires Blast." *Ha'aretz*, July 27, 2006, http://www.haaretz.com/hasen/pages/ShArt.jhtml?itemNo=273898&contrassID=2&subContrassID=1&sbSubContrassID=0 (accessed October 3, 2006).

Schmidt, Alex. "Links Between Terrorism And Drug Trafficking: A Case Of 'Narco Terrorism'?" *SafeDemocracy.Org*. January 27, 2005, http://english.safe-democracy.org/causes/links-between-terrorism-and-drug-trafficking-a-case-of-narcoterrorism.html (accessed October 18, 2006).

Schwartz, Stephen. "Wahhabism and Islam in the U.S.: Two-Faced Policy Fosters Danger." *Middle East Information Center*, March 22, 2005, http://www.middleeastinfo.org/forum/index.php?showtopic=3752 (accessed May 29, 2006).

Siegel, Jennifer. "Sinatra Bio Explores Icon's Jewish Connections." *All About Jewish Theater*, http://www.jewish-theatre.com/visitor/article_display.aspx?articleID=1458 (accessed October 7, 2006).

Sokov, Nikolai and William C. Potter. "'Suitcase Nukes': A Reassessment." Center for
    Nonproliferation Studies (CNS), September 23, 2002, http://cns.miis.
    edu/pubs/week/020923.htm (accessed October 27, 2006).

Stalinsky, Steven. "Sheikh Yousef Al-Qaradhawi in London to Establish 'The
    International Council of Muslim Clerics,' " in *MEMRI*, Special Report-No. 30, July
    8, 2004, http://memri.org/bin/articles.cgi?Page=archives&Area=sr&ID=SR3004
    (accessed July 29, 2006).

Stern, Jessica. "Understanding Terrorism." *Harvard Magazine* (January–February, 2002),
    http://www.harvardmagazine.com/on-line/010262.html (accessed October 5,
    2006).

Tao, Terence. "The Case of the Missing 4000 Israelis." Self-published article, last updated
    August 8, 2003, http://www.nocturne.org/~terry/wtc_4000_Israeli.html
    (accessed February 12, 2007).

The United States Commission on Security/21st Century. "Major Themes and
    Implications." September 15, 1999, "Conclusions" section, article 1, http://
    www.au.af.mil/au/awc/awcgate/nssg/nwc.pdf (accessed October 27, 2006).

Trotsky, Leon. "Why Marxists Oppose Individual Terrorism." http://www.
    socialistparty.org.uk/Trotsky/againstterrorframe.htm (accessed July 19, 2006).

United Nations Office on Drugs and Crime, "Biological Weapons: What's What," June 1,
    2006, http://www.unodc.org/unodc/terrorism_weapons_mass_destruction_
    page005.html (accessed October 20, 2006).

United Nations Office on Drugs and Crime, "Terrorism and Weapons of Mass
    Destruction," June 1, 2006, http://www.unodc.org/unodc/terrorism_weapons_
    mass_destruction_page002.html (accessed October 20, 2006).

Woolsey, R. James. "Iran: Tehran's Nuclear Recklessness and the U.S. Response."
    Committee on the Present Danger, November 15, 2005, http://www.
    fightingterror.org/views/woolsey_15Nov2005.cfm (accessed October 19, 2006).

Xaykaothao, Doualy. "Nepal Maoist Leader: Women Driving Movement." *National
    Public Radio* (NPR), May 5, 2006, http://www.npr.org/templates/story/
    story.php?storyId=5387419 (accessed October 13, 2006).

UN PUBLICATIONS

United Nations, Security Council. "Letter Dated 19 September 2002 from the Chairman
    of the Monitoring Group Established Pursuant to Resolution 1267 (1999)
    Addressed to the President of the Security Council." Document Number:
    S/2002/1050/Corr.1.

Arab Human Development Report 2002. *Creating Opportunities for Future Generations.*
    p. xx, United Nations Development Program.

Arab Human Development Report 2003. *Building a New Society.* United Nations
    Development Program.

Arab Human Development Report 2004. *Towards Freedom in the Arab World.*

Index

D

D Company, 88–89
da Vinci, Leonardo, 129
"data mining" program, National Security
    Agency (NSA), 271
decolonization after World War II, reasons for
    rush to, 22
Degauque, Muriel, 205
demonizing the enemy, 46–48
  co-conspirator, 47–48
  conspiratorial explanations, 47
  scapegoating, 47
Department of Homeland Security (DHS),
    250–251
Department of Homeland Security
    Organizational Chart, 251(chart)
Dev Sol, 59
Dhanu (better known as Thenmuli
    Rajaratnam), 196
DHS (Department of Homeland Security),
    250–251
digital-terrorism, 239
Direct Action, 59
"dirty bomb", 221–222
"Dirty War" (Argentina-1976-1983), 106
divine law versus international rules, 78
Dohrn, Bernardine, 199
Dome of the Rock on the Temple Mount in
    Jerusalem, 81, 82n. 14
domestic terrorism in the United States
  on behalf of the "Old Country", 130–132
    fighting America on its own soil, 131
    Frank Sinatra and the pre-Israel
      Haganah, 130
    introduction, 130
    spraying Congress with bullets, 131
    using American soil to further the Old
      Country's cause, 131–132
  categories of, 121
  ecological terrorism, 128–130
    Animal Liberation Front (ALF),
      128–129
    Earth Liberation Front (ELF), 128, 134n. 11
    escalating radicalism, 130
    Justice Department, the, 129
    specieism, 129
  historical types of, 121, 134n. 2
  history of, 120–121
  John Brown, 120–121

left- and right-wing terrorism today,
    126–127, 134n. 9
left-wing terrorism, 121–122
  Black Panther Party for Self-Defense,
    123, 134n. 4
  M19CO- the combined task force, 123
  Weather Underground, 122
North Valley Jewish Community Center, 119
right-wing terrorism, 123–126
  Alfred P. Murrah Federal Building after
    the bombing, 125(ph)
  attacks foiled by the FBI, 127, 134n. 9
  Christian Identity Movement, 124–125
  introduction, 123–124
  Ku Klux Klan, 124
  Posse Comitatus, 125–126
single issue causes: antiabortion move-
    ment, 127
smallpox-infested blankets, 120
summary, 133
Donohue, Laura K., 266–269
Doomsday Clock, 279–280, 291n 1
Doran, Michael Scott, 163
"dream Team", 83
"dual "wings", 49
Dylan, Bob, 122
Dzhebirkhanova, Satsita, 202

E

Earth Liberation Front (ELF), 128, 134n. 11
ecological terrorism
  Animal Liberation Front (ALF), 128–129
  Earth Liberation Front (ELF), 128
  escalating radicalism, 130
  Justice Department, the, 129
  specieism, 129
economics of terrorism
  entrepreneurship and its rewards, 86
  financing terror, 85–87
  revenue sources, 85
  terrorism financing: fighting back, 85
Edwards, Jessica, 201
EGMONT Group, 85
Ehrenfield, Rachel, 95
El Al, security measures, 260
electromagnetic terrorism, 239
ELF (Earth Liberation Front), 128, 134n. 11
Elisabeth (Austrian Empress), 19
ELN (National Liberation Army), 59